Information Literacy and Information Skills Instruction

Information Literacy and Information Skills Instruction

*Applying Research to Practice in the
21st Century School Library*

THIRD EDITION

Nancy Pickering Thomas, Sherry R. Crow,
and Lori L. Franklin

AN IMPRINT OF ABC-CLIO, LLC
Santa Barbara, California • Denver, Colorado • Oxford, England

Library of Congress Cataloging-in-Publication Data

Thomas, Nancy Pickering.
   Information literacy and information skills instruction : applying research to practice in the 21st century school library / Nancy Pickering Thomas, Sherry R. Crow, and Lori L. Franklin. — 3rd ed.
      p. cm.
   Includes bibliographical references and indexes.
   ISBN 978–1–59884–490–0 (pbk. : acid-free paper) — ISBN 978–1–59884–491–7 (ebook)
   1. Library orientation for school children—United States. 2. Library orientation for high school students—United States. 3. School libraries—Activity programs—United States. 4. Information literacy—Study and teaching (Elementary)—United States. 5. Information literacy—Study and teaching (Secondary)—United States. I. Crow, Sherry R. II. Franklin, Lori L. III. Title.
Z711.25.S36.T48 2011
027.62′5—dc22   2011011066

ISBN: 978–1–59884–490–0
EISBN: 978–1–59884–491–7

15 14 13 12 11   1 2 3 4 5

This book is also available on the World Wide Web as an eBook.
Visit www.abc-clio.com for details.

Libraries Unlimited
An Imprint of ABC-CLIO, LLC

ABC-CLIO, LLC
130 Cremona Drive, P.O. Box 1911
Santa Barbara, California 93116-1911

This book is printed on acid-free paper ∞

Manufactured in the United States of America

To the school library research scholars and professionals who inspired us and to all future school librarians who will benefit from their insights.

For my children and grandchildren, in memory of my parents, and in honor of my students.

—NPT

For my devoted husband, Steve; my loving mother, Rose; and in memory of my inspiring father, Bob.

—SRC

For my husband Edward and children Casey, William, and Matthew—always faithful by my side.

—LLF

Contents

Preface to the Third Edition

The importance of information literacy competence and the continuing challenge of teaching Millennials within the context of emerging and evolving technologies provided the impetus for revising *Information Literacy and Information Skills Instruction: Applying Research to Practice in the School Library Media Center* (published in 2004) and argue for the need to revisit the roots of library instruction, with the aim of updating topics and issues considered in the two previous editions of this book. In addition, emphases on evidence-based practice (Todd 2009) in education and school librarianship and new professional publications, including *Standards for the 21st Century Learner* (American Association of School Librarians [AASL] 2007) and *Empowering Learners: Guidelines for School Library Media Programs* (AASL 2009a), combined to make this an ideal time to update research understandings that can provide school librarians guidance for instructional decision making. This third edition also benefits from insights and perspectives of the book's coauthors, all of whom have extensive practical and professional knowledge that can come only from combining personal experience as school librarians with academic credentialing as active researchers.

The revision process began with the a careful and independent review of the content of the second edition by each of us, followed by collaborative brainstorming sessions framed to consider issues of content and arrangement. A new outline was created to tighten the organization and presentation of ideas and reduce redundancies. A list of new research studies to be included was generated, and the studies were reviewed. Individual chapters were then revised and/or rewritten to reflect insights from library research studies published since the publication of the second edition in 2004.

One important issue we addressed at the outset involved the changing titles used to describe the work performed in school libraries. At the midwinter meeting of the American Library Association in January 2010, the official title of "school librarian" was formally adopted by the AASL Board of Directors as a reflection of the roles inhabited by professionals working in 21st century libraries—roles that align with those described in *Empowering Learners*: leader, instructional partner, information specialist, teacher, and program administrator. Reasons given for the reinstatement of a term widely used in the past included the desire to correct misconceptions held by those both inside and outside the library field and to ensure the consistent use of a title "that is clear to other educators, administrators, and the public, and that presents a common nomenclature for all publications and advocacy efforts" (AASL 2010a).

The AASL used survey data, along with a series of board meeting discussions, to reach a consensus on the use of the approved title (Staino 2010). As it turned out, different states prefer different titles. Florida, for example, uses "media specialist" as the preferred term for school library professionals, while California favors "teacher-librarian." While many practitioners applaud the attempt by the AASL to clarify and standardize the terms the profession uses to define itself, some AASL members, including school librarians, have expressed concern that the newly adopted title posits the school librarian's role as essentially passive rather than emphasizing the action-centered instructional role the use of the word "teacher" evokes (Staino 2010).

Throughout this edition, efforts were made to reflect the new official title. However, in some cases, the title "school library media specialist" or "media specialist" was retained to reflect terminology originally used by researchers. Sometimes, the title "teacher-librarian" is used because this description is also commonly found in our professional and research literature.

As with earlier editions, our book does not recommend a uniform set of curricular mandates nor advance directives to prescribe instruction across school library contexts. Instead, the authors hope that the new edition will inspire scholars and practitioners to improve what we know and do in ensuring that students develop competencies necessary for lifelong learning in the digital age. As Todd (2009) notes, few if any research studies in school librarianship yet meet what he regards as the scientific "gold standard" for guiding educational practice; however, we believe that the directions, focus, and topics that make up the library research landscape can act as springboards for such research in the future.

Introduction

We are at the threshold of a worldwide revolution in learning. Just as the Berlin Wall fell in 1989, the wall of conventional schooling is collapsing before our eyes. A new electronic learning environment is replacing the linear, text-bound culture of conventional schooling. This will be the proving ground of the 21st century mind.

—Peter Cookson

For at least the past 40 years, library professionals have embraced the "brave new world" of an interconnected informational universe in their continued acceptance of a "fundamental responsibility" for providing "the largest possible number of individuals access to and delivery of the largest possible amount of information" (Ghikas 1989, 124). It is this dedication to the twin goals of ensuring information access and teaching information literacy skills that drives research on information seeking and use. Indeed, it is our belief that efforts to create relevant, inclusive, and technologically savvy user-education initiatives at all library levels will continue to be the hallmark of instructional stewardship and define learner-centered library services well into the first quarter of the new millennium. By the same token, the political realities of life in a globally networked world and a volatile economic context create challenges that will undoubtedly continue to affect library practice for decades to come.

For those with a concern for educating the nation's young people, information literacy programs undertaken in public, school, and academic libraries represent an instructional continuum that, ideally, is initiated before children enter school and reinforced during their years of formal education. It is, as Liesener (1985) suggests, the "cumulative effect" of instruction in critical thinking and problem solving "throughout the learner's school experience" that "leads to the development of a self-directed learner able and motivated for life-long learning" (13).

Information Literacy: A Moving Target and an Evolving Construct

In the literature of librarianship and education, the term "information literacy" has evolved alongside the changing meanings of "information" itself. Writing in the 1970s, for example, Zurkowski (1974), defined information literacy as "the ability to use techniques and skills 'for the wide range of information tools as well as primary sources in molding information-solutions to . . . problems' " (quoted in Eisenberg & Spitzer 1991, 264). A decade later, the National Commission on Excellence in Education explained information literacy as "the skills required for new careers and citizenship" and "life-long learning" (Baumbach 1986, 279). By the mid-1990s, the American Library Association's Presidential Committee on Information Literacy was describing an information literate person as one who "recognize[s] when information is needed," has "the ability to locate, evaluate, and use [it] effectively" (p. 264), and has "learned how to learn" (Breivik & Senn 1994, 4). Drawing on a model created by Christina Doyle (1994), the California Media and Library Educator's Association (1994) went on to characterize information literacy as "the ability to access, evaluate, and use information from a variety of sources" (2), while Breivik and Senn (1994) discussed information literacy as the "ability to acquire and evaluate whatever information is needed at any given moment" (4). In their definition, Kirk, Poston-Anderson, and Yerbury (1990, cited in Todd 1995) attempted to indicate the complexities involved by conceptualizing information literacy in terms of six skill areas: "defining the tasks for which information is needed," "locating appropriate sources of information to meet needs," "selecting and recording relevant information from sources," "understanding and appreciating information from several sources," combining and organizing the information "effectively for best application," "presenting the information learned in an appropriate way," and "evaluating the outcomes in terms of task requirements and increases in knowledge" (133).

Whereas most of these information literacy definitions apply to users generally, Loertscher (1996) framed literacy specifically in terms of the information needs of youngsters. Information-literate students are, according to Loertscher, avid readers, critical thinkers, creative thinkers, interested learners, organized investigators, effective communicators, responsible information users, and skilled users of technological tools. A year later, Montgomery (1997) expanded on this theme, acknowledging that information literacy has become an umbrella term encompassing electronic searching and information retrieval skills, library skills, media skills, research skills, reference skills, learning skills, and study skills.

New Directions for a New Century

Whereas the 19th century appreciation for basic skills as life skills were reframed by the end of the 20th century to include recognition of the information explosion and the demands of digital age economics and technologies, the beginning of the new millennium has seen a continuing professional focus on information and media literacy within the varied contexts of education, business, and government. New and compelling are arguments that posit various literacy skills as fundamental for success in an increasingly global economy. For example, the North Central Regional Educational Laboratory lists scientific literacy, technological literacy, visual literacy, cultural literacy, and global awareness along with basic reading and information skills as essential frameworks for a new generation of children. At the same time, the goal of educating citizens to act responsibly in a democratic society has been expanded to include both an understanding of the relationships that exist between and among nations and an appreciation of and respect for diversity in thinking and living in a world made smaller through advances in transportation and communication technologies. In addition, attention that was once focused on ensuring electronic access has shifted to emphasize the critical appraisal of information and information sources—skills that are sometimes referred to as "media literacy."

Even in societies that describe themselves as information rich, there are still many communities and individuals who remain essentially information poor. And this digital divide grows apace with each technological innovation. Indeed, where information providers have managed to keep abreast of emerging technologies, the ability to make effective and efficient use of them has been neither automatic nor unproblematic. Some have even suggested that a new divide based on information *competence* rather than *access* threatens to undermine human progress toward a more just and equitable society (e.g., see Moran 2010).

Helping children and young adults make sense of information and information seeking has long been the special task and achievement of school librarians. Reformulating curricular goals, refining techniques for database as well as Internet searching, capitalizing on student interest in Web 2.0 technologies to both motivate and build technological competencies, and fostering student awareness of intellectual property, research ethics (Dow 2008), and online safety (Moran 2010) are some of the ways school librarians responsibly deal with evolving information contexts.

Assuming responsibility for student learning—which includes the planning, conducting, and assessment of curricular activities—continues to mark these dedicated professionals as equal and equally accountable partners with classroom teachers. In addition, a common belief held by librarians that "age should not be a barrier to the ability to access, receive, and utilize information" (Hooten 1989, 268) has placed them in the vanguard of championing the rights of our youth to unfettered access to and use of the most advanced technologies and virtual resources. With barriers to physical access fading, at least for upper-middle-class children (Carvin 2000a, 2000b; Wilhelm, Carmen, & Reynolds 2002), the critical issue has become one of intellectual access, translated as the ability to think critically and evaluate information and information sources selectively (McDonald 1988). The increasing sophistication and complexity of online research environments argue persuasively for a continuing and vital role for school librarians in preparing students capable of fulfilling the learning goals central to a digital age literacy agenda.

Applying Research to Practice: Value and Benefits

Writing in 2009, Todd created a model for understanding the mandate of evidence-based practice, which classifies school library research studies in terms of three relevancies: "evidence *for* practice," that is, "the essential building blocks" that can serve as the basis of instruction; "evidence *in* practice," the "integration of research into instruction"; and "evidence *of* practice," which considers outcomes for students as a result of information literacy instruction. By combining a review of the theoretical bases for instructional decision making with insights from published library research to inform curriculum planning, the "evidence" reviewed in this edition falls within the definitions of all three of Todd's categories. It is hoped that this review will help school librarians better understand the complexities in teaching and learning information literacy skills as well as anticipate potential behaviors and concerns exhibited by youngsters undertaking research tasks and school-based inquiry assignments.

As with earlier editions, this book brings together the research literature on information skills instruction with particular emphasis on models related to information seeking and the information search process explored in the research of Kuhlthau (1988a, 1988b, 1993b, 2004) and conceptualized by research scholars in library and information studies (LIS). These include *representational models*, which describe the searching behavior of people in naturalistic settings; *instructional models*, which help students learn the "how-tos" of information seeking and searching; and *facilitation models*, which can be used by students to improve their chances of search success. Our goal in providing this updated version of relevant research insights continues to address Comer's (2001) charge to the educational establishment, reframed within the context of information literacy and information skills instruction. "We will be able to create a successful system of education nationwide," Comer contends, "only when we base everything we do on what is known about how children and youths develop and learn."

Studies reviewed for this book include doctoral dissertations, research reports, academic and professional journal articles in LIS and related fields, and the writings of scholars and practitioners relevant to an information literacy curriculum. For "preservice" graduate students seeking certification or licensure, the book provides an introduction to school librarianship as an area of specialization and an overview of its historical development, an introduction to the major models and approaches that currently guide instructional best practices, and an understanding of the social aspects of teaching, learning, and service in school settings. Students and practitioners interested in bibliographic instruction in academic libraries will also find useful the overview of the development of bibliographic instruction provided in the first chapter, particularly the lessons learned with regard to the creation and implementation of the bibliographic instruction curriculum. For practicing school librarians, this text will help clarify issues and identify challenges encountered by others in the field and suggest research-based solutions. For many principals and teachers, this work will serve as an introduction to the contemporary practice of school librarianship and to the instructional activities that are part of the "package" offered by dynamic school librarians. For LIS educators and PhD students, this book will be useful as a literature review that not only confirms the contributions of many LIS researchers but also brings together the growing body of scholarly work as groundings for further research on information literacy instruction. Taking stock of what we know will, we hope, serve as a springboard to new thinking and reveal new directions for research related to information-seeking activities and practices of children and youth. Then, too, Todd (2009) recognizes the potential value that librarians' knowledge of research evidence offers to their school communities while also demonstrating "that they are part of a sustained research culture" (92).

Chapter 1, "Reference Traditions: From 'Personal Assistance' to Instructional Intervention," provides an overview and a history of reference services as they developed in academic and public libraries. Chapter 2, "The School Library Idea:

From Dream to Reality," explores the evolution of school libraries as centralized facilities with instructional responsibilities anchored in professionally created guidelines and standards. Chapter 3, "The Information Search Process: Kuhlthau's Legacy," summarizes traditional approaches to information skills instruction and traces the development of process models as created by Callison (1986), Sheingold (1986) and Kuhlthau (1988a, 1988b). Special attention is given to Kuhlthau's (1993b) research on the information search process and process intervention and the research stream that continues to explore the usefulness of the information search process and its theory base across contexts. Kuhlthau's recent emphasis on the utility of guided inquiry (Kuhlthau, Maniotes, & Caspari 2007) is considered, as is the notion of "third space." In Chapter 4, "Alternative Frameworks for Process Instruction," a variety of conceptual models for teaching information skills are described. Chapter 5, "Evolving Contexts for Teaching and Learning," reviews constructivism as a theoretical grounding for both LIS research and instructional design and considers current "best practices" in terms of instructional contextualization, effective lesson planning, and student motivation. Chapter 6, "Diagnosing Informational and Instructional Needs," presents Grover's model and its utility for identifying learner characteristics and effecting a "best fit" between user needs, instructional approaches, and learning styles. Chapter 7, "Building Information Competence: Designing Instruction for Today's Learners," considers the relationship between Millennials and the Internet, the realities of the "digital divide" as it is now variously defined, and the challenges these pose for school librarians and administrators. Chapter 8, "Creating Effective Inquiry-Based Educational Tasks," seeks to improve the depth of student learning though the creation of information-based tasks that not only engage learners but also involve students in thinking critically and searching effectively. Chapter 9, "Evaluating Library Service and Programs," reviews school reform issues related to assessment options and to contemporary approaches to library media center evaluation. Chapter 10, "Attending to the Social and Emotional Needs of Today's Learners" considers interpersonal communication within the context of the school library and explores the social nature of information seeking and virtual digital reference services as evidenced in the recent work of Radford (2006) and Radford and Connaway (2007). Professionalism, service, research directions, and leadership for school librarians are addressed in the Epilogue.

As much as we might sometimes wish it were so, there is no single instructional formula for raising student achievement and skill levels that will be effective and engaging for all students, at all grade levels, under all conditions, and in all situations. Such formulaic pronouncements, when they are presented, essentially ignore the value of differentiated instructional practices in meeting the many and diverse instructional needs observed in today's students. It is hoped that by careful consideration of research related to information skills instruction, reflective practitioners will be able to create a "best-fit" guide based on their knowledge of evidence-based instructional approaches and professional assessment of the unique needs of the students they serve. Such a review will also succeed in bringing into sharper focus the educational complexity that developing literacy and technical competence poses for students and the many challenges they face in making sense of information—not in the sort of "predigested, carefully selected, or logically organized" libraries and textbooks of their parents' youth but rather within a "vast network of resources" now ubiquitously available to most users (Kuhlthau 2001).

Even though information seeking for lifelong learning ultimately requires that the "seekers" create their own best ways to find, use, and evaluate information for effective problem resolution and decision making, the research literature reviewed here provides ample evidence that learning the skills on which information literacy depends cannot be left to chance. These skills must be taught, and students must receive support and guidance from knowledgeable instructors as the skills are practiced and ultimately personalized within relevant, interesting, and meaningful curricular tasks. It is up to instructional teams made up of teachers and school librarians to ensure that today's youngsters can survive and thrive in the "knowledge society."

1 Reference Traditions

From "Personal Assistance" to Instructional Intervention

A librarian should be more than a keeper of books; he should be an educator.... No such librarian is fit for his place unless he holds himself responsible for the library education of his students.

—Otis Robinson

While programs of instruction are most often considered the special province of academic and school libraries, the realization that public libraries could contribute to the creation of an informed citizenry emerged in American public libraries as early as the 1820s. Indeed, the practice of educating the library user to locate and use appropriate library resources can best be understood as an outgrowth of traditional forms of reference services in public libraries that date back almost two centuries. As chronicled by Rothstein (1955, 1994), Lubans (1974), Hardesty, Schmitt, and Tucker (1986), and others, the first efforts in this direction, which actually predated the adoption of formal reference services by many decades, included provision of all the information requested by library patrons as well as "guidance and direction in" its pursuit (Schiller 1986, 191). Although reference services provided at that time were essentially individual acts of kindness on the part of the librarians and delivered on an ad hoc rather than a systematic basis, they established the practice of courteous "personal assistance," which eventually evolved into the public service orientation that guides contemporary approaches to reference and instruction.

"Personal Assistance" in Public Libraries

Slightly more aggressive patterns of reference service than the sporadic offerings of personal assistance characteristic of the early years first appeared at the Boston Public Library in the 1850s, where "a naive faith in the efficacy of 'good' reading in the preservation of virtue' " (Rothstein 1955, 16) prompted the institution to commit itself to popular education. Although entirely consistent with the values of the times, Boston Public's vision of itself as "a new tool for scholarship" did not immediately usher in a golden age of library service nor inspire the creation of similar projects in other institutions. On the contrary, limited collections and low levels of funding combined to slow the adoption of a reference service ethic by most public libraries until after the Civil War. Nonetheless, it was during this period that libraries first became concerned with demonstrating their value as community resources; and it was not long before they seized on reference services as a vehicle for expanding their usefulness, their horizons, and their visibility.

The next real milestone in the development of "reference" as an important aspect of library activity was a program for reading assistance devised for library users at the Worcester (Massachusetts) Free Public Library, under the guidance of Samuel Swett Green (1837–1913). Green's public advocacy of a more formal approach to reference services came in 1876 in a paper delivered at the first conference of the American Library Association (ALA). Because, Green reasoned, the people who come into the library frequently lack knowledge of library books and the background and skills needed to use the library catalogs, it is the obligation of the library staff to lend them a hand. To this end, Green trained his staff to assist library patrons, stressing the importance of accessibility to materials and "cordiality" in addressing users' questions. Altruism to the contrary notwithstanding, Rothstein (1955) opined that Green was motivated by a sort of self-righteous self-interest in that his efforts were aimed as much at improving the library's public image as they were at elevating the public's literary tastes. In short, Green hoped to do "well" by currying public favor and to gain public funding by appearing to do "good."

Although Green's ideas for a "new method" (Rothstein 1955, 22) were greeted by some of his colleagues as forward looking, others were less sanguine. One librarian, for example, rejected the idea, claiming that the questions of ordinary library users were bound to be largely "frivolous" and a waste of the librarian's energy and time and that in most cases library staff lacked the expertise necessary to assist scholars in any meaningful way. Even so, Green's somewhat tentative move in the direction of instructional services eventually gained support and with it a realization that libraries should employ every means at their disposal to make their resources useful to the publics that funded their activities.

By the late 1880s, the proliferation of Green's approaches to public service was evidenced in Frederick Morgan Crunden's (1847–1911) study of public libraries. One of the founders of the ALA and an early ALA president, Crunden found "a growing sentiment in favor of the provision of personal assistance by the librarian as the most effective form of aid to the reader" (Rothstein 1955, 26). Within the next 10 years, what often began as "casual, intermittent help" came increasingly to be "replaced by specific administrative organization" (28) of such services. Indeed, by 1891, the new service even had a formal name—"reference work"— which replaced the earlier and decidedly more ambiguous "aids to readers" and "access to librarians" (Rothstein 1994, 542) in use before.

Another early proponent of user education in libraries was Charles Ami Cutter (1837–1903), who proposed teaching library patrons to use catalogs and book lists so that they would be able to find their own information and answer their own reference questions. While Cutter's plan served the rather pragmatic end of keeping library visitors from troubling the library staff, Melvil Dewey's "concern over the library's role as an educational institution" was considerably more benevolent and proactive. For Dewey, instruction was seen as a core rather than a "peripheral" activity and "central in the library's responsibilities" (Rothstein 1955, 31). Because of his commitment to improving services in both college and public library sectors, Dewey's work created a bridge between the two that facilitated the spread of his "modern library idea" (quoted in Rothstein 1955, 27) in academic as well as public library circles.

By the 1920s, most public librarians had adopted a dual service model, although reference most frequently consisted of librarians providing answers and information directly to library users rather than giving instruction (unless they specifically requested it). As libraries grew in popularity, however, demands for services also increased. The strain that this new "traffic" placed on reference departments and concerns to maintain both quality and service led librarians to create a number of innovative approaches to reference service provision. In cities that supported multiple library buildings within a single system, some directors farmed out readers' advisory services to the library's branches while retaining responsibility for more "serious" research functioning at the central facility. Others found a solution in the creation of a separate information desk, which could handle directional inquiries expeditiously while channeling more "important" information questions to experts in the reference department. Where funding and staffing were available, reference departments were themselves divided into specialty areas (e.g., science and technology, business, history and genealogy) similar to existing patterns in the disciplinary specialties (e.g., science, history, social science, humanities) increasingly prevalent in academic libraries so that librarians could provide even higher levels of service.

An interesting innovation and one that suggested a degree of engagement seldom encountered in other settings at the time was the creation of positions at the Library of Congress known as "interpretive chairs." Conceived by Herbert Putnam (1861–1955) during the 1920s, interpretive chairs were reference librarians trained to provide "active aid and counsel" to researchers working in the library. The "extra measure of assistance" available through these individuals included advice on relevant sources and special reference materials, suggestions on procedural and stylistic matters related to the creation of the user's manuscript, and "constructive criticism" (Roberts, quoted in Rothstein 1955, 92) of the final product.

During the course of the past half century, reference services in public libraries have developed further to include ready-reference or fact-finding functions undertaken by a centralized reference unit with specialized assistance programs, such as genealogy and local history, often made available in separate units or departments. Many contemporary libraries have also launched aggressive programs of outreach to extend services to populations previously ignored or underserved and frequently offer "orientation-to-the-library" sessions for new users and user groups. Finally, in libraries where homework assistance has become an important aspect of youth services, a specialized form of reference assistance to youngsters has been devised that combines information services and instruction.

Service Traditions in Academic Libraries

The status of the library as a cultural institution par excellence has seldom been questioned. Rather grandly, Francis Lieber (1882, quoted in Rothstein 1955) described libraries as "the bridges over which Civilization travels from generation to generation and from country to country" (11). In higher education, the affinity between the library as cultural artifact and the library as educational workplace seems to have been appreciated even in the earliest days of the Republic. Rothstein noted, for example, that although academic libraries at the beginning of the 19th century were "indifferent" to most activities other than those involved in acquiring materials, "teaching the use of books and libraries did arouse some considerable interest" (14). In 1816, George Ticknor (1791–1871) described the library as "the light and spirit" of the university and its "first convenience" (10–11). "Give me a library," wrote Benjamin Ide Wheeler at the end of the 19th century, "and I'll build a university about it" (quoted in Rothstein, 1955, 11).

Writing about the same time, Frederick A. P. Barnard (1883, quoted in Rothstein 1955), the president of Columbia University, expressed his enthusiastic support for "instruction and aid to undergraduates as shall enable them in all their after lives to do their individual work more readily and more successfully" (14), while the American historian Herbert Baxter Adams (1887, quoted in Rothstein 1955) found highly commendable a course in "bibliographical information" taught to students "by the librarian of their college or university" (14). Finally, the words of Otis Robinson (quoted in Tuckett & Stoffle 1984) reflect the sentiments of the more visionary 19th century library educators:

> A librarian should be more than a keeper of books; he should be an educator. ... No such librarian is fit for his place unless he holds himself responsible for the library education of his students. ... All that is taught in college amounts to very little; but if we can send students out self-reliant in their investigations, we will have accomplished much. (58)

In a very real sense, the transformation of the librarian from archivist to educator facilitated and was facilitated by the transformation of the university library from literary "sanctum" to intellectual "workshop."

The Move to Instruct Users: Justin Winsor's Legacy

Near the end of the 19th century, the development of an instructional model for reference service was advanced at Harvard University, where the "professor of books," librarian Justin Winsor (1831–1897), actively encouraged both library staff and ordinary library users to provide research assistance. According to a procedure created by Winsor, information seekers could post "notes and queries" (Rothstein 1955, 24) on a spindle in the reference room; anyone interested in finding the answer to someone's question could post it for others to read. Winsor also advocated the preparation of book lists "in anticipation of students' essays." "If our colleges would pay more attention to the methods by which a subject is deftly attacked, and would teach the true use of encyclopedic and bibliographic helps," Winsor wrote, "they would do much to make the library more serviceable" (24).

Winsor (1986) also proposed opening the university collections to individual students and faculty and providing instruction in the "use of books and libraries." Although his somewhat modest model for instruction limited library lessons to locating and accessing library materials, Winsor's vision of the library as "the grand rendezvous of the college for teacher and pupil" (7) placed him well ahead of the learning curve; many college and university librarians of his time were not nearly so accommodating. Indeed, it was not until universities began to adopt the German model of lectures and seminars as vehicles for instruction that textbooks came to be replaced by materials that were housed in campus libraries. Interestingly, if perhaps not surprisingly, state universities initially welcomed the establishment of personally assisted reference services with more enthusiasm than did librarians at older and perhaps more conservative private universities.

Another 19th century librarian who championed accessibility to collections and the amplification of services was William Frederick Poole (1821–1894). While to contemporary ears his announcement that his "office door [was] always open" to anyone seeking assistance may sound at best reactive, at the time it must have seemed positively magnanimous. Poole also favored the creation of a university course in the "scientific methods of using books" and sought faculty status for professor-librarians to whom would fall the responsibility for providing this instruction. Following Poole's leadership, Raymond C. Davis (1836–1919) created a course on bibliography and reference tools at the University of Michigan as early as 1881.

Columbia College's Melvil Dewey

As innovative as these instructional courses were, it was Melvil Dewey (1851–1931) who, at the turn of the 20th century, finally regularized reference and established "organized personal assistance" as an integral instrument of the Columbia College library's educational purpose. Writing as early as 1884, Dewey set forth his expectations: in addition to organizing and cataloging library materials and providing reference resources, librarians were to furnish advice and instruction so that students would gain knowledge of the best library resources and be competent "to use them intelligently" and in the proper order. For Dewey, the "first and paramount duty of the Reference Librarian" was to set an example, counsel students, and train library users in the delights of the library and the "habit of hunting" information (Rothstein 1955, 28). The importance that Dewey's imprimatur gave to establishing the legitimacy of library instruction cannot be overstated.

Princeton's William Warner Bishop

It was left to William Warner Bishop (1871–1955), a classical scholar who served as a librarian at Princeton and the University of Michigan, as well as the Library of Congress, to articulate a comprehensive framework for instruction that has an amazingly contemporary ring. Noting the "deluge" of new material published each year, Bishop in 1912 recommended that students be educated in acquiring a scholar's "attitude toward the printed page" (Bishop 1986, 83) through a sequential program of instruction that should begin in elementary school and continue until a student graduated from college.[1]

Vassar's Lucy Maynard Salmon

It was left to another visionary to explore the idea of instructional integration. At the ALA conference in 1913, Lucy Maynard Salmon (1853–1927), a history professor at Vassar, argued persuasively for the incorporation of instruction in books and libraries as part of regular college courses. Salmon believed that because the professors knew individual students and their particular research needs, they were in the best position to provide library instruction relevant to ongoing course assignments and requirements. Not only did it made good sense to "incorporate knowledge of how to use a library with the subject matter included in a particular course" (Salmon 1986, 88), she opined, but it would also save everyone's time. Further, the "knowledge acquired" in the course of instruction would fall "naturally into its place in connection within definite, concrete work" (88) and be more easily assimilated by college students.[2]

In order to put her ideas on library instruction into play, Salmon (1986) created a course for new students that included a library tour and designed "bibliographical work" within a . . . "definitely planned . . . systematically carried out" progression of courses

> directly related to the specific and individual work of every student. From time to time conferences [were] held by members of the library staff and the instructors in history and these conferences enable[d] each department to supplement and complement the work of the other and thus avoid repetition and duplication. (93)

Salmon characterized the roles of the librarian as friend, counselor, guide, and, ultimately, teacher:

> It is often his duty not to give, but temporarily to withhold information; not to answer but to ask questions; to answer one question by asking another; to help a student answer his own question for himself, work out his own problems, and find a way out of his difficulties; to show him how to seek and find for himself the material desired; to give training rather than specific information; to be himself a teacher and to co-operate with other instructors in training the students who seek his help. (94)

Taxonomy of Reference Service Levels

As noted above, the earliest models for reference services developed first within individual academic and public libraries and thus differed widely, depending on whatever patterns of assistance were in vogue there (Schiller 1986). J. I. Wyer (b. 1869) described these differences in terms of the taxonomy of service levels: conservative, moderate, and liberal (Wyer 1930). At the *conservative* level, the librarian was characterized as an "intelligent guidepost," with the "self-development" of the library user as the ultimate goal of any services extended. In practice, librarians espousing a conservative view considered the act of offering more than directional assistance or the "means of gathering information" a disservice in that it "deprived[d] patrons of the invaluable benefits derived from the experience of personal investigation" (Spofford 1990, quoted in Rothstein 1955, 42). According to Rothstein, this service approach was based on an "a priori assumption that the library [as] an educational institution" had a responsibility to provide formal instruction in the use of its resources but that the "truly deserving university student or public library patron" would desire no more assistance than that. As Rothstein (1955) noted, "Presumably readers more egregious in their demands were to be rejected out of hand, or to be brought to realize that less aid really did them more good than more aid" (44). Rothstein himself found this claim "dubious," an example of inverted logic, and contrary to popular wisdom; surely, he thought, increasing services would ultimately mean an increase in the library's popularity and community support!

The conservative model of service was reflected in the public library arena in the work of such early library notables as John Cotton Dana (1856–1929)[3] and Charles Ami Cutter, both of whom judged library users capable of finding the answers to their own inquiries. Although it may be hard to imagine in light of today's professional concern for bibliographic instruction (BI), at the time few disputed the inherent contradictions in these "less-is-more" policies, possibly because, as Rothstein (1955) suggested, as a rationale it tended to fit contemporary practice. Indeed, according to Rothstein, "the 'conservative theory' never ceased to find adherents" (75), particularly in academic library settings. Perhaps for this reason, the real focus of instructional attention prior to World War I was the "inexperienced library user" (45), with guided tours and formalized library courses as the most commonly used instructional methods. Other, less intrusive and less interactive methods of instruction, namely, the creation of subject bibliographies and finding lists, were also standard practices.

Interestingly, where a conservative or limited service model characterized reference practice, it was usually invoked for faculty as well as for students. "Just what educational purposes were being served by denying to faculty more than minimal assistance," Rothstein (1955) suggested, were at best "seldom made clear. Tacitly, however, the policy was undoubtedly based on the old assumption that the mature scholar did not need help—or at any rate *ought* not to need it" (75) and that students did not deserve it (Schiller 1986). In point of fact, the assumption that "the value of a study [ought to be] measured by the personal labor of its author" (Rothstein 1955, 87) was entirely consistent with the social values inherent in a Puritan/Protestant work ethic (Sillars 1991) and an American preoccupation with the self-reliance characteristic of the period. According to Rothstein (1955), direct services in the form of information provision were often saved for those he characterized as the truly "helpless," that is, "foreigners" and the "timid" (75–76).

There were, however, other voices in academic librarianship arguing for reference librarians to assume a more active role in assisting library users with their information tasks. For example, J. Christian Bay (1871–1962), writing in 1924, opined that librarians should "illumine" (quoted in Rothstein 1955, 76) as well as recommend specific sources, an approach that Wyer (1930) would later describe as typical of a *moderate* level of service. The interpretation of information and its utilization, however, continued to be regarded as the responsibility of the library user.

At a third, or *liberal*, level of Wyer's (1930) service taxonomy, the librarian was obliged to use her or his expertise to find the information sought by patrons and to provide direct assistance in establishing the relevance, authority, and authenticity of particular titles. An articulate and enthusiastic proponent for this enhanced service model was William E. Henry (1927), librarian at the University of Washington, who offered as a rationale his understanding that the essential task of scholarship was the creation of a thesis rather than the mechanics of identifying, searching out, and obtaining particular sources. The most immediate consequence of Wyer's "liberal service" idea was the development of academic subject specialties by reference staff so that they could provide a more scholarly level of assistance than had previously been available or expected.

As seen above, academic libraries have, over time, provided varying levels of reference support. Although most did not adopt one mode or level of service over another in a formal statement of library policy, they tended to operate at a moderate level of service, established not by design but by default, often in response to traffic flow. However, the development of subject specialties by librarians with degrees or advanced levels of knowledge in academic domains, which became a part of the organizational pattern in many academic and public libraries during this period, held out at least the possibility that higher levels of service and increased levels of expertise could be made available to library users, at least for faculty. However, as Farber (1995) notes, overall academic librarians tended to expend most of their efforts in acquiring resources and organizing materials to support faculty research. In many institutions, this led to a sort of double standard: personal assistance for teaching and research faculty was modeled on a liberal approach to reference services, while undergraduate students were on the receiving end of minimalist or conservative service levels (Rothstein 1994).

In a departure from the trend of the academic reference librarian's role as "specialist," generalists were hired at Cornell University in the 1930s to assist faculty members in identifying resources outside the scholar's area of specialization and to procure materials from other libraries when necessary. This departure from the specialist model of academic reference work made use of the librarian as a consultant, considered by some to be a step closer to information provider or instructor.

Dissenting Views and Critiques of Reference Services

It is perhaps not surprising to note that the conservative and liberal approaches to reference service were seldom embraced with equal enthusiasm within the same institution. Indeed, across the profession, there has never been anything akin to total agreement as to what constitutes "best practice" in the delivery of user services (Schiller 1986). Over time, the liberal "direct-provision" camp of librarians has promoted its view with eloquence and humor, often dismissing as "ludicrous" the very notion that the library should be in the business of educating users. Jesse Shera (1903–1982), for example, called on librarians to "forget this silly pretense of playing teacher" (1954, quoted in Hardesty et al. 1986, 189), while Rothstein (1964, quoted in Schiller 1986) argued that, although instruction might be defensible for children and youth, adults had "no more reason to be guided in the techniques of finding out than they have in being shown how to fix a defective carburetor" (193).

Service Ambiguities

On a more serious note, Schiller (1986) has asserted that efforts to provide both "instruction services" and "information services" within the same institution are self-defeating because, in his view, the two approaches are inherently "antagonistic." In fact, Schiller believes that attempts to offer a dual model of service are detrimental to both library users and librarians. On the one hand, Schiller implies that maintaining two approaches to service is discriminatory since in many cases librarians have invoked an instructional services model to justify limiting assistance to students, whom they have traditionally regarded as undeserving. On the other hand, the duality bewilders library users because they do not know which of the two approaches they are going to encounter when they seek reference assistance. Expecting or, perhaps, fearing that they will find the "reduced-service" model in place makes users uncertain about the legitimacy and permissibility of asking for help; indeed, it often leads them to modify or abandon their requests altogether. As a result, when users hesitate fully to explain their information needs, librarians have the problematic task of reinterpreting their questions "to discover what is actually wanted" (201).

Inappropriate Content and Audience

Eadie (1990) has objected to BI in college libraries on the grounds that in the long run the content of instructional sessions most often addresses location skills rather than the more challenging and useful cognitive tasks related to "making sense" of the materials located (42). In addition to critiquing BI on instructional grounds, Eadie has argued that the entire exercise is aimed at the wrong goals. Instead of saving "the time of the reader" (Ranganathan 1957),[4] Eadie suggests that library instruction tends to be aimed at saving of the time of the reference librarian! For his part, Dickinson (1981) has dismissed the creation of instructional programs at postsecondary levels because he believes that "students should enter colleges and universities already in command of most of what [BI] programs endeavor to impart." Indeed, Dickinson argues that the teaching of basic library skills is more "properly the responsibility of elementary and secondary school librarians, since it is only they who can deal with it in other than a remedial sense" (854). Ironically, the fact that, indeed, many students do *not* possess these skills when entering the university (Goodin 1987, 1989; Kester 1994; Turner 1990) has been advanced as the rationale for BI by its many proponents.

Information Seeking versus Research

For his part, Stoan (1984) has warned academic librarians against presenting "information skills" as "research skills," which, as he asserts, are not equivalent "nor bear any organic relationship to each other" (105). According to Stoan, activities that academic librarians frequently referred to as "research" are more properly information seeking and "library use," while "research," within the parlance of academic scholars, is a "quest for knowledge" (105) entailing the systematic collection of original "uninterpreted" (100) data, conducted according to methodologies consistent with particular academic disciplines. The appropriate use of library resources within the context of a scholarly research agenda, Stoan suggests, consists of footnote and citation chasing in the secondary literature to find relevant readings. Since it is through footnotes that "scholars communicate with each other," they are more useful as keys to the utility of an article in relationship to a particular topic than are access "tools," such as subject headings and descriptors, which represent a "layer" of interpretation created by "a third party" (103).

Stoan (1984) has also argued against trying to teach students a single, generic research strategy because scholarly approaches to information seeking are personal, domain specific, subjective, and intuitive. In his view, such approaches constitute an amalgam of insights, experience, and luck sparked by engagement with resources encountered (sometimes serendipitously) along the way. Furthermore, Kaplan (quoted in Stoan 1984) has argued that researchers are often unable to describe their own methods of information seeking and frequently employ "logic-in-use" (102) strategies rather than using the indexing and abstracting resources and reference "tools that librarians deem so central to the research process" (101).

20th Century Instructional Initiatives in Academic Libraries

Of course, the qualities and qualifications that make a person a good librarian are not necessarily isomorphic with those that make a good teacher; nor should the acquisition of pedagogical skills be ignored. George B. Shaw addressed these important points in a speech at Drexel University in 1928. In brief, Shaw (1986) argued that librarians must learn the fundamentals of teaching and learning if their efforts at library skills instruction are to bear fruit. Indeed, Shaw called for the development of "an new species [of librarian] which will combine in one individual the librarian's knowledge of books and bibliographical procedure with the instructor's ability in teaching method and in the skilled imparting of information" (109).

The most common approaches to library instruction during the early years were library lectures, which were usually followed by some sort of assignment that required students to use the library and its array of bibliographic tools and resources. It became evident over time that the stronger programs were those in which the librarian worked closely with the college professors. In fact, the importance of professor-librarian partnerships was a central finding of research conducted within the context of liberal arts colleges by Harvie Branscomb and published in 1940 as *Teaching with Books* (Hardesty et al. 1986).

Stephens College's B. Lamar Johnson

An interesting program of library skills instruction was launched at Stephens College (Columbia, Missouri) in the early 1930s by B. Lamar Johnson (1904–1995). Basic to the Stephens approach were clearly articulated objectives that emphasized instruction in the use of the library resources and the development of good study skills as prerequisites for learning. Through his courses, Johnson sought to place library use at the vortex of the instructional process. The fact that Johnson occupied positions as both the college librarian and the dean in charge of instruction greatly facilitated the implementation of his ideas, and he himself admitted that the adoption of his program would have been impossible had he not had the authority to impose it for both faculty and students (Johnson 1986).

Peabody College's Louis Shores

Johnson's faith in the value of the library as the linchpin of a college education was also shared by Louis Shores (1904–1981) at Peabody College for Teachers (Nashville, Tennessee), who in the 1930s and early 1940s launched an ambitious program based on his idea that the library is the college—and the college, the library (Shores 1986). What Shores envisioned was a library college, in which all the teachers would be library trained and in charge of supervising and tutoring individual students in independently conducted reading and research projects. Among Shores's notable contributions to the discourse of academic librarianship were the ideas that learning should be student centered and interdisciplinary and that creating independent learners was the appropriate goal of education. At the time, Shores's program had little immediate impact on the practice of his contemporaries. However, his understanding that library instruction could make a valuable contribution to the achievement of the broader educational goals of the institution aided in the development of a vision for instructional programming in academic and school libraries that was implemented later in the century.

The Mid-Century Information Explosion

Although the explosion of scientific knowledge immediately evident in the years following World War II raised concerns of many mid-century librarians about the problems that this "Niagara" of information might pose for the general public as well as for students, little progress in user instruction in the academic library was made during the next two decades (Rothstein 1955). In fact, in spite of a burgeoning undergraduate

Table 1.1
Summary of Themes and Insights in Early Efforts at Library Use Instruction

- Roles for librarians as teachers, advisers, consultants, and information providers
- Pedagogical training as a prerequisite for "teaching" librarians
- Importance of faculty and librarian collaboration in planning
- Importance of teaching library use skills in context of a research task
- Value of "information use" skills over "location and access" skills
- The librarian as an identifier of relevant resources
- The librarian assists with research products and their evaluation

population and expanding collections, lack of library staff, lack of "a viable conceptual framework" (Hardesty et al. 1986, 148), lack of enthusiasm, and/or lack of instructional finesse (Kirk 1977, cited in Hardesty et al. 1986) together led most academic librarians to limit their instructional efforts to orientation sessions and library tours. When they were available, library education courses were typically taught in stand-alone sessions, with content decisions most frequently based on the expertise and interests of the librarians rather than the information needs of the students themselves. As a result, instructional programs in many universities languished. Even so, insights gained through the implementation of the innovative programs championed by Dewey, Shores, Salmon, Johnson, and others created frameworks for the development of instructional programs to come. (A summary of new roles and activities is provided in Table 1.1.) Especially compelling in this regard were prototypes for librarians that featured active participation in the process of student learning.

Knapp's Experiment

The program that rekindled the flame of interest in BI among academic and school librarians was created by Patricia Bryan Knapp (1914–1972) at Wayne State University (Detroit, Michigan) in the early 1960s. Convinced that "competence in library use" constituted "one of the liberal arts" (Knapp 1986, 156) and recognizing the key role that college faculty played in student use of library resources, Knapp (1966) launched an initiative to "instruct the instructors" in the use of the library, its resources, and its educational value by integrating library instruction into a wide variety of courses in order to demonstrate the applicability of library skills across the curriculum. In addition, Knapp devised a plan to implement these skills through a series of instructional experiences carried out over time, which she hoped would lead students to develop positive attitudes toward the library and an appreciation for its utility.

Featured prominently in Knapp's (1966) approach were assignments based on problem-solving activities rather than paper-and-pencil tests or "make-work" practice assignments loosely linked to course content. In this way, she hoped to emphasize the "intellectual processes involved in retrieval of information and ideas from the complex system our society uses to organize its stored record" (81). And although Knapp's program was essentially librarian initiated, the delivery of BI was truly a cooperative effort between university librarians and the teaching faculty. The program itself called for the articulation of specific objectives, including the organizational schemes used to structure library collections, the identification of

Table 1.2
A Summary of Insights from the Knapp (1966, 1986) Project

- Library use as a multidimensional activity involving knowledge, skills, and attitudes
- The value of teaching library use skills in context
- The value of integrating library use skills within and across subject domains
- The importance of systematic planning for instruction
- The importance of cooperation and coordination between librarians and teachers
- The importance of practicing library use skills within "authentic" tasks
- The importance of evaluation in the use of information resources

essential reference books, and the creation of criteria that could be used to interpret and evaluate the information obtained.

It must be admitted that Knapp's (1966) dynamic instructional program was not greeted with unbridled enthusiasm by Wayne State students and faculty. However, her insights made a major contribution to the field of library and information studies in general and to school librarianship in particular. Especially influential have been Knapp's understandings that library use is a multidimensional activity involving "knowledge, skills, and attitudes" (Farber 1995, 24) and that library use skills are best learned over time and when presented within the context of ongoing classroom assignments. In fact, the systematicity of her instructional program, her emphasis on "process" over "content," and her understanding of the key roles played by course instructors are now regarded as foundational for the successful implementation of instructional programming in school libraries. Table 1.2 lists important insights anchored in Knapp's research.

The Value of Teaching Library Use Skills in Context

BI: The Earlham College Experience

Another major contribution to the development of BI models was the exemplary program of library instruction created at Earlham College (Richmond, Indiana) in the middle 1960s and implemented by librarians Evan Ira Farber, Thomas B. Kirk, and James R. Kennedy. Founded on the bedrock of active cooperation between departmental scholars and college librarians, Earlham's approach to instruction featured three central principles: integration, demonstration, and gradation (Kennedy 1986, 233). Integration was achieved by embedding all library instruction within courses that most often required students to use library resources. Demonstration was chosen as the central instructional strategy and included an introduction to the search process as well as to specific types of library resources. (Annotated bibliographies of course-relevant materials were also created and distributed as part of the instructional program.) Gradation was achieved through the implementation of a planned sequence of instructional sessions, which were conducted over the four years of a student's college career. Elements that librarians viewed as key to the successful implementation of the program included rapport and synergy between the librarians and the teaching faculty, the selection of appropriate courses for library

Table 1.3
Key Elements of the BI Program at Earlham College

- An academic culture that "demands" library use
- Commitment of librarians and teaching faculty to the goals of the program
- Active rapport and collaboration between librarians and the teaching faculty
- Selection of appropriate courses for library skills instruction
- Highly motivated and interested students
- High teacher expectations for student performance
- Small class size
- "Just-in-time" delivery of instructional intervention
- Instructional quality and creativity

skills integration and appropriate projects within the courses, small class size, and a "just-in-time" approach that based decisions related to course scheduling directly on the needs of students. Kennedy (1986) identified the following strategies as contributing substantially to the overall success of Earlham's innovative program: a college culture that "demands library use," the commitment of librarians, the motivation of students, high teacher expectations, and quality and creativity in instructional techniques (see Table 1.3).

Although in many respects Earlham's experience and success reflected the unique qualities of that institution and its librarians, the program created at Earlham resulted in a veritable explosion of interest among academic librarians in the 1970s and continues today. The first tangible evidence of this interest was the creation of an Ad Hoc Committee on Bibliographic Instruction within the Association of College and Research Libraries and the subsequent establishment of the Bibliographic Instruction Section of that organization in 1977. The founding of the Library Instruction Round Table by the ALA in 1977 and a series of conferences, newsletters, and clearinghouses for information on bibliographic instruction followed, some of which included elementary and secondary librarians (e.g., the Library Orientation Exchange).

BI in the 21st Century: Strategies and Techniques

Contemporary strategies for BI include a variety of practices: "library sessions" by teaching faculty within regularly scheduled course offerings; stand-alone courses conducted by library staff; orientation programs and tours, which introduce students to the library facility, services, and resources; research paper seminars, organized to assist students involved in course-related reference assignments; manuals, handbooks, and workbooks for students to use independently; and point-of-use brochures and fact sheets. Library automation and the proliferation of digital and online resources have made Internet-based library tours, information sessions, and tutorials attractive supplements for more traditional and personalized reference services in many academic libraries. Indeed, in recent years, computerized instruction has become increasingly sophisticated. For example, computer-assisted instruction, which is locally produced and tailored to the libraries in which it will be used, frequently employs voice synthesis capabilities as well as digital avatars.

Conclusion

It is apparent from this historical review that the lessons learned in public and academic library settings have contributed significantly to the development of theory and practice in school librarianship. Indeed, although the schools have made instruction a central feature of their mission in ways seldom realized at the academic level, they owe "innovations in most phases of library instruction, including those of conceptualization, design, experimentation, implementation and evaluation" (Tucker 1994, 364), to the efforts of visionaries in academic and public institutions. An appreciation of these contributions, as well as the insightful programs and theoretical frameworks from which they arose, provide useful points of departure for school media specialists engaged in designing their own instructional programs for elementary and high school students. Especially significant are the characterizations of libraries as intellectual centers, learning laboratories, and information bureaus; the recommendation that students rely on primary and secondary sources rather than textbooks; advocacy for increasing the accessibility of library resources; models for individualized guidance; and roles for library users as independent searchers and lifelong learners.

Interestingly, discrimination by rank (faculty or student), which typified many academic approaches to service provision in the past, survives in school libraries in practices and policies that support the offering of direct information services to administration and staff while, at the same time, limiting services offered to youngsters to instruction only. However, current thinking suggests that an important aspect of information literacy and a valid option and research strategy in information seeking is recognizing and making use of the expertise available in the person of the school librarian. It seems clear that in school libraries as well as in their academic and public counterparts, the extent to which library users feel free to seek assistance from library professionals may well depend on the climate of accessibility and acceptance that the librarians themselves manage to create (Radford 1996; Radford & Connaway 2007).

Notes

1. Essentially, William Warner Bishop (1912) blamed the lack of use that college students made of library resources on the lack of grounding in basic library skills: "I have known boys who passed an entire four years in a college with 350,000 books in its library, and who in those four years never entered its doors" (Hardesty et al. 1986, 82).

2. Lucy Maynard Salmon wrote, "To use a homely illustration, an article of food, like butter, that is essential for our physical diet serves its purpose much better when distributed through other articles of food than if taken independently and by itself" (Hardesty et al. 1986, 88).

3. Dana was also noted for his "12 Rules of Reading: 1. Read. 2. Read. 3. Read Some More. 4. Read Anything. 5. Read About Everything. 6. Read Enjoyable Things. 7. Read Things You Yourself Enjoy. 8. Read, and Talk About It. 9. Read Very Carefully, Some Things. 10. Read on the Run, Most Things. 11. Don't Think About Reading, But 12. Read."

4. Shiyali R. Ranganathan (1872–1972), library science visionary and creator of the Colon Classification, described library service in terms of "Five Library Laws: Books are For Use, Every Book Its Reader, Every Reader His Book, Save the Time of the Reader, and a Library is a Growing Organism."

2 The School Library Idea

From Dream to Reality

The mission of the school library program is to ensure that students and staff are effective users of ideas and information. The school librarian empowers students to be critical thinkers, enthusiastic readers, skillful researchers, and ethical users of information.

—American Association of School Librarians (2009a)

In many respects, the publication of *Information Power: Guidelines for School Library Programs* by the American Association of School Librarians (AASL) and the Association for Educational Communications and Technology (AECT) in 1988 was a rite of passage, signaling to educators and librarians that the specialized field of school librarianship had come of age. At last, school librarians had at their fingertips a blueprint that reframed library practice and offered a vision to guide further growth and development of the profession.

Three New Roles: *Information Power* (1988)

The roles for school library media specialists that *Information Power* unambiguously described were information specialist, teacher, and instructional consultant, conceived as a type of powerful, interacting, and evolving triad. The unique responsibility that librarians were to assume was clearly and succinctly stated as well: "to ensure that students and staff are effective users of ideas and information" (AASL & AECT 1988, 1998). As best practice, *Information Power* called on school librarians to replace fixed-schedule, stand-alone lessons delivered in a predetermined sequence with fully integrated information skills instruction, planned in cooperation with classroom teachers and conducted as needed. Perhaps for the first time, school librarians possessed the power to define themselves and their activities and to develop the vocabulary needed to express clearly the relationship between library instruction and student learning. Indeed, in describing school librarians as dynamic instructional leaders, *Information Power* created a new face for school librarianship, with the goal of helping practitioners (as well as teachers and administrators) put aside old-fashioned and frequently negative stereotypes, thereby gaining a new understanding and appreciation for the educational potential represented by proactively presented library programming.

Information Power was also a timely reminder that the earlier goals of creating centralized collections, of selecting multimedia resources, and of hiring professional staff had been reached and that it was time for the field to establish a new vision. Inherent, too, was the realization that providing physical access to what Pierce Butler (1933) described as the "communal store" of our culture was a necessary but not sufficient precondition for supporting the personal, social, and intellectual development of the nation's children (Heeks 1997).

Proving the Value of Library Skills Instruction

Many in the profession entertained high hopes that the use of *Information Power* (AASL & AECT 1988) as the first formal manual, primer, and guide for school librarianship—along with the new roles it identified for school librarians—would result in achievement benefits for students. Unfortunately, research studies conducted during the 1980s failed to prove definitively that library skills instruction results in enhanced student competencies and higher grades. Professional disappointment at this turn of events and anxiety created by shrinking budgets and increasing demands for educational accountability created a sort of crisis mentality, which has in some ways characterized the school library profession ever since.

Librarians' consternation over the lack of studies that might justify continuing support for their programs has been exacerbated by research that directly challenged the educational efficacy of library skills lessons (Kuhlthau 1987). Anecdotal evidence from the field, which indicated that skills initially taught in elementary school had been insufficiently learned to allow their application to reference tasks in junior and senior high school (Shapiro 1976, cited in Carroll 1981) was substantiated in library and information science research in a variety of contexts. For example, Biggs reported that college freshman "lack[ed] all but the most rudimentary library skills" (quoted in Kuhlthau 1985, 35), while Dickinson (1981) found that undergraduates lacked sophistication in their understandings of what doing research entailed and "failed to use logical progression and systematic approaches to checking sources of information" (853). Later in the decade, Goodin (1987, 1991) reported that student learning of library skills neither transferred into new settings nor was being applied to the research tasks that these students encountered as college students.

These same conclusions were advanced by Kester (1994), whose study of 300 college freshmen revealed that, although 85 percent of them "had received library instruction in high school" (15), the "instruction appear[ed] to have little carry over or effect" (17). Specifically, Kester's research revealed that students lacked technical skills related to online public access catalog use and online searching. Additionally, Julien (1999) studied 400 Canadian adolescents and determined that several barriers to information seeking occur for high school students, including her finding that 40 percent of her participants were unsure where to go to locate information for investigating career paths. Perhaps even more compelling were the results of Kuhlthau's (1993b) initial study, which indicated that, in spite of the sincerest efforts of librarians to teach the skills necessary for students to conduct their own research projects, the students themselves approached their research tasks with feelings of dread and frequently did not know how to begin working on their assignments.

Renewed Focus on Teaching and Learning

Although exceedingly disappointing, this research provided evidence for what many librarians had suspected all along: that a scope-and-sequence skills curriculum presented in stand-alone lessons does not translate into information skills children can apply in completing research tasks even when taught every year. But if, as was now evident, the traditional approach was ineffective, what should be introduced in its place? This question led researchers and practitioners to consider a variety of alternatives. Wall (1974, quoted in Carroll 1981) for example, suggested that students be taught the use of "elaborate resource system[s]," not just reference books. Arguing for an improvement in instructional approaches and greater participation by library staff, Wall noted that "simply turning [students] loose with a bag of questions and a lot of resources will not do this. The teacher, the librarian, or the adult has to be actively and sensitively intervening most of the time in some way or another" (119).

Others in the field provided a veritable laundry list of other weaknesses observed in traditional library instruction. Young and Brennan (1978, cited in Carroll 1981) identified the following as problems that should be addressed: the lack of cooperation between teachers and librarians, poor teaching materials, stand-alone lessons and artificial assignments, failure to provide instruction to meet student needs, and lack of research on strategies to improve practice. Davies (1974) listed as significant barriers to effective student outcomes in information skills programs: the lack of library skills integration, limited time for planning, failure to contribute to curriculum planning or curriculum guides, and teachers' reliance on textbooks.

As in the case of bibliographic instruction in academic libraries, not everyone in the school media field immediately or enthusiastically embraced the new focus on instruction or the expectation that librarians assume responsibility for student learning. Liesener (1985), quoting Freiser (1963), urged librarians to "quit this nonsense":

> [I]nstead of forcing kids to spend the majority of their time searching for information with usually poor results, we should give them the information under certain circumstances so that they do have a foundation of good information to work with and, as a result, develop the skills and knowledge necessary to understand, use and appreciate ideas and information sources. The belief is that these skills and knowledge are not only more important but must precede the attempt to develop information seeking skills if such efforts are to be effective. (16)

Although not in favor of abandoning the instructional enterprise altogether, Liesener suggested that the best solution might be to turn the entire enterprise on its head: provide information directly to elementary students and save library skills instruction for upper-level students.

A New Vision for a New Millennium

Unfortunately, recent research by Peter D. Hart Research Associates and Public Opinion Strategies (2005) and others indicates that for many students, library skills education is still not achieving its potential in helping students learn. In Hart's study, which involved students, college professors, and employers, participants observed noticeable deficits in students' abilities successfully to navigate resource-based assignments. Sobering too was a report by Latham and Gross (2008) that, of 800 students who participated in an Educational Testing Service study, only one-third passed at a level sufficient to describe them as information literate. These kinds of outcomes add a sense of urgency to recent efforts by the AASL to strengthen school libraries and instructional programs across the country.

The response of AASL members was the creation of an enriched agenda that allows school librarians to set their sights once again on fresh horizons set forth and skillfully articulated in three publications: *Standards for the 21st Century Learner* (AASL 2007), *Standards for the 21st Century Learner in Action* (AASL 2009c), and *Empowering Learners: Guidelines for School Library Programs* (AASL 2009a). Together, these three documents provide a new structure and present new challenges for practitioners. While the *Standards for the 21st Century Learner* document directly establishes the content and frameworks for information literacy instruction, *Standards for the 21st Century Learner in Action* is designed to assist school librarians in collaboratively planning powerful, inquiry-driven learning experiences that will enhance student skills and increase understandings. Broadly written, this document fills in the details and "how-tos" in the "benchmark" and "indicator" sections of the standards. The third work, *Empowering Learners*, deepens and extends our perceptions of the many hats school librarians don on a daily basis. Taken together, these three publications clearly establish the focus on student learning, delineate the school library program's role in effecting this important change, and provide direction and foundation for school librarians as they educate today's learners.

The rest of this chapter traces the development of the school library idea from its beginnings and charts the evolution of instructional practices in school librarianship from a skills-based model to a dynamic, process-oriented inquiry-driven curriculum. A final explanation of AASL's new publications sets the stage for an in-depth look at research in library skills instruction in the chapters that follow.

School Library Beginnings: Opening the Door

History students may remember DeWitt Clinton (1769–1828) as an early governor of New York State and as the father of the Erie Canal, but he should be doubly honored by school librarians for his vision in recommending, in 1827, the creation of libraries in the public schools. Nearly 100 years earlier, Benjamin Franklin's "student academies" called for establishing the library as a central feature (Gillespie & Spirt 1973). However, it was not until Clinton, along with the 19th century educational reformer Horace Mann[1] (1796–1859), observed Johann Pestalozzi's[2] educational innovations that Franklin's earlier dream was realized through legislation that enabled school districts to purchase library books. The idea caught the imagination of many and spread quickly in the early years so that by 1840 libraries had been established to supplement instruction and promote reading in public schools in New York (1835), Massachusetts (1837), Michigan (1837), Connecticut (1839), and Rhode Island (1840).

Unfortunately, this early enthusiasm was short lived. In New York, the decline of school libraries was directly related to the fact that school administrators (when given the option in 1843) used library funds to pay teachers' salaries. In the other states, the fledgling school libraries were in some sense undermined by the success of public libraries, which were enjoying a period of rapid growth at the time (Cecil & Heaps 1940). Moreover, initial efforts to launch school libraries and sustain the momentum necessary for their continued support were seriously compromised by a lack of identifiable standards, adequate supervision, and trained personnel. Even so, by 1876, 21 states had funding legislation in place to support school libraries as part of public education (Bowie 1986).

As the 19th century drew to a close, interest in establishing school libraries was sustained by concurrent efforts to improve the quality of public education. Among the most influential of the reformers was the German philosopher Johann F. Herbart (1776–1841), who realized, contrary to the conventional pedagogical wisdom of the day, that ideas and intellectual development were ultimately more valuable than the mastery of a specific body of knowledge (Cecil & Heaps 1940). According to Cecil and Heaps (1940), "The Herbartian movement in reading which swept this country, particularly from 1889–1897, was a large factor in the awakening of educators to the potentialities of the library in the school" (50).

Combining School and Public Libraries

During this same period, there was also a good deal of public support for the idea, first advanced by Charles Francis Adams Jr. (1835–1915), that public and school libraries should be combined. Proponents argued that joining the two entities made sense in terms of "economy, convenience, and efficiency" (Carpenter 1905, quoted in Cecil & Heaps 1940, 58). They maintained that, as both types of libraries promoted educational advancement, blending the two would better serve all elements of the community. Enthusiasm for this idea was shared by Melvil Dewey and others, including Samuel Swett Green. While Green stopped far short of re-creating public and school libraries in Worcester, Massachusetts as a single entity, he made overtures to the schools by loaning to students and faculty materials from his public library and by encouraging classes to visit.

In the meantime, many other communities experimented with various forms of interlibrary cooperation or amalgamation. For example, the staffs of some public libraries joined with principals in planning school libraries that the principals then ran themselves. In other instances, public libraries maintained branch facilities within public schools, tailoring collections to meet the needs of adults as well as pupils. In areas without access to public libraries, it was not uncommon for state library agencies to provide "package" libraries of preselected materials to schools (Carroll 1981). During this period, museums in many communities also partnered with school libraries to make their "collections" available to local school districts (Coleman 1989). The collaborative spirit representative of this kind of interagency cooperation continues even today.

Sharing Library Collections

The idea of shared library collections, which seems to have taken hold first at the high school level, spread as more and more schools came to appreciate the value of easily accessible collections of books. A number of administrative models were tried in various districts around the country. A model adopted by some cities provided for central library management of selection and acquisition activities for all the schools in the district.[3] A second model, described above, called for the public library to use high school libraries as branch sites, while a third model created independent libraries in district high schools supervised and maintained by teachers or librarians. However, during the same period, there was little agreement as to how best to provide and maintain resources for children in the primary grades. In many schools, teachers favored classroom collections, arguing that immediate accessibility to grade-appropriate books would encourage reading and the development of reading tastes. Perhaps for this reason, the concept of a centralized collection within the elementary school grew very slowly.

Establishing School Library Services

While teachers, then and now, tended to prefer classroom book collections, the potential of a centralized library in making contributions to the educational environment of the school though reading promotion and direct programs of instruction was realized quite early among leaders of the educational establishment. In fact, the National Education Association (NEA) and the National Council of Teachers of English, in addition to the ALA, helped institutionalize the idea of school libraries through the creation of special "school library" departments within their organizations. Indeed, it appears that "these professional bodies had a clear vision of what school library service could become long before school libraries were a widespread reality" (Dike 1993, 744). For example, advocacy for school libraries was clearly stated in the NEA's conference proceedings in 1912, which asserted that "the school library will be the proof of the educational value of the new curriculum . . . [and] the open door to the opportunity of the present" (Dike 1993, 744). The rationale for such a move was that the curriculum of contemporary high schools was now so broad that textbooks could not provide what could be offered in the "laboratory" of the library (Hall 1912, 1274, quoted in Cecil & Heaps 1940, 62). Perhaps inevitably, the NEA also supported the creation of classroom collections of age-appropriate books as "the most satisfactory means of forming a taste for good literature" (Coleman 1989, 46) among elementary school students. Although this model sounds unremarkable to contemporary ears, it must have seemed positively revolutionary in schools where teachers relied exclusively on textbooks and grade-level readers as the primary medium of instruction. For many years thereafter, a common practice was to house works of literature in the classroom and nonfiction collections in the school library.

20th Century Educational Developments

The first four decades of the 20th century saw a definite educational turning away from more repressive programs anchored in education as discipline, training theory, and rote learning toward a child-centered theory of education based on the principles of active learning. Some educational initiatives founded on these principles included the Gary Plan (derived from the experiential learning ideas of William Albert Wirt [1874–1938] and John Dewey [1859–1952]), the Winnetka Plan (which featured individualized curriculum), and the Dalton Laboratory Plan (created by Helen Parkhurst [1887–1973]), which emphasized the value of individual study. In one way or another, each of these innovative programs placed the school library at the center of the curriculum (Cecil & Heaps 1940).

Still, during the period before World War I, real gains for the school library idea and improvements in existing facilities were modest. Indeed, a survey conducted by the National Council of Teachers of English in 1915 indicated that most school libraries were lacking both adequate materials and helpful services. Later, the Certain Report, *Standard Library Organization and Equipment for Secondary Schools of Different Sizes* (NEA & North Central Association of Colleges and Secondary Schools 1920), published by the ALA five years later, enumerated a spate of problems. Specifically, the report noted the lack of resources in addition to a lack of space for collections, staff, and students. Interestingly, the ALA noted the proliferation of managerial and clerical tasks—what Butler (1933) called the "bittiness" of library practice—that often kept school librarians from providing instructional assistance and library services. In order to improve the overall condition of library materials and strengthen programs of service and instruction, the report also recommended the establishment of centralized facilities to manage the schools' burgeoning collections of audio/visual equipment and media as well as print materials, run by "professionally trained librarians" charged with responsibility for organizing and maintaining the whole. Somewhat prophetically, as it turned out, the report stated, in no uncertain terms, that to require librarians to assume clerical tasks was "wasteful of educational resources and money" (Davies 1979, 398). Clearly, the school library's door to instructional opportunity was now open even if its future was not yet assured.

Inequities in Library Services

While interest in public education and public libraries in the early years of the 19th century held out the promise of improving the quality of life for many Americans, a significant proportion of the population was being systematically denied access to these kinds of public services. Although public education for African Americans was never supported in the South to any great degree, the institutionalization of segregation by the U.S. Supreme Court in *Plessy v. Ferguson* in 1896 ushered in an era of inequality not seen since the days of slavery before the Civil War. In that decision, the Supreme Court established the doctrine of "separate but equal," virtually guaranteeing to black children a substandard education in the same way that literacy requirements and Jim Crow laws had ensured the disenfranchisement of their parents. Thus, while it is safe to say that although many white children in the public schools of the North during this period lacked easy access to books and resources promised by a centralized school library, the obstacles to such access for black children in segregated schools of the South and West were often insurmountable. Where they existed at all, school library collections maintained for black children most often consisted of donated books and frequently the outdated and worn-out castoffs from white schools.

" . . . and the Twenties Roared": Library Standards for Public Schools

The effort to create elementary school libraries was advanced with the publication of the *Elementary School Library Standards*, distributed by the ALA in 1925. However, the primary focus was not on instruction but on creating "a new department" that could "assemble and distribute the materials of instruction' " (NEA & ALA, quoted in Gillespie & Spirt 1973, 9). These standards also stated that "under no circumstances shall the librarian be expected to do clerical work"; rather, he or she is expected to "work in close cooperation with teachers of the school," introducing "children to many kinds of books on many subjects" (Davies 1979, 403–4). In light of these early reports, a number of regional organizations around the nation made school librarianship the focus of their research. For example, school libraries were the subject of an entire yearbook by the NEA's Department of Elementary School Principals in 1933.

The commitment to creating school libraries expressed in published library standards received a momentary setback during the Depression years, but as the country got back on its economic feet concern for this important aspect of public education resurfaced. Private foundations offered some support for school libraries during this period. Notable among these was the Julius Rosenwald Fund, which provided a measure of library funding for black schools in the South through grants to county libraries that could demonstrate equal service for library users of both races (Cecil & Heaps 1940).[4] According to Hanchett (1988), the Fund also provided money to build library collections directly to black schools. Even so, these gifts did little to close the enormous quality gap in public education funding between white and black schools in the South.[5]

Progress toward Centralization of School Collections

In many locations across the nation, the 1940s and 1950s saw continuous movement in many school districts toward the development of school libraries as separate, centralized facilities, sometimes to augment and sometimes to replace classroom book collections. Furthermore, *School Libraries for Today and Tomorrow*, published by the ALA in 1945, "defined the educational purposes of the library" to "participate effectively in the school program" and called on school librarians to provide instruction in the use of the library and library materials in addition to offering reading guidance. Through these activities, the report suggested, students would "become skillful and discriminating users of libraries and of printed and audio-visual materials" (Davies 1979, 38). Nonetheless, studies during this period continued to show that half the nation's children did not have access to a library in their schools. An even smaller percentage had access to the services of a trained librarian.

Perhaps not surprisingly, much of the research in school libraries undertaken during this time considered book collections, library facilities, and professional staffing as measures of quality. The launching of *Sputnik* by the Russians in the fall of 1957 changed everything and proved to be a watershed moment in the history of American public education when, for the first time, the national spotlight was trained on the quality of its schools. The thought of having lost the educational edge to a totalitarian regime considered by many as "evil" was especially galling to Americans proud of the country's educated workforce and its informed citizenry. The initial congressional response was the National Defense Education Act in 1958, which offered matching funds to school districts for professional development of staff and the purchase of instructional resources to support curriculum in math, science, languages, and counseling.

In the National Defense Education Act, many saw an opportunity to improve the quantity and quality of school libraries. A policy statement created jointly by the AASL, the Association of College and Research Libraries, and the Department of Audio-Visual Instruction of the NEA, for example, spelled out the prerequisites for librarians in creating effective library programs: teaching experience; a multidimensional knowledge base related to learning, curriculum, and guidance; "educational administration and supervision"; "mass communications"; and specialized knowledge related to the evaluation and use of media resources. As Davies (1979) asserts, "This policy statement serve[d] as the 'declaration of independence' for school librarians" in its unequivocal acknowledgment that school media specialists must be directly "involved in the teaching and learning process" (368).

The *Standards for School Library Media Programs* (1960): A Turning Point

In 1960, AASL's *Standards for School Library Media Programs* was issued, constituting what Davies (1979) described as the "single most important document in the history of school library development" (38). If the policy statement in 1958 amounted to a "declaration of independence" for school librarians, then the *Standards* constituted an educational "bill of rights" for students. In fact, the *Standards* explicitly recognized the importance of library resources as "the basic tools needed for the purpose of effective teaching and learning" (Davies, 39) and fundamental to the educational experience of all school children. The Elementary and Secondary Education Act (Title II) followed in 1965, providing additional funding for materials and facilities. Ironically and shortsightedly, the act lacked a provision for the hiring of qualified librarians to superintend the selection, acquisition, and organization of library purchases. Nevertheless, government funding for books and equipment throughout the 1960s, together with powerful statements of policy and direction provided by professional organizations, ultimately made it possible for school librarians to reinvent their libraries as media centers.

The Knapp School Libraries Project

Another major event in the 1960s and one that contributed to the proliferation of centralized school libraries was the Knapp School Libraries Project (1963–1968), which created demonstration libraries at 10 selected elementary and high schools. While Knapp's work was aimed primarily at the improvement of bibliographic instruction in academic settings, her ideas made a major contribution to the development of instructional theories related to library skills instruction for school-aged children. Her insights with regard to integrating library instruction into ongoing course work, planning experiences for learning, and providing practice and problem-solving activities directly related to classroom requirements eventually found their way into elementary and secondary library media programs nationwide (see Chapter 1). To support the rejuvenation of school libraries and to aid in disseminating Knapp's vision for their instructional programs, the Knapp initiative provided funding to reimburse the traveling expenses of school teams so that they could attend demonstration sessions. Eventually, this project spawned hundreds of imitators and with it the demand for certified librarians to re-create the project's programs around the country (Gillespie & Spirt 1973).

New Standards in 1969

The move to institutionalize a centralized library facility within the school received another boost in 1969 with the publication of the *Standards for School Media Programs* (ALA), which called for the unification of all library and audiovisual services under one administrative unit (Gillespie & Spirt 1973)—a move suggested in the Certain Report, *Standard Library Organization and Equipment for Secondary Schools of Different Sizes* (NEA and North Central Association of Colleges and Secondary Schools (1920), almost 50 years earlier—and by 1974, studies reported that 84 percent of the public schools in the country now had centralized library facilities (Carroll 1981). Unfortunately for school libraries, economic conditions during the 1970s created an increasing concern for bottom-line issues and focused the public's attention on all types of public expenditures, educational and otherwise. Turner (1990) maintains that budgetary downsizing during this period not only put pressure on librarians to justify the value of their programs but also quixotically persuaded school districts to promote librarians as regular members of the teaching staff in order to allow them to cover for teachers in the classroom during teacher planning periods. Ironically, these changes paved the way for the introduction of formal programs of library instruction and the creation of library skills curricula.

Developing Instructional Programs

Since the major preoccupation of the early years of the 20th century was the establishment of centralized library collections, it is probably not surprising that widespread acceptance of a teaching role for the library media specialist came about slowly. However, the fact that the very first school librarians were concerned about instructing students in library use is evidenced by the volume of journal articles and library guides published between 1876 (the date of the founding of the ALA and *Library Journal*) and 1920 (Farber 1995). These documents urged the introduction of library skills instruction in elementary and secondary school libraries. However, the first paper that dealt specifically with the instruction of schoolchildren in the use of library resources actually came from outside the field in a speech delivered by T. J. Morgan, the principal of a State Normal School at a meeting of the NEA in Chicago in 1887 (Cecil & Heaps 1940). Even during those early years, a desire was seen to prepare students to be active, engaged members in a democratic society: "preparing the future citizens for successful participation in the social order" (Wilson 1933, 739), a substantial goal echoed today in AASL's (2007) *Standards for the 21st Century Learner*.

The fact remains, however, that until the 1960s, the delivery of library skills instruction at the high school level was most frequently managed through English classes. Indeed, English textbooks usually devoted a separate chapter to study skills and the use of library resources. In cases where English teachers felt that their lack of expertise in this area made them unequal to the task, school librarians were often recruited for the purpose of explaining the vagaries of library organization and demonstrating the use of available reference books (Carroll 1981). For the most part, these early library lessons tended to make little if any use of learning theory, and they relied almost exclusively on lectures that "all too often" seemed aimed at making "miniature librarians of the students" (114).

In the aftermath of the civil rights movement and the Vietnam War, the 1960s ushered in a new perspective on the role of the school and its place in the social order, as educators began thinking about learning in new ways. "School," an institution that had for generations been viewed as "a transmitter of the culture," came increasingly to be considered an "agent of change" (Organization for Economic Cooperation and Development, quoted in Carroll 1981, 23). As reported by the Organization for Economic Cooperation and Development, an educational shift was occurring, centered on learning how to learn, learning for a lifetime, and making the school "an extension of the community" (23). Within this context, the acquisition of discrete facts was increasingly thought to be a less important learning task than understanding the principles of knowledge or developing attitudes and skills to support independent inquiry. At the same time, schools gradually came under more pressure to make educational practices more equitable and "culturally relevant" (Dike 1993). Increasingly, the school library media center "was seen as offering the variety of materials required to meet individual needs" (Dike 1993, 744).

School Libraries and School Reform

During this same period, a number of educational innovations were being introduced that would have a profound influence on the development of library skills instruction during the next four decades. These included small- and large-group instruction, the introduction of ungraded schools and open classrooms, the concept of team teaching, the idea of continuous progress evaluation, and an expanded use of media in the delivery of instruction (Carroll 1981). Moves to replace the single-teacher, lecture-textbook format with instructional designs that required students to use a variety of resources and pressures to create instructional units that offered an interdisciplinary approach to curricular topics created both opportunities and challenges for school librarians. Collection development, which had been predicated on the public library model of creating a well-rounded compilation of materials in all subject areas, became increasingly a matter of acquiring resources that directly supported school curricula.

At the same time, renewed emphasis on the instructional role of the school librarian was advanced in the AASL's (1975) *Media Programs: District and School*, which described the "media program and personnel [as including] active, direct involvement in the school's instructional program" (Coleman 1989, 48). It was also during this period that administrators began to "demand more objective data to demonstrate the worth of the school library program" (Aaron 1982, 231) and the concern for educational outcomes of instruction began to surface (Gillespie & Spirt 1973). These changes also put pressure on school libraries to systematize instruction by articulating specific educational objectives for their programs.

Teaching Library Lessons

In general, the overall goals of library skills instruction in the 1970s and early 1980s reflected reform initiatives related to making students self-sufficient users of libraries and information sources (Liesener 1985). The format for the delivery of "learning skills instruction" in the library context took the form, in the elementary grades, of prearranged library sessions. At the junior high and high school levels, however, the "subject" of library skills was still most frequently taught as a part of English and language arts courses. Of course, informal instruction was also provided as needed to those individual students who came to the library by themselves. At the same time, independent use of the school library was often strictly monitored, with activities limited to research for school reports and book selection for leisure reading.

It must be acknowledged that the model of instruction implemented during this period reflected a much narrower vision of the library's function within the school than is the case today. Typically, bibliographic instruction or library skills instruction involved a series of sequentially conducted lessons, which were repeated with increasing degrees of complexity at each level from kindergarten through grade 12. Students introduced to skills and resources in the elementary grades were expected to achieve mastery or competence of these skills as they progressed through their school years. The content of library lessons generally involved the care of books and other library materials, the parts of a book, authors and illustrators, the use of specific resources and reference tools, library organization, location of items on library shelves, alphabetical order, the card catalog, and the Dewey classification system. Not surprisingly, results of a survey by Hyland (1978) indicated that the skills most often included in library instructional lessons involved knowledge of the physical facilities, selection of appropriate materials, use of particular types of materials, strategies to improve reading comprehension, and report preparation. Baumbach's (1986) study revealed that, by 1985, 64 percent of state and territorial respondents reported that some sort of "organized curriculum in information skills" (280) was in place. Of these, the overwhelming majority included research skills, resource tool skills, location skills, and literature appreciation.

New Focus on Student Learning

But important changes in the school libraries' instructional landscape were on the horizon. Thanks in large part to fallout from the "knowledge explosion" (Dike 1993, 744) of the postwar era, a number of practitioners and scholars developed an interest in the concept of information handling and began to explore the relationship between information and learning. For example, teachers in a study by Irving (1978, cited in Carroll 1981) identified learning from library materials or "information use" as an essential educational outcome for their students. In addition, Irving's research drew attention to task definition as one of the most important information skills that youngsters needed to learn. This emphasis on the student's ability to recognize the need for particular information and its use in the context of specific tasks seemed to echo Willson's (1965) assertion that using information for decision making was a more educationally appropriate goal for instructional intervention than simply teaching the skills necessary to locate and access that information. Indeed, a decade earlier, Willson had also noted the fact that decision-making skills were not ordinarily a part of library skills instruction.

A number of articles published in the late 1970s and early 1980s also indicated a need to reform the library curriculum. New approaches in education and library instruction called attention to the importance of considering both the information "user" and the "cognitive environment" of his or her information tasks (Irving 1983, 4). Irving (1980, cited in Carroll 1981) recognized before many in the field that "the development of abilities and skills in thinking" (121) was the ultimate and most valuable outcome of information skills instruction, and Irving recommended placing these information and study skills within a larger framework of information-seeking tasks to make them both relevant and applicable to life. Too often, Irving argued, the student's role in learning and information seeking had been overlooked. Noting that "the depth and meaning of their learning may be rather more influenced by the way they tackle their work than by any actions of their teachers," Irving (1983) suggested that "the relationship between teaching and learning appears more complex than was previously assumed" (12).

This approach represented a shift in paradigmatic focus that had also been realized in other areas of library and information science, where scholars were struggling to make theoretical sense of information behavior in general and information seeking in new media (e.g., electronic resources, databases, and networks) in particular. The idea that librarians needed to help students learn rather than help them find resources to learn—and to focus on the use of library resources to meet educational goals rather than to achieve library goals—represented a significant shift in direction for many school media specialists (Carroll 1981). This shift also made inevitable the preeminence of the school librarian's role as teacher and the information skills curriculum as the centerpiece of school librarianship (Turner 1990).

Although Irving's was one of the earliest voices proclaiming the need for a fresh approach to library skills instruction, hers was not the only one. During the same period, Mancall, Aaron, and Walker (1986) urged that thinking skills replace resource-based curriculum as a focus for library skills instruction. In addition, on the basis of her study of cognitive science and developmental psychology, Kulleseid (1986) argued for the inclusion of both affective/emotional and cognitive/rational domains in aspects of the library media program. Inherent in these initiatives was the realization that learning was not a task confined to formal schooling and that teaching required a commitment to students' intellectual growth as well as to skill acquisition. These were new goals, and they called for the development of new strategies and new outcomes (Turner 1990).

Flexible Scheduling

The 1980s also saw a move to end or modify fixed or rigidly scheduled library class sessions. In their place, librarians sought to provide "flexible" access by inviting students to come into the library, connect with the librarian, and receive instruction individually or in small groups as needed. Under this scheme, teachers could also bring their own classes to the media center to work on research tasks either in partnership with the librarian or with the librarian "on call." Flexible access thus allowed teachers to capitalize on student interests and "teachable moments" and librarians to deliver "just-in-time" instruction—when it was most likely to extend student learning or support students' research activities.

Where it has been successfully implemented, flexible access scheduling has prompted both the integration of information skills instruction within classroom activity and the process of shared planning by teachers and librarians. Indeed, it has become increasingly apparent that the potential benefits inherent in team teaching and collaborative planning cannot be fully realized without some sort of flexible access policy in place to structure library use (Ray 1994). Moreover, the persistence of rigid scheduling in the library is now considered a barrier to student access to information and to "point-of-need" instruction (Kuhlthau 2001).

AASL's *Standards for the 21st Century Learner*

Acknowledging the challenges imposed on school libraries by the spate of emerging technological innovations that now characterize the environments for information agencies of all kinds, in 2007 AASL offered a new set of standards and introduced new resources to guide the development of information age programs and instructional interventions. To a certain extent, these represent an effort to look holistically at learners and learning as well as at the competencies that will engage today's young people in the increasingly global contexts in which they will be living and working.

AASL's *Standards for the 21st Century Learner* (2007) are built on a foundation of common beliefs, learning standards, and strands of learning. They cover a wide range of learning activities and include recommendations for helping students develop "essential skills, dispositions, responsibilities, and self-assessment strategies" within an overall framework of critical and creative thinking, communication, and collaborative problem solving. "The new standards . . . take a fresh approach and a broad perspective on student standards in the school library field by focusing on the learning process, not on the more limited concept of information literacy. They lay out underlying common beliefs, as well as standards and indicators . . . for all learners" (AASL 2009c, 5).

Taken together, the new standards outline nine common beliefs that make up the learning environment:

1. Reading is a window to the world.
2. Inquiry provides a framework for learning.
3. Ethical behavior in the use of information must be taught.
4. Technology skills are crucial for future employment needs.
5. Equitable access is a key component for education.
6. The definition of information literacy has become more complex as resources and technologies have changed.
7. The continuing expansion of information demands that all individuals acquire the thinking skills that will enable them to work on their own.
8. Learning has a social context.
9. School libraries are essential to the development of learning skills.[6]

In addition, the learning standards can best be understood and realized within a beliefs-driven learning environment. These include the ability to "inquire, think critically, and gain knowledge; [d]raw conclusions, make informed decisions, apply knowledge to new situations, and create new knowledge; [s]hare knowledge and participate ethically and productively as members of our democratic society; [and] [p]ursue personal and aesthetic growth" (AASL 2007, 2).

Four strands of learning are embedded in the standards: skills, dispositions, responsibilities, and self-assessment. *Skills* refer to knowledge of process and content that helps learners grow and develop; *dispositions* are learning behaviors, actions, habits of the mind, and attitudes that "transform a learner from one who is able to learn to one who actually does learn" (AASL, 2007, 15); *responsibilities* require students to assume ownership of their own learning and adopt an ethical approach to their use of information; and *self-assessment* requires learners to employ evaluation skills in judging their own work and that of others.

Empowering Learners: Guidelines for School Library Programs

While clearly aimed at information literacy goals in a dynamic, digital age educational milieu, *Empowering Learners* builds upon the programs delineated in both editions of *Information Power* (AASL & AECT 1988, 1998). With a foundational emphasis on the AASL's (2007) *Standards for the 21st Century Learner*, this book provides a refreshed examination of the evolving roles of the school librarian and details actions for developing visions for learning, teaching for learning, building the learning environment, and empowering learning through leadership. Extensive resource listings pepper the book and offer research-based evidence to provide recommendations for practice. The new guidelines also offer support for the core belief that the school librarian "empowers students to be critical thinkers, enthusiastic readers, skillful researchers, and ethical users of information" (AASL 2009a, 5).

Empowering Learners was an outgrowth a "Vision Summit" that the AASL convened in December 2006 to consider the future of school libraries and school library programs. As a result of discussions conducted online to generate ideas and create new directions, a Guidelines Editing Task Force was charged with developing guidelines for a 21st century school media library program (AASL 2009a). In light of Web 2.0 technologies and an increasingly global information context, the task force decided that a reformulation of the AASL's mission was in order. The result is a statement that more clearly articulates instructional outcomes:

> The mission of the school library program is to ensure that students and staff are effective users of ideas and information. The school librarian empowers students to be critical thinkers, enthusiastic readers, skillful researchers, and ethical users of information. (AASL 2009a, 8)

In addition, school librarians are charged with the following:

- Collaborating with educators and students to design and teach engaging learning experiences that meet individual needs
- Instructing students and assisting educators in using, evaluating, and producing information and ideas through active use of a broad range of appropriate tools, resources, and information technologies
- Providing access to materials in all formats, including up-to-date, high-quality, varied literature to develop and strengthen a love of reading
- Providing students and staff with instruction and resources that reflect current information needs and that anticipate changes in technology and education
- Providing leadership in the total education program and advocating for strong school library programs as essential to meeting local, state, and national educational goals (AASL 2009a)

Standards for the 21st Century Learner in Action

The development of multiple literacies is at the heart of *Standards for the 21st Century Learner in Action*. In a move away from a text-based paradigm, school librarians are urged to consider how students learn about, interact with, create, and assess print, digital, media, and visual literacies. "In addition, learners must use critical- and creative-thinking skills to transform the information that they gather into specialized knowledge that they can use to make decisions, draw conclusions, and create new knowledge" (AASL 2009a, 17).

Because 21st century students need very specific skills in order to make sense of (and place into different contexts) these literacies, the AASL recommends inquiry-driven learning. "Inquiry is defined as a stance toward learning in which the learners themselves are engaged in asking questions and finding answers, not simply accumulating facts (presented by someone else) that have no relation to previous learning or new understanding" (AASL 2009a, 17). It is interesting to note that according to the standards' authors, the very stages involved in the inquiry process might be just as important as working within an overall umbrella of an inquiry-based project. "Learners do not have to complete a full inquiry cycle to be engaged in inquiry-based learning. Any time they are questioning, finding answers, discovering new ideas, and constructing their own meaning they are drawing upon the skills of inquiry" (AASL 2009a, 17).

In sum, *Standards for the 21st Century Learner in Action* provides practitioners with a working document that contains detailed information about standards, strands, indicators, and benchmarks. It is designed as a bridge to help school librarians determine how to integrate the new standards into library media instruction and provides examples and step-by-step directions for developing, through collaboration with classroom teachers, instructional modules that take into account skills, dispositions in action, responsibilities, and self-assessment strategies. (For a full explanation of the standards, with coverage of indicators, benchmarks, model examples, and assessments to support school librarians and educator colleagues, see http://www.ala.org/aasl/standards.)

Demonstrating Our Value: An Enduring Dilemma

The past 35 years have witnessed an increased emphasis on substantiating both the operational efficiency and the overall effectiveness of school library programs. The challenge to demonstrate value that L. A. Martin noted in 1984 (40) is today a professional imperative for school librarians: we must provide empirical substantiation for what every librarian knows intuitively; library programming makes a difference in student achievement. Liesener (1985) summed up the situation well when he wrote,

> The older concepts of passive culture repositories or centers for the development of an enjoyment and appreciation for reading good books while identifying very important functions do not appear to be actively responsive to the entire range of needs identified as crucial for survival and achievement in an extremely complex, information abundant and rapidly changing world. The level of expectation that is satisfied with a nice genteel but fairly superfluous resource is no longer relevant or appropriate. (13)

It has always been difficult to estimate the contribution that library skills instruction makes to student learning. A great many variables contribute to student achievement; for this reason, crediting library skills instruction for variance accounted for as measured on standardized achievement tests has proven to be a formidable task. Recent years have seen a number of estimable attempts to provide the sort of statistical evidence that administrators appreciate. Most influential to date among American studies has been the research initiated by Lance, Welborn, and Hamilton-Pennell (2002); these studies are reviewed in some detail in Chapter 8. Lance's (2002) findings have led him to conclude that

> there is a clear consensus in the results now available for eight states: School libraries are a powerful force in the lives of America's children. The school library is one of the few factors whose contribution to academic achievement

has been documented empirically, and it is a contribution that cannot be explained away by other powerful influences on student performance.

More studies will, of course, be needed to establish and understand links between instructional models, academic achievement, and lifelong learning. In an interview with Lance, Callison (2006) argued for more quantitative data and rigorous experimental research methodology as strategies for convincing school administrators of the benefits of school library programs and school librarians. Todd and Kuhlthau (2003), on the other hand, have sought to capture the voices of today's youth in an effort to understand at a deeper level and in their own words how students learn. In this way, Todd (2009) seeks to replace with research evidence the rhetorical and anecdotal claims to learning outcomes advanced by practitioners in defense of their programs.

Interestingly and importantly, the instructional function of the school librarian has been made more complex and more exciting in recent years by increased attention to reading and libraries in the national media. The White House Conference held in 2002 cast a spotlight on school libraries and in some respects raised expectations for their programs not witnessed in many years. However, the conference's apparent failure to focus on information skills instruction as a key dimension of the library program seems to reinforce an outdated conceptualization of the librarian's role. While books and reading indeed remain central foci of school library programs, instruction in information seeking and inquiry learning greatly increases what contemporary models of school librarianship can offer students and teachers.

There appears to be a persistent perception on the part of some educators as well as the general public that providing electronic access to information alone creates equity and parity of educational opportunity for all students. It seems quite likely that this misconception will continue until policymakers come to understand and appreciate the cognitive challenges that exist for students operating in online environments and the complexities involved in information seeking and learning in dynamic information environments.

Notes

1. Often referred to as the father of American public education, Horace Mann at one time served as librarian at Brown University in Providence, Rhode Island.

2. Johann Pestalozzi (1746–1827) was a Swiss-born educator and pedagogical visionary who influenced educational practice in the United States and abroad in the nineteenth century. Believing that access to publicly supported education was the birthright of every child and fundamental to the development of democratic values in a society, Pestalozzi also recognized the importance of parental involvement and encouragement to the education of their own children. In addition, Pestalozzi pioneered the replacement of rote memorization by experiential learning and advocated the ordering of curricular content so that mastery of simple concepts preceded the presentation of abstractions. A precursor of such educational giants as Herbart and Froebel, Pestalozzi adopted a holistic approach to education that fostered the development of physical health and a sense of morality as well as intellectual achievement.

3. In some cities, public libraries also managed classroom libraries in the public schools.

4. The Julius Rosenwald Fund was founded by an Illinois philanthropist in 1917. Rosenwald, who had amassed a fortune as president and chairman of the board of Sears, Roebuck and Co., was one of a number of public-spirited citizens of the period who hoped

to bring an end to racial inequity through investment in public education. In addition to the Rosenwald fund, other major contributors to the effort were the Rockefeller General Education Board, the Anna T. Jeanes Fund, and the John F. Slater Fund, to name only a few. The general approach of these funds was to use their money to leverage local funds from white and black communities in support of black schools. Choosing to work within the social system of the segregated South rather than confronting racism directly, these groups seemed to believe that as blacks achieved parity in education, racism would fade, and the white community would accept blacks as equals. Rosenwald, in collaboration with Booker T. Washington, designed and built dozens of rural schools in the South between 1917 and 1928. After that time, he turned his attention to preparing black educators and, among other projects, established scholarships for black students (Hanchett 1988).

5. Hanchett (1988) writes, "Rosenwald and his fellow philanthropists succeeded magnificently in raising the level of black education in the South. But they failed in their larger goal of promoting equality. Despite the marked improvements in conditions, in 1930 black students were even further behind whites by almost every important measure than they had been in 1915. Though black schools had improved, white boards were improving white facilities much faster" (4). The same was true for school library collections. Hanchett reports that the total expenditure for library books to white schools in South Carolina during the 1925–1926 school year was $26,982.89. Library budgets for black schools during this same year totaled $205.32. Of the 2,330 black elementary schools operating in South Carolina in 1933, fewer than 10 percent had any library books at all; during the same year, more than 60 percent of white elementary schools had a school library.

6. Excerpted from *Standards for the 21st Century Learner* by the American Association of School Librarians, a division of the American Library Association, copyright © 2007 American Library Association. Available for download at http://www.ala.org/aasl/standards. Used with permission.

3 The Information Search Process

Kuhlthau's Legacy

> The objective of library and information services and systems is to provide access to sources, information, and ideas.
>
> —Kuhlthau (2005)

In a review of specific approaches to the teaching of library and information skills, Carol C. Kuhlthau (1987) identified three major models in use for instruction in school library settings in the 1970s and 1980s: the source or library tool approach, the pathfinder or search strategy approach, and the process approach. Whereas the source and pathfinder models involved teaching techniques and tools necessary for the completion of research tasks, process models contextualized library skills and reframed them as strategies for critical thinking and problem solving.

Modes of Instruction: The Source Approach

The source approach to library and information skills features lessons related to the organization of library materials in a particular setting and the location and use of specific reference books, indexes, and other resources that are available there. This "how-to" approach dates from the earliest days of school libraries and is emphasized in the "scope-and-sequence" types of library skills lessons. Because lessons built on this model are generally site specific and carefully tailored to local sources and local situations, library sessions are relatively easy to plan and conduct. However, this approach has some very serious limitations. For one thing, it is often difficult to tailor lessons delivered in a preplanned sequence to the instructional needs of specific individuals or the exigencies of a specific situation. For another, such lessons are conducted in the library outside the flow of ongoing classroom activities in which students are otherwise involved; for this reason, students often fail to see the relevance of what the librarian is trying to teach them. In addition, the practice sessions that ordinarily follow the demonstration of a particular reference resource and its use are basically artificial or "inauthentic" in that they are made up expressly for the purposes of the lesson and taught out of context. Finally, the source model assumes access to a static library collection of preselected print resources; the introduction of research tools in this way does little to prepare students for information seeking outside the context of the specific library or, indeed, in the absence of the specific resources on which the lessons are based.

Modes of Instruction: The Pathfinder Approach

The pathfinder model is a search strategy that requires students to move from an overview or background source, such as an encyclopedia, through a sequence of progressively more specific sources, leading finally to an examination of the most—and presumably the most pertinent—resources. This approach is particularly useful for students who lack content knowledge of a topic because it forces them to investigate the topic holistically before moving on to create a specific focus or thesis statement. It is also useful conceptually, as it serves to introduce students to different types and levels of resources that may be immediately useful to them in completing their projects. However, as Kuhlthau (1987) notes, it is a rather rigid approach and may have limited utility outside academic tasks and school assignments. Nor does the pathfinder approach allow teachers to take account of the cognitive abilities, information needs, learning styles, and information-seeking preferences of individual students. In short, it is a "one-size-fits-all" instructional strategy.

Modes of Instruction: The Process Models Approach

The source and the pathfinder approaches represent examples of a resource-centered view of library service in that their primary focus is on texts and documents within a specific collection. Process models, on the other hand, consider information skills as pieces of the information-seeking "puzzle" and can be both better understood and more fully applied if they are practiced within a larger framework. The focus thus moves from direct instruction of specific resources to a holistic awareness of processes involved as the seeker progresses toward a curricular goal. Such approaches are specifically user centered in that they begin with a statement of the information need as articulated by the student. A number of process models for library skills instruction were developed during the 1980s; the best-known models were created by Sheingold (1986), Callison (1986), and Kuhlthau (1987, 1988a, 1988b). Many of these models rely on inquiry learning, sometimes referred to as discovery learning rather than direct instruction ("receptive learning") (Gordon, 2000), and focus the learner's attention as much on the information-seeking "means" as it does on the end product. A major benefit and outcome of teaching this approach is the student's ability to apply understandings of the process across situations, problems, and projects.

Sheingold's Inquiry Model

Sheingold's (1986) approach is an inquiry model based on educational principles derived from cognitive psychology. As such, it places the learner at the center of instructional interest and makes thinking the central outcome. More specifically, Sheingold asserts that a "child's mind is [not] an empty vase into which information is 'poured,'" nor is the library a place where children go to "get" information. Rather, the library is viewed as an "apprentice's workshop for thinking—a place where" children actively construct their own understandings through interactions with "human, physical," and "symbolic worlds" (80). Within the inquiry process, students come to create meaning by relating what they read to what they already know. Sheingold also suggests that, to be meaningful, the questions that drive the inquiry process should address real-world problems.

According to Sheingold (1986), inquiry is itself a complex, nonlinear investigative, problem-solving "process that includes formulating a problem or question, searching through and/or collecting information to address the problem or question, making sense of that information, and developing an understanding of, point of view about, or 'answer' to the question" (81). Within this framework, student research is a goal-oriented activity in which the learners seek solutions, solve problems, fill needs, or answer questions. The questions children create at each stage in the process serve as frames of reference for information seeking and information collection that drive inquiry forward. These questions, which are "formulated and reformulated as new information is gathered and thought about" (81), later become the basis for evaluating the relevance and utility of information found and resources used. Elements of Sheingold's model are summarized in Table 3.1.

Sheingold's (1986) inquiry model also requires learners to do something with what has been learned in order to keep the knowledge "alive." Learning is thus seen as "self-motivated," "intentional" and "purposive" (82). "Knowing about oneself and other people as knowers," about "the task to be undertaken," and about the "strategies to apply" as well as the monitoring of "one's own performance with respect to the task" (84) are important elements as well. Citing Vygotsky's (1978) notion that a zone of proximal development (ZPD) identifies or targets a particular moment in a student's learning when instructional intervention will result in optimal learning, Sheingold recommends the use of social interaction to facilitate "children's cognitive development" and instructional techniques that enable the child to assume the responsibility for learning "as the child becomes able to do it" (84).

Table 3.1
Sheingold's (1986) Elements of a Quality Inquiry Environment

- Inquiry is a complex process that includes:
  1. formulating a problem or question
  2. searching through and/or collecting information to address the problem or question
  3. making sense of the information, and
  4. developing an understanding of, point of view about, or "answer" to the question
- In an effective inquiry environment, students:
  1. build on their existing knowledge and skills
  2. select topics of interest
  3. explore a variety of resources (i.e., books, maps, primary source documents, Web sites, videos, audios, photographs)
  4. select the best way to communicate their findings
  5. share learning with real-world audiences
  6. are evaluated on both process and product
  7. evaluate themselves, their peers, their resources, and their teachers

Source: Adapted from http://virtualinquiry.com/inquiry/inquiry7.htm.

Table 3.2
Elements of Callison's (1986) Free-Inquiry Model

1. Lessons are planned and taught by librarians and teachers acting together.

2. Lesson objectives are evolutionary and negotiated by student and teacher.

3. Students document the processes of learning and share them with others.

4. Content is driven by questions that students raise and answer by exploring resources in the library and beyond.

5. Teachers provide direction for learning, but students are encouraged to take initiatives and work independently.

6. Time for the learning activity is flexible.

7. Peer tutoring is encouraged.

8. Peer interaction and teaming are supported.

9. Projects are shared with peers and parents.

10. Students may choose to extend their learning.

Callison's Free-Inquiry Model

The "free-inquiry" model advanced by Callison (1986) features a library skills instruction plan that is fully integrated into the curriculum, with the teacher and librarian acting as an instructional team. For this reason, the lessons based on this model require advanced planning and coordination. However, lesson objectives are not prepared in advance; rather, they are created on an individual basis by students and teachers acting together. Evaluation of student performance is also a responsibility shared by instructors and pupils. Based on the work of Victor (1974, cited in Callison), the elements of the "inquiry approach to teaching and learning" (21) are summarized in Table 3.2.

Essentially, Callison's (1986) inquiry model attempts to move beyond instructional tasks that require the use of library resources to the process of engaging students scientifically through activities that afford them experience in posing their own questions, finding their own answers, and sharing the results with peers, parents, and community members. Information seeking itself is initiated in response to questions that students devise, and answers are sought from human as well as text-based sources. Traditionally, students create logs to document their activities and their reflections on the processes as they unfold. Evaluation of sources—whether located inside or outside the immediate library environment—is stressed. The model specifically emphasizes the interaction between students and librarians, students and teachers, and students and their peers. Finally, the model explicitly encourages students to develop the skills to act independently in finding solutions to the problems posed.

Kuhlthau's Information Search Process Model

The most significant contribution to the development of the process approach to teaching and learning in school libraries has been Carol Collier Kuhlthau's (1988a, 1988b, 1993b, 2004) research. As it is the only theoretical model that has been empirically tested, Kuhlthau's information search process (ISP) model represents a watershed in the development of new strategies for the delivery of library skills instruction. Over the course of 20 years, the model has continued to demonstrate its value "as a theoretical construct for examining information behavior [and] ... serves as a diagnostic tool for intervention in different information seeking contexts" (Kuhlthau, Maniotes, & Caspari 2007). For this reason, it deserves special attention and is highlighted here.

In brief, Kuhlthau's (1991, 1993a, 1993b, 1997) studies track the creation and testing of a model for inquiry-based information seeking. Particularly noteworthy is Kuhlthau's concern for understanding the experience of information seeking from the point of view of student learners and for sharing her findings with professional as well as academic audiences. Her purpose throughout has been to find effective ways to assist students in the information search process—the process of learning from information.

Although initially Kuhlthau (1993a) did not consider the model "a formula for teaching" or a "packaged program" (12) of instruction, school librarians were quick to find value in the straightforward description of the ISP that the model provides. Students and teachers have also found in Kuhlthau's work a vocabulary for discussing ways in which assistance and instruction can best be delivered.[1] While Kuhlthau's model of the ISP can be understood as "representational" (Bates, 1979a) of a student's thoughts, feelings, and activities related to the conduct of research assignments, the cognitive processes involved (e.g., critical thinking, decision making, and problem solving) are essentially the same as those identified by scholars as necessary for the development of information literacy. For this reason, Kuhlthau's ISP model has found applications in a variety of informational contexts within and beyond the school library.

Kuhlthau's (1991, 1993b, 2004) ISP model was created on the basis of a series of studies conducted over a 10-year period, designed to consider the experience of information seeking from the point of view of the library user. The initial study involved observation of high school students researching topics assigned for a term paper; in subsequent studies, Kuhlthau broadened her sample to include information seeking by informants engaged in a variety of information tasks in school, academic, public, and corporate libraries. In collecting data, Kuhlthau relied on a number of methods, including observation, case studies, individual and focus group interviews, surveys, journals, and student-produced research papers.

Theoretical Underpinnings

In creating a model to fit her observations, Kuhlthau (1993b) drew from theoretical frameworks in psychology, education, information science, and communication. In particular, her research builds on the personal construct theory of George Kelly (1963), the learning theory of John Dewey (1916, 1933), the cognitive theory of Jerome Bruner (1980), information needs theories in the writings of Robert Taylor (1968) and Nicholas Belkin (1980), and the sense-making model created by Brenda Dervin (1983). (The conceptualizations of information needs in the work of Taylor, Belkin, and Dervin are reviewed in Chapter 6.)

Based on her research, Kuhlthau (1991) posited that, in searching for relevant information, seekers pass through six cognitive stages: initiation, selection, exploration, formulation, collection, and presentation. (A summary of Kuhlthau's model is provided in Figure 3.1.) In creating an instructional model, Kuhlthau (1994, 2001)

Figure 3.1
Kuhlthau's Model of the Information Search Process

added a seventh stage, assessment; at this step, students are asked to reflect on what they have learned about the research topic as well as about the ISP as a whole. Although the model appears linear as drawn, Kuhlthau argues that, in practice, students engage the stages recursively, moving back and forth between them as the process unfolds. Thus, students may have to repeat activities typical of the earlier steps if, for example, they find that they have insufficiently narrowed the topic or failed to locate information sufficient to solve the research problem, and so forth.

Following Kelly (1963), Kuhlthau (2001) was also interested in tracking students' affective or "feelings" processes as well as their cognitive or "thinking" processes. In so doing, she observed that the feelings of information seekers varied across the course of the ISP, changing from anxiety to optimism, from confusion to clarity, from uncertainty to confidence, and from apprehension to satisfaction or disappointment. The complexity of information seeking and the difficulties that students encounter in their research investigations, together with the affective discomforts that such activities often create in novice information seekers, convinced Kuhlthau of the need for instructional intervention by school librarians that would provide "guidance in learning from the information they have located" and support for students far "beyond merely leading students to sources."

Verification of Kuhlthau's ISP

Between 2003 and 2005, Kuhlthau was joined by colleagues Todd and Heinström in reviewing ISP-related research as it has been undertaken over time and across contexts and in considering its continued usefulness as a "pedagogical framework" for understanding information seeking "in new technologically rich information environments" (Kuhlthau, Heinström, & Todd 2008). They also tested the model in a study that tracked the ISP for more than 500 students in grades 6 to 12. Specifically, the researchers sought to observe changes at each stage of the ISP, any interactions between feelings and knowledge construction within "the context of a collaborative inquiry project," and difficulties in searching. The charting of "information-to-knowledge development" was also a research goal. In the study, students reported feelings of "confidence, disappointment, relief, frustration, confusion, optimism, uncertainly, satisfaction and anxiety." Although there were some variations observed, the study verified feelings reported in earlier studies. For students who failed to find a focus, depth of knowledge remained at a specific fact or superficial level; these students also reported negative feelings of "disappointment, frustration, confusion, and uncertainty" during the ISP. "They were relieved at the end but this relief seemed more related to the project completion rather than a sense of accomplishment. . . . " In fact, "not all students progressed through the construction process . . . [but] those who did tended to learn the most." Moreover, "students working in digital environments appear to go through the stages to build knowledge of their topics, but the easy availability of information encourages them to skip stages and thus end up with superficial conceptions of their topics." Overall, the authors conclude, "the model continues to be a useful theoretical and explanatory framework for user studies in librarianship and information science." They also found that the most challenging stages in terms of students in the study were those involving prefocus exploration and focus formulation and concluded that intervention would have been most useful and beneficial to students struggling with these activities.

A Closer Look at Kuhlthau's ISP

Kuhlthau (1993b, 1999, 2004) characterized the first step or stage in the ISP process as *task initiation*. For students, this stage generally begins with the assignment of a research task or question. Kuhlthau's informants indicated that many students experience this particular phase as a time of uncertainty and/or anxiety, particularly when they lack knowledge of the subject and/or an understanding of how to proceed.

The *selection* stage of the model is that point in the process when the students choose a question to explore or a topic in which they have an interest. Students generally experience feelings of optimism during this stage. However, Kuhlthau also found these feelings to be short lived, fading at the *exploration* stage, especially when students begin information seeking on a topic about which they know little. Feelings of confusion are typical because part of the challenge in the exploration stage is to make sense of new information, some of which may conflict with students' prior understandings or preconceived ideas. "As students encounter inconsistent incompatible information that does not match their expectations," Kuhlthau (1997) writes, "they commonly begin to doubt the appropriateness of the topic, the adequacy of the information sources, and their own ability to accomplish the assignment" (713). Kuhlthau has characterized this drop in confidence as "the dip."

The ability to use information obtained in the exploration stage to draw some preliminary conclusions and create personal understandings enables students to create thesis statements and a personal point of view about the topic at *focus formulation*.[2] Quite logically, Kuhlthau (1997) considers focus formulation the most important task in the ISP, as it is the focus that guides students in determining the pertinence of information later on. Kuhlthau notes as well that students with a clear idea of where they were headed at this stage in the search process displayed an increased interest in both the topic and the project.[3] During the *collection* stage, the students Kuhlthau studied went confidently about the task of gathering information pertinent to their research topics and centered on their research focus; at the final or *presentation* stage, as students prepared to organize their information, to make connections among ideas, and to present their work in their chosen formats, they felt relieved that the search was over and either satisfied or disappointed with the search results. Kuhlthau maintained that students' feelings at the end of the process were often directly related to their ability to formulate a personal focus for their projects.

Interestingly, Kuhlthau (1993b, 1997, 2004) found that exploration was a difficult stage for many students. Indeed, impatience with having to do the reading necessary to obtain an overall understanding of the topic sometimes caused students to jump over both exploration and formulation stages entirely and immediately to begin collecting information. Taking time to reflect on information obtained through exploring a topic thoroughly prepares students to create a focus. Unfortunately, as Kuhlthau notes, most information-seeking sessions are not structured to include time for processing information in this way. As noted above, many students confuse exploration (when any topic-related information may seem relevant) with collection (where students should concentrate on making use of information pertinent to their foci). When this happens, students can end up with too much information of a general nature, experience difficulty in deciding what information to use, and consequently have trouble organizing the information in coherent ways. Providing guidance at this stage is extremely helpful to students, especially those in middle school and junior high for whom research as a process may be an entirely novel concept. Two strategies that Kuhlthau suggests may help students work through this stage are (1) reading and reflecting and then (2) preparing a list of topic-related ideas that are of interest and relevance to the information seeker. Building time for reflecting and formulating while students are exploring and collecting ensures that they will not miss "the critical stages of learning" (Kuhlthau et al. 2008). Indeed, Kuhlthau asserts that when students do not take the time to reflect, their understandings remain at a descriptive level, and they simply do not learn as much.

Kuhlthau's (1997) and Kuhlthau et al.'s (2008) research indicates that individuals experience the ISP variously, moving through the stages of the ISP iteratively and at different rates. Indeed, some fail to complete all the described stages. Studies subsequent to the first one also indicated that the confidence levels experienced by some groups were found to deviate from the model as initially proposed. For example, searchers in public library settings expressed more confidence in the initial stage of the search than those in academic and school settings. By the same token, college searchers expressed more confidence in the outcomes of these projects than did students in the high school studies. This finding suggests that the feelings experienced during the ISP may be a function of both the nature of the task and the experience of the searcher. Furthermore, the seeker's failure to formulate a personal perspective might be the result of the assigned nature of the task or students' assumptions that it is the views of the "authorities" consulted and not their own that should be expressed in presenting the finished project. Finally, Kuhlthau (1997) reports findings that suggest "that younger children experience the search process in similar holistic ways," although those "under the ages of eleven or twelve" tend to be more involved in building a knowledge base than in creating "a personal perspective" and "experience formulation less intentionally than teenagers," perhaps because they lack the developmental structures to engage in abstract thinking (713).

Kuhlthau's (1991) efforts to track four of her original high school informants in a longitudinal study revealed that, as more experienced information users, these students noted "that interest in a topic increases as a search progresses; that a topic changes as information is gathered; [and] that a central theme evolves as information is gathered" (368). It was also evident that these students felt more in control of the search process and of their projects and developed a kind of personal "sense of ownership" in the process itself as a "way to learn," above and beyond the more pragmatic goals of fulfilling a school assignment. In a very real sense, the search process became a metacognitive device, wherein the student was made aware not only of stages in the ISP but also of the evolution in his or her own thinking about the topic and in the problem-solving process itself.

Kuhlthau's Research "Moods"

Unique to Kuhlthau's (1991, 1993b) work is her consideration of two attitudes or "moods" exhibited by students in her studies, which she labeled "invitational" and "indicative." When information seekers are in an invitational mood, they are open to exploring their topics, and they eagerly seek and consider new ideas, new information, and new information sources. When students decide that they have enough information to meet their research needs, they move into an indicative mood, which allows them to end the search and proceed with the presentation and assessment phases of the process. As Kuhlthau notes, an invitational mood is especially important at the initiation and exploration stages, when students are trying to understand their topics. An indicative mood, which marks the formulation and collection stages, helps students conclude their searches and is especially important when decisions must be made regarding the creation of a thesis. In Kuhlthau's (1997) view, it is essential that school librarians learn to recognize student moods so that they can intercede if students sustain an invitational mood so long that they are unable to decide on a topic or end a search so early that they select a focus without the necessary reflection. An emphasis on location and access skills in information skills instruction may also serve to encourage students to close down prematurely their information-seeking activities before exploring all their options.

Implementing the ISP

To ensure that research projects are directly related to curricular objectives and course content, Kuhlthau (1993b) posits task initiation as the creation of open-ended questions. Ideally, these questions arise in classroom discussions and resonate with a student's own experience and interests. She also suggests identifying the audience for whom the assignment is being prepared at this stage in the process. The use of student journals is a way to help students preserve aspects of the process, particularly their thinking about possible topics and their feelings; journals can also help students keep track of their searching strategies and their notes. Guidance, coaching, and conferencing provided by teachers and librarians can help reduce student feelings of uncertainty, which frequently arise in exploring the information on a topic for the first time. Kuhlthau (2004) also believes that interaction with the instructor will help students in creating a focus for their topics, constructing a personal perspective, and organizing the information for presentation. In fact, evaluating the process in terms of the use of time and resources should include consideration of the use of the school librarian!

Research Based on Kuhlthau's ISP Model

An impressive number of research studies have drawn on Kuhlthau's (1993b, 1997) pioneering study, and the research stream anchored by Kuhlthau's ISP is unprecedented in the school library literature. When considered together, the insights embedded in study findings have not only extended our understandings of the ISP as Kuhlthau originally described it but can also be used by librarians "in the field" to improve and extend both instruction and service.

In an early study, Kuhlthau's (1993b) model served as a guide to the research process for students in a high school science course team taught by a library media specialist and their science teacher (McNally & Kuhlthau 1994). Science topics served as the focus of student research conducted by junior and senior high students in an action research study[4] conducted by Loerke (1994) and a case study by Watson (2003). McGregor's (1994b) research, as well as Pitts's (1995) dissertation, considered mental models, while Swain's (1996) research focused on the searching behaviors of college freshman. Burdick's (1996) study is notable in that it looked at gender issues in information seeking. Six additional studies of information seeking and children that used Kuhlthau's ISP were conducted by Gordon and Broch, in 2000, Harada in 2002, Holliday and Li in 2004, Heinström, in 2006, and Hyldegärd in 2009.

In McNally and Kuhlthau (1994), Kuhlthau's ISP was presented to students as an instructional model and guide to information-seeking activities. Students were required to keep a log of their activities and their reactions to their readings, and instructors also used individual conferences to monitor student progress. Instructors found that student journals were especially helpful to students as they attempted to find an individual focus at the formulation stage. In implementing the ISP, the teaching team actively encouraged students to be "invitational" in their approach to the research assignment and "to be open to ideas" (57). At the selection stage, when students were expected to find a topic for their projects, the instructors encouraged students to browse current periodicals and newspapers to gain background information. Researchers found that students experienced confusion as their exploration activities led them to identify scientists, gather factual information, and encounter the vocabulary that would assist them in online searching. Providing an opportunity for students to share their searches with one another also helped students build their confidence and "clarify the direction of their work." Strategies that students found particularly useful involved "expressing their thoughts aloud" (58) as well as hearing that others in the class were experiencing similar difficulties. The collection phase of the ISP provided an opportunity for the library media specialist and the teacher to "suggest, introduce, and explain sources as needed" (58–59) in the library and beyond; in the presentation stage, the teacher facilitated the process by helping "students organize their notes" in anticipation of creating a final project. Reflection on the process followed, with students being asked to consider their own study skills and thinking as well as their use of time.

In her study, Loerke (1994) applied Kuhlthau's theoretical frameworks and methods in an "action" study of 120 junior high school students involved in a research project that required the use of library resources. Of particular interest to Loerke were the steps taken by student information seekers, their feelings, and the processes they used to focus their topics. Loerke was also interested in identifying or creating intervention strategies that would help students engaged in the process of focusing. In general, Loerke found that, from the beginning, students experienced feelings that mirrored those of the high school students in studies conducted by Kuhlthau (1993b) and McNally and Kuhlthau (1994); initial uncertainty, which gave way to optimism at the point of topic selection, was followed by a period of confusion during prefocus exploration. Confidence increased as the creation of a focus proceeded and students had a "greater sense of where they were going . . . and felt more confident about what they were doing" (24–25).

Even though, as Loerke (1994) noted, students tended to choose topics with which they had some personal experience, developing a focus represented the most challenging aspect of the process. Seventh graders in the study experienced more problems with this task than eighth graders, particularly those who "lacked background knowledge" (25) of the subject domain of the topic or the topic itself. In addition, "[m]ost of the grade 7 students appeared to be reasoning at [Piaget's] concrete operational stage in their science thinking" (25). However, "providing background knowledge and teacher guidance allow[ed students] to work at more abstract levels" (25). This supports the theory that students can operate at a higher level with assistance than they can if left on their own. Loerke concluded that even though "grade 8 students researched their topics in greater depth, these students also needed the structure of built-in checkpoints to ensure that they were not having difficulties" (25). Based on her research, Loerke recommended a number of strategies that librarians can use in assisting junior high information seekers who are working on a research task. These included assigning research as the "culminating activity" for a unit of study so that students have some content knowledge on which to build, allowing time to enable students to forge links between their topics and their prior knowledge, and keeping response journals throughout the instruction phases of the unit as an aid to topic selection and investigational focus.

Watson (2003) also chose a science topic—the typical science fair project—as the focus of her study of stakeholders' perceptions of such assignments. She interviewed three middle school students, their parents, their teachers, the library media specialist at the school, and the local public reference librarian about their perceptions of the same middle school science fair and found that all parties agreed that the purpose of the fair was to teach *process* rather than *content*, though some thought the assignment emphasized the organizational process and others the scientific process. The author posits that by devising and employing a "step-by-step" approach in researching, "the assignment does not represent the kind of inquiry that real researchers do in making meaning of the problematic as defined by Kuhlthau (1997)" since this kind of planning limits "the ambiguous nature of constructing meaning and gaining understanding." She recommends that teachers and school library media specialists design projects that allow "students to pursue ideas that intrigue them enough to investigate" in more personal and individualistic ways, thus allowing for mistakes and wrong turns that "may offer as much information as successful efforts" (10).

Pitts's (1995) dissertation research used a grounded theory approach to investigate the ISPs of grade 10 students whom she considered novice researchers. Students in this study had been assigned a video production project on a science topic of their own choosing. Pitts determined that difficulties students encountered in completing this essentially unstructured research task were related not only to their lack of background knowledge of the subject but also to their lack of mental models to guide their own information seeking and project completion. Their experiential deficits with research projects of this kind led them to rely on familiar topics and prior interests and the convenience and availability of relevant resources. Another reason for project failure was the fact that students did not automatically consider research projects as vehicles for learning course content.

Students in Pitts's (1995) study were not given any support for information seeking and use, and this lack of instructional input "kept most of them from developing more complex, subject-related mental models." She concluded,

> It is probably true that most people who begin a new research project are at first novices in the subject matter involved. If those people have expert information-seeking and use understandings, however, they know how to use the information skills to strengthen the subject understandings. . . . But if subject understandings and information skills are both weak, . . . students have little chance of being able to progress. . . .

In another study of students' use of mental models, McGregor (1994a, 1994b) looked at the information-seeking behavior of high school students while finding information for school research assignments in the school library, the public library, and home settings. Her conclusions led her to develop a "model of thinking" that confirmed Kuhlthau's assertion of the "non-linear nature of the process" (1994b, 72). In addition, her findings indicated that students followed an intuitive path without being aware of the processes they used, that their purposes for thinking could be either external or internal to the information, and that Bloom's (1956) taxonomy accurately described their thinking processes throughout the different stages of research. She also found that the nature of the research question affected the complexity of students' thinking during the information-seeking process.

Swain's (1996) study of college freshmen enrolled in an English class also sheds some light on information seeking and the information search processes of student researchers. Swain tracked students to compare their information-seeking processes with Kuhlthau's (1993b) ISP. Although students' activities in Swain's research mirrored those that Kuhlthau described, there were some interesting variations. For example, Swain's informants were observed to move through the stages of the ISP recursively and frequently in a different order. In addition, they often combined steps.

While Swain (1996) found that, as their projects developed, the students' thoughts (increasing specificity and clarity and decreasing ambiguity) and feelings (from uncertainty to confidence) followed Kuhlthau's (1993b) model, their speed in moving through the phases varied. In addition, it was observed that students changed topics several times, meaning that task initiation and topic selection stages had to be repeated. Sometimes students moved from initiation to focus formulation immediately. Swain's informants also noted that interpersonal interaction and communication were important to success in developing and focusing their topics. Indeed, discussions with parents and peers also had a direct impact on students' selection of both topics and library resources. This finding is consistent with the implementation of the ISP model in McNally and Kuhlthau (1994), who also noted the importance of interaction with others at a number of points in the search process.

Burdick's (1996) study involved youth in grades 10 through 12 who were engaged in research activities in their English courses. Citing a report published in 1992 that raised concerns that models generally used to guide research projects

Table 3.3
Gender-Related Differences in the ISP Identified by Burdick (1996, 1997)

Girls were:	Boys were:
More likely to seek assistance	Less likely to ask for help
More likely to work together	More likely to express confidence
More likely to be optimistic at task initiation and doubtful and uncertain at completion	More active
More reflective	More emphatic in collecting data and completing assignments
More interested in exploring and focusing topics	More comfortable in expressing personal opinions
Less confident overall in their abilities	

Both girls and boys:

Showed higher degrees of involvement for tasks in which their interest was high

Placed more emphasis on project completion than on focus formulation

Expressed feelings of confidence not necessarily related to the formulation of a personal perspective

Exhibited choice behaviors for topics related to gender

and assignments "might favor males" (19), Burdick elected to test this theory through Kuhlthau's (1993b) ISP. Kuhlthau's model essentially assumes a "generic" information searcher. Using an approach to data collection that Kuhlthau designed when investigating the ISP, Burdick explored gender issues particularly as they related to cognitive and affective information-seeking behaviors and to focus formulation; she found that students demonstrated gender-related differences in their selection of topics, in their searching behaviors, and in the feelings they reported experiencing. (A summary of Burdick's findings related to gender and information seeking appears in Table 3.3.) For example, the girls Burdick observed were "more likely to work together" and were more reflective than were the boys, while the boys were more active in their approaches to research tasks and "less likely" to seek assistance. While Burdick did not include the subject area of the topic as a research variable in the study, the tendency on the part of some girls to prefer affective approaches and some boys' preference for logic suggests that "there might be gender associations with either the information seeking or the subject domain of the class in which the process takes place" (21). In addition, study results provided some evidence that "girls chose topics about either males or females," while "males chose topics only about males."

In terms of student perceptions of the information-seeking tasks, girls in Burdick's (1996) study emphasized the exploration and formulation stages of the ISP, while boys showed more interest in collecting materials and completing the assignment. However, both boys and girls considered the completion of the assignment to be more important than the creation of a focus. Burdick's research also revealed that boys were less tentative than girls about "expressing a personal perspective" (22). While this quality may reflect gender differences related to self-confidence, Burdick suggests that there may also be developmental characteristics that have a bearing on students' abilities to formulate personal points of view, as in, for instance, whether students consider knowledge as something that is "given" or something that is "constructed."

Burdick (1996) identified two approaches to information seeking employed by students she observed; she characterized the students using these approaches as "navigators" and "tourists." Whereas navigators tended to follow the phases of Kuhlthau's (1993b) model quite closely, tourists were much more likely to look for answers to their questions through the exploration and collection stages of the ISP and appeared confident about their activities, even though they failed to create a focus. In terms of feelings, Burdick's female informants were less likely than boys to express confidence in their projects, regardless of outcome, although in general, girls were more likely to discuss their affective responses related to the overall process than were the boys. This led Burdick to conclude that Kuhlthau's theory of "decreasing uncertainty" may "be less applicable to these females" (23). Finally, Burdick noted that interest and personal investment in the topics chosen proved motivating for students in her study and increased their overall involvement and enjoyment of the ISP. For this reason, she considers involvement an important, if previously unrecognized, aspect of the ISP and suggests that the ISP model be extended to include "enjoyment, satisfaction, confidence, and competence" as positive outcomes of the process. While it is important to remember that Burdick's findings are based on a single study, they raise interesting issues that should be pursued further.

Gordon's (2000) small study of grade 10 science students used Kuhlthau's ISP framework with special attention to task initiation and prefocus exploration. Using "think-alouds, interviews, and journals" as data sources, Gordon's quasi-experimental study compared searching efficiency and effectiveness of two groups, one of which had received direct instruction in concept mapping as a presearch activity and one of which had not. Interestingly, the concept mappers made greater use of print indexes in planning electronic searches and came to understand the dimensions and structure of their topics through their exposure to hierarchical arrangement of such topics and subtopics in indexes and in cross-references. The control group, on the other hand, immediately chose electronic searching as an information-seeking strategy, relying on key words. As a group, they were less able to determine the relevance of articles found and ultimately spent more time in searching than did the concept mappers. Other benefits of concept mapping for students included the ability to maintain their foci while searching, improved capacity to "relate new information to what they already knew to be meaningful," and greater gains in background knowledge important for successful focus formulation and information gathering.

In 2000, Broch reviewed the literature on children's use of the Internet as it related to each stage of Kuhlthau's ISP model. She determined that cognitive immaturity in terms of recalling prior searches and terms hampered their ability to modify their searches, while deficits in keyboarding skills, search term selection, sophisticated vocabulary, and Boolean logic led her to conclude that "some of the obstacles that Kuhlthau observed in information seeking are in fact potentially more burdensome on the web." Quoting Fidel et al. (1999), Broch noted that success at task initiation was compromised when students' faith in the Internet led them to conclude "that there was no need to plan ahead" and to rely on search results to guide subsequent searching activities. Searching in this way returned so many citations that students had a terrible time selecting a topic at all and were frequently distracted by the presentation of so many alternatives. By the same token, the easy availability of information was frequently used as the criterion for topic selection rather than any genuine interest on the part of students. "On the web," Broch opined, "it is almost impossible not to collect too much information."

If Broch's (2000) students experienced considerable difficulty selecting a topic, finding a focus at the formulation stage was equally problematic. This led Broch to conclude that efforts to locate pertinent sources replaced the thinking activities that one assumes will occur at this step, undermining the learning that is built in when one is asked to create a personal perspective. So too, at the presentation stage, the creation of the final report often defaulted to a cut-and-paste assembly of information from the sources chosen and the absence of any sort of individual understanding.

Harada (2002) used Kuhlthau's model as a framework for an action research study that looked at the utility of student journals in tracking thoughts, feelings, and actions of elementary school children aged 10 to 11 involved in a complex information-seeking task that grew out of content covered in the classroom. In order to understand the problems and feelings experienced by the children, the researcher used student journals, librarian logs, researcher observations, and teacher interviews.

Before beginning the information-seeking activities, the ISP model was presented as a useful approach to the task. However, students became confused at the exploration and collection stages of the ISP, and it became clear that additional instructional interventions would be necessary. To this end, a wall mural was created that provided a visual of the ISP process, and charts and discussion were also used as aids to understanding. As with students in the Pitts (1995) study, the student's lack of mental models led many to admit in their journals that they did not know "what they were doing." Having students create their own diagrams of the process later proved a useful strategy in addressing this issue, at least for the duration of the project. The actual internalization of the process by the students proved elusive, however, but journal keeping was shown to allow the teacher to assess the learning and plan appropriate interventions.

In 2004, Holliday and Li replicated Kuhlthau's research in an effort to understand the information-seeking behaviors of Millennials. In their study, Holliday and Li observed that students replicated behavior of students observed by Broch (2000) in choosing their topics based on quantity of information that was immediately available to them rather than on personal interest. In addition, these researchers found that students were also less interested in learning outcomes than they were in just completing the assigned task. Another finding was that having full texts of articles available online also resulted in less note taking on the part of students. According to Holliday and Li, "The students who do not go through all the stages of the model, especially focus formulation, have more difficulty conducting research and experience more uncertainty and frustration." They also noted that some students in their study "skipped altogether" a number of the steps, notably focus formulation, and "stopped searching for information in the prefocus stage and built their papers and bibliographies from what they had at hand" (364). Students noted frustration as well when they discovered "that research was not as easy or as seamless as they expected it to be" (363). Finally, students in the study appeared to represent the characteristics noted for Millennials in terms of reliance on the Internet and electronic resources and a "just-enough" rather than an exhaustive approach in searching for information.

Heinström (2006b) used Kuhlthau's ISP to study the information seeking of middle school students and the roles played by motivation (extrinsic and intrinsic) and intention (deep learning or task completion) in their searching behavior. She labeled the searching styles as "fast surfers" and "deep divers." Students this researcher characterized as deep divers tended to be intrinsically motivated to seek information because of an interest in what they were learning and were willing to keep a search open long enough to locate and examine information documents for use in obtaining deep understandings of the topic. Heinström also noted that for some students, the search strategies themselves were also compelling. These students made note of the processes involved in information seeking and evinced an interest in information handling that went beyond the skill level. "Extrinsically motivated students," on the other hand, "tended to adopt a surface approach to studying," relying heavily on the "reproduction of information through rote learning" and consulting "information sources only because they were required to do so (1442)." These students sought and used pieces of information to fill knowledge gaps rather than appreciating single items or documents as stepping-stones to more holistic understandings. Additionally, fast surfers were observed to put forth minimal effort, being preoccupied with task completion and using only the most readily available sources. In terms of Kuhlthau's moods, Heinström noted that motivation determined whether a student stayed in an invitational mood long enough to comprehend a topic or whether the student moved to an indicative mood, narrowing the search to bring the project to a swifter conclusion.

Hyldegärd (2009) found that the ISP model was less useful in understanding the experiences of graduate students when seeking information as members of a small group. Using questionnaires, journals, and interviews to capture informants' experiences, Hyldegärd explored collaborative projects, concluding that affective responses they reported were based on the motivation and expectations of individual group members rather than the group as a whole. While the study tended to confirm the general outline of the ISP, many participants continued to experience feelings of uncertainty and frustration no matter the outcome. Echoing Burdick (1996), Hyldegärd's research seemed to suggest that contextual and social factors also play a role in information seeking not accounted for in the ISP.

Suggestions from the research studies based on Kuhlthau's model are summarized in Table 3.4.

ISP Update

An article by Kuhlthau, Heinström, and Todd in *Information Research* published in 2008 provided an opportunity for Kuhlthau herself to consider the efficacy of a 20th century-based research process to a 21st century "information environment," taking into account the findings in a number of the studies reviewed above and based on qualitative and quantitative data from a new study of Millennials' seeking information within the context of digital technologies. The authors were reaffirmed in the belief in the validity of the original ISP model to describe information seeking and use by students involved in constructing new knowledge in response to the demands of complex tasks and searches, as an instructional medium for guiding searching activities, and as an intervention model for diagnosing the process needs of students and pinpointing times and spaces for instructional focus. In addition,

Table 3.4
Research-Based Recommendations for Implementing the ISP Model

- Exploration of the topic should be built into the research process; for younger students, the research project should probably come after students have knowledge of subject-specific content or the teacher has provided background information on the topic or topics to be investigated.

- Teachers should discuss the use of journals in which students record their responses to the topics and their thoughts throughout the unit; in this way, students can use their recorded thoughts in selecting a topic and creating a research focus.

- The inclusion of regular checkpoints in structuring research assignments provides opportunities for teachers to monitor student progress in thinking about a topic as well as the research project as a whole.

- Students should have time to share their thinking, their ideas for a focus, and their feelings about the process with peers, teachers, and parents—a strategy that will facilitate conversations and make them more focused and productive.

- The structure of ISP tasks should include times for reading and reflection.

- Students should be encouraged to find personal links to research topics; where their thinking may be at concrete rather than abstract levels, student interest and enthusiasm might increase if they are able to select topics with which they have some prior knowledge or experience.

- The development of a focus is essential before students are allowed to move into the collection phase of the ISP; however, the focus may change during the process.

- Student research projects should allow for student individualization of the ISP. Insights and deep learning may result when students are permitted to experiment and devise strategies on their own rather than being made to follow a predetermined "one-size-fits-all" step-by-step research model.

- Motivating students at the outset of the information seeking activity will help ensure sustained searching and deeper learning.

they assert that the model applies when researching involves both traditional and digital resources and venues (Branch 2003). However, improved access to Internet resources and the seemingly instantaneous information available has "changed students' conceptions of the research process, in that they expect to find information quickly and without effort" (Kuhlthau et al. 2008).

Kuhlthau's Intervention Model: Taxonomy of Service Assistance

Kuhlthau's research has contributed many insights to our understanding of the ISP and knowledge of how students learn from information. The fact that students not only need but also welcome such assistance, support, and encouragement, particularly during the initial stages of the ISP, is also an important finding (Kuhlthau 1993b). And this begs a number of important questions for school librarians. How can this intervention best be provided? When and what kinds of assistance would be most helpful? To address these questions, Kuhlthau created the "taxonomy" of assistance, which can serve to guide library media specialists in providing instructional and emotional support for students involved in the ISP. In this way, it is hoped that students and librarians will come to understand that assistance is appropriate and necessary in providing intellectual as well as physical access to information resources.

The Theoretical Basis for Service Intervention

In building a model to guide instructional intervention levels in support of information seekers, Kuhlthau turned to the work of Lev Vygotsky (1896–1934), especially his theory of zones of proximal development. In Vygotsky's (1978) view, there are certain moments in the child's development when instruction is most effective, that is, times during which the child's cognitive elaboration is most likely to occur. Vygotsky called these moments "zones of proximal development." Specifically, each zone creates an instructional space that represents "the distance between" a child's actual "level of development as an independent problem solver and [his or her] potential level of development" (86). At the lower, or actual level, problem solving is achieved by the child working independently, and at the upper, or potential, level, the child can perform more difficult tasks with assistance provided by a more knowledgeable partner.

Vygotsky (1978) believed that through careful observation of a child's present level of functioning, a perceptive teacher should be able to identify, plan, and support learning activities to match each child's proximal zone. For example, the teacher first sets a goal and provides scaffolding in the form of directions, demonstrations, and strategies that the child can use in reaching the goal and then guides the child in enacting the activity. When this initial goal is reached, the teacher offers a new and more difficult one. The central mechanism of learning in such an approach is the transfer of responsibility from the teacher (or more knowledgeable partner) to the child as learning occurs and the task is completed. As the lesson proceeds, the teacher gradually eliminates the supportive explanations, hints, and demonstrations until, in the end, the skill is performed by the child alone. At this point, the child's newly internalized skill acquires its individual character and constitutes the new actual level of development—the foundational level for a new proximal zone. In this context, the teaching is dynamic and reciprocal, a negotiated division of labor aimed at increasing the learner's share of the burden for the attainment of the goal. Thus, in Vygotsky's view, the child does not alone possess a zone of proximal development (e.g., a set level of achievement or an IQ score) but rather shares one with his or her instructor.

Levels of Assistance and Service Roles

Kuhlthau (1993b) has suggested five roles for library media specialists based on a taxonomy of five levels of intervention. These roles and levels are summarized in Figure 3.2 as organizer, lecturer, instructor, tutor, and counselor. The range of intervention techniques that Kuhlthau has devised are based on "physician/patient interaction" model frequently used by medical professionals in choosing appropriate treatment levels (Kuhlthau 1993b, 156).

The appropriate role for the library media specialist in any given situation is to support students as they engage in activities that might be beyond their present levels

Figure 3.2
Kuhlthau's (1993b) Assistance Levels Available to Students during an ISP

| Organizer | The library media specialist selects, arranges, and manages resources; creates a user-friendly, self-service environment; and establishes policies that maximize opportunities for student access to informational resources in anticipation of their information needs. |

| Lecturer | The library media specialist provides tours and orientation sessions focusing on location of departments and collections to acquaint students with organizational schemes and specific reference tools to increase student interest and use of the library and its resources. |

| Instructor | The library media specialist provides one or a series of cooperatively planned lessons on specific reference sources and types of resources related to needs arising from classroom activities and tailored to the students' cognitive levels. |

| Tutor | The library media specialist presents informational resources in ways that show the relationships among different kinds of resources and recommends a sequence for their use. Sessions are provided when student needs dictate and are based on collaborative planning and active teaching by both teachers and librarians. |

| Counselor | The library media specialist actively participates in the students' ISPs and assists and provides cognitive, behavioral, and emotional support for students related to their tasks at initiation, selection, exploration, formulation, collection, and presentation phases of the process. |

of expertise until such time as they can perform the tasks independently. Importantly, the model also creates a diagnostic tool that librarians can use in planning the kinds of assistance a seeker would find most beneficial at any given place in his or her ISP and provides a description of best practices appropriate for librarians in helping students learn from information. In short, the zone idea provides a point of access so that the student's needs for instruction on particular information seeking skills drive the lesson. Since the assistance provided by the information professional enables the students to experience progress in carrying out an assigned task, the model reflects Dervin's (1983) initial view that gaps in understanding can impede an individual's forward progress in meeting personal goals. (See Chapter 6 for an explanation of Dervin's sense-making model.)

Finally, although primarily a diagnostic tool for planning instruction, the taxonomy may be particularly useful to librarians in explaining to administrators the range of instructional alternatives available to students in the school library. In addition, school librarians can use it as an interactional barometer in evaluating their own activities across students, classes, and grade levels.

Organizer Level

Acting at an organizer level, the library media specialist prepares the context for learning by selecting, arranging, organizing, and managing resources so that information is available in a wide variety of topics, formats, and media. Essentially, the librarian creates a self-service facility, perhaps providing maps, diagrams, and library signage. He or she also creates policies that maximize student access to library materials. At this level, the expertise of the librarian is apparent in the creation of collections that support the curriculum and of environments and policies that enable students to search for information independently. In brief, the central tasks for the librarian at the organizer level are managerial and clerical rather than instructional.

Locator/Lecturer Level

When operating at the locater level, school librarians provide students an overview of library resources, services, and policies, with a focus on the location of particular items. Group tours of the library, orientation sessions, scavenger hunts, and locational games are typical of locator/lecturer level support. This kind of assistance serves to call the students' attention to the organizational schemes used in classifying and accessing library materials and the varieties of materials that are available in the library, in the community, and online. In many respects, these activities may increase student interest in the library and its resources, but they fall short of helping students seek information to meet their own information needs or to solve particular problems. To a certain extent, the locater and identifier levels correspond to Wyer's (1930) conservative level of library service since the library media specialist plays a more or less reactive role in the educational process, responding to requests rather than initiating interaction or inquiry.

Identifier/Instructor Level

At the identifier level, the library media specialist provides lessons on specific sources and types of sources and their usefulness to students involved in specific kinds of information tasks. The key to success in planning and conducting activities at the identifier/instructor level is to make information about the library's resources relevant to the individual user by planning one or a series of sessions in direct response to student needs. Planned in advance and in cooperation with the classroom teacher, these services can directly address the requirements of the lessons and the individual needs of the students. Ideally, this kind of source-oriented instruction occurs at the point when students are ready to use the resources to fulfill information tasks.

Adviser/Tutor Level

Providing instruction at the adviser/tutor level requires that the library media specialist plan a series of sessions to demonstrate the sequential use of a variety of informational resources. Basically, this level of intervention is reminiscent of the pathfinder model, in which the librarian helps students understand the relationships between and among various types of resources in the library, and reflects the "moderate" level of Wyer's taxonomy. To be effective, instruction based on a tutorial model requires that teachers provide the context for the lessons and plans with the library media specialist the objectives and outcomes for the lessons taught. Kuhlthau (1993b) recommends a team-teaching approach as the most useful way to conduct these kinds of instructional interventions even though the primary emphasis is still on "location and use" kinds of activities.

Counselor Level

Instruction provided at the counselor level is truly process instruction and is most often conducted over time; instruction in identifying and interpreting information to address an evolving problem requires instructors to "be there" for students, providing active assistance whenever the student feels uncertain as to how to proceed. These types of activities implicitly resemble Wyer's (1930) "liberal" service orientation.

The librarian, acting in the counselor role, structures sessions to support students in learning the processes involved in making information inquiries and in learning from the process as well. Creating a research plan, getting necessary background information, narrowing or expanding topics to create a focus, identifying and evaluating appropriate resource alternatives, and interpreting the information found are the kinds of activities that instructional counselors support. Assessing the students' "moods," reading their emotional reactions, and providing encouragement to students engaged in the complexities of a research task are also appropriate and important.

At the counselor level, the primary focus is to help students become independent library users and problem solvers. It is when the library media specialist acts as a counselor that he or she collaborates on the project and can model the necessary skills, provide feedback, and support students as they learn the skills and the processes necessary to achieve a measure of competence and independence. According to Scheidecker and Freeman (1999, cited in Callison, 1999), great teachers "take the we approach," partnering with students to assess what is wrong when they fail and celebrating with them when they succeed. As Callison argues, "Our own enthusiasm and values have much to do with our students' interest" (37).

Zones of Intervention

As noted, Vygotsky's model of zones of proximal development can also be useful in describing the levels of assistance that students might require at particular points in their ISPs. Figure 3.3 summarizes Kuhlthau's (1993b) suggestions for intervention zones and levels of assistance. In this model, each higher level assumes the provision of services at all preceding levels. For example, students operating in zone 1 require no direct intervention, although their ability to conduct research independently assumes access to a library that is well organized and managed to maximize physical and intellectual access to information. Organizer-level assistance might include comprehensible signs, information sheets, pathfinders, and computer-based "virtual" library tours. When operating in zone 2, a student will require the help of the librarian in locating information to solve a fact-based or ready-reference question. Students with zone 3 information needs will require assistance and instruction in finding and using a number of library resources. At zone 4, the student's information problems will call for the presentation of sources in a specific sequence and instruction in their use. At zone 5, students' information needs may require a conference with the librarian to discuss the processes involved in the ISP and in learning from the information collected.

Figure 3.3
Intervention and Instruction Zones: Activity Based on Student Needs (Kuhlthau 1993b)

Zone 1	No assistance	Organizer
Zone 2	Introduction to the library; reference assistance	Lecturer
Zone 3	Assistance in locating and using a variety of relevant resources	Instructor
Zone 4	Identification and use of relevant resources in a sequence	Tutor
Zone 5	Assistance in understanding the process, in the development of search strategies, in the formulation of a focus, and determining relevance of retrieved items, etc.	Counselor

Understanding the level of assistance a particular student needs and wants at any given time requires sensitivity and keen observational skills. While Maslow's research indicates that students have high affiliation needs, "motivation may be complicated by conflicting needs for independence and dependence" (Callison 1999). (For an explanation of Maslow's hierarchy of needs, see Chapter 5.) Acknowledging what the student does know and is able to do on his or her own at the same time that guidance is being provided is one way that librarians can respond to both of these needs.

Inquiry Learning: A New Framework for Information Literacy Instruction

According to its proponents, inquiry learning centers on the research process (Kuhlthau 2001) but mimics real-life contexts where learners consider problems, develop strategies, and seek solutions. Donham et al. (2001) suggested that "For children to own their own learning, they need to own their own questions" (vii);

these include "What do I already know? What questions do I have? How do I find out? And finally, what did I learn?" (Kuhlthau 2001, 1). Kuhlthau continues, "Inquiry takes students out of the predigested format of the textbook into the process of learning from a variety of sources to construct their own understandings" (1). In short, "inquiry learning enables students to meaningfully accomplish the objectives of the curriculum by preparing them for living and learning in the world outside of the school" ((Donham et al. 8). The emphasis on sharing what children learn "with others in the community" (9) sets inquiry-based learning apart from product-centered research projects. "Children can move beyond consuming of online information products to creating it" term papers exhibits or experiments… shaped in paperless fashion" (Bilal & Watson 1998).

The Impact of Online Resources

Since the 1990s, library and information science researchers have marked the revolution in information seeking made possible by increased access to the Internet. Mancall, Lodish, and Springer (1992) believe that online resources create authentic contexts for learning because their use replicates real-world complexities and provides access to perspectives and viewpoints that stretch students and encourage them to think critically. The availability of online resources in school libraries has also created opportunities for independent learning (Peck & Dorricott 1994). For example, Woronov's (1994) research indicates that computers have been useful in "supporting inquiry-based science teaching, inclusion of students with disabilities in regular classes, interdistrict collaboration, [and] distance learning" (1). The potential that information skills and technological access provide for enabling students to engage in "active, self-directed learning" has also been noted by Kafai and Bates (1997, 104). Indeed, in Morton's (1996) view, access to technological resources provides students with an unparalleled opportunity to exercise critical thinking, create their own perspectives, and take charge of their own learning in ways that make computers "interactive learning extensions of the children themselves" (417).

Irving's (1990) study also confirmed that online resources facilitated children's independent pursuit of academic topics of individual interest, observing that their use provided information for personal decision making when the library's own collection offered little support. Since independently conducted activities allowed students a unique opportunity to control many aspects of their own learning, Bialo and Sivin-Kachala (1996) suggest that the use of electronic resources will enhance both the self-confidence and the self-esteem of students. In addition, Mendrinos (1994) reported that where resource-based learning initiatives were combined with electronic resources, students reported being able to exert a measure of control in meeting curricular objectives. In Irving's study, this sense of ownership seemed to arise from the children's ability to download information they themselves chose.

Guided Inquiry Learning: Moving beyond the ISP

In recent writings, Kuhlthau and her colleagues have paid increasing attention to the uses of a guided inquiry approach to teaching and learning (see Kuhlthau, Maniotes, & Caspari's monograph, *Guided Inquiry: Learning in the 21st Century*, published in 2007). "In guided inquiry students are seen as active agents in construction of their own personal topical comprehension. This view of learning includes motivation and emotion as vital for lasting knowledge construction (Kuhlthau & Todd 2005)"

(Heinström 2006a). A key concept in guided inquiry is "transformation," when a student's understanding of a topic translates into knowledge at a deeper level. The relationship between guided inquiry and information literacy is clear: guided inquiry effectively moves the teaching of information literacy skills to a higher level, instructing students to go beyond managing and analyzing information to the transformative level of understanding. As Heinström notes, guided inquiry casts learning in a "broader perspective . . . where 'students actively engage with diverse and often conflicting sources of information and ideas to discover new ones, to build new understandings, and to develop personal viewpoints and perspectives' (Kuhlthau & Todd 2005)." It is widely held that the projects related to guided inquiry help students develop content knowledge as well as information literacy skills.

4 Third Space

Perhaps the most compelling new building block for ISP work previously carried out by Kuhlthau et al. (2007), however, is the notion of "third space." The knowledge and nurturing of this concept lays the foundation for learners to successfully use the Guided Inquiry (GI) model. Developed for the ISP model from previous work by Maniotes (2005), third space represents the merging of first space (an individual's varied life experiences outside the school setting) and second space (the curriculum content of the classroom) (Kuhlthau et al. 2007, 31). Other researchers have also studied the concept of third space, especially in the area of discourse, as a way to examine the blending of informal and formal talk between teachers and students.[5] It is interesting to note that hints of third space can be seen in Dewey's (1915) discussions of the function of the school in the child's social life: "We all know how self-centered the little child is . . . his horizon is not large; an experience must come immediately home for him, if he is to be sufficiently interested to relate it to others" (18).

Tapping into Dewey's "organic connection," Kuhlthau et al. (2007) explain that inquiry for learning naturally includes all the worlds that the child inhabits. "Through this approach, what students learn in school helps them to understand what they then experience outside of school. And their outside experience is called upon to help them make sense of what they are learning in school" (30).[6]

The concept of third space specifically advances the GI model, helping students make sense and gain understanding as they encounter materials and ideas that they may then construe as part of their evolving schema. Third space in the Guided Inquiry model (Kuhlthau et al. 2007, 32) uses dotted lines to represent permeable boundaries wherein students cognitively (and verbally) cross the lines that separate aspects of their lives as they constantly reconstruct their worldviews within the hybrid classroom environment (see Figure 3.4). Essential to the success of this model are attitudes displayed by teachers and librarians as well as informal and formalized language structures.

The power of the ISP and GI models is demonstrated when digital age students, working with instructors, call upon prior knowledge as they encounter new information to reconstruct understandings and to create meaning in their worlds. Strategies that set the stage for and encourage these reconstructions are outlined in the GI model and include a reiteration of Kuhlthau's (1995) early recommendations for instructional strategies: collaborating, continuing, conversing, composing, and charting.[7]

The idea of learning in isolation is inconsistent with what we know about young learners today. If teachers can provide and nurture environments where the

Figure 3.4
Guided Inquiry Model and Third Space[1]

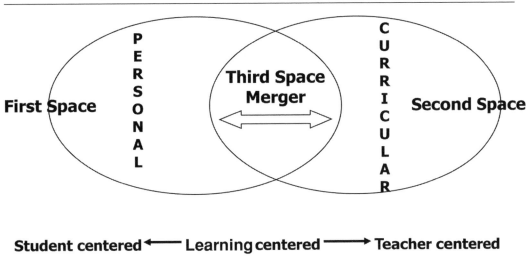

[1]Adapted from models provided in Kuhlthau, Maniotes, and Caspari (2007).

third space concept can flourish, might not their students also learn from the knowledge bases and new co-constructions articulated by one another? Todd (2008b) likens this setting to a "brave new world" and tells us that the school library is a place that provides "exciting opportunities for school librarians and classroom teachers to re-imagine the information-to-knowledge landscape for young people and chart meaningful approaches to instruction and information services" (32).

Conclusion

The changes in our understanding of teaching and learning in the library context are profound. The sophistication of ideas and strategies will serve school librarians well as they continue in pursuit of new strategies to inform practice and assist students in deepening understandings and enhancing competence.

Notes

1. Kuhlthau's research has had enormous impact on both practice and research in library and information science. Kuhlthau (1999) writes that

> reference librarians who have become aware of the stages of the ISP describe important changes in the way they view students and faculty who approach the reference desk. They now listen for an indication of the stage in the process of the user and particularly note when someone is "in the dip" and needs some extra help to explore for learning in order to formulate a research focus. They are especially careful not to give too much too soon and to assist in pacing the use of resources by suggesting strategies for exploring information to form a focus for research.

2. It is important to note that in Kuhlthau's studies, only the more successful students were observed to narrow or refine their topics in ways that provided the clarity needed to pinpoint information needs in preparation for the collection activities that followed.

3. It is also of interest to note here that Kuhlthau's assertion that where a personal effort at sense making and creating a point of view is neither part of a student's process nor an expectation of the instructor, plagiarism through the appropriation of another's words and thoughts is often the result.

4. Action studies represent an approach to research that is intended specifically to explore some aspect of professional practice. As Lindlof (1995) explains, action research in education is frequently employed when teachers wish to study new pedagogical techniques, such as "the introduction of new technology," in order to "diagnose problems, engage in collaborative analysis of data, and engender problem-solving skills" (110) so that instructional techniques can be modified or improved. Action research studies have certain limitations; they often although not always lack a theory base, and they are site specific, meaning that research findings are not transferable or generalizable to other situations or populations. However, such studies are extremely useful in that they often suggest new issues, topics, and avenues for other researchers to explore.

5. For a review of third space research, see Pane (2009).

6. Two other researchers recommend the same approach but do not label their assumption third space. Asselin and Doiron (2008) call for a merging of literacies developed both in and out of school settings. "We know the new literacies are active in students' out-of-school lives, and we know the critical place of new literacies in the workplace. It is time to situate the new literacies of the real world in schools and make school libraries the bridge between in-school and out-of-school literacies" (15).

7. For a complete explanation of the concepts of GI and third space concepts, see Kuhlthau et al. (2007).

4 Alternative Frameworks for Process Instruction

...there are no generic kids.

—Chelton (1997)

Since the mid-1980s, a number of library media specialists and library and information scholars have developed process models for use in teaching information literacy skills. These models are based on the experiences of practicing librarians and designed to improve the educational value of the kinds of information-seeking activities typically assigned in the classroom. Taken together, these models constitute a nexus of effective alternatives to stand-alone library "lessons," especially when they are aligned directly with classroom curriculum and delivered in response to students' immediate instructional needs.

As discussed in the previous chapter, Kuhlthau's (1993b) information search process model is a seminal work that grew out of her observations of high school students involved in a complex research task. It is also the first model that explicitly acknowledged the "holistic" nature of information seeking, dealing directly with thoughts, feelings, and actions (Kuhlthau 1999). Kuhlthau's original information search process model described the search process itself, specifically that portion of research activity beginning at the initiation of the assignment and ending at the point when students are ready to organize their information and begin writing. The addition of an evaluation step made the model more comprehensive in its application.

Over time, a number of other process models have been created to provide more comprehensive guidance for students in completing school-based assignments. All of them are instructional in nature (Bates 1979a); that is, they suggest a "best practice" for students as they engage in information seeking and research projects, and all emphasize "higher-order" or critical thinking skills and inquiry strategies. For this reason, school librarians, teachers, and students may find any or all of them useful at different times and under different conditions, depending on the context, the task or problem, and the student or students involved. Among the best known of these are the term paper and REACTS models created by Stripling and Pitts (1988), Joyce and Tallman's (1997) I-Search model, the Pathways to Knowledge model created by Pappas and Tepe (1997, 2002), and Yucht's (1997)

FLIP IT! As noted, each of these models provides a framework for research projects in their entirety, covering the writing of a paper or the creation of a project as well as the information-seeking processes that precede it.

Although the process approaches proposed by Irving (1985) and Eisenberg and Berkowitz (1990) can also be applied to research paper projects, these authors believe that their models have applications beyond school-based student research. For example, Irving suggests that information skills are, in fact, "life skills" (115) and that her model can be successfully used by students in conducting a wide variety of tasks, not only those related to their schoolwork. By the same token, Eisenberg and Berkowitz regard their Big6 Skills model as flexible enough to use in many kinds of everyday decision making.

The Handy 5 model (Kansas Association of School Librarians Research Committee 2001) was created as a framework for projects across the curriculum. Based on the Big6 Skills, the Handy 5 model used Kansas state guidelines as they applied to all school subjects to create a common approach to problem solving. The Handy 5 is typical of many regional and state initiatives that aim to reduce confusion and create links among and across curricular areas.

As with the reports of the research studies explored in this book, the descriptions of the models below are meant as introductions to the authors' ideas and frameworks and invitations to further reading. Full accounts of each model can provide school librarians and teachers with valuable strategies, and several also include lesson plans to extend understanding and suggest appropriate applications. For these reasons, readers are urged to read Irving's (1985) *Study and Information Skills across the Curriculum*, Eisenberg and Berkowitz's (1990) *Information Problem Solving, the Big Six Skills Approach to Library and Information Skills Instruction*, Stripling and Pitts's (1988) *Brainstorms and Blueprints: Teaching Library Research as a Thinking Process*, Joyce and Tallman's (1997, 2006) *Making the Writing and Research Connection with the I-Search Process*, Pappas and Tepe's (2002) *Pathways to Knowledge® and Inquiry Learning*, Alice Yucht's (1997) *FLIP IT! An Information Skills Strategy for Student Researchers*, the Kansas Association of School Librarians Research Committee's (2001) *The Handy 5: Planning and Assessing Integrated Information Skills Instruction*, James McKenzie's (2000) *Beyond Technology: Questioning, Research and the Information Literate School*, and Tony Stead's (2005) *Reality Checks: Teaching Reading Comprehension with Nonfiction K–5*.

Irving's Study and Information Skills across the Curriculum

Ann Irving, a British librarian with many years of experience, developed a nine-step model for elementary school students to use in the completion of a range of school-related assignments, from relatively simple ones to those of considerable complexity. Although Irving's (1985) intent was to link information skills directly to the kinds of curricular activities "which form a substantial part of a pupil's school life" (25), she was quick to realize that information skills are "inherently present in all learning tasks" (23) and immensely important. In her view, information handling is key to enabling all students "to participate in the control of [their] future" (157). The nine steps in Irving's (1985) model (see Figure 4.1) create a cycle of learning that takes the student from the beginning of an assignment or project through to its completion and evaluation. As described by Irving, each of the steps serves as "a signpost to a wider range of skills" (31) and creates a framework for appropriate questions and activities.

Figure 4.1
Summary of Irving's (1985) Nine-Step Model for Completing Assignments

Step 1: Defining Tasks	"Formulation and analysis of the information need"	"What do I need to do?"
Step 2: Considering Sources	"Identification and appraisal of likely sources of information"	"Where do I go?"
Step 3: Finding Resources	"Tracing and locating individual sources"	"How do I get to the information?"
Step 4: Making Selections	"Examining, selecting, and rejecting individual sources"	"Which resources shall I use?"
Step 5: Effective Use	Interrogating, or using, individual sources	"How shall I use the resources?"
Step 6: Making Records	"Recording and storing information"	"What shall I make a record of?"
Step 7: Making Sense	"Interpretation, analysis, synthesis, and evaluation of information"	"Have I got the information I need?"
Step 8: Presenting Work	"Shape, presentation, and communication of information"	"How should I present it?"
Step 9: Assessing Progress	"Evaluation of the assignment"	"What have I achieved?"

Step 1 of the model, "Defining Tasks," is "primarily a thinking stage" (42), which acknowledges the importance of understanding the nature of the assignment and the criteria used to evaluate it. Irving (1985) firmly states that it is the responsibility of the instructor to provide "a clear and understandable statement of the task," the task outcomes, and the assessment techniques and rubrics. Instructors must also check with students to be sure that "everyone understands exactly what is required" (33). At this first step, students should also be furnished with a rationale for the assignment so that they can understand its significance. In Irving's view, "[A] knowledge of purpose . . . helps to structure the information-seeking, reading, note-taking and presenting" (35) activities to come. In addition, the explanation of the assignment should contain information on the intended audience for the finished product, the amount of time the students have for task completion, and the level of detail (e.g., general overview or in-depth coverage) acceptable or expected in the finished work.

Topic selection is also a part of step 1 in Irving's (1985) model. Irving believes that instructors must ascertain the state of the students' existing knowledge base at the outset of the project and provide guidance and support for students as they undertake this important activity. In her view, "[C]hoosing a topic, or narrowing down one which has been chosen by a teacher" (41), demands considerable cognitive effort, and its significance lies in that it is the basis of subsequent work. Essential as well is the identification of appropriate vocabulary terms related to the topic so that students will have some starting points and initiate the task of searching.[1]

The central issue addressed in step 2 of Irving's (1985) model, "Considering Sources," involves finding the best resources appropriate for the task and putting them to the best use. At this stage, an important consideration for students is the physical (e.g., location and time constraints) and the intellectual (e.g., reading level and complexity) accessibility of potential resources. In fact, Irving suggests that mapping the possible alternatives (e.g., local agencies, museums, public libraries, community resources, and types of print and electronic media) is a useful activity for students to undertake before actually beginning their investigations.

At step 3, "Finding Resources," Irving (1985) suggests that students use their knowledge of classification schemes to find appropriate information sources. In Irving's view, the key to successful completion of this step is an understanding of how libraries are arranged. However, Irving points out that instruction should be directed at teaching the *concept* of "systems" and the "concept" of classification rather than the idiosyncrasies of a single system (e.g., the Dewey Decimal System).[2] In addition, students need to understand how they can use signs, labels, and guide words to navigate their ways through the library, its catalogs, and the subject indexes that describe aspects of each field of knowledge.

Irving's (1985) step 4, "Making Selections," requires students to select appropriate resources by taking into account their "scope, suitability, reliability and level" (68) and by considering information in a variety of appropriate formats, from realia to encyclopedias. "The crucial skill," Irving writes, "is not that of finding a book, but rather that of being able to reject a book which is unsuitable" (76). In this regard, students may find indexes, book jackets, media labels, and introductory sections of sources helpful in estimating the relevance, currency, and bias of the resources they encounter. "Reading, viewing, listening, and understanding" (76) are the essential skills Irving identifies as constituting step 5, that is, making effective use of the resources located at step 4. Strategies and activities necessary for successful completion of this step include skimming, scanning, viewing, and listening.

Irving's (1985) step 6, "Making Records," refers to thinking, understanding, and identifying those elements in selected resources that are important as well as to the physical activity of taking notes. This notion of selection is essential since, as Irving tells us, a student's "desire to include everything often prevents the retention of anything meaningful" (88). Irving also believes that "knowing when to quote is a skill in itself, and should be developed rather than ignored." Finally, note taking can take any number of different forms, from mind maps and webs to tables and diagrams, and may range from student-devised shorthand techniques to "near-verbatim" (89) accounts.

Step 7, "Making Sense," in Irving's (1985) model is "the most intellectually demanding" (93) since it asks students to organize their notes in a way that aids learning, usually by interpreting it, reflecting upon it, analyzing it, and synthesizing it. These cognitive activities require students to link new information from their reading, viewing, and/or listening to what they already know. In fact, Irving contends that "synthesis can only occur when new information is matched with existing information or perceptions, and when students are confident enough to generate personal opinions on their learning" (97). For this reason, reflection and discussion may help students draw together the strands of their thinking. Additionally, students performing step 7 activities must decide if the information they have obtained is sufficient to address the requirements of their assignments. Finally, each student must determine if her or his information has been synthesized in a useful way and if the end result matches the intent of the assignment as originally described.

"Presenting Work" is step 8 of Irving's (1985) model. Although essays and written reports are traditional ways of demonstrating learning and showing the results of student research, many creative alternatives—such as streaming videos, PowerPoint projects and dramatic productions, electronic slide presentations, posters, dioramas, and social networking outlets—now exist that are appropriate for the expression and sharing of student ideas and learning.

Step 9 of Irving's (1985) model, "Assessing Progress," provides for an evaluation of each project or performance by the teacher, by the student, and by other students. In addition, this assessment should include the student's estimate of his or her learning related to the topic chosen over and above the quality of the finished project. Irving believes that the students' self-assessments are "absolutely vital if they are to develop as learners" (105) and must include reflection on all steps in the process in addition to assessment of content learned.

Irving (1985) acknowledges that not all curricular assignments will require the completion of the entire nine-step cycle. Furthermore, in instances where the attainment of particular skills may actually be masked when these activities are embedded in comprehensive assignments, librarians and teachers may wish to focus instructional attention on only one step. For example, it may sometimes be useful for students to practice analysis and synthesis tasks on information furnished by the instructor. Irving also emphasizes that the research process is most frequently an iterative nonlinear one. For this reason, it is likely that application of the model and its steps will depend on the exigencies of the situation and the educational needs of the students involved.

Although not formalized into a separate step, Irving (1985) suggests that an "evaluation feedback—a 'how am I doing?' intermediary stage"—would help students track their own progress as their research activities proceed. At the same time, such a step would remind students of "the continuing possibility of improvement" and give teachers an opportunity to intervene in the process and adjust its direction when necessary "to avoid disasters" (31).

Eisenberg and Berkowitz's Big6 Skills[3]

Eisenberg and Berkowitz's (1990) Big6 Skills is an instructional model currently being used by thousands of school librarians worldwide and "is a central focus of information literacy instruction on the K–12 level" (Newell 2010) in American school districts. Although the Big6 model draws on the theoretical frameworks, structures, and applications suggested in Irving's (1985) model, it is far less cumbersome and for this reason has been adopted with enthusiasm by students and teachers alike. Since it provides a straightforward summary of activities related to information seeking and project completion, the Big6 serves as an extremely user-friendly approach to what are often extremely complex tasks. Big6 creators emphasize the model's utility for teaching technology skills (Eisenberg, Johnson, & Berkowitz 2010) and have studied its application in academic settings (Cottrell & Eisenberg 2001).

According to Eisenberg and Berkowitz (1990, 1996), student assignments that require the use of multiple informational resources are essentially information "problems" which can be resolved through a systematic process of thinking about the task at hand, the activities and resources required for task completion, and the nature of and expectations about the project or product involved. For this reason, the Big6 works well as a cross-situational model in that the same process can be used for real-world decision making as well as for school reports and projects (see Berkowitz & Serim 2002 and Eisenberg & Berkowitz 1996).

Essentially, the Big6 Skills approach ties cognitive levels (Bloom 1956) to various stages of the information-seeking process by identifying needs (knowledge level), relating resources to aspects of the problem (comprehension level), selecting channels and sources (application level), identifying salient elements within and across information sources (analysis level), restructuring and communicating information (synthesis level), and making judgments about the information obtained "in relation to specific needs" (evaluation level) (Eisenberg & Berkowitz 1990, 12). In effect, the model calls for application of a six-step strategy that requires students to *define the task* that has been set for them and the expectations in terms of the quantity and quality of the product that they will produce; *select strategies* and resources for finding the information they are going to need; *locate* and *access* relevant and appropriate information resources; *use the information* by "engaging" or *extracting* it through reading, note taking, and highlighting and by determining its relevancy for the task; *synthesize* the information in making a decision or creating a project, writing a paper, or producing a performance or exhibition; and *evaluate* the process and the project in terms of its effectiveness in meeting the criteria established by the teacher or school librarian in addition to the efficiency with which the project was carried out. The steps in the Big6 model are summarized in Figure 4.2.

Although the Big6 appears to be an iterative linear process with one step preceding the next, its creators argue that it can be used recursively as a student's searching activity progresses; for example, students' evaluations of what they are doing are activities appropriate at all stages, and location and access tasks may have to be repeated any number of times. The model's implicit understanding of information seeking as a recursive activity recognizes and accommodates variability in student learning styles.

The Big6 also emphasizes the importance of student-instructor interaction in brainstorming ideas and the desirability of using human as well as print and electronic information resources. The model also supports a variety of search strategies, making this an appropriate choice for teachers and librarians who hope to address the needs of a variety of student learners. Further, when truncated to the "Super3" ("plan, do, review"), the model can be used successfully with and by students at all grade and developmental levels.

Ideally, Big6 Skills lessons are created through collaboration between librarians and teachers to make the most of library resources and student research time. Indeed, one of the model's major advantages is its apparent simplicity, which helps

Figure 4.2
Summary Chart: Super3 and Big6 Skills Models for Information Problem-Solving

students grasp the six steps quickly and in such a way that they can conceptualize the process as a whole as well as their own location within it at any given point in time.

First introduced in 1990, the Big6 Skills approach has proven so popular that it has spawned a variety of support structures, including a newsletter and an active website on the Internet (http://www.Big6.com), which is devoted to answering Big6-related questions, providing news and research updates, providing information on Big6 conferences and workshops, identifying and describing exemplary Big6 programs, and listing articles published on Big6 model applications and success stories. A website for children, http://www.big6.com/kids, has also been created.

Stripling and Pitts's REACTS Model for Term Paper Preparation

The REACTS model was originally devised by Barbara K. Stripling and Judy M. Pitts for use by students engaged in researching and writing term papers. As practicing librarians, the authors were concerned primarily with using the research project, a staple in many high school English and social studies courses, as a way to help students develop cognitive creativity, critical thinking, and metacognitive skills. In their view, research assignments could be improved if they were structured and planned to promote student thinking along a continuum ranging from simple to complex. The result of their collaboration was a "taxonomy of thoughtful research" (Stripling & Pitts 1988, 3), which arranges research activities from "fact-finding" assignments requiring thinking at the level of recall to "conceptualization" tasks in which students

Figure 4.3
Stripling and Pitts's (1988) REACTS Taxonomy of Thoughtful Research Tasks

Level 1	Fact-Finding	Reporting on the information	Recalling
Level 2	Asking and Searching	Posing who, what, where, and when questions and finding answers	Explaining
Level 3	Examining and Organizing	Posing why and how problems and organizing information to fit the project	Analyzing
Level 4	Evaluating and Deliberating	Judging information on the basis of authority, significance, bias, etc.	Challenging
Level 5	Integrating and Concluding	Drawing conclusions and creating a personal perspective based on information obtained	Transforming
Level 6	Conceptualizing	Creating original solutions to problems posed	Synthesizing

are called upon to synthesize their information in creating research projects. A summary of the REACTS model is provided in Figure 4.3.

At the level of "fact-inding" in the REACTS model (Stripling & Pitts 1988), learners seek specific information on a topic in one or a variety of library sources and create reports on the basis of what they find out. At the level of "Asking and Searching," students create specific questions (e.g., who? what? when? and where?) about a topic and then seek information in the library to answer these questions. In this way, students are required to do something with the information that shows that they understand it; frequently, this takes the form of creating a summary or expressing the information in their own words.

At the "Examining and Organizing" level, students seek answers to more sophisticated "why and how" questions and then reorganize the information in a way that fits the requirements of the particular assignment. Thus, students may be asked to explore cause and effect, to compare and contrast, to demonstrate problem solving, or to make predictions. Assignments that require research at the "Evaluating and Deliberating" level call on learners to evaluate the information on a set of criteria (e.g., accuracy, authority, significance, and bias) that they or others establish. "Integrating and Concluding" types of research tasks provide students with an opportunity to "draw their own conclusions," form a personal opinion, or frame the results in a "personal context" (Stripling & Pitts 1988, 6).

The most sophisticated research projects occur at the level of "Conceptualizing," which calls for the creation of original solutions to the problems the learners pose for themselves. Research tasks at this level are similar to those undertaken by scholars and scientists. Working in a group and engaging in "practical, community minded problem solving" can challenge students to think at the "conceptualizing level" (Stripling & Pitts 1988, 6). Although all levels of the taxonomy may prove of educational value under certain circumstances and at different times, it is only in response to questions posed at the higher levels (Levels 3 to 6) that students will be required to think critically.

Stripling and Pitts (1988) have also created a process model for the preparation of resource-based research: a 10-step guide that takes students from topic selection through project completion. The model is summarized in Figure 4.4. In general, it calls on students to do preliminary reading and information seeking in preparation for narrowing the topic, creating a thesis, and writing research questions (Levels 1 to 5). At Level 6, students themselves must develop action plans to structure their own searching activities. Level 7 finds students locating and selecting information resources. Note-taking activities take place during Level 8, culminating in the compilation of a bibliography of their information sources. Level 9 involves students creating an outline based on conclusions drawn from the information, with final creation of the project or paper and project evaluation occurring at Level 10. One of the strongest features of the Stripling and Pitts model is the reflective aspect, which is provided in the questions students ask themselves at each step of the process. It is this sort of metacognitive device that educators have found so valuable in extending learning experiences and for helping students deepen their understanding of information processes.

Pappas and Tepe's Pathways to Knowledge®

Pappas and Tepe (Pappas 1997; Pappas & Tepe 1997) originally created a K–12 information skills model—Pathways to Knowledge®—under the auspices of Follett Educational Services (Follett Software Company) and marketed it at professional conferences, workshops, and in-service sessions. The authors later published the model in *Pathways to Knowledge® and Inquiry Learning* in 2002. According to its creators, the Pathways model attempts to present the information search process in a holistic way, emphasizing the nonlinear path that most often characterizes the ways we find, use, and evaluate information. The original model was keyed to the information literacy standards adopted by the American Association of School Librarians and the Association for Educational Communications and Technology AASL/ AECT in 1998. While Follett is no longer involved with Pathways, an Internet site for children is available at http://www.sparkfactor.com/clients/follett/home.html.

Pathways to Knowledge® comprises a variety of strategies that students can employ heuristically as the search proceeds. The strategies themselves are grouped as Presearch, Search, Interpretation, and Communication. As originally envisioned, the authors suggest that two other stages, Appreciation and Evaluation, are actually transcendent phases or steps present in each of the other steps and extending throughout the student's search process. Appreciation is the fostering of interest and imagination and often begins with a teacher/librarian-generated activity meant to spark students' curiosity for a topic. It continues throughout the searching process as students' own "appreciation grows and matures" (Papas & Tepe 2002, 4).

Figure 4.4
Stripling and Pitts's (1988) 10-Step Model for Term Paper Research Projects

Level 1	Select a broad topic	
Level 2	Obtain an overview of the topic	
Level 3	Narrow the topic	"Is my topic a good one?"
Level 4	Create a thesis statement	"Does my thesis statement of purpose represent an effective overall concept of my research?"
Level 5	Formulate research questions	"Do the questions provide a foundation for my research?"
Level 6	Develop a research plan	"Is the research/production plan workable?"
Level 7	Locate and evaluate information sources	"Are my sources usable and adequate?"
Level 8	Evaluate sources, take notes, and create a bibliography	"Is my research complete?"
Level 9	Draw conclusions, create an outline	"Are my conclusions based on research evidence? Does my outline logically organize conclusions and evidence?"
Level 10	Create the project or product or write the paper	"Is my paper/project satisfactory?"

At the Presearch stage, students develop an overview of their topics or projects and explore the relationships among related concepts, essentially enabling them to make connections between their prior knowledge and this topic. The exploration of general sources, the formulation of initial questions, and the identification of key terms and words related to the topic are recommended. The creation of webs and outlines and the clustering of ideas are strategies that help students organize their thinking.

During the Search stage, students are urged to plan their information-seeking activities by identifying available information sources and to then "plan and implement a search strategy" (Papas & Tepe 2002, 8) that will enable them to find the information they seek. These might include government and consumer agencies, museums and historic sites, as well as libraries and the Internet. Selecting resources from these alternatives is a next step, followed by the search process itself.

The Interpretation stage begins once the information has been gathered. Since "information requires interpretation to become knowledge" (Pappas 1997), emphasis on "analyzing, synthesizing, and evaluating information" is essential if students are to select relevant resources and information and use them in meaningful ways. As Pappas asserts, "If critical thinking is not a part of the learning plan, there is no need to interpret information and searchers are stuck at the knowledge level of learning" (2). Through interpretation and reflection, the learner develops personal meaning from the information found (Papas & Tepe 2002), while at the Communication stage of the Pathways model, students must apply what they now know to solve the problem, organize the information they have gathered, or answer the question and then share their new knowledge with others.

Within the Pathways model, Evaluation by self and peers occurs through formative and summative activities. These include assessing the project and evaluating the process so that students assess their own abilities in making information decisions regarding searching and problem solving. In this way, students are supported as they develop the skills necessary to become independent information seekers.

Joyce and Tallman's I-Search Model

Joyce and Tallman (1997) have also created a model to guide student research, but their approach differs in a number of significant ways from the models proposed by Irving (1985), Stripling and Pitts (1988), Eisenberg and Berkowitz (1990), and Pappas and Tepe (1997, 2002). In all the others, there is an explicit or implicit assumption that the topics of research attention are either assigned by a teacher or chosen by students within the context of subject domains or curricular content and that the resulting reports and projects are formally and traditionally presented. In the case of the I-Search model, the research topic is identified by the students on the basis of special personal interest or personal connection. In this respect, the topic can be seen to choose the student as well as the student choosing the topic. In addition, the resulting research report is presented not in the formalized style typical of academic writing but in the form of a first-person narrative, which not only presents the student's perspective on the specific topic but also chronicles his or her information-seeking and data collection strategies.

Initially intrigued by the connections they saw between writing process models and contemporary research models and troubled by the student apathy that all too frequently accompanied the announcement of a research assignment, Joyce and Tallman (1997) set about finding an approach to the research process that would be personally meaningful for students. Like Stripling and Pitts (1988), Joyce and Tallman were particularly interested in sense and meaning making and in the intellectual benefits to be realized for students engaged in metacognitive activities.

In the I-Search model, Joyce and Tallman saw a way to use writing and research "to foster critical thinking" (16) and personal investment on the part of their students.

Although they reviewed a number of process models for writing and research, the authors eventually chose Macrorie's (1988, cited in Joyce & Tallman 1997) I-Search model, which asks students to select and research topics on a need-to-know basis and to write up the results in a narrative form. An important part of the narrative is the account of how the information students collected was "selected, evaluated and used" (17). In creating their model, Joyce and Tallman also drew on theoretical frameworks suggested by Murray (cited in Joyce & Tallman) and Kuhlthau (1993b). In defining writing as a special case of information processing, Murray's process-writing model provided the conceptual link between writing and information-seeking tasks. According to the authors, Kuhlthau's research on the information search process was also particularly helpful, especially as her methodology had originally been based on models employed in process-writing research. In addition, Kuhlthau's emphasis on metacognitive activities, the importance she places on feelings as well as searching behaviors, and her use of interviews and conferencing techniques as a way of tracking individual student progress also became parts of Joyce and Tallman's approach. For example, the journals suggested in Kuhlthau's work were adapted by Joyce and Tallman, who asked students to maintain learning logs as records of their actions. Students used the logs to track their thoughts as their searches proceeded, and instructors used the logs in creating writing prompts and posing questions to stimulate student thinking and discussion. Joyce and Tallman also employed the use of webbing as a conceptual frame and a process device at several key steps. An I-Search Process Web involves four central tasks: selecting a topic, researching the topic, using the information found, and completing a research project.

Because of the personal nature of the research topics and the individual nature of student processes, school librarians and teachers play keys roles in the I-Search process through conferencing activities. Information skills instruction fits into the model at times when students need particular skills or specific resources in conducting their research activities. The major elements of the I-Search Process Web are summarized in Figure 4.5.

At Step 1, "Topic Choice," or topic selection, students explore their own interests through webbing activities and discussions with parents, peers, and teachers. The skimming and scanning of resources in the media center to identify items of potential use follow these activities. It is at this stage in the process that information skills can best be taught, with instructional approaches based entirely on student needs and skill levels. At Step 2, "Finding Information," students generate research questions, do background reading, create bibliographies of pertinent resources, and then enrich their knowledge through reading and interviewing. Step 3, "Using Information," can be undertaken in a number of ways, including highlighting and note taking. Reflection is encouraged at this stage and facilitated through conferencing and the use of learning logs. The final project is prepared at Step 4 and includes the opportunity to share the experience and the project with peers.

Insofar as personal interest drives the selection of the research topic and interviewing data as well as other informational resources are used by students in answering their research questions, Joyce and Tallman (1997) believe that the I-Search process creates the sort of authentic instructional environment that is most compatible with forms of assessment that are also considered authentic. In addition, the I-Search model stresses interaction and reflection with peers and parents as well as

Figure 4.5
Summary of Steps and Activities in Joyce and Tallman's (1997) I-Search
Process

Step 1: Topic Choice
Explanation of the I-Search process
Webbing activities to pinpoint student interests
Preliminary investigation of library resources
Conferencing with teacher/library media specialists
Sharing topic choices with peers and parents

Step 2: Finding Information
Generating research questions
Background reading
Preparing bibliographies
In-depth reading
Interviewing

Step 3: Using Information
Highlighting text
Double-entry drafting
Reflecting and conferencing
Using learning logs

Step 4: Preparing the I-Search Product
Using the first person
Telling about search
Using learning logs
Editing by peers
Transferring the research

with teachers and the school librarian. All these strategies are consistent with the intent of authentic assessment, and inquiry approaches lend themselves readily to the creation of rubrics for evaluating the product and the process.[4]

Grassroots Models for Teaching the Research Process

Clearly, the creation and use of models are the approaches of choice in contemporary efforts to reframe the teaching of information literacy skills. Not only do we now have a number of wonderfully useful models from which to choose, but the emphasis on the process approach and the demand for curricular connections and collaboration between teachers and librarians and inquiry learning inspired practitioners to innovate and strategize. In general, the proliferation of grassroots models reflects the local nature of education and the value placed on tailoring instruction to the instructional needs of specific groups of children. Some are local adaptations of major models described above. Some are relatively simple and straightforward iterations of research process steps, and others are more elaborate and tied to library standards as well as content standards, such as language arts, math, science, social studies, and so on. Assessment rubrics are also provided in many models.

Yucht's FLIP IT!

Yucht's (1997, 2002) FLIP IT! model is a commonsense problem-solving model for student research created in 1988 and based on observations the author made during her career as a practicing library media specialist. The title for the model is an acronym and a mnemonic "to keep the thinker on task" and can be used as a guide and strategy for individual decision making as well as a variety of school activities and research projects. The four steps of the model can be summarized in four words: "Focus," "Links," "Input," and "Payoff." Students are to specify what they know about a topic or problem and what they need to find out or do, consider (strategize) the best research (connections) sources and locate them, investigate the topic by sorting and sifting the information found, and produce a solution to the problem and present the results. The "it" in the model stands for "intelligent thinking and the central question the model poses for students: If? . . . Then? What do I already know that will help me here?"

Yucht (2002) describes her model as nonlinear, "goal oriented," purposeful, and strategic. Yucht writes,

> The phrase FLIP IT!™ has been so successful as a mnemonic because it's easy to remember, it sounds just silly enough to obviate any serious thinking fears, and it reminds the problem solvers that they will need to flip back and forth: evaluating, rethinking, and revising as they work through their information needs and activities.

As with other practice-based models, Yucht has made an effort to keep the model current by tying the stages and activities of the model to standards published in the AASL's (2007) *Standards for the 21st Century Learner* and to Web 2.0 technologies. Information on the FLIP IT! model is available online at http://www.aliceinfo.org/flipit.

The Handy 5

The Handy 5 model, first published by the research committee of the Kansas Association of School Librarians in 2001 and revised in 2007, is an example of the effort of one state's professional organization to make sense of the information literacy standards published in *Information Power* (AASL&AECT 1998) within the context of state standards in math, reading, social studies, science, writing, and the arts. The authors also provide a rationale for changes in teaching and learning created when educators adopt constructivist theory as a basis for curriculum, especially in the expectations of responsibilities for students within the context of a constructivist classroom.

Using Eisenberg and Berkowitz's (1990) Big6 Skills as a foundation, Grover, Fox, and Lakin (Kansas Association of School Librarians Research Committee 2001) combined Big6 model steps 3 and 4 (location and access and extraction and use) to create a five-step model that practitioners can use in planning curriculum-based integrated instructional units as well as in guiding youngsters through the information-seeking and task completion processes. A key element in the Handy 5 model is collaboration between librarians and classroom teachers and the sharing of responsibility for planning, teaching, and assessment tasks. As the authors suggest, "[T]he terms in the integrated teaching/learning model represent a common language for discussing and planning instruction with teachers from various subject areas" (9). Steps in the Handy 5 include the assignment, the plan of action, doing the job, product evaluation, and process evaluation. Special emphases of the Handy 5 as an instructional tool center on ensuring that students "have a clear, complete understanding of the assignment"; create an action plan that represents consideration of the most appropriate strategies and resources; undertake the assignment based on the first two steps; and then complete the task as understood.

One of the strengths of the model is the framework the authors have devised for the systematic evaluation of student progress. To this end, a set of rubrics was created on a five-point scale and tailored to the specific standards and language used within the specific context or content of the assignment. A rating of NA indicates that "there is no evidence that the student has attempted to do the work" or that "there is no basis for evaluation" (Kansas Association of School Librarians Research Committee 2001, 11). A rating of 1 indicates that "the student demonstrates an awareness of knowledge of the process or product" (11) and signals significant misunderstandings or misconceptions. A rating of 2 indicates, through omissions or errors in the assignment, that the student's understanding of the problem or the process is "partial or incomplete" (11). A rating of 3 is the benchmark, or "expected level of achievement." The student at this level "has a substantial and acceptable measure of learning," with "evidence provided by behavior and/or example(s)" (11). The highest rating on the scale is a 4, denoting a level of achievement beyond what is expected and demonstrated by the student's "thorough and complete understanding" of the task or assignment. In short, a level 4 student "has integrated knowledge and is able to apply it in a real-life situation" (11).

Under the supervision of a research scholar, the model was field-tested with library media specialists and teachers in an elementary school, a middle school, and a high school. Results indicated that the model "effectively provides a step-by-step framework for planning, building, and delivering a unit that integrates information skills and curricular content" for children in grades K–12. The model was effective with low- as well as high-achieving students, had a positive impact on student attitudes, promoted higher-order thinking skills, and provided a useful way to assess student progress. In terms of teaching and collaboration, the model facilitated collaboration, provided a structure for planning, saved time, and improved communication between and among teachers and library media specialists. However, as with other instructional strategies, the research indicated that the model requires both training and practice for effective use and a school culture receptive to collaboration.

McKenzie's Research Cycle

An example of a schoolwide research model is McKenzie's (1999, 2000) Research Cycle, which was expressly created to take advantage of the information-rich environment made possible by the installation of a wide area network. An explanation of the Research Cycle (available online at http://questioning.org/rcycle.html) depends on active collaboration between teachers and school library media specialists. The research tasks themselves are undertaken by students working together in research teams. The model specifically takes into account the possibilities and problems that students encounter when searching online. For example, in order to avoid the sort of information glut that can result from indiscriminate downloading of information from the World Wide Web, research teams "only use the Internet when that is likely to provide the best information. In many cases, books and CD-ROMs will prove more efficient and useful" (McKenzie 1999). Steps in the model include "Questioning" (reframing research topics as problems to solve: "How might we restore the salmon harvest?"), "Planning" (consideration of the best and most reliable sources and how to store information retrieved), "Gathering" (making relevance judgments and structuring the information found as an ongoing activity), "Sorting and Sifting" (the "systematic scanning and organizing of data" to find "that which is most likely to contribute to 'insight' "), and "Synthesizing" (arranging and rearranging information until "some kind of picture begin[s] to emerge"). "Evaluating" (deciding if more information is needed to answer the questions) and "Reporting" (creating the finished projects) are the final two steps in the model. McKenzie (1999) writes of them,

> As multimedia presentation software becomes readily available to our schools and our students, we are seeing movement toward persuasive presentations. The research team, charged with making a decision or creating a solution, reports its findings and its recommendations to an audience of decision-makers (simulated or real).

A complete explanation of the model is presented in a monograph first published in 2000 titled *Beyond Technology: Questioning, Research and the Information Literate School* (McKenzie 2000).

KWL-RAN©

KWL-RAN is a modification of the KWL model: the "what do I know, what do I want to know or find out, and what have I learned" strategy that has been used by many classroom teachers for decades, especially as a structure for information-seeking tasks in the early grades. In spite of its utility and the appeal of its simplicity, it is Stead's (2005) view that the KWL model may not help young information seekers when their knowledge of a topic is sketchy or nonexistent. In order to engage children in understanding topic content at a deeper level, Stead created the RAN© chart, an acronym for "Reading and Analyzing Nonfiction." Stead's (2005) model has been published in *Reality Checks: Teaching Reading Comprehension with Nonfiction K–5*.

Stead's (2005) model consists of a five-category chart that youngsters can use to record their understandings of a topic as the information-seeking task proceeds (see Figure 4.6). Before reading begins, the student is asked to think about what he or

Figure 4.6
Reading and Analyzing Nonfiction (RAN Strategy)

What I Think I Know	Confirmed	Misconceptions	New Learning	Wonderings
Children state information they think to be correct about the topic	Children research to confirm prior knowledge	Children research to discard prior knowledge	Children research to locate additional information not stated in prior knowledge	Children raise questions based on the new information gathered

she may already know about the topic. Once reading has commenced, students can begin to consider their initial understandings and sort out *confirmed* facts (information verified in nonfiction sources) from *misconceptions* (information that they initially believed to be true but that, on the basis of reading, they now learn is false or erroneous). Students enter new facts and understandings as *new information* in a fourth column, while in the fifth column, *wonderings*, students can record new questions they now have, sparked by their new understandings about the topic. The KWL-RAN strategy has been used successfully with both large and small groups of youngsters.

Conclusion

Carey (1997) has argued that the most appropriate and valuable instructional role that teachers and librarians can have in creating students capable of lifelong learning is to offer students an array of models and strategies so that they may construct for themselves a personal approach to solving information problems. This idea has found more recent expression in Markless and Streatfield (2007), who urge librarians to encourage metacognitive activities that help students "think about their skills and how to apply them" in "plan[ning] activities to meet goals, anticipat[ing] obstacles, monitor[ing] their own progress, approach[ing] information critically, [and] evaluat[ing] information during the problem-solving process" so that "by these means" students can "develop a personal information style." Indeed, Jacobson and Ignacio (1997) have asserted that, especially in online environments, "librarians and teachers cannot follow a prescribed theoretical model" if they are "to teach students to be effective searchers" (793). Instead, Carey has suggested that teachers should provide problem scenarios that have intrinsic interest for learners, model information-seeking strategies, facilitate interaction among students as they collaboratively consider effective alternatives, and then provide "scaffolding" and support as solutions are developed.

The models reviewed in this chapter and in Chapter 3 offer attractive alternatives that librarians can use when they meet with teachers to collaborate on plans for research activities. Additionally, they constitute a rich array of tools on which school librarians can draw in helping students become independent learners. It is evident from this review that the models vary in emphasis, scope, and complexity. However, each one "assumes learning as an active and creative process, and each promotes the development of critical thinking skills" (Thomas 2000a, 1). Offering some options as structures for information seeking is one way teachers and librarians can avoid applying a "one-size-fits-all" approach across children and contexts. There may be generic models, but as Chelton (conversation with the author, August 24, 1997) reminds us, there are no generic kids.

Notes

1. The importance of mutual understanding between instructor and student regarding the task and the topic has been highlighted in a study by Gross (1995), who also suggests that librarians working with students who are researching imposed (or assigned) questions will need to be sure that student expressions of the need reflect what was intended in the original assignment. A student's ability to execute information tasks that are incompletely understood may be undermined still further when the student articulates this "version" of the information need to a third party, such as the librarian. Including the librarian in

planning assignments is one way a teacher can ensure that the school librarian fully comprehends the intent and expectations of the research task and can assist students in an effective manner even when the teacher is not present.

2. Originally, Dewey set out to classify all knowledge. In so doing, he created a system that would allow resources to be arranged on the library's shelves in ways that maintained what he considered to be the relationships among all elements of that knowledge system. In recent times, the notion of knowledge as a compilation of separate subject domains and the compartmentalization of subjects in this way have been challenged; in many instances, the distinctions between categories have become extremely fuzzy. To attempt to justify the relationships that Dewey established can be difficult given the number of resources that do not fit single categories. Under these circumstances, asking students to memorize Dewey's system seems problematic.

3. The "Big6™" is copyright © (1987) by Michael B. Eisenberg and Robert E. Berkowitz.

4. The value of creating a meaningful (to students) product as a result of the information search process is addressed by Oliver and Oliver (1997) in an experimental study involving 11- and 12-year-old schoolchildren. Specifically, the researchers studied the retention of information, "higher levels of knowledge acquisition" (519), and the learning that resulted from a research task when the task itself involved the creation of a meaningful information product. Drawing on Brown et al.'s (1989, cited in Oliver & Oliver 1997) model of situated cognition, the authors argue that "meaningful learning will only take place if it is embedded in the social and physical context within which it will be used" (521), preferably when the contexts have "relevance to the ways the information might be used in later life" (525). While the study results failed to find an increase in comprehension among students in the experimental group, they did note the "minimal cognitive processing" and retention of information when "the focus of research questions was not linked to any context or purpose" (525). "It is evident," state Oliver and Oliver, "that the factor underpinning the achievement gains experienced by the students . . . was the level of engagement and cognitive processing the activity encouraged" (525). Finally, "the context in which the activity was phrased was a significant factor in motivating the students to locate and retrieve information and to read and analyze that information for their own purpose" (525). On the other hand, "the lack of need to use the retrieved information for any purpose other than display for assessment purposes appeared to limit the degree to which the students [in the control group] engaged in reflective and cognitive processing."

5 Evolving Contexts for Teaching and Learning

[W]hen schools are organized and run in ways that fit the school to both the learning and developmental needs of children, both children and schools are successful; but when schools attempt to cram learning into students without regard to their developmental needs, children fail and so do schools.

—Howe (1993)

Although the instructional nature of the school librarian's job description emerged at a relatively early stage in the development of school librarianship, it did not achieve priority status until the American Library Association published of *Information Power: Guidelines for School Library Media Programs4* (American Association of School Librarians & Association for Educational Communications and Technology) in 1988. Over time, Stripling (1995) and others have gone on to argue that "library programs must be based around learning, not around libraries" (Pitts 1994, cited in Stripling 1995, 163). This assertion is a succinct acknowledgment that, by empowering students to attain personal inquiry and curricular goals, teacher-librarians provide essential and foundational support for the learning process.

If there is a theme that runs through the contemporary research literature in library and information studies (LIS), it is the centrality of concern for the library user (Jacobson 1997). In school settings, where the library's mission is by definition responsive to the school's curricular goals, this concern has been shaped by theoretical frameworks defined as "constructivist." Indeed, LIS researchers who have come to consider information seeking as a cognitive process through which students create meaning and achieve understanding (Kuhlthau 1993b, 2004; Smith 1987) have adopted constructivism as a basis for redefining student information seeking and consequently for reframing information skills instruction.

Because of its assumptions of learning as an active, cognitive process, constructivism has gained a primary theoretical basis for contemporary process models and information skills instruction. This chapter looks at constructivism and then considers other trends that mark contemporary practice, including the contextualization of library skills lessons, the value of process models, new roles for teachers and students, and the contemporary emphasis on critical thinking and inquiry learning. Finally, the chapter discusses the critical importance of motivation to student learning outcomes and offers research-based suggestions for school librarians in their quest to foster motivation in today's learners.

Constructivist Principles Drive Curriculum Decision Making

According to Von Glasersfeld (1995), constructivism is a theory of knowledge that has its roots in the domains of philosophy and cognitive psychology. Although constructivism has been variously defined in the literature, most scholars consider theoretical constructs in the work of John Dewey (1916, 1933), Jean Piaget (Inhelder & Piaget 1958), George Kelly (1963), and Jerome Bruner (1975, 1977, 1980) as seminal and recognize a set of assumptions they share. For example, constructivists generally hold that learning is "something which the individual *does*" (Dewey 1916, 390), that learning involves an act of personal construction, and that knowledge is the creation of meaning based on the experience of the learner. Thus constructivists assert that learners are active participants in their own learning rather than "passive receivers" (Kuhlthau 1993b, 24) of knowledge imparted to them by teachers and others. For this reason, constructivists consider the ability of the student to create a personal focus or "perspective" on a subject or topic as the hallmark of his or her understanding and learning. In fact, the ability to develop a personal viewpoint is, according to Sauer (1995), "the ultimate goal" (140) of education generally and of library instruction in particular. When viewed in this light, learning becomes less a matter of acquiring a set of skills than of developing a "deep understanding" (Von Glasersfeld 1995, 10). According to Kuhlthau (1997), "the constructivist approach seeks to foster deep learning that goes beyond the ability to respond to a text, to application in daily living" (710–11).

How Children Learn

Constructivists argue that, to be effective, learning activities must not only connect to what students already know but also have meaning for the learner at the time of the learning (Irving 1985). Indeed, most constructivists would argue that learning cannot occur in a vacuum but is inherently interactive and built upon a knowledge base of previously learned concepts (see Table 5.1). Their emphasis also includes the social context and the role of learning communities (Bruner 1986) in the creation of knowledge structures. Thus, an understanding of the social nature of teaching and learning provides important clues to how instruction may proceed within constructivist environments and thereby helps define the framework for instruction. For this reason, constructivist educators call on teachers to rethink their roles in the classroom and to implement new models for instructional delivery in order to accommodate this new understanding of how learning occurs.

As noted, constructivists focus primarily on the "cognitive" aspect of learning. However, they also recognize the importance of the "affective" (Kelly 1963) nature of learning tasks and recognize the need to provide emotional support for student learners. While these principles are sometimes advanced as something new in education, Von Glasersfeld (1995) reminds us that, in point of fact, "constructivism" actually supplies the theoretical grounding for activities and strategies that gifted teachers have long employed without fanfare.

Table 5.1
Constructivist Assumptions about How Children Learn

- Learning is an active and constructive process.
- Learning is the internalization and personalization of knowledge.
- Learning is the meaning that is made from experience.
- Learning involves understanding at a deep level.
- Learning involves the ability to apply new knowledge.
- Learning activities help students relate new information to past experience.
- Learning involves cognitive (thinking), social (interactive), and affective (feelings) dimensions.

Contextualizing Instruction

Although constructivism is certainly not the only theoretical framework upon which school librarianship draws, few would dispute the extent of its impact on practice or its value to the design of learning experiences in the school library. As we have seen, the acceptance of constructivism as "the fundamental theoretical foundation" (Kuhlthau 2001) for library programming has led most school librarians to replace context-free "scope-and-sequence" approaches to "bibliographic instruction" with an emphasis on information literacy (Walter 1994), critical thinking, information organization, and information use. Stand-alone "library" instructional sessions involving location and access skills have, in most places, been superseded by educational practices that call for the "contextualization" of skills within the curriculum: instruction presented at the point of need within ongoing classroom content instruction. This means, for example, that instruction on the use of a particular library resource is not introduced until it is required for the successful the completion of curriculum-related tasks (Bowie 1990, cited in Callison 1994; Engledinger 1988). Perhaps more importantly, "contextualization" means that library skills are considered "information skills" that are taught within the framework of an overall process model for information seeking (Irving 1985; Kuhlthau 1993b). An essential value of implementing a process approach to information tasks is in helping students to understand "that knowledge is something" they themselves construct in "collaboration" with "the sources they find to inform their thesis" (Fister 1990, quoted in Sauer 1995, 142) rather than a collection of factoids they compile to satisfy a teacher or complete an assignment.

Disappointingly, research in the area of teaching information literacy has shown that instruction provided within a skills-based library curriculum has not provided sufficient learning to allow application to research projects undertaken in the same or different educational contexts (Goodin 1987, 1991; Kester 1994). Furthermore, Pitts, (1994, cited in Stripling 1995) research shows that "instruction in information seeking and use must be integrated with content for subject matter learning to occur" (164). There is a growing body of research evidence that substantiates this claim. For example, this finding was corroborated in Todd's (1995) study where, "for the specific students involved, integrated information skills interaction appears to have had a significant positive impact on students' mastery of prescribed science content and their ability to use a range of information skills to resolve particular information problems" (137). And in an experimental study of information seeking in research projects among primary school students, Brien (1995) found that teaching the complex skills to information seeking and use within the structure provided by class-related projects reduced "cognitive load" for students and resulted in significant gains in student learning. In addition, a study by Todd, Lamb, and McNicholas (1993), cited in Todd (1995) suggests that "an integrated information skills approach to teaching and learning can have a positive impact on" such "learning outcomes" as test scores, recall, concentration, focus, and reflective thinking (133). Additionally, these findings corroborate earlier studies indicating that integrated skills instruction results in higher achievement on library skills tests (Becker 1970; Nolan 1989) and an increase in student self-confidence (Nolan 1989).

The Focus on Process: Implications for Teaching and Learning

As was evident in the discussion of process models in Chapter 4, the constructivist concern for "process" has created a shift in what is considered curricular content, that is, a concern for the processes involved in learning as well as—or, in some cases, as opposed to—a concern for the final "product" or project. For this reason, instructional designs that educational "constructivists" tend to promote employ the use of multistage curricular units. Implementing instruction in this way provides opportunities for students to engage in "authentic" problem-solving activities rather than through traditional and generic instructional sequences that proceed without reference to learners or context (Jonassen, Myers, & McKillop 1996). Loertscher (1985) and Eisenberg and Berkowitz (1990) have suggested the use of "collection mapping" as a way to target units and topics in all curricular areas and collect the resources to support them. Research indicates that this approach to instructional design is effective because it promotes comprehension, depth, and breadth in course content (Pappas, Kiefer, & Lewiston, cited in Winograd & Gaskins 1992).

Presenting information-seeking activities in the form of a comprehensive model is important in that it helps "students gain an understanding of the overall" process (Eisenberg & Berkowitz 1990, 15) as well as the relationship of specific subskills within the processes as "a series of instructional experiences" (17). This approach permits students to consider the "means" (e.g., steps in the process), not as meaningless hurdles or portions of the task to be "rushed" through, but instead as problem-solving skills that they can apply to other complex tasks in other contexts and situations.

Using a research model also creates a systematic approach to and structures for information seeking; in so doing, children develop a "vocabulary" to use in discussing the search process and their place within it. By the same token, an understanding of the process itself enables students to predict the activities that lie ahead and to visualize the goal of the research and the projects they will create. Research in LIS underscores the importance of this understanding to the meeting of curricular goals. For example, Pitts (1995) found that students' lack of a "mental model" of the steps involved in undertaking a curricular activity proved to be a serious obstacle to their success in completing their research projects. McNally's (2004) dissertation study of high school students engaged in online searching supports Pitts's conclusions. Given the complexity of most research tasks and the fact that teachers making the assignments may themselves be operating on outdated knowledge of available resource options or "flawed" models of information search-ing instruction (Tallman & Henderson 1999), it is not hard to understand why chil-dren and adolescents experience so many difficulties in information-seeking tasks.

New Roles for Instruction and Services

Within a constructivist approach, the teacher-librarian's primary responsibility is to provide structures and opportunities for learning and support and guidance for learners. Although not denying the necessity or appropriateness of direct instruction in supporting specific learning styles, constructivism emphasizes the coaching role of the instructor in planning appropriate learner-centered activities and structures, cre-ating supportive environments, demonstrating important skills, modeling successful performance behavior, providing opportunities for student performances and reflec-tions, motivating students, and providing feedback for students as they attempt to perform their learning tasks (Kuhlthau 1997; Means & Olson 1994). As noted above, this approach to instruction is based largely on the work of Russian psychologist Lev Vygotsky (1896–1934). In essence, Vygotsky (1978) viewed the process of education as a joint enterprise that involves both the teacher and the learner acting together. "Every function in the child's cultural development," Vygotsky believed,

> appears twice: first, on the social level, and later, on the individual level;
> first, between people (interpsychological) and then inside the child (intra-psychological). This applies equally to voluntary attention, to logical
> memory, and to the formation of concepts. All the higher functions origi-nate as actual relationships between individuals. (57)

This emphasis on the constitutive nature of language, the importance of culture, and the primacy of social interaction in learning distinguishes the work of this theorist from many of the constructivists. However his insights into links between culture and to thinking and on the constructed nature of knowledge creation have made him an influential contributor to instructional reform in the fields of educa-tion and school librarianship.

Effective Teaching

Effective instruction within Vygotsky's (1978) model is tailored to each child's "zone of proximal development," defined as that "distance between the actual developmental level as determined by independent problem-solving and the level of potential development" (86) that the learner may attain with assistance by a knowledgeable helper. At a first stage of a lesson framed in this way, the learner receives assistance in completing a task and comes to understand what is involved in carrying it out. At a second stage, the learner completes the task independently by following the directions and managing the process for herself or himself. In the third stage, the various aspects of the task are integrated, the learner having internalized the learning so that his or her responses and skills are automatic.

Within Vygotsky's approach, teachers prepare contexts for student learning by creating "scaffolds" or structures that take students beyond the limits of their own competence and experience. In effect, these structures provide the support neces-sary for the students to begin an activity or project; as each student's competencies and confidence grow, the teacher "withdraws," gradually relinquishing control so that the student can take over the responsibility for the project. Thus, for Vygotsky, learning is an interactive, interpersonal activity that involves the "transfer of responsibility" (Rogoff & Gardner 1984, quoted in Belmont 1989, 144) for "reaching the current goal" from teacher to student. This facilitative strategy creates opportunities for the teacher to learn how "the instructional activities are being interpreted" so that subsequent activities and practice are informed by what students are learning or failing to learn (Driver et al. 1994, 11).

When applied within a school library context, Vygotsky's (1978) framework provides strategies for planning and conducting instruction as well as a model for interventional support in information seeking and learning from information. The importance of student-instructor interaction has also been recognized by Kulleseid (1986), who describes as "dynamic learning situation[s]" those opportunities that involve instructors in modeling and "stimulating cognitive activity" (43). These kinds of learning contexts allow students to see firsthand those strategies that either work or fail to work and to talk through processes with others to "expose conceptual misunderstandings" (Jacobson & Jacobson 1993, 128). Such opportunities resemble the kinds of group activities that students are likely to encounter in real-world work environments.

Stripling (1994b) describes the facilitation role of the school librarian in terms of a six-step process for "effective teaching." The steps that Stripling advocates include conducting preinstructional activities, modeling the research process, and guiding student practice. In addition, Stripling suggests that teachers provide checklists for student evaluation and create additional projects that allow students to apply skills learned in new situations and different contexts.

Activities that provide "real-life" tasks and situations reflect instructional strategies sometimes referred to as "cognitive apprenticeships and collaborative learning" (Jacobson & Jacobson 1993, 128). In these kinds of instructional approaches, teacher guidance is implemented through "situated modeling, coaching, scaffolding, and fading" in ways that support both interactive peer discussion and cognitive reflexivity. As Jacobson and Jacobson observe, conceptualizations of the information-seeking process that are "learned by students [only to be] repeated on tests" rather than to be applied in activities that necessitate their use are effectively "rendered inert [and] unavailable for application in new situations" (125).

According to Bertland (1986, cited in Mancall, Aaron, & Walker 1986), the zone of proximal development provides an ideal opportunity for the teacher-librarian to demonstrate and model metacognitive behavior and show strategies for tackling unfamiliar tasks. These strategies might include estimates of difficulty, goals, action steps, and elaborative plans. In addition, the coaching role gives the instructor the opportunity to provide feedback, stimulate student questions, and prompt students to summarize their readings and monitor their own understanding of the material. In a study by Palincsar and Brown (1984, cited in Belmont 1989), the use of this sort of "reciprocal teaching" "resulted in improvements in children's daily independent reading comprehension" (146).

Information Search Process Strategies That Support Students

As noted in the discussion of Kuhlthau's (1993b) information search process and intervention models reviewed in Chapter 3, Kuhlthau has invoked Vygotsky's (1978) model of zones of proximal development in creating a hierarchy of intervention strategies that provide direction for librarians operating in constructivist library environments. Interventional activities that Kuhlthau (1997, 2001) suggests as useful in framing support at the highest or counseling level include "collaborating, continuing, conversing, charting, and composing" (Kuhlthau 1997, 714).

Collaborating (Kuhlthau 1993a) acknowledges the value of social interaction in information seeking and critical thinking, as students brainstorm, mentor, coach, network, and learn together while working on joint projects. *Continuing* acknowledges the ongoing nature of information seeking within projects that extend over time and the series of cognitive events that students experience as they move from "uncertainty" to "personal understanding" (Kuhlthau 1997, 716). *Conversing* recognizes the importance of interpersonal communication to the process of information seeking. Student-teacher and student-student dialoguing helps teachers gauge student progress and encourages students to think aloud and to "think more deeply" (717) as they focus their research topics. *Charting* provides learners with a model or mental "picture" of the entire information search process as well as the stages from initiation to evaluation. Charting can be accomplished in a number of forms. Graphic organizers, including concept maps, semantic webs, and Venn diagrams, are tools that help students in categorizing ideas, understanding relationships among aspects of topics or steps in the process, and conceptualizing thinking processes. For example, a time line can provide students ways to predict events and structure activities. Finally, Kuhlthau (1993b) advocates *Composing*, or journaling, as a strategy that allows students to track their thoughts, reflections, decisions, conversations, and readings in a systematic way. Of course, the use of student journals also allows librarians to monitor student progress (McNally & Kuhlthau 1994) and changes in students' feelings as well. Providing encouragement when students experience uncertainty or anxiety and providing feedback on the process, as well as direction on "how to do it correctly" (Carson & Curtis 1991, 65), are also valuable strategies. By the same token, posing questions for students (Joyce & Tallman 1997; Mark & Jacobson 1995; Stripling 1995) in their journals can demonstrate for them the strategy of self-questioning, which, as Bondy (1984) concedes, is a skill that must be both activated and practiced if students are to embrace metacognition—the act of thinking about thinking.

The rationale for supporting students as they engage in active learning tasks is established in the LIS research. For example, a number of studies indicate that the job of narrowing a topic called for within information process models such as Kuhlthau's (1993b) ISP may be very difficult for some students, suggesting that guidance, direction, and support for students engaged in this task are important services that school librarians can provide (Loerke 1994; Mark & Jacobson 1995). Irving (1985) has argued that "selecting appropriate information sources is impossible without some knowledge of which are available, accessible and relevant" (43). As this is the very area in which librarians have in-depth knowledge and expertise, Irving proposes that librarians share with their students the techniques they themselves use in acquiring this knowledge. Engledinger (1988) believes that this has been an important outcome of the constructivist movement in education. Within constructivism, collaboration is multidimensional, encompassing group activities for students, interactive relationships between students and teachers, and cooperative planning and team teaching between and among instructors. In short, collaboration in all its many and various iterations and configurations changes how education is done.

Perhaps not surprisingly, the desire to make instruction more effective and learning more profound has led LIS researchers to advocate for collaboration in the planning and teaching of library and information skills (Kuhlthau 1993a; Stripling 1995). Indeed, there is research to suggest that library skills instruction is more effective when it is implemented to meet curricular goals and delivered in sessions that are collaboratively planned and cooperatively taught (Haycock 1992). Collaboration and cooperative teaching by teacher-librarian dyads also holds the promise of improving the nature of classroom assignments, particularly in terms of the kinds of questions/problems that students are asked to answer/solve. For this reason, school librarians must be "involved in the educational and developmental processes that begin and end outside the library door in the structure, use, and especially the creation of knowledge" (Sauer 1995, 137). Recent work by Kuhlthau, Maniotes, and Caspari (2007) suggests that, in guided inquiry activities, instructional teams should more properly include additional teaching specialists with relevant expertise.

Where collaboration has been successfully implemented (Kuhlthau 1993a), research indicates that a well-equipped library resource center, time for teacher-librarian planning, student motivation and time on task, administrative support, and an understanding and appreciation of a process approach to information seeking are all contributing factors. Elements that Kuhlthau (2001) identifies as enablers of collaborative projects include clarity in the roles that teachers and librarians will play as they team teach, "a mutually held constructivist view of learning," "a commitment to inquiry–based learning," and "competence in designing and implementing inquiry activities." Hartzell (1994) and others discuss the importance of professional trust and the value of personal relationships in creating and maintaining a culture that supports successful collaboration because, in a very real sense, it changes fundamentally the way education happens. For example, true collaboration between teachers and librarians assumes shared responsibility for assessing student performance on research projects as well as joint teaching. Understood in this way, collaboration may appear "threatening" to some teachers where subject-specific curricula and self-contained classrooms constitute the norm. In such cases, school librarians must develop and use considerable interpersonal and social skills as well as professional expertise in enacting new models for teaching and learning.

An approach to engaging instructors in an academic library setting, as suggested in Engledinger and Stevens (1984), may provide clues for establishing productive relationships in elementary and high schools. These researchers found that instructors who were uncomfortable in teaching library reference skills actually welcomed assistance by academic librarians once they understood that their feelings were shared by other instructors. They also appreciated being given background information on library skills instruction and strategies to further cooperation between themselves and the members of the library staff. In addition, the researchers found that time for discussion allowed peers to create solutions to problems and that honest evaluation of cooperatively planned lessons resulted in "better projects" (598). Providing teachers with the experience of finding information for and by themselves in unfamiliar settings and on subjects about which they knew little was also an effective way to draw attention to the value of a librarian's assistance with information tasks.

Moving beyond the basic collaboration models described in the research is the vision of the guided inquiry team described by Kuhlthau et al. (2007), who comment, "Although two-member collaborations between one librarian and one teacher are commonly used, three-member instructional teams are highly desirable for the most productive collaborative planning and teaching" (48). They go on to note that this third team member might be an expert teacher, such as a reading specialist, technology specialist, and even subject-area specialists (e.g., art, drama, or music teachers).

Active Learning: New Directions and Frameworks

Within constructivist environments, learning tasks also change. For example, non-constructivist activities require students to "give back" information to the teacher, whereas constructivist activities present problems to be solved by active learners. In short, knowledge, within the constructivist view, is a process of construction rather than an act of reproduction (Jonassen et al. 1996). As noted above, this emphasis on the student's control of the learning tasks extends to include "meta-cognitive" processes in which students monitor the activities, reflect on their experiences, and evaluate their own progress in learning. Vygotsky's (1978) description of the transfer of responsibility as the student is led to take over the tasks at hand essentially posits a kind of cognitive apprenticeship, particularly where the information problems that students are asked to solve are in some sense "real" problems that require the collection of primary data. Peer tutoring, brainstorming, and collaboration between and among class members all call for students to contribute to their learning communities and play mentoring roles as well. This provides practice in monitoring the self and others and in giving feedback—activities similar to those they will encounter when entering the real world of work (Bruffee 1984). The concept of real-world problem solving as a strategy for student research projects is considered more fully in Chapter 8.

Motivating Today's Learners

Teachers have long understood the importance of motivation as it connects with student learning. Studies support this belief, showing that students who are motivated enjoy not only the benefit of higher academic achievement (Boggiano et al. 1993; Flink, Boggiano, & Barrett 1990) but also other, less obvious benefits; these include more positive emotionality (Patrick, Skinner, & Connell 1993), higher self-esteem (Deci, Nezlek, & Scheinman 1981; Deci, Schwartz, Scheinman, & Ryan 1981), and greater creativity (Koestner et al. 1984). Certainly, motivating students to learn is an important part of the instructor's task. This is especially true in information seeking, as the tasks involved are complex and can be frustrating (Kuhlthau 2004); at the same time, we know that motivation is the key to creating independent, lifelong learners—and that goal is at the very core of the school library program's mission. But how can teachers and school librarians motivate learners? What motivational strategies does the research offer?

Motivation Theory: Two Approaches

Motivation theories address why people and animals think and act the way they do (Weiner 1992) and can be categorized into two basic approaches: *mechanistic* and *organismic*.

The Mechanistic Approach

The mechanistic approach to motivation began with the earliest motivational theories—the drive theories—which assumed that an organism's responses are governed by the interaction between its own physiological drives (such as sex, hunger, thirst, and the avoidance of pain) and the environmental stimuli around it (Freud 1925, 1957; Hull 1943). Over time, it became clear that people (and animals) exhibited many complex behaviors that could not be explained through drive theories, thus leading to the organismic approach to motivation theory.

The Organismic Approach

The organismic approach to motivation presumes an active role for the organism, one that is volitional and involves initiating behaviors. The organismic view sees outside stimuli not as causes of behavior, as did the mechanistic view, but rather as opportunities for the organism to satisfy its needs (Deci & Ryan 1985). It is this approach that led motivational theorists to create new definitions and concepts of motivation, specifically the concept of intrinsic motivation. Expectancy-value theory (Vroom 1964), curiosity (Berlyne 1960), flow theory (Csikzentmihalyi 1975, 1990), and self-determination theory (Deci & Ryan 1985) are all examples of intrinsic motivation theories.

LIS researcher Small (1998, 1999) took an organismic approach by using the ARCS model of motivational design (Keller 1987) to explore K–8 library media specialists' use of motivational strategies in library skills instruction and the consequential effects on the on- and off-task behaviors of their students. ARCS, founded on expectancy-value theory (Vroom 1964), identifies four components of instructional motivation: attention, relevance, confidence, and satisfaction. Keller, a professor of instructional systems, posited that instruction embedded within teaching strategies designed around these four aspects would be motivating to learners on an organismic level. In her early study, Small (1998) observed nine exemplary library media specialists teaching library skills to students in third to eighth grade. She found that the specialists used a significant number of motivational strategies during lessons (averaging 24 strategies per 30-minute lesson) and that middle school specialists used more motivational strategies than their elementary school counterparts. She also reported that only 2 percent of the motivational strategies used were considered to stimulate behavior based on *intrinsic* motivation (Small 1999).

More recently, in a study conducted in New York school libraries that continued LIS studies of motivation with an organismic lens, Small, Snyder, and Parker (2009) reported that there was a significant correlation between the school library media specialist's perception of the library media program's "ability to motivate students to learn and the importance he or she places on teaching basic information literacy skills" (8), and that the school libraries and librarians in the study positively influenced students' motivation for research and inquiry, their reading development, and their development of reading interest (Small, Shanahan, & Stasak 2010). They also found that elementary school library media specialists use "significantly more motivation strategies than either secondary or K–12 [school library media specialists]" (8); this finding reverses conclusions drawn from data in the 1998 study. In a related finding, elementary and middle grade students saw the school library program as having had a greater total impact on their motivation than was reported by the high school students (Small & Snyder 2009).

Interest in the Task

Because intrinsic motivation involves both a task and an organism, it can be defined in terms of the interest in the task and the satisfaction gained by the person when engaged in the task. Koch (1956, 1961) theorized that actions can be motivated by simple *interest in the task*, or engagement that is absorbing to the individual for the mere pleasure of doing it (Deci 1975). More recent theorists (e.g., Csikszentmihalyi 1975; Hidi & Baird 1986; Krapp & Fink 1992) have continued in the tradition of Koch to explore characteristics of activities that make them interesting, the individual interests of people, as well as the effect this "interestingness" has on the learner (Renninger, Hidi, & Krapp 1992).

A prominent theory based on interest in the task is *flow*. Csikszentmihalyi (1975, 1990) explored the characteristics of activities that cause flow, or a state of complete absorption. He found that these activities have clear goals and rules appropriate to the activity and that usually flow activities provide feedback that is immediate and unambiguous. He also found that the skills needed for the activity align with the participant's abilities. His research indicates that the results of engaging in activities of high interest and flow are un-self-consciousness, serenity, joy, involvement, and happiness (Csikszentmihalyi 1975) as well as higher comprehension (Schiefele & Csikszentmihalyi 1995). Csikszentmihalyi and Hermanson (1999) applied flow theory to develop a "formula" for learning in museum experiences. The formula includes "the hook," opportunities for involvement, conditions for flow, and growth complexity in consciousness.

School library researchers have also found that interest plays a part in successful information-seeking behavior. Burdick (1996) noted that a majority of the youngsters she studied evidenced a bored attitude and a lack of interest in the research task, concluding that students' focus and involvement had a direct bearing on their success (or lack thereof) with information-seeking projects. Similarly, Heinström (2006a) reported that students in her study who employed a deep (as opposed to a surface) approach to information seeking found the research process to be easy and enjoyable because of interest in their topic. "What was striking among the students with a *deep* approach was the prevalence of topical engagement and ownership" (6).

Kuhlthau (2004) has theorized that, with the mediation of librarians and teachers, students can overcome the natural anxiety caused by the searching process and develop a personal interest in the topic being explored. Silverstein (2005), in her "Just Curious" study, reported that students (especially those of elementary and middle school age) using digital reference services to answer self-initiated questions were highly motivated to do so primarily because of the interest stimulated through informal learning environments. Lu and Gordon (2007) and Gordon and Lu (2008) found that high school students who participated in a Web-based summer reading program read more than they had in previous summers when they were given traditional summer reading lists. They suggest that this increase was due partially to a greater number of books from which to choose, thus allowing for the likelihood that students would find titles that were of interest to them. Crow (2009a) found that upper-elementary-aged students who were identified as intrinsically motivated to seek information had undergone a point-of-passion experience, most at the age or four or five. A point of passion is an interest-igniting episode that stimulates a child to explore more information on a specific topic for many years.

Satisfaction of Needs

The other prong in intrinsic motivation research focuses on the satisfaction gained by the person when engaged in a task. White (1959) proposed that actions such as visual exploration, crawling, grasping, language and thinking, exploration, and manipulation of surroundings are motivated by the organism's psychological need to "interact effectively with his environment" (329), or its sense of *competence*. LIS researcher Bilal (2005) found that students experienced a high level of motivation while exploring the World Wide Web, primarily because they enjoyed the challenge of searching and discovering new information. Another recent study (Arnone & Reynolds 2009; Arnone, Reynolds, & Marshall 2009) suggests that eighth graders' perceived competence in their information literacy and reading skills contributed to their intrinsic motivation to do research. Gordon and Lu (2008) reported that average achievers and honors students acknowledged the benefit of summer reading because of the new knowledge they gained from reading self-chosen nonfiction books, perhaps suggesting a newfound sense of competence.

Additional research studies into intrinsic motivation based on the satisfaction of the person's needs are those by Harter (1980, 1981) and Lepper, Corpus, and Lyengar (2005). Harter's studies focused on five dimensions of students needs, and her findings indicate that there is a significant and progressive decline in intrinsic versus extrinsic motivation across elementary and middle school years, perhaps because the needs that stimulate intrinsic motivation (such as curiosity, challenge, independent mastery, and independent judgment) are not being met. Lepper et al. (2005), in a large study of ethnically diverse third through eighth grade public school students, found that extrinsic motivation for academic activities remained relatively stable across grade levels, whereas intrinsic motivation—positively correlated with higher grades and test scores—steadily and significantly decreased throughout the grades. LIS researchers Fourie and Kruger (1995) identified the psychosocial, cognitive, and affective needs behind the information seeking behavior of secondary school students. They theorized that the fulfillment of these developmental needs is the basis of adolescents' motivation to choose particular books and media. Agosto and Hughes-Hassell (2006a, 2006b) similarly found that urban teens seek information in order to facilitate fulfillment of their developmental needs in seven areas: social self, emotional self, reflective self, physical self, creative self, cognitive self, and sexual self.

Self-determination Theory

Many studies about intrinsic motivation and youth are based on the Self-determination Theory (Deci & Ryan 1985). Self-determination theory is an organismic theory that categorizes motivation into three basic types spread across a spectrum: *amotivation, extrinsic motivation,* and *intrinsic motivation.* The theory points to three innate psychological needs: competence, autonomy, and relatedness; it posits that people living in social contexts that provide opportunities to meet these basic psychological needs are optimized not only for motivation but also for performance and development (Ryan & Deci 2000).

Table 5.2
What School Librarians Can Do to Foster Intrinsic Motivation

- Provide students with individualized opportunities, not a one-size-fits-all approach to learning
- Use teaching strategies and exhibit an attitude based on play (including a sense of humor) and create playful environments
- Offer creative outlets for project completion, collaborate with music and art teachers, and provide access to materials about creative people and pursuits
- Provide choices to various media (including authentic objects)
- Educate parents/guardians in the role of information-seeking "anchors" and notify them when a child is showing an affinity for creativity or a particular interest
- Pay attention and be proactive in connecting students to resources (including people) based on their interests
- Initiate low-key research experiences with the very young
- Use constructivist teaching methodologies (such as problem-based learning and inquiry strategies)
- Reduce extrinsic motivators in the learning environment

Source: Adapted from Crow (2009a).

A recent LIS study based on self-determination theory examined the experiences of students who were self-motivated to explore information about the world around them (Crow 2009b). Using the Self-Regulation Questionnaire for Information Seeking, Crow identified fifth graders who were indicated as highly and distinctly intrinsically motivated to seek information. Based on student interviews and analysis of the children's artwork, Crow found that all the students exhibited an affinity for play, tended to be creative, and were noncompetitive in nature. They all perceived themselves to be competent (though not always in school subjects), and the study suggests that their relatedness needs were met through "anchor" relationships—people who supported their information-seeking interests.

An important principle espoused in self-determination theory is that extrinsic motivators, while effective in promoting motivation for rote and routine tasks, actually results in decreased levels of intrinsic motivation (Deci & Ryan 1985). Several authors have examined the motivational aspects of Accelerated Reader (AR) (e.g., Biggers 2001; Krashen 2003; Mallette, Henk, & Melnick 2004; Robbins & Thompson 1991; Schmidt 2008), a computer-generated reading program in which students select a title based on reading level and then are awarded points upon successful completion of an electronic comprehension quiz about the book. Schools traditionally offer prizes when students reach point goals. Biggers (2001) sees the program's focus on external rewards as a "Skinnerian . . . system of literacy learning that poses the threat of extinction once the rewards are withdrawn" (73). In a study of the school library media specialist's (SLMS) role in managing the program, Everhart (2005) explored the relationship between the implementation of AR and student motivation, then applied her findings to the leadership role that school library media specialists can play in the program's administration. She recommends that those SLMSs who already work in AR schools can be instrumental in its proper implementation, "particularly in the area of book selection, reading guidance and motivation, organization of materials, and teacher professional development" (12). She recommends that school library media specialists in non-AR schools use her study to support collaborating directly with teachers to help students set reading goals outside the AR program. Crow (2004, 2010) suggests that children's choice book award programs are preferable to AR as motivational tools because students are empowered by the act of voting for their favorite book, the programs are based on student choice (a powerful intrinsic motivator), and the act of reading a common list of books creates a sense of camaraderie, all factors that build intrinsic motivation (see Table 5.2).

6 Diagnosing Informational and Instructional Needs

Despite massive and rapid scientific, technological, and social change, children have the same needs they always did: They must be protected and their development must be guided and supported by the people around them. They cannot rear themselves.

—Comer (2001)

We need to begin asking the "why questions" about youth and information-seeking behavior and taking young people more on their own terms than exclusively on terms dictated to them.

—Bernier (2007)

Teachers are being challenged as never before to tailor instruction to meet the educational needs of an increasingly diverse population of young learners and to make sense of the differences in cognitive development and ability, cognitive style, social and cultural experiences and traditions, as well as language variations.[1] Diagnosing instructional needs and customizing instructional approaches for information literacy education assumes the presence of "reflective practitioners" (Schön 1983) who are able to apply educational theory to practice. As has been noted in previous chapters, school librarians have proven themselves to be both reflective and resourceful in reframing resource-based "library skills" to focus on information seeking, process learning, critical thinking, and problem solving (Bodi 1992; Kuhlthau 1993b) and guided inquiry (Kuhlthau et al. 2007).

There are, of course, many ways to differentiate instruction. In the research literature of library and information science, individual differences have frequently been viewed in terms of "user needs" and information-seeking behaviors. Within the educational literature, differences have been identified related to cognitive and personal development and learning styles. Research in sociology, communication, and other disciplines suggest worldview, culture, socioeconomic status, and gender as foundations of difference. Understanding each of these dimensions can help school librarians design effective learning sessions. This chapter takes as its touchstone the diagnostic model created by Grover (1993, 1994), the implementation of which allows instructors to create programs and services based on the needs of specific information seekers.

Grover's Diagnostic Model

Robert Grover (1993, 1994) has proposed a useful approach to instructional customization that takes account of differences in thinking and learning. In essence, Grover's model reframes the standard reference interview as a "cycle of service" that shifts the focus of attention from the characteristics of the library's resources to a concern for the information seeker and his or her particular information needs. Originally aimed at re-creating reference interactions as user-centered activities in public and academic libraries, the model can be used by school librarians in lesson planning because, as Grover (1994) suggests, "information skills instruction is an educational service" (176).[2]

In creating his model, Grover (1993, 1994) invoked a clinical approach developed by doctors to diagnose, prescribe for, and treat their patients. In Grover's adaptation, the service cycle begins when a librarian and an information seeker first encounter each other and ends with the librarian's evaluation of the services provided. Two elements in the model specifically address accountability issues and deserve special notice. The first is that, from the outset, the librarian assumes responsibility for the successful outcome of the service interaction or information search process. The second is that it is the library user, not the librarian, who determines what constitutes "success" in terms of service or search outcomes.

The four steps in Grover's (1993, 1994) model are diagnosis, prescription, treatment, and evaluation (see Figure 6.1). At *diagnosis*, the information provider must inquire into the what, where, and when of the user's information topic or need. However, the central question to be answered is "who?" According to Grover, factors to consider include the individual's literacy level, developmental level, cognitive style, worldview, format preference, culture, and technological skills. Age, gender, communication style, and English-language proficiency may also be germane at the diagnosis phase. This information is then used in the second, or *prescription*, stage of the model in determining the relevance and appropriateness of specific resources (available in the collection, online, or in another library) that will meet the user's need.

The information seeker and the resources identified by the librarian are brought together at the *treatment* stage of the cycle; at *evaluation*, the librarian assesses the service process in light of the user's satisfaction with the resources provided. The essential questions to be answered at evaluation, however, relate to the information need initially expressed: Has the user's need been met? Has the user's problem been resolved? If the answer to these questions is "no," the diagnostic process begins over again and is repeated until the user is satisfied. Greer, Grover, and Fowler (2007) note a wide range of potential theories necessary for the most accurate information needs diagnosis: learning theory, cognitive theory, life-type theory, brain theory, information theory, and role theory. Also recommended as relevant in providing insights into the ways librarians meet users' needs are theories and models from the fields of psychology, sociology, social psychology, linguistics, physiology, cultural anthropology, ethnography, and cybernetics.

When applied in a school context, diagnosis of a student's needs must additionally involve initial assessments of his or her reading level, prior knowledge of the

Figure 6.1
Grover's (1993, 1994) Model for Diagnosing Information Needs

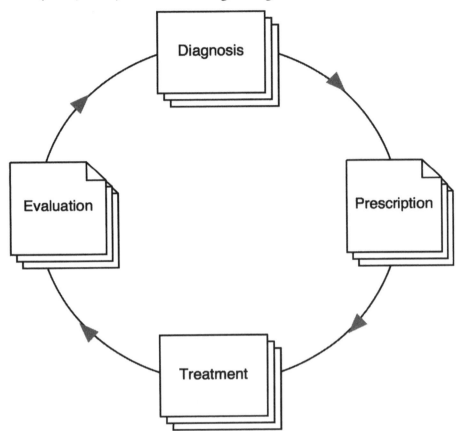

topic or subject, and preferred learning style (Grover 1994) so that lessons that address specific curricular objectives and standards and that meet the instructional needs and preferences of individual students can be created. The implementation of the lesson corresponds with the treatment stage of Grover's model. Evaluating the outcomes of instruction concludes the cycle; at this stage, the school librarian and teacher can assess student learning in relation to the objectives established earlier. This assessment can then serve as a basis upon which to plan further activities or make necessary modifications to instructional strategies.

Student progress and learning may be assessed through observation, interviewing, student journals or learning diaries, portfolios, student projects, paper-and-pencil tests, and teacher, peer, and self-evaluations. In the event that assessment measures show that objectives have not been met or that skills have not been learned, a new round or rounds of planning, instruction, and assessment can be carried out until such time as students achieve mastery. In sum, Grover (1994) proposes *diagnose, design, teach, assess, reteach,* and *reassess* as steps in an instructional adaptation of his service cycle.

In addition to conceptualizing reference services and lesson planning in useful ways, Grover's (1993, 1994) model invites school librarians to select and apply a variety of theoretical frameworks in creating "best-fit" instructional strategies for their students. In fact, the importance of diagnosing the information needs and knowledge states of individual learners faced with an information task probably cannot be overstated. Without knowledge of the information search process and with inadequate background and lack of understandings of the research topic (or both), students have little chance for success in terms of searching and task completion (Harada 2002). When deficits in terms of both process and content knowledge are ignored, professionals may be overly optimistic in terms of expectations on the one hand and fail to provide adequate support to learners on the other. In an information vacuum, the fallback strategy may be limiting service to providing location assistance of resources that may or may not be relevant, and students may be left with the impression that the information they seek does not exist, or even worse that no real help is available from library professionals.

Dimensions of Difference

Successful implementation of Grover's model calls for a theoretical grounding in library and information studies (LIS) and related disciplines as a way to advance student learning and individualize instruction. In the LIS research literature, individual differences have frequently been viewed in terms of user needs and information-seeking behaviors as conceptualized by Taylor, Belkin, and Dervin. Within the educational literature, differences have been identified related to psychology (Maslow), cognitive development (Piaget, Bloom, & others), cognitive processing and activity (e.g., laterality) (Buzan), multiple intelligences (Gardner), learning modes and approaches (e.g., Kolb & Pask), worldview (Anderson), and gender (Gilligan). Understanding each of these dimensions can help school librarians design effective learning sessions. In a very real sense, they also reveal the layers of complexity embedded within activities that may appear, on the surface, to be straightforward and unproblematic.

Information Needs

A useful place to begin an examination of approaches to library and information skills instruction is a discussion of information needs. Theorists in LIS (Taylor & Belkin) and communication (Dervin) have made major contributions to our understanding of needs as an important aspect of information behavior.

Taylor's Levels

In one of the foundational articles in the literature of LIS, Taylor (1968) explored the process through which information *needs* of users are transformed into the kinds of questions or *queries* that can be successfully addressed in a library setting. To this end, Taylor described information needs as a set of hierarchically arranged levels based on the seeker's ability to express the need and the clarity of that expression. According to this taxonomy, Taylor identified as *visceral* those needs that are unexpressed and inexpressible; needs at this level may be experienced simply as a sense of uneasiness or dissatisfaction with a situation. In the event that the feelings persist, they will eventually come to the surface; needs at this level Taylor identified as *conscious*. Users with conscious needs can articulate or talk about them and relate them in a general way to specific subjects, topics, or situations (e.g., "I need information about . . . "). As the need becomes clearer in the user's mind, it becomes more focused and can be *formalized* as a rational statement or a specific question (e.g., "I need specific information on . . . "). Once the information need can be stated in this way, it can be reformulated or *compromised* into vocabulary (e.g., keywords or Library of Congress subject headings) to which an information system can respond. Taylor's model is useful in that it raises awareness of the difficulties that users may experience in expressing their needs in a library setting. At the same time, it suggests that librarians have a role to play and expertise to offer in helping users articulate their needs, especially at formalized and compromised levels. In a very real sense, the traditional reference interview was an acknowledgment of and framework for this role.

Belkin's Information Problems: Anomalous States of Knowledge

For Belkin and his colleagues (Belkin 1980; Belkin, Oddy, & Brooks 1982a, 1982b), the information problems that individuals experience are best described as *anomalous states of knowledge* (or *ASK*). An information science theorist interested in the design of electronic information retrieval systems, Belkin argues that information needs can more usefully be addressed if they are considered information "problems" that arise when a person realizes that "his or her state of knowledge" is not sufficient to make a decision, solve a problem, or reach a goal. The challenge this poses for the information seeker is that the specific information or resource necessary "to resolve the anomaly" (Belkin, 1978, quoted in Dervin & Nilan 1986, 13) may not be known. As it is difficult for people to request assistance when they themselves are unsure what it is they are seeking, Belkin suggests asking users to describe what they do know about the topic or situation to determine what is "missing." When the information seeker is allowed to tell his or her own story in a reference interview, it may be possible for the information professional to understand and thus address the need and identify relevant resources to satisfy the unarticulated question.

Dervin: Information Seeking as Sense Making

One of the first theorists to introduce the idea of customized services as a goal for reference librarians was Brenda Dervin (1983, 1989). A communication scholar, Dervin sees information seeking as sense making. Within this framework, information seeking is initiated when individuals encounter gaps in their knowledge sufficient to impede, prevent, or stop their forward progress through time and space (see Figure 6.2). These gaps may be perceived as dilemmas, confusions, or

Figure 6.2
Dervin's (1983) Situation-Gaps-Uses Model

uncertainties of the sort that people face as a part of daily life. The "sense" or understandings that they ultimately construct from the information they obtain in information encounters provide the "bridge" that enables them to proceed with their activities or decision making.[3]

In Dervin's view, what people require when they find themselves stuck in an information gap is personalized information and assistance based on their interests, their views of the problem, and whatever barriers they expect to encounter. As information problems do not arise in a vacuum but are tied to situations in which people find themselves, Dervin suggests that librarians create and pose one or a series of neutral questions (Dervin & Dewdney 1986) that will uncover the seeker's situation, the gaps in understanding, and the intended use. Neutral questions are a subset of open-ended questions that professionals can use to guide information seekers in explaining their information needs, their situations, their knowledge gaps, and their intended plans of action in their own words.

Maslow's Hierarchy of Needs

Abraham Maslow (1908–1970) conceptualized individual needs as physiological and psychological or "human" rather than strictly informational. In Maslow's (1970) model, needs are ranked hierarchically, with the physiological and physical dimensions of human experience at the base or bottom levels and self-actualization at the highest or top level. Originally, Maslow posited only five levels of needs; later, he added two dimensions to self-actualization: the need to know and the need for beauty and order. Maslow holds that failure to have needs met at any of the first four levels compromises an individual's successful achievement or fulfillment of needs at higher levels (see Figure 6.3).

The lowest or base level of needs comprises those *physiological* elements that support and sustain life: the need for food, water, rest, warmth, and shelter. Needs at the next higher level involve personal *safety* issues, including the needs for environmental and personal stability and physical and psychological *security*. At a third level are *love and belonging* needs, which are fulfilled in family relationships, friendships, and acceptance by one's peers. *Esteem* needs occupy a fourth level and are realized in acknowledgments of our personal competence by others and resulting feelings of self-respect and self-worth. *Self-actualization* needs arise in feelings of self-acceptance and frequently are expressed in self-enhancement activities and activities that allow the exploration of personal values. The *need to know* and the *need for beauty and order* often translate into love of learning and the pursuit of personal interests, while the need for beauty is often realized in art appreciation, literature, and music. Maslow conceptualized this highest state as episodic rather than static and characterized by peak experiences of creativity, spontaneity, happiness, and the fulfillment of potential that punctuate our existence. Maslow's hierarchy of needs makes acutely apparent the reasons why a hungry child may not demonstrate much intellectual curiosity or why one who has been belittled at home or is worrying about the acceptance by peers at school may not take an interest in abstract notions of beauty or justice. Comer (2001) acknowledged the continuing value of understanding children's needs in school settings. "Despite massive and rapid scientific, technological, and social change," Comer writes, "children have the same needs they always did: They must be protected and their development must be guided and supported by the people around them. They cannot rear themselves."

Figure 6.3
Maslow's (1970) Hierarchy of Needs

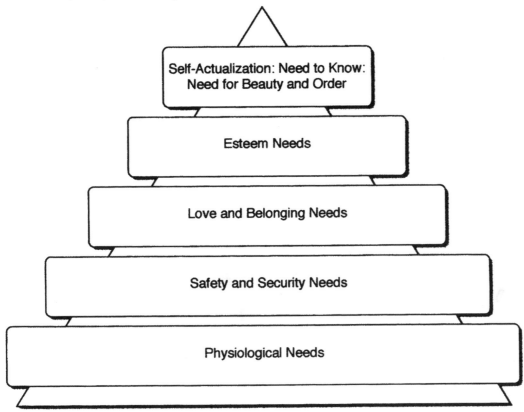

Applying Theories of Information Needs in the School Library

In her studies on the expression of information needs by school-age children, Gross (1995, 1997) drew on the work of Taylor (1968) and his conceptualization of levels. Her findings suggest that although the ways in which information needs have been understood in the literature of LIS illuminate the evolutionary process through which self-generated questions pass as they move from visceral to compromised levels, the information questions that teachers pose for students to answer present entirely different kinds of problems. If, for example, the question the student brings to the librarian is stated unclearly, it may be because the student lacks the background knowledge (possessed, presumably, by the teacher who created the question) to clarify the nature of his or her information need. Under these circumstances, the task of helping the student formalize the need (restate the need as a question) may be extremely difficult no matter how well or compassionately the librarian conducts the interview. Indeed, the question that the student poses when seeking assistance will reflect his or her *interpretation* of the teacher's intent, an interpretation that may or may not reflect the teacher's understanding of the task or question. Obviously, relevance judgments of resources and information provided to answer these kinds of requests are compromised as well. This is particularly true when information that matches the question cannot be found in student-appropriate resources.

Furthermore, the student's request or question is also interpreted by the school librarian through layers of meaning based on the librarian's prior knowledge of the teacher, the subject, or the assignment. When both the teacher and the assignment are unknown to the librarian and the student's understanding is incomplete, both the librarian and the student will be left to speculate on the teacher's intent.

Gross (1995, 1997) believes that understanding the ways in which a teacher-imposed question differs from a self-generated question will assist school librarians in providing guidance to students. For a start, it demonstrates how sensitive librarians must be to the *possibility* that the students themselves lack an understanding of the very questions they are asking. In her study with elementary school students, Gross found that determining the origins of their requests was not at all straightforward because the children in the study interpreted even this question in a variety of ways.

The sorts of confusion that assigned questions can engender can be ameliorated to a great extent if the school librarian and the classroom teacher work together to establish assignment objectives and create the potential research questions. Another, perhaps better solution would be to make the students part of decision making so that the objectives of the assignment are understood by all parties before the library activity actually begins. But even in cases where the questions appear to adults to be clearly and unambiguously stated, the school librarian must check for student understanding before acceding to requests for help. Indeed, Gross (1995) argues that librarians need to interview "all students who come to the reference desk regardless of whether they are the first, fifth or twentieth person to make that request in a given day" (242).

Whereas Gross's (1995, 1997) research considered children's information seeking and needs related to instruction, Walter's (1994) study was concerned with identifying the information that children need for daily living (e.g., personal safety and life choices). Citing the richness of the LIS literature on adults as information seekers and the lack of research on children's information needs, Walter set out to explore this issue. At the outset, she made two assumptions: first, that, like adults, "children have information needs that, if met, would enable them to solve problems and resolve particular difficulties" and, second, "that children are frequently unaware of their needs" (115).

In the absence of field-tested strategies and guidelines as to how to implement such a study, Walter (1994) organized her research around interviews that she conducted with 25 adults (other than parents) who were involved in working directly with and/or planning services for children. In each case, the adults were asked to discuss what information they thought the children should have, how they thought the children were getting their information, and what information gaps existed for children.

Walter (1994) justified her decision to interview adults rather than children about children's needs because, in many instances, children lack the experience necessary to know that an information need exists. Kuhlthau's (1993b) research confirms that children are often unable to express their needs in ways that will help them initiate the search process, while Moore and St. George's (1991) study demonstrated the problems children have in extracting and using information they find, even when the research topics themselves are preselected. "Imagine the obstacles," as Walter (1994) directs, "when children must also" (115) initiate information seeking and explain the original information need. It is for this reason that Walter asserts that "adults must articulate those needs for them" (113).

Walter's (1994) study revealed that, indeed, school-aged children do have information needs and that many of these needs are not being met. In reviewing the interview data, Walter determined that the articulation of needs closely resembled the hierarchy identified by Maslow (1970). Specifically, Walter found that children's needs for information on health, hygiene, and disease (AIDS) prevention, substance abuse, and child abuse[4] are expressions of needs experienced at a physiological level.

Children's safety needs were reflected in information on avoiding crime, safety procedures of various kinds, literacy skills, and traffic laws. Belonging needs identified in the study related to information on interpersonal relationships, multicultural issues, emotional awareness, and recreation. The esteem needs that Walter (1994) reported related to "multicultural awareness, emotional awareness, social system knowledge (legal, economic, etc.)" (120) and to information on values and ethics. Finally, at the level of self-actualization, Walter noted children's needs for education, recreation, values and ethics, and "cultural" opportunities related to reading, art, and music.

In Walter's (1994) work, sex education was mentioned by so many of the interviewees as being related to "so many different contexts" (122) that she considered this an information need at every level except self-actualization. Of interest as well was Walter's finding that adults in the study emphasized physiological and safety needs as being of primary importance for the development of skills necessary for basic survival. They also mentioned the *misinformation* supplied to children through the media and from uninformed or ineffectual caregivers, service providers, and peers as a central problem.

Walter (1994) also identified a number of barriers to children's information seeking; these included inadequate services, absence of adult-child interaction, and ineffective information programs and providers (especially noted were lack of rapport between service providers and children and failure to provide appropriate instructional approaches). It is significant to note that some adults in Walter's (1994) study considered children's needs as relational rather than informational and did not see a role for the library to play in improving the situation. But if, as Walter asserts, all children are "information poor" (126), is there not a role for library professionals to play in helping children meet these unmet information needs? Walter, of course, thinks there is.

Although Walter (1994) is interested mainly in improving public library services, school librarians, most of whom have direct access to children on a daily basis, are in an excellent position to address these needs. In addition, they can do so through the information skills curriculum. For example, creating "authentic" information tasks directed at addressing the information gaps children have could be easily incorporated into various content or subject areas assigned to meet classroom objectives. In addition, collecting pamphlets, periodicals, and magazines as well as nonprint resources that support such an information-rich and authentic curriculum and making them easily available to children through the library, the classroom, and wherever children congregate would serve as well. Secondary school librarians often provide such pamphlets as a matter of course, but the availability of such information products has been observed less frequently in elementary school libraries.

Harmon and Bradburn (1988) discuss information needs in terms of kinds of information that adolescents require in completing developmental tasks. Citing the work of Havighurst (1953) and Abrahamson (1970), these researchers suggest that the needs unique to teenage youth pertain to social and gender identity tasks, the need to establish both emotional and economic independence, intellectual skills and ethical values, life skills, self-control skills, and coping skills. From these tasks,

Harmon and Bradburn have identified three categories of needs: research needs (for academic and personal intellectual use), recreational needs (media resources in all formats), and information needs (life skills and coping skills). In their view, a problem with meeting all these information needs is the complexity of the adolescent tasks themselves.[5] It is interesting to note that the information needs that Harmon and Bradburn identified in 1988 as needs of adolescents did not include the concerns for survival or personal safety identified by the informants in Walter's (1994) study.

Socioeconomic Issues and Children's Information Needs

Jonathan Kozol (1994, 1996, 2000, 2006) has written extensively about the needs of children in low-income neighborhoods where deficits in the availability of print resources and access to knowledgeable adults who can stimulate reading interests and guide information seeking are continuing problems. In discussing the importance of school libraries, Kozol notes that, without them, the children "who ha[ve] the least to stimulate their reading appetites at home . . . find much less to stir their love of learning in their public schools." He speaks of this kind of deprivation as a form of "theft of stimulation, cognitive excitement, and aesthetic provocation" that is catastrophic. He writes that

> school libraries developed with the artfulness of skilled librarians—remain the clearest window to a world of noncommercial satisfactions and entice-ments that most children in poor neighborhoods will ever know. To shut those windows is to close down one more opening to democratic amplitude and one more opportunity for fully realized cultural existence.

Such an eventuality clearly limits underprivileged children's access to the higher levels of Maslow's hierarchy.

Neuman and Celano (2001) studied access to print resources in middle- and low-income neighborhoods. In particular, they looked at the nature of the all kinds of texts available in each of these environments. Drawing on the work of Rogoff, Bronfenbrenner, McCloud, and others, Neuman and Celano believe such texts "shape children's first literacy experiences." As such, they constitute the very "architecture of everyday life," which "embed opportunities for children to learn and develop through observation and apprenticeship" (11). Their intent was to examine "access to literacy as a potential contributing factor for explaining differences in interaction, behaviors, and ultimately achievement for these children" (11).

Particularly germane to some of the issues addressed in this book were Neuman and Celano's (2001) descriptions of the disparities between the school libraries in the neighborhoods included in their study. Chief among the differences were numbers of resources per capita, condition of print collections, availability of computers, presence of a certified library media specialist, and hours of operation. Statistical significance was observed in number and condition of books, number of days open, and availability of computers. School libraries in low-income neighborhoods lacked certified librarians; school librarians in middle-income neighborhoods held master's degrees. Their data suggest that "children who live in already print-rich environments tended to have school libraries that offered more books, more computers for research, better trained librarians with more experience, and more hours to visit during the day" (22).

Although clearly family interactions are immensely important to children's access to resources, the larger social settings within which families live exert tremendous pressures as well:

> Pervasive poverty, institutional settings like the workplace, and social welfare systems act as indirect environmental influences on children's interactions. They may affect the physical and emotional resources provided to the child (e.g., stress levels due to lack of work), adult responsiveness, and involvement in daily activities. (Hart & Realey, 1995; McLoyd, 1990)." (Neuman & Celano 2001, 23)

When it comes to content on the Internet, a report by The Children's Partnership (Lazarus & Mora 2000) provides some insights into what children of "underserved Americans" (defined as low-income, rural, limited education, or racial or ethnic minorities) want the Internet to provide. Included on the list were participation and self-expression, high-impact packaging with interactivity, multimedia, and youth-friendly tutorials, easier searching and usability, encouragement, and involvement. The study's finding that "young people instinctively see the Internet as an entertainment source rather than an information source" also presents school librarians with additional considerations in framing information literacy skills agenda for this generation of information seekers. Finally, the study found that children as well as adults

> want coaches and mentors to guide them in finding what they want on the Web, suggesting sites or activities to get started, helping use a tutorial and the like. Moreover, they want an environment where they can get literacy support or help with English if they need it. They want to be in a place where others in their community are doing the same thing and where they can count on coaching and support to build their confidence, answer their questions, and guide them in new directions. (21)

As McDonald (1988) noted, the inaccessibility of information is compounded in electronic environments; for this reason, the role of the school library in providing access, instruction, and guidance in information use is crucial to the searching success of today's youngsters.

Of special interest with regard to children's everyday information needs is the work of Agosto and Hughes-Hassell. In their study of inner-city youth (2006a, 2006b), they found that the informants' developmental needs drove their information seeking and that this was finding was similar across contexts for advantaged, nonminority youth (2006b) as well as for minority children. Their research suggests that information needs of youth are universal across socioeconomic, geographic, and cultural lines.

Theories of Cognitive Development and Complexity

Although, as Kuhlthau (1993b) argues, information seeking and learning from information have behavioral and affective as well as cognitive dimensions, the primary concern of information models in LIS is with children's capacity to think critically. For this reason, Grover (1993) and others recommend that school librarians consider theories of learning as they plan for information literacy instruction. Of particular value in this regard are the frameworks provided by theorists Jean Piaget (Inhelder & Piaget 1958) and Benjamin Bloom (1956).[6]

Piaget's Theory of Cognitive Development

Piaget (Inhelder & Piaget 1958) believed that cognitive development is dependent on physical maturation and interaction with the environment and proceeds for all children according to an orderly succession of learning states. Within Piaget's framework (see Figure 6.4), learning structures or schemata develop in response to the child's concrete experience of his or her world and are extended with each new experience through the mechanisms of accommodation and assimilation. Accommodation involves modification of schemata in response to new information. Assimilation is the integration of new knowledge into what is already known. For Piaget, maturation can best be understood in terms of developmental stages, which are thought to be invariant across culture and gender, although children may pass through them at different chronological ages and at different rates.

Figure 6.4
Piaget's (Inhelder & Piaget 1958) Stages of Cognitive Development

Sensorimotor (0–2 years)	Children's actions are instinctual and reflexive Children manipulate concrete items Children exhibit limited language development
Preoperational (2–7 years)	Children employ preconceptual thinking (cannot classify) Children operate in the present Children are animistic Children acquire language Children exhibit egocentricity
Concrete Operational (7–11 years)	Children can classify concrete objects Children develop a sense of time and space Children understand conservation and reversibility
Formal Operations (11+ years)	Children can deal with hypotheticals and abstractions and begin to think critically

Piaget (Inhelder & Piaget 1958) described the development of children's intellectual skills or "mental operations" as a progression of accomplishments related to perception (the ability to detect and organize information through the senses), memory (the storage and retrieval of information), reasoning (the ability to use knowledge to make inferences and draw conclusions), reflection (the ability to evaluate the quality of ideas), and insight (the ability to see patterns and to recognize and understand relationships among ideas). As they grow biologically, children move from a sensory stage where learning is accomplished through direct experience and the manipulation of physical objects in an egocentric universe to a state of formal thinking wherein a child is able to consider perspectives different from his or her own and to do mentally (by thinking) what as a younger child he or she had to do physically (by doing).

During the *sensorimotor* stage, the largely reflexive behavior of the newborn progresses to include responses to observed objects and the differentiation of self and other. Children at this stage become increasingly able to explore the world through their senses and begin to learn language. During the *preoperational* stage, language development continues, and children grow in their ability to classify or group objects. Preoperational children are egocentric, however, seeing everything from their own points of view. They learn by imitating the behavior they observe in others, and they are very busy exploring the environment. During the *concrete operational* stage, children continue to learn through the manipulation of tangible objects; but they also begin to develop a sense of time, and their thinking becomes increasingly logical. They begin to understand cause-and-effect relationships and can classify objects based on more than one characteristic. As their cognitive "operations" become increasingly "formal," children learn to take the point of view of others and to think abstractly and critically. It is at this stage that they become able to consider a number of solutions in solving a problem and develop the capacity to compare alternatives and consider hypotheses. As *formal* thinkers, children are able to consider their own lives from different perspectives and to think about and evaluate their own thinking (metacognition).

Bloom's Taxonomy

Whereas Piaget considered the development of thinking skills as maturational, Benjamin Bloom (1956) proposed a taxonomy of mental activities, independent of physical development, which ranked thinking tasks on the basis of mental complexity or cognitive load. These levels are summarized in Figure 6.5. Bloom ranked *recognition* at the basic or beginning level. As explained by Bloom, thinking at the level of recognition allows an individual to distinguish one entity from another and to give the entities names or labels. Thinking at the second level, *knowledge*, constitutes the ability to recall information or report facts. At the next level, *comprehension*, thinking is described as an understanding of concepts. At the third level, *application*, thinkers are able to take what is known or has been learned in one situation and use it to solve problems in a variety of other situations. *Analysis* is the ability to look at a whole by examining its constituent parts, while *synthesis* is the ability to construct new knowledge or new understandings out of disparate ideas or facts. At the highest level, *evaluation*, thinkers are able to make judgments regarding the value of an idea, an activity, or a project. "In this model," as Fitzgerald (1999) notes, "each skill potentially exercises all of the ones below it in the hierarchy."

Figure 6.5
Bloom's (1956) Taxonomy

Recognition	Remembering and labeling

Knowledge	Recalling facts

Comprehension	Understanding important concepts

Application	Using what is known in a variety of situations

Analysis	Understanding the whole through an examination of its constituent parts

Synthesis	Making something new out of separate ideas or facts

Evaluation	Judging the value of an idea, concept, or project

Revising Bloom's Taxonomy

Recognizing changes in how students interact with technologies and considering research demonstrating best practices for educating students, Marzano (2000) has provided an update for Bloom's Taxonomy that takes into account motivation and metacognition. His revised system does not necessarily proceed in a linear fashion, and it echoes the learning processes that students undergo. Whereas Bloom's Taxonomy includes the ordered steps of *knowledge, comprehension, application, analysis, synthesis*, and *evaluation*, Marzano (2000) has created a nonlinear model, labeling his conception "A New Taxonomy of Educational Objectives," comprised of three main systems and a *knowledge domain*. His model, which builds on earlier work that he completed on a "dimensions-of-learning model" (Marzano 1992), posits that five dimensions of thinking influence the learning process and proceeds in a nonlinear fashion. These dimensions are *positive attitudes and perceptions about learning*, *acquisition and integration of knowledge*, *extension and refinement of knowledge*, *meaningful use of knowledge*, and *productive habits of the mind*. Marzano's model holds that, in fact, learning categories do not build on each other in a linear way but instead exist with equal importance in the overall learning process. He explains,

> The three systems are the Self-System, the Metacognitive System, and the Cognitive System. When faced with the option of starting a new task, the Self-System decides whether to continue the current behavior or engage in the new activity; the Metacognitive System sets goals and keeps track of how well they are being achieved; the Cognitive System processes all the necessary information, and the Knowledge Domain provides the content.

Other researchers have also proposed changes or updates to Bloom's Taxonomy. Anderson and Krathwohl (2001) recommended combining both the cognitive processes and the knowledge dimensions originally described by Bloom. They list the following items, among others, as key to their "upgrade" of Bloom's work: *recognizing*, *recalling*, *interpreting*, *exemplifying*, *classifying*, *summarizing*, *inferring*, *comparing*, and *explaining*. Wiggins and McTighe (1998) also considered possible changes to Bloom's original work when they detailed the "Six Facets of Understanding" as a model for curriculum design processes in an effort to bolster student understanding of content. They label these facets as *explanation*, *interpretation*, *application*, *perspective*, *empathy*, and *self-knowledge* and include specific performance indicators as well as common vocabulary for assessment of learning.

Learning Styles and Learning Modes

While it is useful to consider thinking in terms of developmental stages and complexity levels, approaches that focus on styles of learning and knowing can help school librarians create activities that take advantage of students' preferences, "potentials," and strengths. The inclusion of alternative ways of knowing and being in the world (McCarthy 1996) within curricular assignments also raises teacher and school awareness and appreciation of the many kinds of intellectual gifts that students possess while honoring differences in ways that enhance both the learning and the learner. The following sections consider cognitive diversity in terms of learning styles (Kolb 1983), problem-solving skills (Pask 1972, 1975), hemisphericity (Bogen 1969; Buzan 1991), and multiple intelligences (Gardner 1996, 1999, 2003).

Kolb's Learning Modes

Kolb's (1983) theory of learning styles is based on the work of the Swiss psychologist and psychoanalyst Carl Jung (1875–1961), who theorized that people function in the world in four ways: by thinking and reasoning, by feeling and relating, by perceiving and sensing, and by intuiting and imagining. As interpreted by Kolb, the ways people implement these "vantage points of human consciousness" (McCarthy 1996, 47) create for them individual patterns or "modes" of thinking, which Kolb labeled as concrete experience, reflective observation, abstract conceptualization, and active experimentation (see Figure 6.6). Kolb and Fry (1975) argue

Figure 6.6
Kolb's (1983) Modes Learning

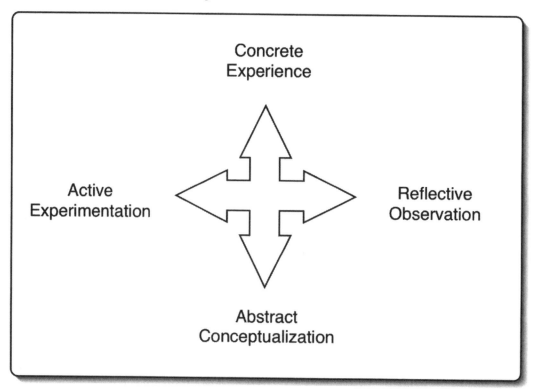

that effective learners possess all four learning modes to some degree. Indeed, there are no age levels attached to these different patterns of functioning, and there is no intimation that one way of thinking is better than another. For this reason, Kolb's theory is considered "experiential" rather than "developmental."

According to Kolb (1983), every person has the capacity to function in all four modes. However, individuals develop preferences for one mode over the others and find that operating in that mode seems entirely ordinary and natural. Indeed, when individuals are asked to think outside their preferred modes, Kolb believes that they have to work harder to make sense of the learning task at hand. On the other hand, many individuals have the cognitive flexibility to use alternate modes, depending on the subject, the situation, or the level of stress. Figure 6.7, which is based on Kolb's theory, shows the relationship of the modes to one another. Here, ways of thinking and learning are represented as two continua of experience. The horizontal axis, extending from action/participation (doing) to reflection (watching), represents how learners process information. The vertical axis, extending from concrete (sensing and feeling intuitively) to abstract (analyzing and reasoning conceptually), represents how learners perceive reality. Kolb maintains that the intersection of the two continua not only defines four distinct learning abilities but also creates a four-part or four-step model of learning (see Figure 6.8). Kolb argues that learning can begin in any of the steps in the cycle.

In Kolb's view, *concrete experiencers* enjoy problem solving in real-world situations, and they tend to personalize task experiences, emphasize feeling over thinking, rely on intuition, and enjoy creative approaches to decision making. People

Figure 6.7
Kolb's (1983) Approaches to Learning

Concrete
(Sensing and Feeling)

Action   **Reflection**
(Doing)   (Watching)

Abstract
(Analyzing and Reasoning)

Figure 6.8
Kolb's (1983) Four-Part Learning Cycle

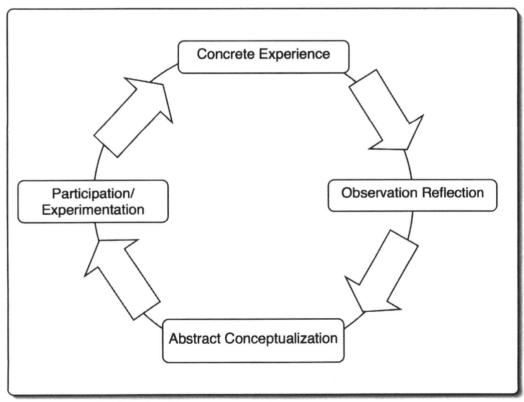

who prefer this approach tend to relate well to others and enjoy working under flexible as opposed to highly structured conditions. Kolb's *reflective observers* like to learn by watching others and observing situations and events. Individuals who take this approach to learning are thoughtful rather than pragmatic, frequently seeking understanding, meanings, and truth rather than "what works." Reflective observers prefer contemplation to action in problem solving, and they frequently excel at being able to see the implications of situations or actions within a wider context or frame. Reflective observers are self-reliant, preferring to work alone and depending on their own judgment rather the opinions of others when making decisions. The mode of learning used by *abstract conceptualizers* emphasizes logic and thinking rather than feeling, favors analysis and quantification types of activities, and approaches problem solving in scientific and systematic ways. These kinds of learners are often task oriented and highly productive. Finally, Kolb's *active experimenters* learn by doing and favor hands-on activities that allow them to use the ideas and theories they encounter for practical tasks and pragmatic problem solving. Active experimenters are often risk takers and change agents, and, since they are often results oriented, they enjoy setting goals and completing projects.

Few learners actually exhibit the "ideal" behaviors implied in Kolb's (1983) model, tending instead "to develop [an] orientation to . . . one of the poles of each dimension" (Smith 2001). To take this into account, Kolb and Fry (1975) acknowledge the existence of four learning styles (see Figure 6.9.), which mark positions people can take between concrete and abstract thinking and between action and observation. In brief, these characterizations describe four ways in which people like to learn. "Convergers" are pragmatists who combine active participation with an ability to think abstractly. "Divergers" are watchers, who enjoy learning through

Figure 6.9
Learning Styles Identified by Kolb and Fry (1975)

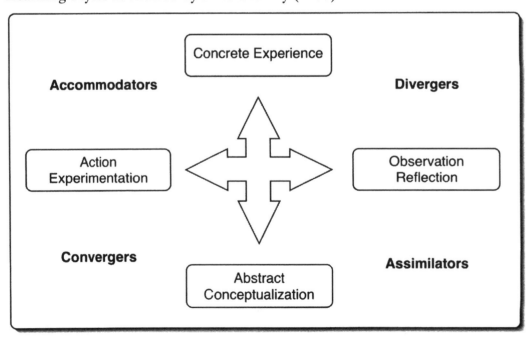

observing real-world activities. "Assimilators" are thinkers who learn best through reflecting on abstract concepts, while "Accommodators" like to learn by doing.

While many educators acknowledge the value of Kolb's models to the creation of instructional strategies, critics have pointed to a lack of research verification for the theory itself. In addition, they argue that the model fails to account for individual motivation, cultural characteristics, aspects of the task, and contextual differences experienced by specific learners. Dunn, Beasley, and Buchanan (1994) have reviewed the educational literature on learning styles and achievement and assert that "most students can learn anything when . . . they are interested in the topic, begin learning with their preferred processing style," receive reinforcement through their "secondary or tertiary modality," and "apply new information" to the development of "a new instructional service," such as the creation of a game, play, poem, or "set of task cards" (12). Still, Kolb has contributed a great deal to our understanding of the very real differences that exist in the ways people learn.

The 4MAT Learning System

Berniece McCarthy (1996) has created the 4MAT Learning System, which incorporates elements of cognitive learning-style theory (Jung 1923; Kolb 1983) and brain research on cerebral laterality and hemispheric dominance (Bogen 1969; Buzan 1991). While many people appear to favor one side of their brains over the other, some learners integrate both sides when solving problems (Wilkerson & White 1988). McCarthy believes that "every learner needs both for the fullest possible understanding of experience" (31) and that training can modify "the tendency to use a particular hemisphere during problem solving" (Wilkerson & White, 358). With this in mind, McCarthy calls for the inclusion of a variety of instructional approaches so that the needs of all students are met in all instructional plans (Hagopian et al. 1996).

In creating a vehicle for the delivery of instruction (McCarthy 2000), 4MAT explicitly tailors the presentation and implementation of the curriculum to the needs of diverse learners in two ways: by asking teachers to use multiple instructional options and by asking instructors to provide alternative assignments for students to use as proof of learning (McCarthy 1987). Although interest in learning-style preferences and hemispheric dominance theory has gained attention and proponents across the educational spectrum, McCarthy's 4MAT Learning System is apparently the only one that translates "the available research into instructional strategies" (Wilkerson & White 1988, 358).[7]

Pask's Holistic and Serialistic Problem Solvers

Pask (Pask & Scott 1972) construes differences in thinking and learning in terms of problem-solving orientations. In brief, Pask suggests that people prefer to think either holistically or serially when considering information to resolve an issue or dilemma. Holists take a global view of a problem, seeking to understand "the whole" and how a problem may be linked to other problems or topics. As information seekers, holists are top-down processors who survey systematically and exhaustively all possible information resources and then examine each in turn (Eisenberg & Berkowitz 1990). Holists tend to thrive on complexity and enjoy hypothesizing. Serialists, on the other hand, reach understanding through an orderly process of sequential steps, identifying constituent elements and focusing on specific details.

These learners favor simple and straightforward solutions to problems they face. As information seekers, serialists may find and use resources in a linear fashion, viewing a succession of items and quitting when they perceive that they have found a sufficient number.

Cerebral Laterality and Multiple Intelligences

A number of learning theorists consider structures in the brain the foundation of differences in thinking and learning. Major frameworks anchored in physiology include cerebral laterality theory and split-brain theory, left-brain/right-brain dominance theory (Bogen 1969; Buzan 1991), and multiple-intelligences theory (Gardner 1983, 1996, 1999, 2003).

Theories of difference involving left-brain and right-brain orientation are anchored to scientific evidence that locates mental functions and patterns of cognitive activity within specific areas of the left and right hemispheres of the brain. Stated briefly, split-brain theory recognizes that for most right-handed people, the left side of the brain is responsible for analytical tasks, such as separating a whole into its constituent parts. The left brain thinks logically, rationally, and sequentially. Verbal and computational skills are also considered left-brain functions in these individuals. By the same token, the right brain manifests abilities to integrate elements into a whole, to find patterns and relationships, and to perform spatial and visual tasks. Aesthetics and intuition are considered right-brain activities, as are the abilities to recognize faces and remember tunes. The two sides of the brain work together to perform mental tasks, "shifting back and forth" (Gedeon 2000, 260), depending on the skills required to complete the task at hand.

The theory of cerebral laterality was first posited in the 19th century by pathologists and neurologists who were treating patients who had sustained brain injuries. Twentieth century advances in medicine and neurology allowed researchers to observe and study the brains of normal people as well as split-brain patients who, from injury or surgery, have lost function of the corpus callosum, a band of tissue that links the two hemispheres

Brain or cerebral dominance theory holds that the left side of the brain is the leading or dominant hemisphere because it controls language and speech (Springer & Deutsch 1993). However, Gedeon (2000) explains the theory of brain dominance in this way: "As one grows intellectually, tendencies develop for hemisphere preference. These tendencies, influenced by an assortment of social and genetic considerations, generally become more entrenched with maturation" (260). Although the preference of one hemisphere over the other can be very strong, Gedeon cites Johnson and Daumer (1993) in suggesting that "it is possible to cultivate use of the less dominant hemisphere" (260). Psychopathologists have noted the relationship between hemisphere dominance and illnesses such as schizophrenia and bipolar disorder.

Research in cerebral laterality offers practitioners some suggestions for tailoring direct instruction to the needs of individual learners. As discussed above, left-brain learners tend to think analytically, rationally, logically, and critically; possess special facility in the use of language; prefer verbal and written instructions; like hands-on activities; enjoy learning facts and details; and excel at classifying, comparing, contrasting, and sequencing. They appreciate structure and understand processes best when they are presented in terms of a sequence of orderly steps. As noted above, those for whom right-brain functions are dominant tend to think holistically, creatively, and intuitively, rather than analytically, and are especially adept at creating visual images, recognizing patterns, making connections, and pulling ideas together. They enjoy inventing, predicting, and imagining alternatives. Such learners like to use metaphors and are talented at synthesizing activities.

Recent research in brain function recognizes hemisphericity as it is related to the task, to the individual, and to culture. Task hemisphericity recognizes the specialization of functions within areas of the brain. Individual hemisphericity relates to an individual's preference in performing a specific task. Cultural hemisphericity acknowledges cultural preferences in thinking styles that typify specific groups (Gordon 1996). While it is safe to say that the complexities of brain functioning are masked in models that sort functions into neat arrays of abilities and capacities, the simplicity of such models does assist in making them comprehensible to nonspecialists.

Another cognitive model identifies four *cerebral modalities*: visual, auditory, kinesthetic, and tactile (Dunn & Smith 1990). Characteristics of *visual learners* include the ability to recognize words by their shape; an interest in visual display, graphics, and media; the tendency to concentrate attention on faces; the practice of making of lists; and recall based on the location of information on a particular page. *Auditory learners* prefer verbal instructions, class discussions, and talking through problems and issues, and they often use music and rhythms as mnemonic aids. Storytelling and group work appeal to these learners. Individuals who enjoy role playing, dramatics, and games and find sitting for extended periods a hardship are exhibiting behaviors of *kinesthetic learners*, while *tactile learners* enjoy hands-on activities and use the act of writing—as in note taking or outlining—as an aid to memory.

Gardner's Multiple Intelligences

One of the most influential of the "cognitive theories" in contemporary psychology and education is the theory of multiple intelligences. In *Frames of Mind*, Gardner (1983) challenged the conventional wisdom shared by supporters of Binet's testing methodology that IQ is a genetically based and stable characteristic, retrievable and measurable through an examination of a person's verbal and analytical skills. On the contrary, Gardner defined intelligence as the *ability to solve problems* and *to create intellectual products* that closely reflect skills valued by families and communities that surround the learner. Thus, for Gardner (1996), frames of intelligence represent "biological and psychological potentialities"—"relatively autonomous intellectual capacities" that can be "realized to a greater or lesser extent as a consequence of the experiential, cultural, and motivational factors that affect a person" (2).

While acknowledging the impact of social factors on the development of special abilities, Gardner (1999) limits the designation of "intelligence" to those talents that can be shown to have a biological basis and that meet eight specific criteria:

1. Potential isolation by brain damage
2. Existence of savants, prodigies, and other exceptional individuals
3. An identifiable core set of operations—basic kinds of information processing operations or mechanisms that deal with one specific kind of input
4. A distinctive developmental history, along with a definite set of "end state" performances

5. An evolutionary history and evolutionary plausibility
6. Evidence in support from experimental and psychological tasks
7. Evidence in support from psychometric findings
8. Susceptibility to encoding from a symbol system

Gardner originally identified seven intelligences (Lazear 1991). However, in *Intelligence Reframed: Multiple Intelligences for the 21st Century*, Gardner (1999) proposed the existence of an additional "intelligence," naturalist, and discussed the possible addition of a ninth, existentialist[8] (see Figure 6.10). *Linguistic intelligence* is shared by writers, poets, and debaters, whose verbal gifts and interests in words and grammar make them good readers and articulate communicators. *Musical intelligence*, which emerges earlier in a child's development than other forms, includes the ability to sing, to detect perfect pitch, to discern rhythms, and/or to create original compositions. *Logical-mathematical intelligence*, which is traditionally tested and thought to measure "intelligence," includes the ability to reason and to think through problems in logical and sequential ways. Individuals with *visual-spatial intelligence* possess the ability to visualize patterns, to create maps and diagrams, and to use flowcharts. This group includes architects, designers, and artists. According to Gardner's (1983, 1999) theory, dancers, athletes, actors, and others who can use their bodies in skilled ways or who have highly developed fine and gross motor skills exhibit *bodily-kinesthetic intelligence*. Gardner also identifies sensitivity to others and sensitivity to self as forms of intelligence. Thus, those with *interpersonal intelligence* have a keen sense of the moods of others and are adept at both personal communication and group facilitation processes, while those with *intrapersonal intelligence* are highly self-reflective and especially good at metacognitive tasks. *Naturalists* have a highly developed sense of the natural world, abilities that manifest themselves in affinity with the biological sciences as well as in activities such as hunting and farming (Hoerr 1996); those with *existential* intelligence possess the ability to consider those questions that relate to the meaning of life and to the nature of human existence.

Although individuals vary to the extent that they exhibit to a high degree one or several of the intelligences, Gardner (1996) asserts that everyone possesses some ability in each of the "intelligence" areas and that these constitute potentialities that can be strengthened in children if they are exposed to appropriate educational strategies and support. While Gardner argues that multiple-intelligences theory can be productively used to alter instructional approaches in ways that "reach more students, and give those students the opportunity to demonstrate what they have understood" (3), he does not suggest them as a replacement for curriculum nor as a shortcut to learning. The central task for teachers, as Gardner sees it, is to provide support for learners so that they can use their own unique sets of capacities in mastering the tasks and skills that will allow them to succeed in contemporary society.

Theories of Social and Cultural Difference

Many researchers look to culture, ethnicity, and social status as frameworks for considering individual differences. Some scholars believe that ethnicity and culture shape not only the development of cognitive skills in children but also their approaches to school tasks and behaviors (Hale-Benson 1982). Others have pointed

Figure 6.10
Gardner's (1999a) Theory of Multiple Intelligences

Verbal-Linguistic	The sounds and meanings of words, grammatical structure	Writing, journaling spelling, reading poetry, debate, word games, puns, and jokes
Logical-Mathematical	Inductive and deductive reasoning, problem solving, sense of numerical order, discernment of patterns, abstract	Logic, mathematical fluency, scientific projects and activities
Visual-Spatial	Imaging and imagining, mapping and pattern making, visual-spatial relationships	Art, architecture and design, sculpture, wayfinding, photography, filmmaking
Bodily-Kinesthetic	Mimetics, coordination, motor skills, role-playing	Dance, athletics, dramatics
Musical-Rhythmic	Melody, structure and tone, pitch, and rhythm	Composing, music making, singing, humming
Interpersonal	Communication skills, awareness and concern for others	Teaching, parenting, counseling, politics, social engagement
Intrapersonal	Mindfulness, metacognitive awareness, self-awareness, personal understanding	Contemplation, self-reflection
Naturalist	Environmental awareness, biological aptitude, attunement to the natural world, classification of species	Farming, gardening, hunting, biological sciences, outdoor activity
(Existentialist)	Philosophical aptitudes, contemplation of questions related to life's meaning	Philosophical thinking, spirituality

to the impact of social and economic contexts as keys to understanding the different ways that children learn. As will be seen later in this chapter, cultural, social, and ethnic dimensions of learning have tremendous implications for teaching and learning in an information skills curriculum. It is well to note at the outset that any general statements made about groups is always tempered with the realization that no group is monolithic—that there are differences among members of any one cultural or ethnic group just as there between members of disparate social groups.

Anderson (1988) understands differences in thinking and learning as differences in "worldview" and relates these differences to cultural traditions and values, which he characterizes as "Western" and "non-Western." Among groups Anderson classifies as Western thinkers in the United States are most American males of Anglo-European descent and those members of various minority groups, including women, who have become acculturated into the dominant Anglo-European traditions and value systems to a high degree. In Anderson's analysis, populations considered non-Western include American Indians; Americans of Mexican, African, Vietnamese, Puerto Rican, Chinese, and Japanese descent; and many Anglo-European females. Anderson frames his comparison of the two groups on a variety of dimensions, involving values, social orientation, and cognitive style; these dimensions are summarized in Table 6.1.

According to Anderson (1988), the differences in worldview he has identified are expressed in the classroom in a number of ways. For example, non-Western thinkers tend to perceive separate elements of a phenomenon holistically—that is, as the constituent parts of a complex picture; for this reason, they prefer to begin learning tasks with an overview of a topic or project so that they can see how the subsets or elements are related to each other and to the whole. This orientation is sometimes referred to as field dependence. In addition, they value "affiliation and conformity" in classroom activities over "individuality and competitiveness" (Clark and Halford 1983, 281) and perform best on verbal tasks. Hale-Benson (1982) points to African traditions as the wellspring for the importance of personal

Table 6.1
Anderson's (1988) Dimensions of Non-Western and Western Worldviews

Non-Western	Western
• Emphasis on cooperation/group achievement	Emphasis on individual/competition
• Social orientation	Task orientation
• Emotionally expressive	Emotional expressions are limited
• Strong extended family relationships	Strong nuclear family orientation
• Values harmony with nature	Values mastery and control of nature
• Time is relative	Time provides an invariant structure
• Religion permeates culture	Religion is separate from culture
• Accepts worldviews of others	Believes that the Western worldview is superior
• Holistic/relational thinking	Analytical thinking
• Field-dependent thinking	Field-independent thinking

connections and social interaction in the learning preferences of black children. Learning that is personally situated and that involves a human aspect is preferred by many non-Western students to the more impersonal, objective, and detached view that typifies the Western approach to topics and subjects. Finally, for many non-Western students, performance in school is highly influenced by authority figures. This may make them especially sensitive to expressions of confidence and expressions of doubt from teachers, administrators, and other adults in the school environment.

Western thinking, on the other hand, is analytical, with elements perceived as separate from the background or "whole" and distinct from one another, an orientation that is known as field independent. Students who exhibit a Western worldview tend to enjoy working more independently and are less likely to be affected by the opinions of others.

Claxton (1990) also recognizes the differences between Western and non-Western worldviews, which he characterizes as two distinct "ways of knowing" (7) that have both sociocultural and cognitive dimensions. Echoing Anderson (1988), Claxton characterizes the Western way as intellectual, detached, and analytical; while the non-Western way is affective, relational, and attached. While Claxton believes that most people feel fairly comfortable with the idea of *learning styles* related to cognitive development, discussions of learning differences related to the social, cultural, and ethnic experience of learners tend to make many educators, community groups, and politicians uneasy. In Claxton's view, educators fear that calling attention to the learning styles of "minority students" will contribute to racial and ethnic stereotyping in ways that undermine demands for educational equity or that justify educational "tracking." However, Claxton argues that a teacher's understanding of the instructional needs of individual children can be deepened through an appreciation of and regard for the differences created by culture and experience. Indeed, he maintains that, as long as educators realize that individual differences within groups negate generalizations across groups, they can employ alternative approaches to learning "which are highly functional in the [students'] home environment" (Gorden & Allen 1988, quoted in Claxton 1990, 6) and ultimately improve their school performance. Understood in this way, knowledge of learning styles can actually validate learning-style differences among students while helping teachers individualize teaching and learning.

Claxton (1990) notes that the dichotomy between Western and non-Western worldviews also resonates with the work of feminist scholars such as Belenky et al. (1986, cited in Claxton 1990), who have argued, like Anderson (1988), that males and females in Western culture tend to view the world from two disparate perspectives. Belenky et al. (1986) characterize these differences as "Separate Knowing," which emphasizes impersonal, rational, and objective perspectives, and "Connected Knowing," which is seen as understanding, subjective, personal, and relational and "requires the learner to see the other person in his or her own context" (Claxton 1990, 7).

One of the most outspoken and influential psychologists in the United States is Carol Gilligan, who was among the first to call attention to the fact that the major developmental theorists based their descriptions of human development exclusively on research from which females and female experience had been excluded. Since the appearance of Gilligan's (1982) book *In a Different Voice*, many scholars have developed a research interest in the experience of women and girls (e.g., see Burdick's research discussed in Chapter 3).

The importance of providing "culturally responsive instructional techniques" has been addressed by a number of scholars who have studied the instructional needs of African American, Hispanic American, and Asian American youth. Irvine and Irvine (1995) have outlined the difficulties that exist for African American and other minority youngsters when schools fail to take their differences in worldview and culture into account. As "Black children's ways of doing and knowing often conflict with and are antithetical to the ways in which schools do and know" (133), the kinds of cultural discontinuities that can occur in the classroom can lead these children to experience both "psychological discomfort and low achievement" (134). In particular, Irvine and Irvine argue that where cultural "otherness" in learning and knowing is "not recognized" or is "rejected," educational contexts can prove alienating and diminishing to minority youngsters. On the other hand, research indicates that where teachers personalize the educational experience, encourage active participation, contextualize instruction, and link curriculum concepts to the "social, cultural, historical and political reality" (138) of "students' everyday experiences" (137), minority youngsters thrive.

Specifically, Irvine and Irvine (1995) argue that minority youngsters who are "predisposed to learning" through "movement, variation, creativity, divergent thinking approaches, inductive reasoning, and a focus on people" are especially at risk where classroom activities and assignments promote only an "analytical style" and emphasize "rules and restriction of movement, standardization, conformity, convergent thinking approaches, deductive reasoning, and a focus on things" (135). In explaining the sorts of misunderstandings that can arise when teachers view stylistic differences in a negative light, the authors offer as an example the elaborate "stage-setting behaviors"—such as "looking over the assignment in its entirety; rearranging posture; elaborately checking pencils, paper, and writing space; asking teachers to repeat directions that have just been given; and checking perceptions of neighboring students" (135)—that often attend initial task engagement for field-dependent students. Such activities are often misconstrued as "avoidance tactics, inattentiveness, disruptions, or evidence of not being prepared to do the assigned task (Gilbert & Gay 1989, 277)" (136).

Understanding behaviors and being sensitive to cultural patterns and preferences will make school libraries safe places for all students. Group projects, class discussion, and allowing time for student storytelling and the relating of personal experiences as well as positive feedback and interaction with instructors are strategies that will support African American students. Finally, teacher expectations are particularly important in the development of positive self-images in black students. It has been shown that positive racial attitudes by teachers are associated with greater minority achievement (Forehand, Regosta, & Rock 1976). Low teacher expectations have been shown to reduce the motivation of students to learn. Perhaps the most damaging consequence of low teacher expectations is the erosion of academic self-image in students. Indeed, "Black youth are more influenced by teacher perceptions than by their own perceptions" (Garrett-Holiday 1985, quoted in Kuykendall 2001).

In stressing the need for culture appropriate teaching strategies, Hale-Benson (1982) noted that classrooms that depend primarily on technology, texts, learning centers, drill and practice sessions, television, and programmed instruction at the expense of socially interactive learning activities and people-oriented learning place many children of African heritage at educational risk (Kuykendall 2001).

Using Cognitive, Cultural, and Social Theories in a Library Context

The theories presented above have important implications and applications for school librarians in crafting information skills programs and tasks. For example, many of the process models created to guide information seeking and student research are highly sensitive to students' cognitive levels as described by Piaget, Bloom, Marzano, and others. That is, most require students to have achieved formal operations and be capable of higher-level thinking in that they demand that learners examine information sources critically, synthesize information, and evaluate their own thinking as well as their own projects. Assignments that require students to explore a topic, construct research questions, narrow a topic, create a focus, and evaluate the process and its outcomes are complex indeed, and librarians and teachers need to be especially concerned that the complexities of their assignments do not so far exceed a child's present level of cognitive functioning that frustration and failure result. Used by reflective practitioners, knowledge of developmental levels helps school librarians diagnose instructional needs and creates scaffolding activities that will support the children in doing with assistance what cannot be managed by the child acting alone.[9] Finally, expectations that students will learn the information search process within the context of a single research project are also bound to end in disappointment (Harada 2002).

Bloom's (1956) taxonomy provides an extremely useful tool to use when considering the levels of thinking required in carrying out instructional tasks and activities of any kind. Indeed, taking the taxonomy into account is especially important in implementing a successful information skills curriculum, as the processes involved in information searching and the creation of research projects are specifically intended to provide opportunities for students to develop and practice critical thinking skills.

Especially relevant to school librarians has been the work of Hensley (1991), who has applied Kolb's (1983) model of the four learning modes in the library context. Thus, for Kolb's *concrete experiencers*, librarians might want to provide affirmation for the user's request for assistance and respond to requests in empathetic and personalized ways. As *reflective observers* enjoy considering alternatives, librarians should be prepared to listen with patience to the students' explanations and thought processes as they work through assignments and projects. Because Kolb's *abstract conceptualizers* often like to work independently, Hensley suggests preparing printed instructions that describe searching techniques and resource options. In providing personal assistance to these learners, Hensley suggests that librarians offer a rationale for suggestions they make and provide a number of alternatives. For *active experimenters* who enjoy learning by doing and prefer practical and simple explanations, librarians can offer instruction at the same time that they demonstrate or present appropriate resources.

Matching Learning-Style Preferences to the Information Search Process and Information Search Process Models

In planning instructional interventions and in choosing process models to help guide students in information-seeking activities and research projects, it is important to be sensitive to the different approaches students use in solving real-world problems and to consider allowing students a range of choices. In fact, it is interesting to consider the process models described in Chapters 3 and 4 in relation to preferences for teaching and learning. Indeed, when taking into consideration Kuhlthau's (1993b, 2004) information search process model, which emphasizes reflection and meaning making; Eisenberg and Berkowitz's (1990) Big6 Skills model, which provides a conceptually neat, analytical and scientific emphasis; Stripling and Pitts's (1988) model, which features thinking and reflecting; Joyce and Tallman's (1997) I-Search model, which focuses on the personal experience of the student in determining topic and format for the project as well as in presenting the final project—all can be seen to reflect differences in approach similar to the learning modes described by Kolb (1983).

4MAT in the School Library

The relevance of the 4MAT Learning System for the teaching of library and information skills is that it involves children in their own learning and creates awareness that learning is a constructive process. Metacognitive strategies such as these, as Kuhlthau (1995) suggests, "substantially increase" children's "confidence and competence" as information seekers (96). In addition, by ensuring a presearch space for "brainstorming and preliminary discussion" of topics and concepts (perhaps alternative "search terms") among students, 4MAT supports Callison's (1995) assertion that this sort of preliminary activity contextualizes a project and facilitates subsequent information-seeking activities.

The fit between 4MAT and the Big6 Skills (Eisenberg & Berkowitz 1990) approach has been explored by Thomas (2001b). The Big6 adds an important component to 4MAT in that it provides a structure for steps that students can follow in researching, synthesizing, and creating projects that is assumed but not described in the 4MAT model. Since information seeking and project completion are complex activities, successful management of the "task requires knowledge of the information retrieval process" and the "range of appropriate strategies" (Moore & St. George 1991, 168) that can and should be taught to students as their projects unfold.

Library Applications for Gardner's Multiple Intelligences

Knowledge of Gardner's (1983) theory of multiple intelligences certainly argues for school librarians to move beyond the more traditional forms of instruction to provide multimodal approaches to teaching and design information projects that permit students to present their learning in different ways. In so doing, students can build their competence in all areas and demonstrate those gifts not ordinarily valued in school or in school-related assignments and assessments (Lazear 1999).

Recently, the move to permit students to present their learning through project options beyond the written report or term paper has made it possible for children and youth with special abilities to maximize their own interests and talents. Other strategies would include the use of games and role playing in addition to pencil-and-paper "seat work"; graphics and visuals, manipulatives, and class discussion in addition to lectures; journal writing and the use of graphic organizers, flowcharts, and time lines in addition to formal, text-based outlines; and group activities and cooperative learning opportunities in addition to individual activities. These strategies naturally take into account the visual, auditory, and kinesthetic preferences of students and create a context of support for all kinds of learners. It is well to note also that accommodating children's differences in these ways is "culture-fair" (Ford 1996, 19).

Exceptionalities

An important difference to be accounted for within the context of information seeking and information skills instruction relates to cognitive, physical, or sensory ability levels of students in contemporary classrooms. It is estimated that 10 percent of American students receive some sort of "special education" support for conditions that include mental retardation, visual or hearing impairment, chronic illness, speech pathologies, and learning disabilities of various kinds. Since the mid-1970s when Congress passed the Education of All Handicapped Children Act (Public Law 94-142, amended in 1986 by Public Law 99-457) and the Individuals with Disabilities Education Act (Public Law 101-476) in 1990, providing for children with special needs has been a mandate for public education. In effect, these laws required schools to create instruction for children with disabilities in the least restrictive environment possible in accordance with the IEP (Individualized Education Program) created for each exceptional learner. This practice assumes that each adult with whom the child interacts within the school setting has an opportunity to contribute to the child's educational experience.

Two approaches used to structure education for children with disabling conditions are mainstreaming and inclusion. Mainstreamed youngsters spend a portion of the school day in a regular classroom. Inclusion provides all children an opportunity to have their instructional needs met within the regular classroom regardless of disabling conditions. Inclusion presupposes that special needs students may receive support within that setting. Research indicates that the mainstreaming/inclusion of exceptional students results in an improvement in student performance when instruction is tailored to the cognitive and social needs of these students and cooperative learning techniques (peer tutoring, learning buddies) and technology are part of the instructional repertoire (Slavin 1990).

Callison's (1990) review of the research literature in school librarianship and special needs children in the early 1990s cited a number of unpublished doctoral dissertations that dealt with the library collections for special needs students (e.g., Davie 1978; Vinson 1983) and the practice and perceptions of school librarians with regard to exceptional students (Buckley 1978). At that time, Callison called for increased attention in this area of school librarianship. While there have been a number of practice-based articles and books (e.g., Wesson and Keefe's [1995] *Serving Special Needs Students in the School Library Media Center*) that contribute to our understanding of the special needs or exceptional students within the context of library and information literacy instruction, research studies in this area have been rare. Much work needs to be done to support school librarians and students in this important aspect of library service.

Relating Cultural and Social Differences to Instructional Design

In dissertation research that sought to test a variety of instructional approaches to the teaching of library skills, Bobotis (1978) compared the effectiveness of oral (lecture), visual (overhead transparencies), and performance approaches to instruction with 21 classes of Hispanic (Mexican American) and Anglo-American seventh graders. Her findings revealed that Mexican American students in her study learned more when information was presented using performance-based methods that more clearly reflected "real-world" types of activities. For this reason, she concluded that there might be a relationship between ethnicity and learning-style preferences in the acquisition of library skills. Lin (1994), who studied cultural differences in an academic library, reached a similar conclusion. Lin's research suggested that Asian (Chinese) and other Non-Western, holistic thinkers might benefit for an overview of the library as a system before being introduced to library routines, library resources, and searching skills.

Citing studies that indicated that there are gender differences (Canada & Brusca 1991; Diem 1986; Freedman 1989) and ethnic differences (DeVillar & Faltis 1991) related to attitudes and the use of computers, Freedman and Liu (1996) found that there were "cultural differences in learning with computers" (57) when they studied a group of middle school Hmong youngsters. In observing the exchange of e-mail messages between their informants and minority students in other cities involving their ethnic traditions, family life, and school experiences, the researchers found that cultural values of the Hmong students created difficulties related to course content, the role of the instructor, and inquiry learning strategies. Content issues related to the assignment surfaced because the students in the study had been raised according to "a strictly patriarchal system" within which males are regarded as "keepers of cultural knowledge" (48) of the sort that students were supposed to investigate. Since the possession of this kind of information is exclusively a male prerogative, "both boys and girls were concerned about the girls learning things about Hmong culture traditionally outside of their accepted range of knowledge" (54). In addition, restrictions on access to cultural traditions meant that in many cases Hmong students lacked knowledge of their own culture to share in response to questions that their "key pals" asked of them. Negotiation with students and parents was necessary to overcome these impediments to information seeking and learning.

The role of the teacher in the learning process also proved problematic for this group of youngsters. For example, even though learning the use of the computer was the intent of the course, many students were reluctant to ask for assistance because to do so would have been to admit that they "lacked computer knowledge" (Freedman & Liu 1996, 52). Rather than "lose face" in this way, students tended to ask one another for help. Similarly, the Hmong students did not like others to watch "over their shoulders" while they were working, lest they be observed making errors. Finally, whereas Anglo students tended to jump into assignments and use a trial-and-error method when using computers, Asian students were reluctant to undertake an assignment without specific direction.

Experiential learning and an expectation of the participation of all students in learning tasks were also problematic. For example, since the values of this particular group included strong group identity, family loyalty, and respect for authority, male students whose fathers were community leaders acted as group leaders, and this influenced the ways that the girls "treated these boys." In addition, their "interest in supporting the common good" (Freedman & Liu 1996, 52) led the more expert students to take over and do the work of their less knowledgeable peers rather than tutoring the novices or demonstrating for them appropriate searching techniques. Asian American students in the study also were inexperienced in asking questions of their respondents, even though they were quite candid at answering questions addressed to them. "The cultural background of the Asian American students, particularly on the part of the girls, tended to limit verbal investigation" (52). And, although some did become adept at asking questions once they understood the importance of posing questions to elicit information, "none of the Asian American students were really comfortable with this part of the project" (52).

These kinds of differences pose challenges for teachers and librarians in planning instruction for groups of minority students unless they have knowledge of approaches to learning that are part of the cultural experience of these students. Where there are differences between the content and processes of instruction and the ways of knowing and learning, the differences will have to be discussed so that students and parents see value of the assignments and develop a level of comfort with what may be for them entirely novel instructional situations. By the same token, changes in practice to ensure the personal and cultural confirmation of minority students are also appropriate; these might include the use of same-sex grouping, turn taking with regard to leadership roles in group activities, and the explanation, modeling, and implementation of peer tutoring activities.

Clearly, the challenge of differentiating information skills instruction is multidimensional, and much more research on information-seeking behavior will have to be done before there will be definitive answers about how differences in learning styles can be best accommodated in instruction and supported in action. However, the research reviewed above provides a foundation and a rationale for the development of user-centered instruction. Students need to be made aware of the processes that underlie information seeking and to have opportunities to discuss with others the projects in which they are involved (Irving 1985; Kuhlthau, Goodin, & McNally 1996a). Indeed, many scholars believe that the reflection on the process is essential for the retention and application of learning across situations and settings. Others would argue, with Delpit (1995), that attention should also be paid to the products created by students in demonstrating their learning as well since in many cases it is by project completion that adults are evaluated in the larger world outside the school. School librarians who can take individual differences into account will be able to make a genuine contribution to the success of all students and model a type of inclusivity that honors "the many different ways students learn and process information" (Teele 1996, 65). Indeed, the library should be a safe place for the expression of these differences.

Differentiating Research Tasks

A useful way to accommodate the learning styles and capitalize on learning strengths that individuals bring to learning tasks within the context of library-based information-seeking tasks is to reframe or have students reframe research questions based on their own preferences. Handling research assignments in this way ensures that students actually have to interact with and apply the information they find to resolve a specific issue and present a synthesis in their own words. Planning a variety of questions to guide student research will accommodate learning-style differences because alternative questions permit students to investigate a subject or engage a topic based on personal interests and perspectives (Thomas, Vroegindewey, & Wellins 1997). Such an approach has the added advantage of promoting a type of inquiry learning that is "founded in gathering information for the purpose of seeking various perspectives, not just a single conclusion" (Callison 1994, 55) and to do so in ways that reflect "the way we learn in 'real life' " (Donham et al. 2001). Kuhlthau, Maniotes, and Caspari (2007) promote the seeking of many perspectives rather than a transmission approach to teaching that "emphasizes the right answer, memorizing specific facts, and repackaging information" (14). Such an approach also reduces the likelihood that students will find either useful or relevant information that they simply copy or download from print and online sources.

However, it should be noted that generating research questions is often a very difficult task and requires practice (Irving 1985). For example, the ability to consider alternative points of view will pose a considerable challenge for concrete thinkers. For this reason, it is appropriate to offer younger students an array of alternatives in research approach from which students can choose. On the other hand, changing the ways that questions are asked may provide students with practice in creating a focus for their topics (Irving 1985), which Kuhlthau (1993a, 1993b) considers *the* crucial element in the successful implementation and completion of the information search process.

When generating a thesis statement and developing a personal focus are objectives within the overall assignment, teachers can assist students by providing models to serve as catalysts for student thinking. By assisting teachers in the development of alternative questions, librarians can use their expertise as instructional consultants to add value to the projects students create. Past research has tended to focus on two-member collaborative teams consisting of the teacher and school librarian. However, Kuhlthau et al. (2007) recommend three-member instructional teams (consisting of the teacher, school librarian, and an additional specialist) as "highly desirable for the most productive collaborative planning and teaching" (48).

Collaborating with teachers in creating research projects for students that permit student choice in terms of topics and approaches is a way of ensuring culture-fair practice in information skills instruction. Moreover, providing an overview of the search process and a rationale for its use are strategies that will be appropriate for many minority youngsters whose thinking is consistent with non-Western cognitive patterns. Finally, making sure that minorities and minority history and traditions are fully represented in the topics chosen as vehicles for student learning as a standard part of the curriculum (not just the focus of Black History Month) and in the organization and patterns of classroom activity will help subvert institutional racism, which many educators see as compromising the ability of minority youngsters to achieve at high levels.

Insights from the research in education and LIS can be summarized as including the following themes: that learning involves personal construction, that learning builds on prior experience or knowledge, that learning proceeds in a nonlinear fashion, that learning is inherently social as well as psychological, that children can understand at a number of levels, that they can perform at higher levels if they are assisted by knowledgeable others, that they learn differently, that intelligence can take multiple forms, and that differences in learning styles are related to biology, culture, motivation, and experience. To create assignments supportive of only one style of information behavior is a discriminatory practice that works to disadvantage students whose cognitive styles and strengths reflect other orientations and interests. This fact demands that school librarians consider multiculturalism and its complexities in ways that truly support and extend learning rather than merely to engage in cultural "tourism" of the type represented by sporadic, once-a-year tributes to ethnic heroes, multicultural food festivals, and multiethnic literature fairs. Although these gestures no doubt make multiculturalism objectives visible, their use addresses the artifacts of culture rather than reflecting cultural values and alternative ways of knowing[10] and constitutes a nod in the general direction of minority students rather than an invitation for them to dine at an educational table prepared with their instructional needs in mind. "We can continue to view diversity as a problem," Delpit (1995) writes, or "we can recognize

Figure 6.11
Strategies for Multidimensional, Student-Centered Learning

Environmental

Provide formal and informal seating
Vary the lighting from bright to subdued
Provide "quiet" and "noisy" spaces

Cognitive

Ground new learning in what students already know
Explain tasks in advance and provide an overview
Divide complex tasks into smaller, sequential steps
Provide oral and visual as well as written instructions
Use modeling, demonstrating, and role-playing in explaining activities
Provide multisensory approaches to learning
Provide activities that encourage exploration and challenge thinking
Provide activities that call for both analysis and synthesis
Provide structured and unstructured alternatives to the same assignment
Where appropriate, emphasize collegiality over authority
Provide choices of projects, resources, activities, and equipment
Include time for both classroom discussion and reflection

Emotional

Expect responsible behavior in the completion of tasks
Make learning activities relevant to student interests and concerns
Express confidence in student ability
Provide positive feedback and support

Social/Cultural

Plan for both individual and small group work
Use same-sex groupings where cultural asymmetry related to
  gender hampers development of information seeking and computer skills
Explain and negotiate instructional strategies when cultural differences
  in approach prove problematic
Interact with students as they work on projects
Be sensitive to stylistic differences in behavior
Provide research topics that are racially and ethnically inclusive
Invite community speakers/local experts to visit school

Physical

Allow for activity as well as reflection
Provide interactional games as well as written activities
Take account of energy levels of students
Vary activities and include some break time

that diversity of thought, language, and worldview . . . can not only provide an exciting educational setting, but can also prepare our children for the richness of living in an increasingly diverse national community" (66).

Modeling Support for All Students in Library Design and Instruction

Support for the use of individual differences in planning library spaces for library instruction appears in research by Dunn and Smith (1990). In their study, these researchers employed a 23-element construct of learning styles developed by Dunn, Dunn, and Price (1985). The elements, which can "affect a person's ability to absorb, process, and retain information" (Dunn & Smith, 33), can be grouped along five dimensions: environmental (sound, light, temperature, and design), emotional (motivation, persistence, responsibility, and structure), sociological (sociability in terms of self, pairs, peers, teams, adults, and variety), physical (perceptual, nutritional, temporal, and mobility), and psychological (hemisphericity, impulsivity and reflexivity, and analytical and global). According to Dunn and Smith state that "the most important aspect is the potent contribution to individualizing instruction" (36) made possible through applications of this construct. This seems entirely consistent with the goal of customization promoted in most contemporary media centers and many schools.

Conclusion

The work of the many theorists and research scholars reviewed in this chapter offers library media specialists a variety of approaches and strategies to use in tailoring instruction to the needs of individuals and groups they serve. Some practical suggestions gleaned from this review are presented in Figure 6.11.

Notes

1. The contemporary term for individualizing instruction is "curriculum differentiation," a strategy that calls on teachers to alter course content and processes, instructional environment, learning products, and assessment measures in response to the interests and abilities of individual students. Interdisciplinary approaches to content, independent activities, critical thinking, active exploration, and challenging assignments are current priorities in curriculum differentiation.

2. When employed in this context, the model assumes that lessons proceed within the context of ongoing classroom activity and draws attention to the necessity of project coordination and cooperative planning with the classroom teacher.

3. In recent thinking and writing on the topic of sense making, Dervin has moved from conceptualizing gaps as obstacles in everyday life to an emphasis on the "hows" of sense making as a "methodological tool" (Savolainen 2003, 697). For a complete explanation of Dervin's current use of sense making, see Dervin (1999).

4. Of interest in this regard is a recent (2002) Kaiser Family Foundation study presented ("See no Evil: How Internet Filters Affect the Search for Online Health Information) citing Generation Rx.com's report that 75 percent of young adults (ages 15–24) relied on information obtained online to fulfill their health-related information needs with fully 44 percent seeking information on birth control and sexually transmitted diseases. The Kaiser report studied three levels of Internet filters (least restrictive [blocking pornography] intermediate [blocking pornography, nudity, and discrimination] and most restrictive [blocking these categories in addition to profanity, drubs, and alcohol]. Filters assessed to be most restrictive incorrectly blocked 50 percent of sites dealing with safe sex and sexual health issues (as opposed to 9% for least restrictive filters) and 60 percent of gay health sites. Significantly, the kinds of information most often blocked related to sexually transmitted disease, pregnancy and birth control, and safe sex.

5. Julien's (1999) study of adolescent career decision-making supports this view. In addition, career decisions, as well as health decisions, require youth to make sense of information from an often bewildering array of sources: "parents, siblings, other family members, family friends, peers, guidance counselors, teachers, school and public library resources, the mass media, and government career centers" (p. 38). Add to this the social

pressures, socialization patterns, and lack of self-confidence that accompany children into adolescence and one begins to understand the complexities of information-based decision-making.

6. The theoretical frameworks related to moral and social development in the writings of Lawrence Kolhberg, Erik Eriksen, and others are also relevant to issues of differentiation of instruction. Readers are encouraged to explore these theories in: Lawrence Kohlberg's Stages in the *Development of Moral Thought and Action* (New York: Holt, Rinehart and Winston, 1969); and Erik H. Eriksen's *Identity, Youth and Crisis* (New York: Norton, 1968).

7. While noting the contribution to thinking that each "brain" makes, McCarthy (1990) argues "every learner needs both for the fullest possible understanding of experience" (p. 31). In addition, there is some research evidence to show that training can alter "the tendency to use a particular hemisphere during problem solving" (Wilkerson & White 1988, p. 358). "According to Torrance (1981)," for example, "a child's preferred style of learning and thinking can be modified over 6 to 10 weeks (Reynolds & Torrance 1978)" (p. 358). Within McCarthy's framework, Kolb's Divergers are "Type One" or "Imaginative" learners; "Type Two" or "analytical learners" are analogous to Kolb's Assimilators; McCarthy describes Kolb's Converger's as Type Three or "common sense" learners; while Kolb's Accommodators are described by McCarthy as Type Four or "Dynamic learners."

McCarthy (1987, 1990) has used the knowledge of Jung's (1923) learning modes to create an eight-stage cycle or "wheel" teachers can use to prepare instructional plans applicable to any curricular area or grade level (Wilkerson & White 358). Briefly stated, lesson plans based on the 4MAT model provide a wheel of activities that are divided into four quadrants. Each quadrant is also divided, in order to provide for both left-brain and right-brain cognitive functioning. By providing activities in each quadrant that reflect right- and left-brain cognitive activity, the "cycle appeals to each learner's most comfortable style in turn, while stretching her or him to function in less comfortable modes" (McCarthy 1990, 33). In this way each student is encouraged to develop "a broader repertoire of problem-solving skills" (Wilkerson & White 1988, 358). In addition, the inclusionary nature of the 4MAT model makes diversity in the classroom an asset for learning rather than an impediment or a deficit.

Thanks in part to its capacity to accommodate diverse learners with a single instructional model and within a single instructional setting, McCarthy's (1990) 4MAT System for Teaching and Learning has been adopted in many school districts nationwide (information on 4MAT is available at http://www.excelcorp.com). Although research into the efficacy of the model as an instructional strategy is in its formative stages, studies in several school districts have shown that 4MAT can have a positive effect on elementary student achievement in geometry (Lieberman, 1989), math (Hagopian et al. 1996), language arts and student attitudes (Wilkerson & White 1988), and reading (Hagopian et al. 1996).

8. At this time, Gardner reports that designation of this last intelligence is "in limbo" as it has not as yet met all the criteria demanded for its permanent inclusion as an independent intelligence.

9. A study by Cooper (2002) takes into account frameworks created by Piaget, Vygotsky, and Kuhlthau in exploring the information seeking behavior of second graders. Specifically, Cooper was interested in observing how students, operating cognitively between preoperational and concrete-operational levels, find information in a school library. The research tasks undertaken by the youngsters included searching for books on general and specific topics on the library shelves and for information on the same topics in a CD-ROM encyclopedia. Cooper found that scaffolding techniques of encouragement and suggestions provided by the school librarian as the electronic searches proceeded enabled pre-abstract thinkers to operate more successfully and confidently in the "metaphysical world" of electronic searching. In addition, computerized searches, which channeled the seekers directly to relevant information, reduced the cognitive demands experienced when new readers negotiate finding aids such as titles, indexes, and tables of contents before actually locating information. Cooper's work also provided evidence for Kuhlthau's (1993)

assertion that feelings are an important aspect of the ISP for "novice information seekers." Her observations led Cooper to conclude that "children tend to favor browsing types of strategies in their information seeking;" that they "rely on visual information if it is available to them rather than using textual information;" and that they can use "meta-information in textual format to find information if it is presented in a very directed manner."

10. Ford (1996) presents Boykin's (1994) list of cultural values and styles as follows: spirituality ("the conviction that nonmaterial religious forces influence people's everyday lives"), harmony ("the notion that one's fate is interrelated with other elements in the scheme of things so that humankind and nature are harmonically conjoined"), movement ("a premium placed on the amalgamation of movement, (poly)rhythm, dance, and percussion embodied in the musical beat"), verve ("a propensity for relatively high levels of stimulation and for action that is energetic and lively"), affect (the centrality of affective information and emotional expressiveness and the equal and integrated importance of thoughts and feelings"), communalism ("a commitment to the fundamental interdependence of people and the importance of social bonds"), oral tradition ("the centrality of oral and aural modes of communication for conveying full meaning and the cultivation of speaking as performance"), expressive individualism ("the cultivation of a distinctive personality and a proclivity for spontaneity and genuine personal expression"), social time perspective ("a commitment to a social construction of time as personified by an event orientation") (pp. 85–86).

7 Building Information Competence

Designing Instruction for Today's Learners

In the libraries of old, the Dewey Decimal System got you started in research. But there is no card catalog for 2.0. To use the Internet as a library you need new research skills: the ability to pick out reliable sources from an overwhelming heap of misinformation, to find relevant material amid an array of options, to navigate the shifting ethics of creative commons and intellectual property rights and to present conclusions in a manner that engages modern audiences. ... Without a dedicated guide, [students] end up, in the words of professor Henry Jenkins, as "feral children of the Internet raised by Web 2.0 wolves."

—Moran (2010)

Now the roller coaster really begins as we deal with the next generation—those "born with the chip"—who have grown up in the 1980s with computers and don't think of them as technology. They are part of their cultural DNA.

—Abram and Luther (2004)

The profound changes wrought by digital technology have created opportunities for students unparalleled in the history of education. Our ability to connect students with an ever-expanding, increasingly "interactive informational universe" (Huston 1989, 19), has transformed the concept of "library" from a place to a "function" (Ely 1992) and has vastly increased the contributions school libraries can make to teaching and learning. Indeed, late 20th century preoccupations with library automation, Internet access, and expanding electronic resources (Kafai & Bates 1997) have given way to millennial efforts to integrate technology across the curriculum and help students make sense of Web 2.0 technologies within a climate of school reform characterized by both severe budgetary limitations and demands for increased accountability. At the same time, the ability to access electronic resources has brought into sharp relief the layers of complexity surrounding online searching and the challenges that confront school librarians when helping students find and use information to meet academic and personal needs.

Creating Competent Students: An Instructional Imperative

Basic to research in the area of technology and information skills instruction is the assumption that a contemporary definition of information literacy must include the ability to locate, retrieve, and use *electronic* as well as print-based resources and that, in addition to *information* literacy, students must also develop "digital, visual, textual, and technological" literacies (American Association of School Librarians [AASL] 2007). While our commitment to helping children learn the skills they need to be successful in school still holds strong, school librarians must also ensure that students can succeed in the workplaces of today and of tomorrow (AASL 2009a; Kuhlthau 2001).[1]

In an article in *Forbes'* electronic journal, columnist Mark Moran (2010) cited a *New York Times* story that "chronicled the 21st century school librarian as web curator and information literacy specialist" for the nation's children. While it is indeed good news that the contributions to education that school librarians make on a daily basis has been so publicly acknowledged, Moran's article went on to bemoan the prevalence of "clueless administrators [who] persist in maintaining that a search engine is an adequate substitute for a trained research teacher." Writing for a lay rather than a professional audience, Moran made his case in this way:

> In the libraries of old, the Dewey Decimal System got you started in research. But there is no card catalog for 2.0. To use the Internet as a library you need new research skills: the ability to pick out reliable sources from an overwhelming heap of misinformation, to find relevant material amid an array of options, to navigate the shifting ethics of creative commons and intellectual property rights and to present conclusions in a manner that engages modern audiences. . . . In addition to learning how to phrase a search query, students need to learn how to protect themselves online, and how to share their work through wikis, videos, and other interactive media. Without a dedicated guide, they end up, in the words of professor Henry Jenkins, as "feral children of the Internet raised by Web 2.0 wolves."

In a nutshell, Moran has summarized the new competencies needed by contemporary youngsters in navigating the dynamic and complex information landscape that the Internet represents while also articulating what is most problematic in using the very resources that so many school administrators are apparently counting on as substitutes for school libraries.

The new standards introduced by the AASL in 2007 were created to meet the challenges of contemporary and evolving information environments and together identify the technological competencies that students need to develop in today's schools. The instructional imperative, which Moran (2010) so clearly articulates, also sets a high bar for library professionals in engaging Millennials and helping them overcome the issues and challenges manifest in obtaining the benefits of technology set forth above. Research studies have identified the many challenges that technology poses for young searchers. It is hoped that the review provided below will initiate discussion, drive objectives, and identify outcomes for instructional programs that will directly address the learning needs of students for whom Moran advocates to passionately.

Because most contemporary observers consider today's learners as a unique group with needs and perspectives that differ in significant ways from those of students in preceding generations, this chapter begins with a description of the "Net Generation" and how these contemporary youngsters understand and use digital technology and behave when seeking information online. Also considered are the ways in which technology has revolutionized teaching and learning in classrooms and school libraries and the need for new and sophisticated skill sets and research-based instructional intervention to ensure searching success. Strategies for helping students deal with the ethical uses of information found online are included. A concluding section discusses issues relating to hardware, software, and maintenance of computer equipment and the challenges these may present in running the school library.

A New Generation of Learners

Contemporary observers have labeled today's students variously as the Net Generation ("Net Gen"; Tapscott 2009), the Information Generation, digital natives, and Neo Millennials (Asselin & Doiron 2008). Whatever the sobriquet, most argue that the term generally applies to students aged 12 through 18 and born after 1982 who constitute a unique group distinguished by attitudes, dispositions, and propensities related to their enthusiasm for technology. Net Gen natives are also more ethnically diverse, have more discretionary money to spend, and are more socially "connected" than teens in the generations that have come before.

It is interesting to note that the nation's young people were among the first to embrace the use of computers in the school library. While some of their elders were mourning the passing of the "card catalog," youngsters were eager to search the library collection electronically (Armstrong & Costa 1983) and could do so successfully (Borgman et al. 1995; Marchionini & Teague 1987; Solomon 1994) from an early date. As long ago as the 1990s, for example, Tapscott (1998) sensed a change in computer expertise that often made teenagers more technologically adept than their parents and teachers. In the years since, student access and comfort with technologies of all kinds have increased, just as the ages at which children are developing relatively sophisticated skill sets continue to decrease.

Tapscott followed up his original work *Growing Up Digital* (1998) with a large-scale mixed-methods research study that examined the habits and activities of the Net Generation. His team interviewed students between the ages of 13 and 20 as well as members of the Gen X population (aged 30 to 41) and baby boomers (aged 42 to 61). In *Grown Up Digital*, Tapscott (2009) addresses those who would bemoan the potential issues displayed by students who daily interact with digital technologies—that is, a possible lowering of intelligence, a growing lack of social skills, the blurring of concept of privacy within evolving social conventions, interference by so-called helicopter parents, the violation of online intellectual property rights, cyberbullying, online violence via gaming behaviors, the lack of a work ethic, increased narcissism, and an overall lack of moral and civic values.

The portrait painted by Tapscott (2009), instead, describes today's Net Gen students as interactive, collaborative, and savvy learners whose needs are not being met by educational practices that were developed long before technologies became a pervasive part of daily life. The evidence he offers, through survey, interview, and focus-group data, presents a vital group of learners bored with formal schooling and who may be learning more within the digital landscape than within the walls of brick-and-mortar schools.

Tapscott (2009) describes eight characteristics of today's digital age learners, which he terms "*net gen norms*." They prefer *freedom* to create and perform work when and where they please. They *customize* hardware and software to make their preferred technologies work in ways that suit their personal needs. They use *scrutiny* to determine the worth of information and goods: "They compare and contrast product information online, and look for the cheapest price without sacrificing value. They read blogs, forums, and reviews. They're skeptical about online reviews. Instead, they consult their friends" (81). Tapscott describes *integrity* as meaning that today's digital users are tolerant, open to alternate viewpoints, and quick to examine corporate misbehavior. (It is interesting to note, however, that here Tapscott provides several statements from students and young adults who comfortably provide justification for illegally downloading music, videos, and other content from Internet sources.) These students also express a need for *collaborative* experiences, whether they occur in an actual, physical place, or in online environments where many users from different geographical locations may come together to work on projects or gaming. Tapscott warns, "The current model of pedagogy is teacher focused, one-way, one size fits all. It isolates the student in the learning process" (91). Net Gen students also have a need for *entertainment* both in personal and in work situations, which in part explains their proclivities toward "engaging in 'netivities' simultaneously, such as chatting with friends on MSN while listening to their media player and surfing the Net" (92). These same students also greatly value *speed* in terms of connectivity and response time for instant messaging and social networking. Additionally, they seek out *innovation*, looking for newer and better ways to conduct the business of their lives. Tapscott tells us that it is not unusual to see young people upgrade media players, for example, every time a newer generation with more features is released for sale.

Tapscott's (2009) somewhat rosy descriptions of Net Gen students make for fascinating reading. His overall tone, however, is one of awe and wonder when it comes to what he describes as an increasing power of Net Gen students to make significant changes in our world. In addition, he appears to have been especially influenced by the behavior and views of his own children. A more balanced view of the Net Gen population and its promise in terms of cognitive gains for students awaits additional research and the examination of perspectives held by teachers, school librarians, parents, and employers who interact and work with this population on a daily basis.

That said, it is clear that the computer expertise that today's students bring to the classroom and library has changed the dynamics and direction of instruction in both settings. While as individuals Millennials are remarkably diverse, school librarians can capitalize on the technological prowess many members of this group of youngsters display in the development of dynamic teaching models that will assist these learners to develop 21st century literacy competencies.

Understanding Millennials

What kinds of preferences and enthusiasms do Millennials exhibit, and how can our understanding of their worldviews and computer use assist us in providing learner-centered programs and services? In terms of learning style, research indicates that many Millennials prefer visual information formats and favor participatory problem solving and active learning to teacher/librarian-led didactic instructional approaches. In addition, multimedia and multitasking (Lohr 2006) are watchwords for this generation of young people. Cell phones are their "most preferred method of tool-mediated communication" (Agosto & Hughes-Hassell 2006), and their information needs center on "schoolwork, time/date, social life, and weather" (Fisher et al. 2006, 2). Used to the fast pace and instant response made possible by improved Internet service providers and available hardware, instant messaging, and texting capabilities, Millennials tend to be impatient in informational transactions and desirous of multiple stimuli in their environment.

Whereas their parents may have been content to be information consumers, Millennials prefer to construct their own knowledge and distribute it using a dazzling array of Web 2.0 tools. This means, of course, that "the literacy education provided in the past by parents and teachers will no longer equip [them] for success in the altered world in which [they] live" (Selfie & Howisher 2004, cited in Asselin and Doiron 2008, 1). What was necessary and sufficient to know and understand in a print-based and often finite set of information resources is today not in any way helpful for students who must navigate constantly evolving networks, evaluate websites, choose search engines, select hyperlinks, and compare "information across sources" (Asselin & Doiron, 2).

Web 2.0: An Information Space for Children and Youth

If there is one single behavior that typifies technology use by today's young people, it is their obsession with social networking sites (e.g., Facebook, Twitter, and MySpace), virtual worlds (e.g., *Farm World*), multiplayer gaming (e.g., *Call of Duty*, *World of Warcraft*, and *Halo*), online collaboration (e.g., wikis and Google Docs), and journaling (e.g., blogging), mashups, zines, and video sharing, to name a few, and the seemingly seamless ways in which these are integrated "into all aspects of their lives" (Asselin & Doiron 2008, 1).

Finally, graphics and the interactive features of Internet searching are particularly popular among today's Web-surfing youngsters. Interactivity and animation reflect the active learning style of many children, while the graphics help them to make sense of the information, especially when a child's interest level exceeds her or his cognitive ability and reading proficiency.

How Students Think about and Use the Internet in Information Seeking

What does the research tell us about the Internet use by children and youth? In 2001, the Pew Internet and American Life Project (Pew Research Center 2001) interviewed students from across the country to determine information-seeking behaviors and experiences. The studies provided statistical evidence for what most educators already suspected—students were using the Internet in ever-increasing numbers, and most of them were thoroughly enjoying the experience. For example, 94 percent of the teenagers who reported having access to the Internet indicated that they relied heavily on online information for research tasks; 71 percent of them used "the Internet as the major source for their most recent school project"; "58% had used a Web site set up by school or a class; 34% had downloaded a study guide; and 17% had created a Web page for a school project." As Bilal and Watson (1998) observed, "[T]he Web's ease of access, speed of finding information, convenience of access from home and richness in graphics" so appeal to 21st century youngsters that their continued participation online for school-related research, personal information seeking, and entertainment is virtually guaranteed.

A number of earlier studies also demonstrated the popularity of electronic and online resources and preferred searching strategies. For example, a study by Newbold (1993, cited in Bialo & Sivin-Kachala 1996) reported not only that children preferred researching the electronic encyclopedias to their print counterparts but also that the use of these electronic sources was related to positive attitudes about the library and about writing. Interestingly, Large and Beheshti (2000) found that their informants preferred using the Web as a research resource even though they reported that it was harder for them to use than print sources. In addition, Sutton's research (1991, cited in Martinez 1994) found "some evidence that [for] disadvantaged students" "computer technology [was] especially engaging" (399). It is perhaps for this reason that students surveyed by Todd and Kuhlthau in the Ohio Research Study (Whelan 2004) emphasized technology support and instruction as such an important aspect of their school's library program.

Although many researchers have frequently commented on the motivational value of Internet use and electronic searching capabilities, this does not necessarily mean that today's youngsters have abandoned print resources. In fact, not all research supports the notion that students *uniformly* prefer the use of the Internet to books and other media for information seeking. Latrobe and Havener (1997) found that books, magazines, and television all were used more often than were electronic resources by high school honor students in meeting their information needs. Both Large and Beheshti (2000) and Gross (1999) found that younger students did not have the same affinity for using the computer for information seeking as their high school counterparts. In a more recent study, Crow (2009b) found that upper-elementary students who were intrinsically motivated for information seeking were all users of computer technology, but fewer preferred electronic information sources over print materials. It remains to be seen if future studies will confirm these patterns and preferences.

The Experience and Meaning of the Internet for Children and Youth

Research indicates that children's search experience online is multidimensional, engaging them in cognitive, behavioral, affective, and social activities. For example, the thinking about and choosing of a topic and coming up with search terms to describe it, as well as keeping track mentally of search options and determining relevance of retrieved items, are tasks that engage children on a number of cognitive levels. At the same time, behavioral demands of Internet use relate to eye-hand coordination, keyboarding and typing, mouse management, and operating peripherals (e.g., printers and jump drives). Children are also engaged on an emotional or affective level, particularly when screens freeze, printers jam, and searches result in an avalanche, or a dearth, of "hits." Perhaps because they have been conditioned by technological advances and/or media hype to expect near-instantaneous responses from information systems, speed seems to be an issue and an expectation for many Millennials. Outdated equipment and insufficient bandwidth can combine to produce slowdowns in retrieval that exasperate students, especially when connection time in school is limited to one or a portion of a class period.

Finally, children's use of the Internet has a social dimension in that they enjoy assisting one another and sharing ideas, information, and websites. Interestingly, they also seek and appreciate website recommendations from teachers and library media specialists (Hirsh 1998) when such assistance does not jeopardize student self-image or "face" (Goffman 1967).

Student participants in the Pew Research Center (2001) study themselves described the Internet variously as a "textbook and reference library," a "tutor," a "study group," a "guidance counselor," and a "locker." These metaphors and the images they evoke provide useful insights into what the Internet means to many contemporary youngsters. In the first instance, the Internet represents access to a world of primary, secondary, up-to-date, and state-of-the-art sources that students and teachers believe are essential for engaging in school-related research tasks. A second benefit is the online availability of assistance in the form of "how-to" technology information, homework shortcuts, and online term papers. Indeed, Pew researchers reported that some students see in "the Internet . . . a way to complete their schoolwork as quickly and painlessly as possible, with minimal effort and minimal engagement . . . [and] as a mechanism to plagiarize material or otherwise cheat."

On the other hand, students also find the Internet a resource for education, life, and career decision making and as a source for health-related information. Many students interviewed in the Pew Research Center (2001) study reported that, for them, the Internet functions as a kind of virtual study hall, providing an opportunity to communicate with peers online, collaborate on school projects, share notes, and study together for tests. Students also spoke of the Internet as a "virtual locker, back pack, and notebook"—as a "place to store their important school-related materials" as well as to send papers to peers and teachers, keep track of their schedules, stash course syllabi, and check assignments. In short, students in the Pew study found that the Internet "help[ed] them navigate their way through school" and to balance school tasks and extracurricular activities.

The Pew Research Center (2001) study informants also identified a number of challenges inherent in using the Internet in school. These included restricting access to specific times, places, and conditions; the proliferation of filters that "raise barriers to students' legitimate educational use of the Internet"; and the lack of parity in terms of at-home access to computers that makes teachers reluctant to require Internet use for homework. These students also considered surveillance and prohibition on e-mail use as reducing the value of Internet access at school. For these reasons, many students in the Pew study considered Internet use an "at-home" activity.

Research Focus on Information Seeking in Electronic Resources

Research interest related to technological issues in library and information studies has been very high, for there is still much to be learned that will help designers create more user-friendly retrieval systems in the "brave new world" of high-tech school libraries. Over time, research on children's information seeking online has progressed to keep pace with the new and emerging technology. Thus, studies that once centered on children's use of automated catalogs (online public access catalogs) have given way to research into their use of CD-ROM encyclopedias, electronic databases, search engines, and, finally, the World Wide Web. Many of the studies are exploratory in nature, with small and "purposive" samples of students. Although there are some studies that have strong theoretical frameworks, many are action projects designed to solve a practical problem. This means that in many instances, the findings lack generalizability to other populations and contexts. While these limitations argue for more and more robust studies, school librarians can use the insights provided so far in designing instruction to support children's online research tasks.

Online Searching Behavior of Millennial Students

In addition to the Pew Research Center (2001) study, a number of library and information research studies provide clues to the online behavior and preferences of Millennial information seekers that reflect their experiences and expectations with regard to Internet speed, searching activities, and standards for searching success. For example, a key issue in terms of the persistence, personal investment, motivation, and enthusiasm for searching online seems to be the interest that students have in the search task itself (Agosto 2002; Hirsh 1998). In other words, it seems to matter whether students feel personally connected to the topic being investigated or whether they look on the research task as an assignment to be "gotten through." In a few cases, information seeking is not seen as a prelude to learning. On the contrary, Shenton and Dixon (2003) report that the British primary, middle, and high school–aged youngsters they observed "were generally intent on retrieving sufficient information to meet the need with the minimum inconvenience" and tended to close down their searches once a single relevant source had been retrieved "rather than forming a pool of information from various sources" (1041) to enrich understanding.

Being content with a minimum amount of information also typified students whom Agosto (2002) observed in a study that she conducted to explore the searching behavior of 22 ninth- and tenth-grade girls who were involved in a leadership institute. Her findings led her to conclude that the theory of bounded rationality could be applied to information seeking with this group of students. In brief, the theory states that because of constraints of time and patience, information seekers will rarely attempt to find every bit of information or even the best information when searching; instead, they tend to settle for information that is "good enough." Students in Agosto's study used two strategies to cope with the information retrieved: "reduction" and "termination." Students reduced the cognitive task of reviewing information by using familiar or recommended websites, reading site synopses and summaries, reading descriptions supplied by search engines, and skimming. They found the categorization of sites in terms of "personal websites, scientific websites," or "best for science, for math, for fun" as particularly useful. Termination strategies involved truncating searches as soon as an acceptable website was located. This behavior is consistent with the notion of "satisficing" first introduced by Simon (1955, 1956, cited in Agosto) and typical of approaches many adult users employ in online searching.

Nor do students evidence much patience online. For example, high school searchers in Fidel et al.'s (1999) study made relevance judgments on the basis of a cursory look at a site, examining the images at the top of the page; this behavior reflects that of students in Bilal and Watson's (1998) research who rarely bothered to scroll down through the entirety of an online text. Ninth and tenth graders in Agosto's (2002) study and Hirsh's (1998) fifth graders evinced similar behavior, relying "heavily on summaries describing Internet links" or reading "the first paragraph of an Internet document" (69). One of Hirsh's students summed up this approach in this way: "I don't like to take the time to read the whole thing" (70).

Other online searching behavior observed revealed preferences for search strategies that are more serendipitous than planned. For example, a number of studies have shown that many children are successful browsers, whether they are searching online public access catalogs (Armstrong & Costa 1983; Borgman et al. 1995), electronic encyclopedias (Cooper 2002; Liebscher & Marchionini 1988; Marchionini, 1987, cited in Borgman et al. 1995), or the Internet (Bilal 1998, 1999, 2001, 2002a, 2002b; Hirsh 1998), perhaps because browsing "requires less well-defined search objectives than does directed keyboard searching" (Armstrong & Costa 1983). Children also use key words as search terms rather than focused queries or controlled vocabulary (e.g., subject headings) and prefer the use of natural language queries and key words to subject lists, subject categories, Boolean operators, or other functions offered by search engines.

While the capacity of Millennials to engage with technology in increasingly creative ways seems endless, their ability to retrieve relevant information online does not always rise to a level of expertise that translates into searching success. Perhaps this is related to a Millennial preference for "speed and convenience" as criteria for searching online (Holliday & Li 2004) or their disinterest in tracking search processes and search history (Armstrong et al. cited in Holliday & Li 2001). For these reasons, Asselin and Doiron (2008) suggest that although "students are savvy in many aspects of the new literacies of the Internet, research shows they are not as proficient as popularly thought" (3). In contrast to Tapscott's (2009) account, Asselin and Doiron (2008) actually paint a rather dismal picture of contemporary Internet searching by today's youth.

Computers and Learning: Benefits and Challenges of Online Access

Morton (1996) asserts that "the value of a computer environment is not so much the improvement of students' achievement through computer use as it is the improvement of students' ability to achieve" (419). Political rhetoric to the contrary notwithstanding, "[c]omputers in themselves do not automatically change the nature of teaching and learning" (Woronov 1994, 1) nor improve the quality of education (Broch 2000) or learning (Oliver & Oliver 1997). Rather, it is the ways in which their use is integrated into classroom activity that have educational yield for students (Todd 1998). Indeed, in Neuman's (1995a) view, the costs of technology in terms of energy, money, and time "can be supported only to the extent that the resources contribute to what schools are all about—learning" (1). It is for this reason that it is so critical that school librarians orchestrate instructional opportunities for students to engage with technology in learning centered and meaningful ways.

Many studies conducted since the 1980s have led educators to conclude that the use of technology can benefit students in a number of important ways (see Table 7.1), including the promotion of critical thinking skills, the development of writing skills, enhanced opportunities for language development, and an increase in student motivation. Although it is useful conceptually to consider these benefits as separate entities, research shows that they are interrelated.

Research studies aimed at showing the relationship between use of computers and cognitive development emphasize the possibilities for critical thinking and problem solving (Means & Olson 1994). Researchers also point to growth of student learning in the area of oral and written language development. For example,

Table 7.1
Educational Benefits of Access to the Internet and Electronic Resources

Internet access at home and school:

- Motivates students
- Improves attitudes toward reading and writing tasks
- Improves language skills (reading, writing, spelling, and vocabulary)
- Provides an audience for student work outside the classroom
- Creates opportunities for inquiry learning, student independence, and differentiated instruction
- Increases student choice and sense of control of their own learning
- Provides immediate access to resources not available locally
- Provides access to other points of view and invites critical thinking and evaluation
- Promotes collaboration between and among students.

a study by Bialo and Sivin-Kachala (1996) found that the use of computers for word processing helps "students produce high quality writing" (52). In their study, Kafai and Bates (1997) observed that the opportunity to exist online as creators of information provides an incentive to students to improve their written work.

Other research indicates the importance of social interaction among students working together on computer-based activities in the same classroom (Clements & Nastasi 1988; Dwyer 1994; Irving 1990; Morton 1996; Nastasi, Battista, & Clements 1990; Turkle 1984) in improving thinking skills, developing vocabulary, and increasing conversational competence (Bialo & Sivin-Kachala 1996; Irving 1991). In her study, Irving (1990) found that "on-line searching requires careful and logical query description in order to avoid difficulties," leading many children to discuss together the alternatives and the vocabulary itself, which resulted in "a good deal of language development" (31). Language benefits were also shown in a study conducted by Diaz (1984, cited in Kleifgen 1989), which demonstrated that "strong gains in English" were made by students when their learning activities included "complex computer tasks." Finally, Bialo and Sivin-Kachala (1996) found that reading achievement as well as spelling improved as a result of computer use and that the "use of on-line telecommunications for collaboration across classrooms in different geographic locations has been shown to improve academic skills" (52).

Challenges for Students in Using Electronic and Internet Resources

While the potential for learning in the classroom and the library in tapping the information resources on the Internet cannot be overstated, researchers have identified a litany of problems children encounter online. In spite of E-Rate funding and an expansion in Internet access in the nation's schools, there are still inequities and barriers that jeopardize the ability of many children to make educational use of online information. And in spite of increased computer skills of Millennials, children still encounter search failure based on skill deficits of one kind or another.

Barriers to Information Seeking: Ethical Issues in Information Seeking

Inequities in educational opportunities due to community socioeconomics directly affect students' access to information in print and online sources (Kozol 2000; Neuman & Celano 2001) and to the use of the Internet for school research tasks. Even though nearly 100 percent of U.S. classrooms now have Internet access (Wells & Lewis 2006), the disparities between those with easy access to computers and the Internet and those without persist, with children from low-income homes having less access to personal computers than students from high-income families. The Pew Research Center (2001) study also indicated that because not all students have computers at home, teachers have often been reluctant to make Internet-based assignments. In order to improve Internet access to students, an increasing number of schools have created after-school programs, particularly in areas serving low-income students. In addition, many communities are providing Internet access and technology training through local agencies, such as community technology centers, libraries, and churches, some funded by the Bill and Melinda Gates Foundation. Lazarus and Mora's (2000) informants appear to want the support that these kinds of centers are designed to provide, that is, "coaches and mentors to guide them in finding what they want on the Web, suggesting sites or activities to get started, helping us a tutorial, and the like" (21). Minority adults and youngsters in Lazarus and Mora's (2000) study spoke of seeking

> an environment where they can get literacy support or help with English if they need it. They want a place where others in the community are doing the same thing and where they can count on coaching and support to build their confidence, answer their questions, and guide them in new directions.... [It appears that] the circumstances through which people get information is [sic] as important as the medium. (21)

These kinds of initiatives may eventually help to level what remains a very unequal educational playing field for many American youngsters.

Another aspect of the "digital divide" relates to online content. For example, a significant barrier to information seeking for some students is the predominance of English as the language of the Internet. Lazarus and Mora (2000) report that fully 87 percent of the content on the Web is in the English language and that only 2 percent of the sites surveyed were multilingual. This is particularly poignant in light of the fact that 32 percent of Americans speak a language other than English. They also found that even where sites have some bilingual sections, the links provided often take information seekers to sites that present information exclusively in English. Moreover, Lazarus and Mora report that some "areas on Yahoo! Español, such as education, family, government, and jobs, did not contain the same amount of useful (practical and local) information in Spanish" (23) as was available in their English counterparts. The fact that the Internet is primarily text based makes successful information retrieval online a problem for all children but especially for those for whom English is a second language. On the other hand, these researchers also found some "sophisticated multilingual Web sites that offer online learning tools . . . [where] students can listen to English world pronunciations . . . practice grammar and receive immediate feedback" (24).

In an article championing the professional resource embodied in each school's librarian, Moran (2010) has drawn attention to ethical issues surrounding information access and has reframed the digital divide in terms of access to media literacy instruction. In fact, Moran's own experience of corporate America has led him to conclude that "Students do not know how to find or evaluate information they need on the Internet." Yet "I know that without adequate media literacy training, kids will not succeed in a 21st century workplace." The stakes in the kind of administrative myopia that results in a school district "abandon[ing] its professional guides," as Moran suggests, are high.

Problems for Students in Online Searching

That youngsters experience difficulties as novice searchers should not be surprising when one considers that they are now expected to negotiate complex online systems that not so long ago were the exclusive province of highly trained professional intermediaries (Huston & Oberman 1989). Ironically, even sophisticated computer skills do not automatically translate into searching skills. Patterns in the research reveal a panoply of difficulties; some relate to the nature of the online environment itself, some relate to deficits in literacy and information-seeking skills, and some relate to the students' lack of domain or topic knowledge and the disconnect between children's information needs and skill levels and the sophistication and reading levels they encounter online. The following sections offer insights from the research into the special problems children encounter when searching online and are followed by some research-based suggestions for improving children's chances for searching success.

Navigating the Online Environment

Until relatively recently, difficulties with typing (e.g., Chen 1993; Kafai & Bates 1997) and keyboarding (Chen 1993; Marchionini 1989; Solomon 1994) made computer-assisted information seeking difficult for many children. While these kinds of problems have been successfully addressed for most youngsters through computer classes and personal experiences with computers at home, complex issues persist, many of which relate to basic misunderstandings of the nature and structure of the Internet, to difficulties in implementing effective and efficient search strategies, and to dealing with search "output." Also problematic for students have been the evaluation of websites and online information and the determination of the relevance of retrieved information items.

Denning, Shuttleworth, and Smith (1998) assert that scrolling and links make "the navigation task more complex for the user . . . and may be particularly cumbersome or disorienting" (Broch 2000) or distracting. Broch (2000) posited that on-screen "clutter" in the form of pop-up advertisements tend to "reduce the amount of space available for information" and forces children to scroll down through successive screen "pages" or to follow a series of hyperlinks, some of which take users to online booksellers or other kinds of Web vendors. However, it is also true that adults and children have different "tastes" when it comes to Web page design. The adults interviewed by Lazarus and Mora (2000), for example, preferred "succinct, uncluttered information, whereas younger users want Web sites that have fast-moving imagery and sound" (21). Noting the difficulties that students have traditionally experienced when using print resources, Neuman (1995a) found that these carried over into "electronic" library materials as well. For example, Neuman reported that students often fail to identify classification numbers and other kinds of information on computer screens that would assist them in continuing their searches. Similarly, Edmonds, Moore, and Balcom (1990) documented the difficulties youngsters had in following online instructions.

Ineffective Searching Strategies and Techniques

According to Nahl and Harada (1996), "a growing body of research" in the use of information-seeking skills among elementary and secondary school students shows that these youngsters consistently demonstrate a "lack of general information seeking strategies" (199–200) in their inability to select appropriate search terms, especially when they are searching complex and abstract topics for which there are no direct and obvious matches (Moore and St. George 1991; Walter 1996, cited in Kafai & Bates 1997). Other related studies show that children lack skills in generating alternative search terms and synonyms (Fidel et al. 1999; Moore & St. George 1991; Nahl & Harada 1996; Neuman 1995a; Solomon 1993); in handling variant spellings (Solomon 1994), abbreviations (Chen 1993), and homonyms (Solomon 1994); and in using available thesauri (Moore & St. George 1991). Walter, Borgman, and Hirsh (1996) and Chen (1993) highlighted language skill deficits as creating problems, noting particularly the discrepancies between the terms that youngsters frequently use and those that indexers typically assign as subject headings.

A similar problem observed by Irving (1990) was the "particular difficulty" children had in "developing questions that were both sufficiently specific and efficiently expressed" (87). Many youngsters found extremely troublesome the use of search commands (Fidel et al. 1999; Irving 1990) and the creation of search protocols to which the systems they searched could respond (Kafai & Bates 1997; Nahl & Harada 1996).

Chen (1993) noted the failure of students to extend searches beyond the terms originally chosen and to use subject headings and tracings as keys to appropriate alternatives. Students in Neuman's (1995a) study also noted failure to "switch" approaches or to employ other terms when their searches got "stuck" or when their search terms produced an insufficient number of "hits." These results were confirmed by student search behavior in Fidel et al. (1999), who noted that students frequently changed their topics rather than do the intellectual work of finding suitable alternatives to describe the topics originally chosen. This would seem to support Eaton's (1991, cited in Fidel et al.) finding that successful searches may rely on the searchers' abilities to change and detach themselves from unsuccessful strategies and then to continue the original search in a different manner. It also suggests that the invitational (open) mood, essential to continuing the information-gathering phase of the information search process (Kuhlthau 1993b), demands a degree of cognitive flexibility not usually acknowledged.

Lack of computer skills as well as an inability to create effective "search statements" by students observed by Nowicki (2003) inhibited their retrieval of relevant information. This led Nowicki to conclude that "[i]f users cannot define the information for which they are searching, no search engine will return relevant results." Thus, it is important that searchers learn the nature and capabilities of specific search engines as resources of value in addressing specific kinds of information questions.

As one might expect, not only do today's youngsters use the Internet as the court of first resort, but recent studies indicate that they "tend to rely almost exclusively on Google as their search engine, and use natural language as search terms" (Rowlands & Nicholas, 2008; Stenton, 2007)" (Asselin & Doiron 2008, 3), browsing serendipitously through Internet texts in what Asselin and Doiron describe as of "digital grazing" (7). Whereas "older generations tend to search the web to complete a given task, . . . Millennials see the 'web as their information universe . . . [and] prefer the global searching of Google to more sophisticated but more time-consuming searching provided by the library' (Lippincott 2005, p. 13.3)" (Radford & Connaway, 2007, 5). In fact, "they want easy access to full-text documents and become impatient with complex searching that yields citations or abstracts" (5).

Kafai and Bates (1997) found that students were more "receptive to learning" about "differences between search engines" after they had actually encountered search failures (100). However, it should also be noted that where mechanical difficulties frustrate the search, the "extensive cognitive energy required" to overcome the difficulties involved in simply getting to the information may leave little energy, "time or patience to perform advanced cognitive operations on that information" (Neuman 1995a, 12). Under these conditions, it is easy to understand why some children conclude that it is finding, downloading, or copying information (rather than its analysis, synthesis, and use) that are the major goals of the research task or project (Irving 1990).[2]

Handling Search Output

Since information overload frequently leads adults to premature abandonment of online searches (Wiberley & Daugherty 1988, cited in Oberman 1995), it is fair to assume that less experienced information seekers will find excessive search output intimidating as well. In point of fact, managing search results has indeed proved to be a daunting task for many students (Liebscher & Marchionini 1988). Studies show that the sheer volume of search "hits" (Oberman 1995), as well as the prospect of reading through long texts online (Irving 1991), makes selecting relevant items difficult. Perhaps for this reason, student searchers frequently stop with the first screen they encounter, using it as a sort of index or abstract of the site rather than scrolling though successive screens to locate the information they need (Fidel et al. 1999; Schacter, Chung & Dorr 1998). Information overload and students' strategies to cope with it have also been documented in studies by Akin (1998), Gordon (2000), and Agosto (2001). Asselin and Doiron (2008) describe Millennial handling of retrieved information in this way:

> They approach the results list with a "click and grab" strategy by most often selecting the first source on the list with minimal or no review and evaluation of its relevance or quality. . . . (Guinee, Eagleton & Hall, 2003; Henry, 2006). Students spend little time in reading the source; instead skimming and scanning are typical reading processes. . . . Once within a website, becoming distracted by both internal and external hyperlinks is a greater risk than in print sources of information. Finally, cutting and pasting rather than rewording and recording are dominant processes when students are taking notes from online information sources. (3)

Evaluating Online Information Sources

Many youngsters lack the conceptual skills to understand that the Internet sites and resources are not centrally created but are the work of different providers with different motives (Asselin & Doiron 2008). This leads many youngsters to accept what they find online without question. In fact, a concern for determining the authoritativeness and factual accuracy of online information does not characterize the mind-set of most young information seekers (Watson 1998), who are often are oblivious to the need to question the origins of resources they locate via electronic searching. In their study, Wallace and Kupperman's (1997, cited in Hirsh 1998) sixth graders accepted what they found on the Web at face value and judged the utility of sites based on whether or not the search terms they were using were repeated in the online text. Schacter et al. (1998), Todd (1998), Kafai and Bates (1997), and Shenton and Dixon (2003) reported similar behavior on the part of their informants. "As with books," Shenton and Dixon found that "the children were quick to assume everything they found about their topic on the Internet was correct just because it was there" (101). However, with guidance and experience, many students were eventually able to "distinguish sales and marketing sites from more neutrally informational sites" (109).

Hirsh (1998) suggests that children's acceptance of Web-based information can be partially explained by the fact that her fifth-grade informants "were in the concrete operational stage of development, which means it is difficult" for them to "question authority" (59). However, this probably does not excuse Fidel et al.'s (1999) high school students, who showed a similar disinclination to challenge information retrieved online.

Kuhlthau (1997) believes that the sheer amount of information on the Internet is a barrier to evaluation. In Kuhlthau's view, when information is available in such "abundance," it is "particularly challenging for a library media specialist (LMS) or teacher to convince an unmotivated student to distinguish between an adequate and a better than adequate source" (Broch 2000).[3] In their study, Kafai and Bates (1997) found that children under 10 years also experienced difficulty with evaluation tasks, including the ability to articulate evaluative criteria. However, once criteria (e.g., "easy to read") were suggested, these students could evaluate the sites they visited.

It might be well to note that unless youngsters are taught and also expected to appraise critically the resources they find on the Internet and pursue research questions rather than fact-finding tasks, the potential for inspiring the development of higher-order thinking skills represented by the activity of Internet-based searching will remain largely unrealized.

Judging Relevance

In their evaluation of information sources, "relevance" seems to be a particularly difficult concept for children to determine, though there is indication that some are able to learn this skill especially when their interest levels are high. Hirsh's (1998) study indicated that children can articulate criteria for relevance, although these may differ significantly from those that adult or expert searchers might use. The three most mentioned criteria identified by Hirsh's students included topicality, novelty, and interest. Novelty as a relevance category translated as "new information" for Hirsh's informants. In other words, if a source provided facts not previously encountered that they needed to complete a research assignment, the information was considered "new." By the same token, an assessment of "interesting" in terms of texts and (especially) graphics was taken to mean that the information was of personal interest to the searcher. Some students also considered peer interest as a mark of relevance. Following Kuhlthau's (1993a) finding that student interest increases during the information-searching process, Hirsh noted that relevance judgments changed as the research proceeded with "interesting" replacing "topicality" as the information search neared completion.

Hirsh's (1998) study (as mentioned above) showed that highly motivated fifth graders "were generally able to articulate their reasons for selecting relevant information in both text and graphic formats." These students made use of "metadata and other descriptive elements" in searching in "an online catalog, an electronic encyclopedia, an electronic magazine index, and the Internet" (58), at home, and at school. As concrete thinkers, Hirsh's fifth-grade informants judged topical relevance on the basis of "exact matches" between search terms they used and the vocabulary used by the teacher and the retrieved documents. Students also had difficulty in recognizing the larger categories within which their topics or subjects might fit. For example, "when the book titles [reviewed] did not include their athlete's name," they did not identify the book as relevant. This behavior mirrors that of students in Wallace and Kupperman's (1997) study (cited in Hirsh 1998) and Hirsh (1996, cited in Hirsh 1998), where children looked for matching terms in the subjects of retrieved bibliographic records.

Agosto's (2002) informants also considered relevant any information they found that fit with personal convictions, opinions, and beliefs and also made choices of relevance and usefulness based on the tone of the site (e.g., friendly, patronizing, humorous). This led Agosto to conclude that "personal preferences are an aspect of the affective side of information seeking, as these preferences are based on personal feelings (such as personal dislikes for particular colors), rather than on cognitive or behavioral information seeking" (18). For this reason, Agosto sees a role for "adult intermediaries who work with young people and information" (25) in explaining evaluative criteria and providing search training.

Literacy Issues

Deficits in basic literacy skills have also been identified as limiting student effectiveness in online searching. For example, in many studies, difficulties related to reading skills (Chen 1993; Irving 1990), alphabetizing (Edmonds et al. 1990), spelling (Chen 1993; Irving 1991; Kafai & Bates 1997; Nahl & Harada 1996; Solomon 1992, 1993, 1994), and vocabulary (Solomon 1994) all proved debilitating for students attempting to search electronically. Irving's (1990) students also encountered difficulties when skimming online texts to find the main idea within a screen of information, a difficulty that Fidel et al. (1999) also mention as a problem for students. In the same vein, Kafai and Bates (1997) noted student problems in extracting information from child-"unfriendly" websites, defined by the students themselves as those pages that employ "big words and lots of text without pictures" (108).

Complexity of Online Resources

Neuman (1995a) noted the problems the sophistication of many online resources pose for young learners. As newcomers to "the subject matter areas they are in

Table 7.2
Challenges for Students When Searching Electronically

* Difficulty in choosing search engines other than Google
* Limited knowledge of databases and their arrangement
* Lack of understanding of the Internet as a collection of resources
* Difficulties in evaluating online sources
* Difficulty in determining relevance of resources to research question
* Difficulties operating in online environments
* Lack of knowledge of searching strategies
* Difficulties in handling search results or output
* Lack of basic literacy skills

school to master," Neuman explains, students frequently need basic texts, which provide an overview of a subject rather than "cutting edge research results" (6) of the sort generally retrieved from database or Internet sources. In addition, information found online frequently demanded reading comprehension that far exceeded the skill levels of young students (see Table 7.2.).

The complexity of the information systems and their patterns of organization are difficult for novice searchers to manage as well, both conceptually and mechanically. Irving (1990, 1991) found that children lacked understanding of the design of online systems in addition to more basic concepts related to searching, such as how computers are used in information retrieval. Although children observed by Keil (1979) and Borgman et al. (1995) were able to make sense of hierarchically arranged topics presented online, student searchers in Neuman's (1995a) study experienced difficulties with file arrangement. Further, Neuman's informants frequently failed to select databases appropriate for their topics or use them in an appropriate order.

Improving Children's Chances of Searching Success

Although at least some of the difficulties that students encounter clearly relate to the idiosyncrasies of specific online resources, the good news is that most student-centered problems can be overcome through instructional intervention and careful planning on the part of teachers and school librarians. It is clear that students need to develop skills related to the mechanics of searching, including at least some knowledge of search commands and basic keyboarding moves. Of equal importance, however, is an awareness of how information is organized and represented in online search environments. This awareness will aid them not only in selecting appropriate databases but also in finding information in useful formats (e.g., titles, abstracts, extracts, or full text). In addition, providing instruction in terms of process models, new conceptions of the library and its resources, and attending to domain knowledge will greatly improve children's chances of searching success.

Process Models as Structures for Learning

An important finding in the work of Irving (1990, 1991) and others is that just as searching online "bring[s] into a more prominent position the need for information-handling skills" (Irving 1990, 5), it also calls for an understanding of the overall search process. Students apparently need to conduct their searches as a sequence of activities and to understand the underlying search "concepts and strategies that transcend individual products" (Neuman 1995b, 297). Other researchers have made similar observations. In his studies of the use of database software by social studies classes, Ehman et al. (1991, cited in Bialo & Sivin-Kachala 1996) concluded that to ensure effective and efficient searching, instructors must provide an overall structure for student tasks as well as "clear expectations with a sequence of activities." In addition, explaining and modeling essential elements of the problem-solving process and offering students opportunities to practice these elements within a framework of supervision were deemed both appropriate and necessary. In her dissertation study, Pitts (1995) found that her informants' lack of mental models for information seeking compromised not only the entire research process but also the learning that was to be derived from the research task. McNally (2003, personal conversation) confirmed that the lack of mental models for the process, task, and environment compromised search success.[4]

A process approach to the teaching of research, particularly as provided in models created by Kuhlthau (1991, 1993b, 1994), Eisenberg and Berkowitz (1990), Irving (1985), Stripling and Pitts (1988), Pappas and Tepe (1997, 2002), and others, constitutes a useful structure within which online searching activities can be planned and implemented. Kuhlthau's model is valuable in its specific emphasis on gaining a view of the topic through exploration as a prerequisite for data collection. In addition, its consideration of affective, behavioral, and cognitive aspects of information seeking makes it a useful tool for teachers and librarians in helping students plan and cope with the frustration and stress—as well as the high cognitive demands—created by the use of electronic resources. Eisenberg and Berkowitz's (1990) Big6 Skills, having been successfully applied to searching in electronic environments, is particularly useful in matching particular databases to specific topics at the point of planning information-seeking strategies, a stage which research indicates has been a problem for student searchers in the past. However, it is well to note that in the final analysis, students will have to create their own mental models as frames for independent problem solving online. Providing students with an overview of the options is a place to start in engaging students in this crucial information-seeking activity.

Another useful strategy within the context of an overall process of information seeking is understanding how much information is "enough" to create the understandings that the tasks were assigned to accomplish. Of course, how much information is too little, too much, or just right depends in large part on the learning style and the cognitive level of the information seeker, the demands of the task, and the information context. In considering information seeking online, Kuhlthau (1999) notes the changes created by access to the Internet:

> What is enough [information] may have been a fairly straightforward notion when a person could gather all there was to know on a problem or topic in a contained collection. The concept of enough is quite a different matter in the present information environment. (6)

"Enough," then, is an individual determination based on "what is enough to make sense for oneself within a context and to accomplish the task at hand" (6) and should be considered at each stage of the information search process. In a very real sense, the ability to assess for oneself "what is enough" is an important information skill that children need to acquire and relates directly to the ability to bring closure to a search task. To a certain extent, the concept of enough may help to answer the question often heard in the classroom and library: "How many sources do I need to use?" Depending on the situation, the concept may turn out to be liberating for both instructor and learner.

Understanding the Library and Its Online Resources

In the days when children's research tasks were based solely on resources available in the school library, information seeking was relatively straightforward. Children used standard "tools" to locate information in print and media formats on hand. The library was "a collection" in its strictest sense, for in most instances the resources had been painstakingly, even lovingly, selected by informed adults with the developmental needs, domain knowledge, language requirements of students, and the specifics of the curriculum in place at a particular school in mind. In such an environment, students could assume the authority, accuracy, and truthfulness of the resources they used. Online catalogs and electronic encyclopedias that signaled the library's entry into the information age were essentially extensions of this early controlled, well-structured library environment (Hirsh 1998).

Searching on the Internet today assumes none of these characteristics (with the exception perhaps of websites created to offer a number of carefully selected links for children's use). In fact, it is an activity of an entirely different sort. The old saying that "on the Internet no one knows you're a dog" seems particularly apt in this regard. Today, anyone can create a website or other Web-based information space and represent him- or herself in any way for any purpose. Many websites that appear informational are, in fact, commercially produced and purposed. By the same token, even informational websites "sell" a point of view by selecting to focus on a specific slice of the experiential pie; in this context, reality is what the creators of the site say that it is, complete with inherent and often hidden biases. While Mancall, Aaron, and Walker (1986) and others have pointed to the benefits of being able to access different points of view, such access also calls for development of new and more sophisticated evaluation skills. "Since the Internet has no built-in filters to publishing and children are making greater use of the Internet for their school assignments, children need to understand how information is placed on the Internet and how to verify" (Hirsh 1998) its authenticity, accuracy, and timeliness. In addition, search engines tend to provide access to a unique and limited portion of the websites out there. For learners who expect to search exhaustively online, the information scatter that characterizes the Internet may be especially perplexing.

Both Pitts (1995) and Oberman (1995) concluded that, for many students, misconceptions of libraries as warehouse-like entities with a finite number of resources on a limited range of topics actually kept them from appreciating either the types of information currently available, how that information was organized, or the possibilities for information access that now exist in the contemporary media center. In fact, students assumed that their failure to find relevant titles in one electronic resource meant that the information on the topic was simply unavailable in that setting. Fortunately, this deficit can be directly addressed through programs of information-seeking instruction and should be included as a standard part of any introductory sessions and reinforced as needed throughout the children's information-seeking activities.

The Importance of Background, Domain, or Topical Knowledge

Research related to online searching underscores the importance of domain knowledge and generally holds that students who "jump into" online searches without taking time to develop some familiarity with topic-related concepts and topic-related vocabulary (Fidel et al. 1999; Irving 1991; Solomon 1993, 1994) severely compromise their chances of a successful search experience (Gross 1997; Hirsh 1997; Loerke 1994). Because background knowledge enables students "to recall more concepts and integrate these concepts more readily into their cognitive structure" (Chi, Hutchinson, & Robin, 1989, cited in Borgman et al. 1995, 666), "building adequate content knowledge [is] a critical first step in successful information searching" (206), regardless of whether the research tasks are self-selected skills to research tasks or imposed by others.

Research indicates that when children lack essential frameworks, they experience difficulties in identifying an interest to pursue and, later, in narrowing, focusing, or refining their topics (Kuhlthau 1993b; Oberman 1995; Scott & VanNoord 1996). For this reason, Kuhlthau in particular recommends that students explore their topics thoroughly before beginning the tasks of collecting sources and gathering information. Domain knowledge as a preliminary to successful information seeking was also addressed by Neuman (1995a), who noted that a student's understanding of the topic determines not only the types of the resources that the student needs most but also the relevance of the information and resources eventually located.

Indeed, a lack of background knowledge sets the stage for a variety of problems. For example, Solomon (1993), Moore and St. George (1991), and Irving (1985) found that children who lacked knowledge of their topics were unable to pose appropriate research questions or select appropriate search terms. These findings underscore the emphasis that Chen and Kuhlthau (1994, cited in Nahl & Harada 1996) place on identifying "descriptors and alternative subject headings" (200) as prerequisites to a successful search process.

Irving's (1985) research indicates that teaching subject knowledge alongside online searching is one way to ensure that students know enough about topics to undertake initial searches. Widely appreciated in other kinds of instruction, this strategy has been successfully applied to searching tasks described by Ruggiero (1988, cited in Bodi 1992) and Mark and Jacobson (1995). Hayes (1994, cited in Mark & Jacobson 1995), for example, found that getting students to consider all the areas that could be covered within particular topics made students more aware of "how broad" their topics actually were.

Selecting Topics and Tasks That Are Developmentally Appropriate

It is clear from the research that difficulties in accessing and using online information sources are related to cognitive development. Oberman (1995) noted problems her informants experienced in dealing with abstractions, whereas Walter et al. (1996) found that "the only topics that were consistently easy for children to find were concrete subjects that were [also] easy to spell" (108). Related to concrete operational thinking is the assumption that many youngsters make that the title of a book or article reveals its content in a straightforward way. Yet many books and magazine articles carry "catchy" titles that give no hint as to what they are actually

Table 7.3
Key Competencies for Searching Success

- Knowledge of the library and its print and online resources
- Knowledge of the information search process as a structure for searching
- Knowledge of database organization and design
- Background knowledge of the topic of the research question
- Time for information seeking online

"about." The obscurity of titles was found to be a problem for searchers in a study by Kafai and Bates (1997), and Hirsh (1998) confirmed that when her informants used titles as indicators of relevance, their ability to evaluate retrieved items for relevance was seriously diminished.

Allowing Time for Information Seeking

For more than three decades, Irving (1990, 1991) and others have noted the importance of class scheduling for online searching, because children need time for learning how to search; for practicing search techniques, protocols, and procedures; and for applying newly acquired searching skills to research tasks. Once-a-week class sessions were simply insufficient to provide students the time needed to develop searching competence. Not only did this sort of scheduling magnify the impact of system failures and mechanical difficulties, but the intervals between library sessions also increased student forgetfulness of procedures and strategies, which necessitated the repetition of instruction.

Time was also an issue for students in the Pew Research Center (2001) study. These youngsters reported that even when there was sufficient school access to computers, their involvement in curricular activities in the classroom left little school time for online research. Sometimes, equipment was a problem as well. One middle school girl complained, "[W]hen I go to school, it takes a long time to get online, and by that time, the project you're trying to do is already half over. It's no use anyway." The time issue surfaced as well in Broch's (2000) review of search engines designed for children's use. Specifically, Broch discussed the time it takes students to review the potentially large number of "hits" that sometimes result when searching online. (See Table 7.3.)

Searching time issues for students in Bilal's (2000) study related to the slow response of the Yahooligans! Web search engine. However, Bilal found that time constraints experienced by youngsters were exacerbated by their lack of research skills and by the search engine's complexity. These results confirm the importance of technical and searching competencies as essential literacy skills. Informants in Todd and Kuhlthau's (2003) study of Ohio school students, for example, reported that instruction in Internet information evaluation "enables them to save time in the research process by not having to deal with junk information" (11).

Developing Competent Searchers: Instructional Strategies

The research related to student searching provides some insights into the skills students need and the kinds of lessons that may be the most valuable in helping students reap the positive outcomes that can be gained by accessing electronic resources. Given the range of problems that children encounter in searching online, Chen's (1993) insightful observation that "merely emphasizing the mechanical aspects of online technology will probably not serve students very well" (38) seems particularly appropriate. Clearly, as Moran (2010) argues, when left to their own devices, students will not develop information competencies on their own. Professional instruction and guidance is clearly necessary. Thus, it is up to school librarians to apply their expert knowledge of information resources and search techniques, curricular goals, instructional design, and student abilities in planning instruction and guiding students in seeking information. In addition, they must create and sustain a climate for searching success while also documenting problems so that their own instructional strategies (and perhaps even the systems themselves) can be redesigned to reflect a more student-centered, child-friendly, and differentiated focus. These are complex responsibilities indeed.

Fortunately, lessons learned from recent research studies provide many clues to student information needs in electronic environments and can help school librarians develop curricular strategies. As noted above, we cannot expect students to pick up the information skills they need without instructional intervention (Entwistle 1981; Nahl & Harada 1996) no matter how computer savvy they may appear (Moran 2010). In addition, studies by Irving (1990, 1991), Kuhlthau (1993b, 1997), McNally and Kuhlthau (1994), Fidel et al. (1999), and others repeatedly underscore the need for school librarians to play an active role in assisting youth in information seeking and learning from information sources.

The Importance of Differentiating Instruction

Perhaps the biggest challenge for school library professionals lies in planning and implementing a coherent program of instruction that not only meets the needs of students with vastly diverse computer skills, search experience, and interests but also encourages "deep" as opposed to "surface" understandings of the processes involved (Entwistle 1981). Tailoring instruction to fit skills levels will be increasingly complex as the range of student experience with computers and Internet searching continues to widen. Sitting through instruction on basic computer operations will be every bit as frustrating for experienced "surfers" as advanced instruction would be for already angst-ridden novices. The basis of instruction at any level must be the enactment of active learning, which requires learners to relate new information to what they already know, link abstractions to experience, and evaluate the ideas they encounter in light of their relevance and utility (Entwistle 1981).

For their part, Nahl and Harada (1996) believe that students need direct instruction and activity for learning the skills required to conduct successful searches and that written instructions may not be as effective an instructional approach as face-to-face interaction. Irving (1990) came to the same conclusion in noting that the children in her study proved reluctant "to read manuals and detailed handouts before searching computerized files" (Norton & Westwater 1986, cited in Irving 1990, 14). In order to increase the educational value of online information tasks, these researchers also recommend that students submit printouts of searches, justify their choices of relevant materials, and demonstrate an understanding of the differences between academic and technical journals, popular magazines, and ideological tracts.

Collaboration as an Information-Seeking Strategy

Just as an improved knowledge of information and use in electronic environments creates new kinds of models, formats, and levels of interaction for school librarians, new instructional models may be needed in teaching students how to navigate the sometimes treacherous technological waters. According to Neuman (1995a), collaborative searching involving both librarians and students as well as peer mentoring can be effective additions to the librarians' repertoire of instructional strategies. Morton (1996) asserts that allowing students to take the lead in pursuing personal lines of research enables librarians and teachers an opportunity to participate as colearners: intellectual sojourners "who also [do] not know the answers" (Irving 1990, 115).

With the possible exception of studies in the 1990s by Saracevic, Mokros, and Su (1990) and Mokros, Mullins, and Saracevic (1995), which considered the dynamics of interactivity when professionals and students interact around an electronic search, there are few research studies that inform librarian-student interactions. Given the sensitivity that characterizes most adolescents and the pride in their own technology skills that they often perceive to be stronger than those of school librarians, it behooves the research community to consider giving more attention to deference and demeanor issues as well as to "facework" (Goffman 1967) when balancing collaboration and instruction in the school library. (See Chapter 10 for a more complete explanation of Goffman's work as it has been used by Radford [1996, 2006] in her research into librarian-user interaction.)

Studies related to student use of electronic resources and online searching suggest that essential elements of a dynamic and effective information skills curriculum include: instruction about the information search process, an emphasis on the presearch phase of the process, a thorough exploration of the research topic, instruction on critical strategies for evaluating Web-based information, attention to basic literacy skills, attention to searching strategies, and an emphasis on information handling skills and information use.

Presearch Activity: An Essential First Step

It seems evident that the activities that precede actual searching are more than simply opening moves in the analysis of the research task at hand. Over and over again, studies of electronic searching portend the importance of presearch planning (Nahl & Harada 1996), question creation, search term generation, and strategy selection. In addition, providing a presearch "space" in the overall project makes good instructional sense in that it allows students the opportunity to capitalize on what they already know and make personal connections with important aspects of topics before proceeding.

It is also possible that the presearch phase of information-seeking assignments should include time for librarians and teachers to review the specific process model that youngsters are going to use in carrying out research tasks. Newell (2010), for one, has also pointed to the necessity of direct instruction by school librarians on the overall process of information seeking as a basis for enacting coaching and facilitation roles that are helpful later on.

Instructors can help students learn to become planners by providing activities that stimulate thinking about the topic and the research process and that allow students to practice making research decisions. For example, Irving (1990) found brainstorming to be valuable for both librarians and students in that these activities helped the instructors consider the informational dimensions of the research task, the kinds of resources that would be needed, and the "range of topics in which the students were interested" (64). Graphic organizers and other types of "visual representations," which allow students to "see" facts from a content area in meaningful patterns (Clarke, Martell, & Willey 1994, 70), have also been found helpful to students in exploring possible search topics, formulating search questions, and selecting search terms when used as a part of the presearch planning (Irving 1990) process. In fact, Irving concluded that these activities enhanced the opportunities for successful searching and for information seeking in general. Indeed, the generation of "alternative terms" was itself "a valuable exercise" in exploring student "understanding of the subject matter" (88).

The importance of creating a focus or narrowing a topic has proven to be of even greater importance as a presearch strategy in online environments because within this context, the possibility of retrieving literally thousands of items is a distinct possibility. According to Creanor et al. (1995), "The sheer volume forces users to think more precisely about the topic and about their own needs, to make qualitative decisions on the nature of the material at every step, [and] to rely on their own judgment to a much greater extent" (5) than was necessary before.

Creation of focused questions assumes that children can discern the difference between broad and narrow topics or questions and between objective and subjective questions (Oberman 1995). A group exercise that provides practice for students in recognizing the differences might include presenting students with a list of focused and unfocused research questions and asking them to identify and discuss them as alternatives to a topic, then to select broad and narrow search terms based on the questions. The identification of key words, which is an important strategy in creating search protocols or "strings," can be facilitated by providing practice in main idea identification (e.g., underlining the nouns in a passage, crossing out unnecessary words, and identifying key concepts) and the selection of key words. The expansion of this key word list through the use of synonym finders and the matching of search terms with subject headings or descriptors are also useful presearch activities.

Once children have a general understanding of the topic and have generated key words to use in searching particular aspects, they will require assistance in constructing effective search statements and browsing techniques. Although Boolean searching can be a difficult concept for young children to grasp initially, school librarians and teachers have found creative and "concrete" activities to allow children to conceptualize the strategy and practice this skill. For example, one teacher in Irving's (1990) study successfully presented the concepts of the AND/OR/BUT NOT operators by having the class divide and regroup itself according to eye color and hair color. This makes particularly good sense in light of the research findings by Sein and Bostrom (1989) that concrete thinkers who may have low visualization skills find analogic models more effective as instructional aids than abstract visualizations.

For teachers and librarians, presearch activities provide time and opportunity to assess student knowledge of the topics, their general skill levels, and their mental models of the information search process. Instructors can also use the presearch "space" as a time for activities that alert students to the many pitfalls that may await them in accessing information online and to make students aware of the range and levels of assistance that school library professionals can provide. Supplying students with information on the strengths and limitations of available databases as well as Internet resources is also important since, as Fidel et al. (1999) found, students sometimes have unrealistic expectations of both a library's resources and its librarian. For example, students researching topics assigned for homework believed that the librarian knew exactly where the information was and could lead them directly to it. Using presearch activities to help students plan in advance may alert students to the realities of the information universe in addition to reducing the "cognitive load" (Marchionini 1987, 70) for novice searchers.

Loranger (1994) said that good thinkers "make plans for learning." However, research indicates that preplanning of sequential activities is not a part of the repertoire of novice searchers (Grover et al. 1996; Marchionini 1989), who often tend to rely instead on system feedback. For example, high school students in Fidel et al.'s (1999) study believed that "there was no need" for planning the search in advance, as they expected to follow whatever leads and links presented themselves as a result of inputting their original search terms.

Skill Development for Online Searching

Online searching studies have helped produce a laundry list of skills that students must develop to ensure that they become effective and efficient searchers; not surprisingly, among the most important of these are basic literacy skills related to reading, spelling, writing, and language use. While the lack of such skills may not hamper the initial searching activities of youngsters who have access to iconographic interfaces and other types of "kid-friendly" online public access catalog software, computer software, and websites, the lack of such skills will create barriers as the complexity of search tasks increases. The abilities to read for comprehension, to scan a paragraph for the main ideas, and to see the relationships between ideas and concepts on a given topic are precursors to the ability to generate key words as search terms and understand synonyms as well as the ability to handle alternative word forms—all of which are essential to search success.

Reinforcement of good study skills is also a prerequisite to successful searching and the effective use of retrieved information. There is some research evidence to show that note taking is a valuable way to extract information from a text and is preferable to reading or underlining because it "requires greater cognitive effort and a deeper level of processing" (Loranger 1994, 354) and serves as an aid to the recall of information. In fact, "according to Anderson and Armbruster (1984), the very act of writing aids in the processing of new information because it focuses attention" (354–55).

Research on the searching behaviors of students from elementary through high school demonstrates the need for instruction in the critical appraisal of Internet sources. Specifically, Hirsh (1998) identified the "need to learn to analyze and challenge the authority of documents found on the Internet" (54). A strategy that Jacobson and Ignacio (1997) found useful in raising student awareness of evaluative criteria such as authority, accuracy, and the like was to have students themselves design Web pages.

Search Strategizing

Over time, researchers have created an impressive literature on the information-seeking behavior of adults. Among the most helpful have been studies that examined the ways in which end users go about seeking information in online environments. In an often-cited study by Bates (1989), it was found that in actual search situations, end users rarely followed a linear course but rather invoked an iterative, "berrypicking" process that evolved and changed as their searches unfolded. Research on information seeking and children (Borgman et al. 1995) suggests that searches conducted by children on their own also tend to follow nonlinear patterns. However, Kafai and Bates (1997) noted that student searchers need assistance and support with many aspects of their search process, including "scanning text and using hypertext links" (107). The problem for novice searchers in Neuman's (1995a) view is that they often lack either the domain knowledge or the cognitive flexibility to allow them to change their perspective, their focus, or their direction without some assistance. These problems can be complicated by the reluctance many children have to asking for help, particularly as they enter adolescence. For this reason, young searchers might welcome and benefit from the instruction that includes the "idea tactics" that Bates (1979a) suggests (see Chapter 8).

While it would appear that children's difficulties with electronic resources result from cognitive and skill deficits, an equally cogent argument could be made that their problems are created by the failure of database designers to create accessible, user-friendly information systems. While waiting for systems to improve, school librarians must plan programs of intervention that will provide a level of support for young searchers seeking information in potentially "disabling" information systems. The children will be well served if school librarians seize every opportunity to advocate for them in suggesting to vendors and designers the need for improving the systems designed for student use.

Although many search strategies are generic and can be applied to information-seeking tasks in print as well as to online resources (Irving 1990), some aspects of electronic resource searching are unique. Assignments that are planned to capitalize on the specific challenges that the uses of such resources pose and the possibilities for learning that they engender should be encouraged. In fact, Mark and Jacobson (1995) suggest modifying student assignments to take advantage of learning opportunities offered by specific kinds of electronic resources—activities that, in the process, will reveal their advantages and their limitations. In some instances, there may be a tendency by some teachers to require that students use electronic resources exclusively without realizing that such resources are most valuable when they are "integrated" (Markless & Lincoln 1986, cited in Irving 1990, 14) with "books, magazines, newspapers, video and audio tape, slides, posters, museums, historic sites, [and] field trips" (7). Problems also occur when students are searching for very specific information. According to Mark and Jacobson, without asking students to think critically about the relevance, utility, and authority of the resources they consult, the requirement to use a particular number of sources is meaningless.

Journaling

The use of teacher/librarian-monitored journals to chronicle student experience and to track projects and problems has been effective in helping all ages of students from primary school to college (Mark & Jacobson 1995). Kuhlthau (1991, 1993b), for example, found that journals provide a means for the recording of students' thoughts, problems, and concerns. In addition, a student's journal becomes a permanent artifact of the process and a resource that can be used by him or her as a springboard to the next project and consulted as a tutorial for review before the next project begins. Students can also use these notations as a basis for evaluating the research process and the final project or product.

By the same token, teachers and librarians can use journals as venues within which to pose questions that will stimulate student thinking. Hayes (1994, cited in Mark & Jacobson 1995, 29) found that relating questions to specific aspects of Kuhlthau's information search process was particularly useful. Appropriate questions might include the following: Does the focus relate to the reading and to the topic? Should the focus be narrowed further (or broadened)? Do terms and keywords relate directly to the focus? As the work and instruction continue, teachers can pose other types of questions to check for student understanding.

Mark and Jacobson (1995) also recommend the use of student journals and class sessions devoted to presearch discussion of research topics. While journaling and discussion are time consuming, Hayes (1994, cited in Mark & Jacobson 1995) found that their use "improved [both the] focus of the student's first drafts" and the "quality of the final papers" (29), while Mark and Jacobson (1995) report that teachers' responses in student journals promote "a stronger focus and can prevent a disappointing final product" (28). In addition, student complaints recorded in journals can pinpoint weaknesses in the collection, in instruction, and in programming. A view of library resources and insights on instruction and intervention strategies from the perspective of students can be powerful tools for improving the quality of services in the school library.

Changes for School Librarians: Instructional and Service Roles

The informational and technical needs of students involved in online searching should at last put to rest vestigial models of librarianship that claim that collecting and organizing informational materials, creating an information environment, and teaching library skills necessary for library use encompass all dimensions of the school librarian's job. Current research confirms the need for variety and dynamism in instructional strategizing and for introducing additional levels of assistance and service. In point of fact, roles for school librarians in supporting students in searching online will appropriately include instruction, facilitation, advising/counseling, and occasionally, information provision. Since research has shown that in online environments student access to resources is reduced where personal assistance is not provided (Edmonds et al. 1990, 31), there may even be ethical issues involved when school librarians fail to anticipate and supply the degree of assistance that novice searchers require for successful curricular outcomes.

Within the context of instruction for electronic and online searching, school librarians should count on teaching the mechanics of searching, presearch planning (such as identifying key words and creating search questions), selecting search strategies and databases, and managing search results. In addition, librarians can help students in reviewing lists of citations, interpreting output, assisting with the redesign of the search when necessary, and helping students make relevance judgments (e.g., using criteria such as depth of information, length, reading level, and up-to-dateness in addition to "aboutness") (Smith 1987). Finally, research indicates that students may need encouragement and assistance with "end-game" activities, which involve organizing and using the information obtained (Irving 1990, 1991).

The value of support provided by knowledgeable school librarians—who not only understand search techniques but also possess an understanding of the possibilities and idiosyncrasies of online resources—should not be underestimated.

And, because online searching of bibliographic records yields citations and abstracts for which the full texts may ultimately be desired, knowing how the documents can be obtained quickly and cheaply requires professionals who are capable and willing to acquire them through interlibrary loan. Neuman's (1997) research in particular illuminates a central issue in online and electronic environments: matching the database of resources to the information needs of the students. The truth is that school librarians must stay ahead of the learning curve in understanding both the technical aspects and the instructional implications of new electronic resources in order to keep pace with a rapidly accelerating technological context (Bruce 1994).

The problems that await student learners in seeking information in online environments argue for librarians to anticipate, diagnose, and remediate student skills. In turn, "this type of diagnostic learning requires information-searching experiences that are introduced, reinforced, and expanded upon across grade levels and content areas rather than presented as 'one-shot' instruction" (Nahl & Harada 1996, 206) sessions. It also argues for documenting instructional intervention as a part of a coordinated program of information literacy and the creation of carefully articulated lesson plans that provide for the assessment of student and class progress (Markuson 1986, 39).

New Competencies for a New Age

Key to the use of technology in the workplace are the skills needed for the effective use of Web 2.0 technologies, hence the need for new instructional objectives and learning outcomes. A case in point relates to copyright and ethics issues for students (Dow 2008). Technological innovations that now help students create and share—as well as to consume—information "products" makes their understanding of intellectual property rights a matter of considerable importance and interest. For instance, with mashup applications (wherein two or more creative entities are merged into a new product or presentation), questions occur regarding actual copyright ownership for the newer versions. Because conventional copyright laws are based on the concept of original authorship, creative endeavors such as mashups are the cause of considerable copyright confusion (Kapitzke 2009). In today's online-based creative playgrounds, it is interesting to note trends toward tighter intellectual property and copyright controls, even while government policies recommend the use of collaborative creative problem solving. As Kapitzke notes, "[t]he trend towards privatizing information through strong copyright law is also at odds with the eruption of creative self-expression afforded by social networking tools" (99). In their role as technology and ethical information use experts, school librarians are poised on the front lines to teach students how to navigate knotty issues regarding copyright and intellectual property in the "global world of information" (Dow 2008, 49).

However, students will be ill served by fear of punishment for displaying creative license in mixing elements from a variety of sources found online. "Clearly, commercial piracy of cultural materials is wrong and should be prohibited, but regulatory environments that prosecute young people for tinkering with text (language, image, or sound) by sharing digital resources as part of their meaning-making universe are socially dangerous" (Kapitzke 2009, 103). For this reason, handling questions concerning intellectual property and copyright law in Web 2.0 environments requires finesse, creativity, and sensitivity. Suggestions offered by Kapitzke include an appreciation for and understanding of changes occurring to traditional producer-user relationships as well as knowledge and support of alternate copyright frameworks, such as open-source software and Creative Commons licensing. Creative Commons materials are easily located via the Internet (http://www.creativecommons.org), and the organizational mission makes clear its encouragement and promotion of using materials protected and guided by totally new legal parameters:

> Creative Commons is a non-profit organization dedicated to making it easier for people to share and build upon the works of others, consistent with the rules of copyright. We provide free licenses and other tools to mark creative work with the freedom the creator wants it to carry, so others can share, remix, use commercially, or any combination thereof. (Creative Commons 2010)

Involved in Creative Commons rights are the following:

- Issues surrounding attribution, such as giving the original author credit after modifying and distributing materials
- Noncommercial intent
- No derivatives, meaning that words might be modified and provided to users but not for the purpose of creating derivative works
- Share Alike, a concept wherein new producers modifying and creating derivative works must make the changed products available to users within the same licensing terms as outlined in the original work (Kapitzke 2009, 204)

These suggestions are important and compelling in an environment where more than 300 million creations are labeled with Creative Commons licensing and are available for mass consumption via the Internet.

Kapitzke (2009) also recommends using critique as a tool for fine-tuning understandings of copyright protections and how transformative creations fit into the equation. She suggests that within the federal mandates of No Child Left Behind[5] legislation, schools mistakenly lean toward more conservative approaches to copyright compliance, returning to what she considers to be "compliant, safe spaces of conformist copyright education practices" (106). She adds, "Restricting access to the raw materials of creative endeavor is culturally shortsighted and counterproductive if society is genuinely to value enterprise and innovation in a global knowledge economy" (106).

Teacher-School Librarians as Collaborative Partners

As noted in previous chapters, research has extended our understanding of the importance of collaboration between school librarians and teachers in helping students make meaningful and ethical use of information they find online and integrating electronic resources into curricular units (Heeks 1997; Irving 1991). Interestingly, Heeks (1989, cited in Irving 1990) reports that collaboration between teachers and library media specialists on student assignments "helps to make [student] searches result in more relevant retrieval" (14). However, successful integration assumes that teachers themselves understand the process of information seeking, the range of electronic resources available, and the characteristics of these resources as well as the potential difficulties online searching poses for students. In fact, Irving (1990) found than many teachers lacked knowledge of the research process and of information skills generally. This may be the case even among more technologically adept educators. For example, Fidel et al. (1999) reported that, in their study, teacher-designed online searching tasks were fill-in-the-blanks activities that amounted to little more than electronic scavenger hunts. Where situations such as those Irving and Fidel et al. describe exist, school librarians may have to "educate" some teachers to the benefits of using a "model" for research and assist teachers in creating assignments that facilitate rather than finesse the important learning opportunities such projects can provide. Teachers unfamiliar with the vicissitudes often experienced in information seeking online may need assistance in designing assignments that take into account the additional time required when searching electronically and the instabilities many information systems experience at certain times of the day (Neuman 1997).

In the mid-1990s, Barron (1994) noted the phenomenon of technophobia (48) among school staff. This problem has abated over time as younger and more technologically savvy teachers have entered the instructional arena. In fact, Means and Olson (1994) found that student access to electronic databases caused teachers in the study to create more complex assignments. It is probable that the greater a teacher's experience and effectiveness in searching for information online, the more likely it is that the use of electronic resources will be incorporated within research tasks in meaningful ways.

Hardware and Software in the School Setting

Successful online searching requires an environment that supports its use: demonstration hardware and software for large and small groups, facilities that enable online interaction and group activities, and funding equal to the financial demands of providing online services (Irving 1991). The availability of technical support and policies that promote staff development opportunities and permit flexible scheduling of online searching activities are also elements essential in maintaining educationally valuable, information-rich environments (Chelton 1997).

It goes without saying that a school climate that supports instructional innovation is also necessary if inquiry learning is to be successfully implemented (for a discussion of inquiry learning, see Chapter 3). In the *Library Power* experience outlined by Bishop (2001), the importance of "buy-in" by stakeholders was essential to its success. Limberg's (1999) study of library-based school reform in Sweden underscores the importance of this kind of support. Limberg reported that even where model libraries had been redesigned in line with the expectations and needs of the school, these changes were perceived as threats by teachers wedded to traditional pedagogy and instructional roles.

Technological Troubleshooting: A Continuing Challenge

An unanticipated dilemma for librarians created by the transformation of the library from cultural storehouse to technological nexus has emerged: the increasing percentage of the media specialist's day devoted to technological troubleshooting and the concomitant reduction of time available for teaching (M. J. McNally, conversation with author, January 1997; Chelton 1997). Time *spent* clearing paper jams, rebooting frozen computer screens, and monitoring Internet use is time *unavailable* for enacting the instructional role so carefully articulated in the literature of school librarianship over the past quarter of a century. While no one would wish to reinstate a "retro" view of the librarian as custodian of resources and general school factotum, it is increasingly evident that the responsibility for "riding herd" on technological bulls is an exercise best undertaken by library aides under the careful supervision of the librarian. If not, the profession stands to lose much of the instructional momentum that has been building over the past decades. The expertise of the librarian in making the resources educationally useful and instructing students in the skills they will need to survive in the workplace and the university is simply too valuable a resource to have it dissipated in the "bittiness" of media center odd jobs.

Conclusion

Moran (2010) redefined the digital divide in terms not of access to online resources but of adequate instruction that helps students successfully develop search acumen and judgment—skills that will in turn translate into benefits and knowledge that form the basis for future successes in school, jobs, and life. "While," as Moran notes, "not every school librarian is yet adapting to the new reality of what is demanded of the role, thousands of dedicated librarians . . . are turning school media centers into 'learning commons' where students seamlessly use state-of-the-art Web tools to consume and produce content."

The learning gap that Moran (2010) warns of is created when "elite" students in well-funded school districts and private schools are "learning critical 21st century skills" while in "budget-stressed school districts" youngsters without school librarians are being left to fend for themselves. The result, as Moran opines, is "[w]hat a University College of London study called a 'new divide,' with students who have access to librarians 'taking the prize of better grades' while those who don't have access to school librarians" show up "at college beyond hope, having 'already developed an ingrained coping behaviour: they learned to 'get by' with Google." Predicting that "this new divide is only going to widen and leave many students hopelessly lost in the past, while others fully embrace the future," Moran concludes that schools that rely exclusively on classroom teachers who are "stressed by assessment testing and ever-growing paperwork burdens" to "help students figure this all out" will not only fail their students but also fail in their mandate to educate students for a century's worth of new information challenges.

Notes

1. The Department of Commerce asserts that the K–12 years are critical in generating student interest in "information technology and the career opportunities now possible for students with the requisite skills and access to computer technology" (Twist 2004).

2. Everhart (2003) discusses the problem presented by student plagiarism in an electronic world and some policies that school librarians might adopt to reduce cheating. Quoting Minkel, Everhart reports that when they have access, 94 percent of middle and high school students use the World Wide Web for their research projects, and for 71 percent of these students, the Web is "the main source." For many of these students, cheating has become "irresistibly easy and pervasive." "Plagiarism can take many forms," Everhart tells us, "copying without referencing the information, citing improperly, and even

purchasing term papers online" (43). Indeed, research by McGregor and Streitenberger (1998, cited in Everhart 2003) indicates that direct instruction in quoting, paraphrasing, and citing sources is needed to limit student copying. That is the bad news. The good news is that where teachers and librarians provide instruction on research ethics and the mechanics of citing, support for students in searching for information, authentic research projects, and time to undertake those projects, student's research and their ethical behavior improve (Gordon 1999, cited in Everhart 2003). Dutilloy (2003) describes a comprehensive approach to the problem of plagiarism by the United Nations International School in New York City, where attitudes for using another's work have cultural as well as ethical dimensions. The school has devised and publicized school policies and penalties related to student plagiarism and provided both instructional intervention on information seeking and citation form, and staff development for teachers on plagiarism and on the design of appropriate assignments. Dutilloy concludes, "At UNIS, all community members are involved in the development of a plagiarism-free school—the administration, by supporting new policies and enforcing them; the teachers, by creating assignments that encourage independent thinking; and the SLMSs, by providing tools to avoid plagiarism. To encourage and enhance these attitudes, SLMSs must maintain effective communication with all departments" (45).

3. Todd (1998) cites Burbules (1997) in describing "the Net as an indiscriminate mix of five types of information, where quality, importance and reliability of information is [*sic*] difficult to determine. These types are: Information: factual, clearly sourced; bears all the traditional hallmarks of reliability and quality. Misinformation: information judged to be false, out of date, or incomplete in a misleading way. Malinformation: potentially dangerous or damaging information, inappropriate information; information people feel uncomfortable with in openly accessible circulation. Messed Up Information: poorly organized and presented information; sloppy design; problematic navigation. Useless Information: (recognizing one person's trash is another person's treasure) Information that appears to serve little informing purpose."

4. It is perhaps instructive to note here research on the mental models of electronic resources (such as databases) that school librarians use and the effect these models have on the structure and goals of lessons they plan for students. In a study by Tallman and Henderson (1999), school librarians' acknowledgment of the need to change their mental models did not automatically translate into new strategies for subsequent lessons. Research findings such as these give credence to a claim by Dixon (1994) that "worldwide, school is a puffer belly locomotive chugging incongruously through a high-tech landscape" (quoted in Todd 1998, 16).

5. An educational initiative created in the No Child Left Behind Act of 2001 and signed into law by President George W. Bush in 2002, the act was created in hopes of improving educational opportunities for all children but especially those considered "disadvantaged" through the imposition of federally mandated standards for public schools.

8 Creating Effective Inquiry-Based Educational Tasks

In the real world, information seeking takes a long time. It is characterized by blind alleys and false scents, and answers often need to be constructed following critical consideration of the available information.

—Moore (1993)

This chapter brings together research-based instructional designs that require students to think deeply and critically as they learn from information-seeking tasks. Learners' levels of searching expertise and subject content knowledge are essential starting points when planning inquiry-based assignments, while building in self-evaluation as a metacognitive component enhances the learning potential of assigned tasks. Being able to call on effective strategies for seeking and using information are also important competencies, and offering students proven search tactics is key to their searching success. Here, the models by Bates, Ellis, and Foster will prove of special interest. Information-seeking activities that spark curiosity as well as those that give students opportunities to engage in real-world problem solving are also ways of increasing student enthusiasm and content knowledge. These issues and topics constitute the focus of this chapter (Key points appear in Tables 8.1 and 8.2.).

Components of Effective, Research-Based Assignments

Research paper assignments or "source themes" have long been a staple in secondary school curricular programs in history/social studies or English/language arts that seek to provide students experience in the use of primary and secondary sources and the structures and mechanics of formal writing. At least since the 1980s, these kinds of projects have been scaled down for use with ever-younger populations of schoolchildren. Indeed, it is not unusual to see information age kindergarten youngsters engaged in library activities requiring them to "research" sets of specific facts.

While most assignments for primary schoolchildren are based on finding information in one or two sources from a "contained collection" (Kuhlthau 2001), older youngsters are admonished to find information in a wider variety of print and networked resources. Citing Marland (1978), Moore (1993) describes this instructional strategy as "the project method," in which

Table 8.1
Characteristics of Effective Student Research Assignments

Effective Assignments:

• Are developmentally appropriate for each student

• Do not arise in a knowledge vacuum

• Present clear objectives/outcomes and evaluation criteria for process and product

• Make explicit the reasons for required components (e.g., numbers of sources, types of sources)

• Create a context for the development of process and project skills

• Arise in a systematic program of research within the context of ongoing classroom curriculum

• Are directly and explicitly connected to course content

• Offer gender-fair and culture-fair choices related to student interests

• Offer options that acknowledge learning style preferences

• Are meaningful to students and linked to student experience

• Involve students in critical thinking rather than recalling or reporting

• Take the affective needs of students into account

• Are broken down into manageable elements and supported by teachers and library media specialists

• Provide opportunities for group discussion and activity

• Are structured to allow time for searching and task completion based on a realistic appraisal of source and system availability

students are typically given a topic to research, generally a person, place or event, and are told to use resources from the library, take notes, make an outline, and produce a report. [Sheingold] makes the point that the kind of topic assigned in this context is often a category (Switzerland, music, the 18th century, spiders . . .) and the task can be completed by reviewing a limited number of resources, writing about a few appropriate subcategories, and producing an attractive cover page. (2)

In Moore's view, these kinds of activities "demand a fairly superficial interaction with information, not necessarily the critical information gathering and use essential to the research and inquiry skills supposedly developed through project assignments" (2). A major flaw in information-seeking activities predicated on this model is that children develop an expectation that their hunt in the library will eventually uncover a source that provides "the exact answer to their questions in the exact format required" (17).

However, even when students understand the synthesis aspects of the task (Gordon 1999), they expect to do little more than report what they find and create some concluding statements based on their reading. Moore (1993) believed students in her study created simple rules for the research task: "Think of a question, identify its keywords, look up the subject index for a Dewey number, go to the shelves and

Table 8.2
Questions to Answer in Planning Student Research Assignments

- What cognitive skills do students bring to research tasks?
- What will the research project contribute to student learning and skill development?
- At what point in the curricular unit should the research project take place?
- What are the intended goals and objectives of this particular project?
- What research topics and questions will resonate with learners?
- How can the research topics and questions be designed to elicit students' use of higher-order thinking skills?
- How can the project be structured to ensure time for student planning and reflection and minimize student stress?
- What outcomes in terms of process and projects will students realize as a result of the research task, and how can these best be explained to students?

find the answer. . . . If any part of that sequence failed," Moore continued, her students "often seemed surprised and confused":

> In the real world, information seeking takes a long time. It is characterized by blind alleys and false scents and answers often need to be constructed following critical consideration of the available information. Few of the children [in the study] were prepared to do that. (28)

Given student understandings of school projects, it is perhaps not very surprising that they often bring little enthusiasm to the research task and that teachers and librarians often observe little evidence of "synthesis" and a good deal of plagiarism. In teaching information literacy skills through the creation of student-conducted information-seeking tasks, teachers and librarians may be making unwarranted assumptions about student learners. This has led Moore (1993) to conclude that "project assignments should be set with the purpose of promoting an understanding of thinking processes rather than the product alone" (29).[1] She also suggests making "explicit the problem solving nature of the task and promot[ing] the notion that there are many ways of reaching a solution" (28).

What does the research tell us about the framing of research assignments and its impact on search success and skill development? What kinds of research tasks will have the most educational punch? In planning research tasks, which elements should command our attention? In short, how can we design projects to ensure the achievement of information literacy standards so that our students develop the necessary competencies to become effective and efficient users of information?

Research studies in the field of school librarianship point to the following factors as components essential to successful project completion: the framing of developmentally appropriate research tasks, the timing of the project within curricular activities or units, and the relevance of research tasks and topics to students' experiences and interests. Other factors include explaining the project in terms of its value for learning, making the project goals and expectations clear, reframing research topics as questions that require students to think critically, structuring the project to allow time for presearch planning, giving attention to process learning and product creation, and providing opportunities for student evaluation. A key to success is the process of planning ahead by the teachers and the school librarian so that all are clear as to instructional roles and responsibilities and learning outcomes.

Certainly, it makes sense to begin planning the research task with students' developmental levels in mind. Hirsh (1999) noted particularly the appropriateness of the research assignment (a sports celebrity) for fifth-grade students operating at Piaget's (Inhelder & Piaget 1958) concrete operational stage. "The assigned topic was concrete and relatively unambiguous," Hirsh wrote, and "the topic was also one that generated high levels of interest and excitement" (1278). Understanding how the research activity contributes to the development of children's content knowledge will direct instructors to place the research task within a unit of study. For example, a number of scholars have drawn attention to the importance of content knowledge as essential grounding for information searching. In other words, research assignments should not be fact-finding expeditions that precede direct instruction and in-class reading on a topic; rather, they should be timed to build on and deepen understandings once students have developed a measure of knowledge of a given subject.

Research indicates that when students lack prior content knowledge, their ability to conduct independent and meaningful inquiry based on that content is seriously compromised. For example, McGregor (1994b) found that the student's prior knowledge of a topic "influence[d] the ability to narrow a topic" and to search effectively for "pertinent information" (72). In addition, having students engage in front-end activities such as brainstorming and planning has been recommended by Kuhlthau (1985) and others as important preliminary scaffolding for information seeking. Significantly, Wesley's (1991) research indicates that student planning prior to searching helps to minimize student anxiety and frustration that can subvert or even derail research activities.

In many cases, the student's background readings on a given topic will be textbook based. To increase student interest and also acquaint students with other information resources, Callison (1994) suggests moving beyond "textbook generalities and teacher-led discussion" to include the sharing of "books, newspaper articles, films, guest lectures" (51) and the like to help build content knowledge as a preresearch activity. In this way, students' knowledge of their topics will increase, serving as a basis for in-class discussion and setting the stage for subsequent exploration and learning.

It is clear that students are more successful when the goals and outcomes of an assignment are clearly stated (Thomas 1993) and when they understand assessment criteria and the reasoning behind research tasks. Irving's (1985) research indicates that children need to know up front what is being required of them. Without this knowledge, Irving believes that youngsters will lack the framework for "self-evaluation, which is essential to the development of good learners" (35). Beyond this, the instructions created for each assignment should indicate the "level, depth, scope, and approach[es]" the students are to take because this information will help them "structure [their] information-seeking, reading, note-taking and presenting" (35). Students should understand the value and the reasons for the subskill tasks that are set before them as well. Indeed, "the admonishment 'use more than one book' carries little weight or value if it is not properly qualified; for example 'use more than one book in order to collect different views of the topic' " (26–27). To this end, instruction in the relative value of alternative sources should also be provided (Mark & Jacobson 1995).

The ability to analyze and synthesize information in a variety of sources demands thinking at the high end of Bloom's (1956) taxonomy. Research projects that do not push students to engage intellectually with course content have little value. Critical thinking is not an option, Norris (1985) asserts; rather, it is "an indispensable part of education" (40). For this reason, research assignments must be designed to ensure the use of higher-order thinking (Honebein 1996; Jay 1986) in completing the research task rather than permitting students merely "to recite facts related to a topic" (Clarke, Martell, & Willey 1994, 70) obtained in a "search, print, and run" library activity (Jacobson & Mark 1995, 116). Assignments that do not reach this intellectual level actually "reinforce" fact-oriented learning—a practice that can be antithetical to critical thinking. Perhaps the hardest lesson that students will learn "is that information is not the same as knowledge and that facts are not understanding" (Sauer 1995, 142). But this is an important lesson and one that teachers and librarians must learn as well.

The importance of evaluation as a part of the process of learning is well established in the literature of school librarianship (Callison 1994; Eisenberg & Berkowitz 1990; Grover 1993; Kuhlthau 1994) and education (Thomas 1993). Its purpose, Kuhlthau (1993b) writes, "is to identify what learning has taken place and where further instruction and practice are needed" (59). Self-assessment by students is essential. This philosophy is affirmed through the prominent placement of self-assessment strategies in *the Standards for the 21st Century Learner* (American Association of School Librarians [AASL] 2007). As Irving (1985) notes above, the evaluation tasks for student researchers include not only a critical review of information sources relevant to their projects but also assessment of their own learning as demonstrated in the completed project. Other library and information science (LIS) researchers and scholars (Craver 1989; Eisenberg & Berkowitz 1990; Kuhlthau 2001; Pitts 1995) agree. When evaluation of product and process is in place, there is a balance in emphasis among product, content, and skills that many educators feel is both essential and culture fair (Delpit 1995). Without this feature, students lack the opportunity to learn from their mistakes (Irving 1985) or to gain awareness of themselves as learners. Indeed, they may focus their time and energy on activities that, in the end, have little educational impact. For example, students in studies conducted by McGregor (1994b) and Pitts (1995) were so focused on product generation that the value of the subject content and process skills they were meant to learn were ignored. Students saw the research task as "a job," McGregor asserts, "rather than as an opportunity for learning" (74). The focus on learning and the learning process has another payoff: according to Kuhlthau (1997), students who are aware of the importance of process skill development are not as likely to copy informational texts verbatim.

This begs the question: When should students assess their learning, and to what issues and behaviors should students attend? Kuhlthau (1993b) suggests that "evaluation should take place immediately following the completion of the research assignment" (59) and consider students' abilities to create a focus for their papers, to make good use of their time in planning and carrying out the research activity, and to make use of available resources, including the expertise of the school librarian. Callison (1994) also suggests that students evaluate their information sources in terms of their usefulness, the effort expended in obtaining resources, the transfer of skills to other projects, and the value added to the educational experience (54). To facilitate self-assessment, Kuhlthau recommends the use of time lines (to help students "visualize the stages in the process"), flowcharts (to help students track their progress), and conferencing with the school librarian and the creation of a "summary statement" (to assist students in evaluating their participation in the process and their creation of a final product).

When student research projects are carefully planned and structured "as a planned series of intellectual challenges, rather than as a rote series of tasks" (Clarke et al. 1994, 70), students have multiple opportunities to practice and use the information skills they are acquiring. This underscores the value to students of practicing skills within assignments that are meaningful to them rather than in make-work sorts of activities that were the warp and woof of the old "library skills"/"scope and sequence" library curriculum.

Assignments That Motivate the Searcher

According to Irving (1985), an effective lesson is one that has relevance and meaning and reflects the learner's "knowledge, ability, level [and] interests" (112). Moreover, "motivation implies relevance, and relevance implies an understanding of both learner and learning material" (112). Hirsh (1999) attributed to student choice and topic of interest her informants' ability to personalize their searches, their eagerness to undertake the research task, and their care in evaluating the search results. "Students were absorbed in the search process," Hirsh wrote, "and generally did not settle for the first piece of information they found" (1278). Perhaps for this reason, Schack (1993), Giese, Cothron, and Rezha (1992), and Solomon (1994) suggest that assignments be structured to allow students to select topics based on their interests and that the introduction of the project might better serve both the students and the project if it began with a survey of student interests and hobbies rather than with background on the subject or topic.

Crow (2009b) also found interest in a topic to be an important motivator for students. In her study of 10-year-olds who were identified to be intrinsically motivated to seek information, she requested that informants name their favorite two information-seeking episodes and then asked them to give the reasons why they named those specific experiences as their favorites. The most frequent reason given was their interest in or relevance of the topic. Other reasons they listed were (in order of prevalence) "working in a group, the experiences of the information seeking itself, creating the final product, choice of aspect within topic, and no time limit" (101). It is interesting to note that none of the children gave "working individually" as a reason for preferring a research episode, pointing to the fact that relational needs outweighed the need for autonomy for this group of students.

Jakobovits and Nahl-Jakobovits (1990) call attention to the salience of student affect (e.g., "how we feel about and value learning experiences") (Jacobson & Mark 1995, 108) as a concomitant to success in information-seeking tasks. Kuhlthau's (1993b) work also emphasizes the affective nature of the search task, specifically the feelings of uncertainty, confusion, and anxiety as common experiences for novice information seekers. In planning student assignments, librarians should anticipate these feelings of insecurity and allow time and space for students to discuss them as the information-seeking task unfolds. This kind of guidance and feedback along the way are absolutely essential if children are to understand the value the teacher and school librarian attach to the learning process—as well as to students themselves—over and above the project that comes at the end (Pitts 1995).

Table 8.3
Effective Assignments from the Student's Perspective

Students want:

- A choice of topic and assistance with choosing a topic
- Assistance with the research process and opportunities to practice research skills
- Explicit ties between course content and particular research topics and tasks
- Explicit goals and evaluation criteria for the research project
- Opportunities to engage in social interaction and group work

In her study, Burdick (1997) raised the issue of gender as it relates to information seeking and the character of student research assignments. Citing the work of Gilligan (1982) and Pipher (1994) related to the socialization of adolescent girls in the United States, Burdick particularly noted the need for school librarians to support girls in creating and expressing their own personal perspectives in their research projects, to include women as well as men as researchable "topics," and to legitimate connectedness and syntheses, which often characterize a feminine approach to learning, in addition to the informational approach and logical argument formats, which tend to reflect a male perspective. These themes resonate with the work of Ford (1996), who has noted the need to expand curriculum to include all races and ethnic groups. Ford reminds us that "students learn through acts of omission and commission; they learn from what is present in and left out of the curriculum" (143). Where topic choices fail to acknowledge "the contributions [to history, literature, science, etc.] of various racial, cultural, and economic groups" (143), the "invisible veil" (193) of monoculturalism effectively masks the biases that such omissions portend.

Effective Assignments from the Student's Point of View

Garland's (1995) study of information seeking in school contexts sought to tap the information-seeking experience from the point of view of the students involved. Specifically, Garland was interested in finding out how 387 high school students in 18 classrooms studying a range of subjects from physiology to composition regarded the research task and those elements that related to student achievement and feelings of satisfaction. The tasks themselves were as "heterogeneous" as the students and subject matter and included formal papers and a variety of creative presentation formats. Table 8.3 summarizes the elements that Garland identified as important to students: choice of topics, which gave students "a sense of control" (178); experience with the type of project assigned; background knowledge of the topic; access to assistance in choosing a topic and understanding the research process, particularly if the task "required a higher level of thinking" (176); an explicit connection between course content and the topic; explicit goals and processes for task completion; specific evaluation criteria; and opportunities for social interaction and group work. Interestingly, both Garland and Crow (2009b) found that topic choice was the most important aspect of the research project to both pools of students in their separate studies, though Garland's was on the secondary level and Crow's informants were elementary school aged. (See Table 8.4.)

Table 8.4
Strategies for Building Motivation in Information-Seeking Projects

- Stimulate interest in the activity at the outset in an engaging way based on individual differences in interests, learning styles, media/format preferences, and the like

- Ensure relevance through the use of clearly articulated learning outcomes tied to search success and academic success and appropriate and reflective of student experience, culture, and values

- Increase student confidence by explaining what is expected, what students will be doing, and the availability of assistance, expertise, and emotional support provided by teachers, librarians, and peers

- Ensure that expectations are achievable—challenging but not overwhelming—and that the achievement of goals lies within students' ability levels

- Recognize students for effort and improvement

- Inspire intrinsic motivation by encouraging student enjoyment of the research experience and discussing the value of the activity to other school-related and life-related tasks

- Judge the outcomes of the task in gender-fair and culture-fair ways

- Provide opportunities for students to practice important skills and to revise unsuccessful projects

Authentic Research: Building Competencies through "Real" Tasks

"Reporting has masqueraded as researching for so long that the terms are used interchangeably" Gordon wrote in 1999, with the result that the ever-popular research project has become a bromide, "analogous to 'Take two aspirins and call me in the morning.' . . . Educators adjust the dosage for older students; the length of the paper grows with the time allotted to the task but the prescription is the same." As Gordon notes, students have come to view the research task as a writing assignment in which factual accuracy, grammar, and writing style are emphasized over individual thoughtfulness or creativity in problem solving.

Alternatives to "secondary source" research papers have been explored by Gordon (1999) and Schack (1993), both of whom advocate authentic research projects that involve students in gathering information from "primary sources," and address real-world problems "of personal interest for which there is no known answer" (29). Within Schack's meaning, information seeking becomes data collection, and information-seeking skills become data collection skills. Within an authentic context, interviewing, surveying, observing, and analyzing documents—which are not usually included among information skills taught in elementary and secondary schools—are important additions to the more usual tasks and skills related to information handling. In addition, Schack recommends instruction in the fundamentals of "original" research design.

The use of "authentic" research assignments is consistent with current trends in education that center on experiential learning. Examples of experiential learning include inquiry or discovery learning (Kuhlthau, Heinström, & Todd 2008), situated learning (Brown, Collins, & Duguid 1989), cognitive flexibility and cognitive apprenticeship (Collins, Brown, & Newman 1989), anchored learning, and problem-based learning. There are a growing number of national, Web-based centers that feature the papers of middle and high school students involved in researching real-world problems and issues in health, community life, and the like.

Gordon's (1999) study involved a group of tenth graders in an action research project as part of "a performance-based assessment task, including rubrics, student journals, and peer editing." The goal of Gordon's action research was to "elevate the quality of students' research papers" and "to heighten the awareness of teachers and librarians in their roles as reflective practitioners who use the same research methods they are teaching . . . to assess the design of" research assignments. In the process, it was hoped that students would also learn the difference between report preparation and original research. Essentially, the researcher wanted to know the following:

> [C]an students successfully use primary research methods to collect their own data? What if teachers and librarians designed research assignments that distinguished between information and data—that is, between fact and ideas recorded in books and electronic sources—as evidence or data collected firsthand by the student researcher? What if teachers and librarians became reflective practitioners who saw the research assignments as an opportunity to . . . evaluate and revise the learning task?

Before beginning their research projects, students in Gordon's (1999) study attended a 10-session "advisory" class to learn the fundamentals of action research: research design, proposal writing, research questions, research methods, and data collection and analysis. Results of the Gordon's research indicated that students need time to write and reflect; they also require instruction in the correct form and use of citations and practice in Internet searching and keyword use. The study also provided additional evidence that student research is an iterative, idiosyncratic, and messy process that involves students in rereading background information at various times and modifying research questions as the task unfolds. Importantly, the authentic nature of the "research assignment raised the level of appreciation of teachers for the complexity of independent student work" (18). For this reason, Gordon asserts that presenting the research process as a simple and finite sequence of steps is not helpful for students or teachers. As with more conventional research assignments, Gordon also advises that students build "prior knowledge of the topic" as preparation for authentic research tasks.

Gordon's (1999) study also revealed student preferences when undertaking research. Most often mentioned were additional time to complete the task during the school day; timing the project earlier in the school year; in-school assistance; the use of forms, charts, and organizers in keeping track of sources; assistance with database and Internet searching strategies; and assistance with formulating research questions.

Competencies for Independent Research in the School Library

Kuhlthau (2001) states that "teacher-librarians play a vital role in creating inquiry learning that prepares students for work, citizenship and daily living in the

Information Age." She also notes that "[i]nquiry shifts the focus of learning from a right or wrong answer to the process of learning and investigation" (AASL 2009a, 25). For his part, Loertscher (1996) describes the "information literate student" as "an avid reader," a critical and creative thinker, and "an interested learner" who uses technology skillfully and investigates, organizes, and communicates what is learned in a responsible manner (192). In many respects, this description provides a useful introduction to thinking about program development in school media centers, for it taps into the competencies identified by Doyle (1994) and Irving (1985) as frameworks for the "information skills curriculum." Among those identified by Doyle are the abilities to identity the information problem or need; formulate strategies to guide the search process; locate appropriate information sources: read, use, and evaluate the relevance of the information obtained; and apply the information created to new understandings of the topic in solving the problem or carrying out the task. According to Irving, student learners must also be critical thinkers, competent readers, perceptive questioners, resourceful information searchers, skilled information handlers, and accomplished presenters.

Taken together, Loertscher (1996), Doyle (1994), and Irving (1985) have identified a range of skills that not only inform information skills instruction but also are, as Irving argues, the same skills "inherently present in all learning tasks" (23) and "decision-making activities" (24). For this reason, their integration within curricular units, subject areas, and extracurricular problem solving is both natural and useful. Callison (1994) has challenged school librarians to take advantage of the important relationship between critical thinking and information skills instruction by moving beyond activities that "support, supplement, or enhance" (47) critical thinking to initiate programs and assignments that teach this important skill by placing "critical-thinking activities at the forefront of lesson planning" (Bowie 1990, cited in Callison 1994, 46).

It is worth noting that when students are sent to the library to look up "facts" and report them back to the classroom, when they are required to participate in a scavenger hunt, or when they are given skills worksheets that essentially require them to "fill in the blanks" (e.g., questions that ask students to list, name, define, or describe), they are seldom being asked to operate above the knowledge or recall levels. Although these levels of thinking may occasionally be appropriate for the very youngest information seekers, it does little to extend the thinking and learning capacities of older children and youth, nor does it prepare students to engage in "authentic" and independent information-seeking activities upon which, as Walter's (1994) research indicates, their educational success may well depend.

Critical Thinking and Investigative Stance

What is critical thinking? The skills identified by scholars and educators as dimensions of critical thinking include the ability to set goals, to adjust strategies, to carry out tasks, to distinguish fact from opinion, to establish the authority of sources, to assess the accuracy and relevance of information, and to detect bias and underlying assumptions in data found in information sources and online. In a very real sense, these are the sorts of skills that support information literacy and information literacy instruction.

The positive relationship between critical and metacognitive thinking and student achievement and school success has been established in the research literature

(Lavoie & Good 1988). Indeed, as Norris (1985) suggests, critical thinking requires students "to assess their own view" as well as the views of others, "to seek alternatives [and to] make inferences" (44); and Mancall, Aaron, and Walker (1986) argue that critical thinking skills are essential to success in developing "insight and facility in structuring successful approaches to solving information needs" (22).

Helping Students Develop Evaluation Skills

How can evaluation skills be taught? What strategies can school librarians use to encourage their development? These are significant questions, and professionals intent on improving the educational value of their information skills programs must find practical answers. Many scholars agree that critical thinking can neither arise in nor exist separate from subject matter and experience and that it involves a complex of "considerations" including the "disposition to think critically" (Norris 1985, 44). For example, Bodi (1992) has suggested that critical thinking is the thread that ties curricular concerns for course content and the process aspects of information seeking firmly together; Craver (1989) reminds us that "substantive knowledge of the particular subject" (13) is not only the result of critical thinking but also its basis. Moreover, this theorist asserts that "reading, writing, speaking, and group interaction play important roles in the development of higher order thinking" and "techniques such as questioning, tutoring, oral recitation, group discussion, and writing are successful in improving the ability of students to think critically" (16).

Evaluation skills are at the highest of Bloom's thinking levels and are essential components of literacies of all kinds. Bloom et al. (1956, cited in Fitzgerald 1999, 3) describe evaluation in this way:

> Evaluation is the making of judgments about the value, for some purpose, of ideas, works, solutions, methods, material, etc. It involves the use of criteria as well as standards for appraising the extent to which particulars are accurate, effective, economical, or satisfying. The judgments may be either quantitative or qualitative, and the criteria may be either those determined by the student or those which are given to him. (185)

Within the context of an information search task, the criteria relevant to evaluation of information "might include aspects of information quality such as objective content, sufficient depth, and clear articulation (Eisenberg & Small, 1993, Taylor, 1986)" (Fitzgerald 1999, 3).

As important as evaluation is in so many instructional contexts, it is not an easy skill for many students to develop. According to Fitzgerald (1999), knowledge of the domain, knowledge of the processes of decision making, the context, the culture, the amount of time to devote, the nature of the problem, the willingness to expend effort, the level of support ("instruction, practice and cues"), developmental level, and educational (or reading comprehension) level all have a bearing on a student's ability to evaluate information.

Fitzgerald's (1999) study highlights the difficulty many students have in evaluating information. Her extensive literature review led her to consider evaluation in terms of the subskills involved: understanding task goals, a willingness to undertake the task, recognizing some aspect of the information found that "signals" a problem (e.g., surprise, puzzlement, or ambiguity), and deliberation. Deliberation is itself a complex process that involves a process of thinking through the information in a logical way and then making a decision as to its value or truth. Since children have a tendency to trust adults as authority figures and often believe that " 'there is an absolute correspondence between what is seen or perceived and what is' (pp. 47–48)" (King & Kitchener 1994, quoted in Fitzgerald 1999), evaluating information created by adults can be bewildering. For this reason, many, "elementary school-aged children are particularly unlikely" to question the information they find unless prompted to do so (Markman 1979, cited in Fitzgerald 1999). Having said that, studies by McGregor (1994a) and Pitts (1994, cited in Fitzgerald 1999) noted the failure in older students to consider the quality of the information they encountered. Carey (1985, cited in Fitzgerald 1999) ascribes this failure to a lack of domain knowledge "rather than an immature way of thinking."

Fitzgerald (1999) believes that school librarians can play an important role in helping children with evaluation tasks. In addition to noting the fit between children's developmental levels and the cognitive demands of research tasks, school librarians can challenge students to think more deeply about information and the information task and create structures to assist children as they learn the important subskills necessary for effective evaluation. They can also call children's attention to the following: the influence emotion may have on decision making or evaluation; the "flawed reasoning" that can result when they apply their subjective beliefs and biases in making judgments about new information; and the tendency to believe information that they encounter either first or last or that supports rather than challenges beliefs they already hold ("confirmatory bias").

Finally, Fitzgerald (1999) makes a case for teaching evaluation within the context of ongoing classroom activities. "Few topics could be more boring or incomprehensible to children than critical thinking or argumentation taught out of context," she writes. "The best approach is to choose a subject area of current controversial interest to the student in a given class and integrate the suggested strategies into a unit about that topic." Fitzgerald recommends the following teaching strategies (see Table 8.5): teaching evaluation strategies one or a few at a time and spread out over a number of sessions, providing specific examples, teaching subskills involved in the evaluation, providing practice with well-defined and ill-defined problems, clarifying

Table 8.5
Fitzgerald's (1999) Strategies for Teaching Evaluation Skills

- Teach a few strategies at a time
- Reinforce learning through repetition and practice over time
- Provide specific examples
- Teach the subskills involved in evaluation tasks
- Use well-defined and ill-defined problems
- Discuss the types of biases that students might encounter
- Practice arguing both sides of controversial topics
- Provide a variety of research opportunities
- Involve children directly in the production of media

the biases that might be involved in information texts, providing practice in arguing both sides of controversial questions, assigning a variety of research tasks on a regular basis, and involving children in the production of a variety of media.

Reading Skills

Research in the literature of LIS and education consistently acknowledges the importance of reading (Krashen 1993, 2003) and reading comprehension skills as essential to developing competence in information seeking and learning (Kulleseid 1986). The selection of reading materials that reflect the experience and reading levels of student learners has always been an important aspect of school librarianship. Another is the creation of library activities that enrich and extend that experience. Research in reading suggests a number of activities that school librarians can use in helping youngsters increase reading performance and comprehension. For example, Tierney and Cunningham (1984) recommend the use of prereading activities to stimulate student interest, to focus attention, and to activate student thinking. Tailoring the reading assignment "to the child's level of understanding," assisting the learner to focus on the main ideas in the passage, and promoting readers' awareness of their own comprehension by asking questions and activating their "schemata" in prereading exercises have been suggested by Baker and Brown (1984). These strategies help students maintain a focus, reflect on the new information, and relate this information to the "knowledge they already" possess (375). In some instances, "advance organizers, structured overview, story preview, use of text adjuncts, pretesting, and setting objectives" (Kulleseid 1986, 43–44) have helped students improve reading comprehension. In addition, Kulleseid recommends asking questions about content, visualizing narratives through "diagrams and pictorial representation" (44), reading aloud, using study guides, and facilitating group discussions as techniques that promote understanding.

Stimulating student interest and providing "interesting reading materials" are also essential prereading activities since, as Wigfield and Asher (1984) suggest, they can help students overcome their "insufficient knowledge base" (375) and improve reading performance. Yet McGill-Frantzen, Allington, Yokoi, and Brooks (1999) assert that the availability of books in the classroom and library are "necessary but not sufficient" in promoting literacy. Training teachers to create inviting book displays, read aloud, plan literacy activities, and provide encouragement resulted in "a richer print environment" than merely providing print materials without these strategies. Perhaps ironically, these are just the kinds of strategies that school librarians learn in their children's literature and services courses in library school!

Writing activities can also improve students' reading comprehension, especially when these activities help focus the students' attention and extend the time they spend on reading tasks. Among the most valuable writing exercises are summarizing, "abstract writing," "outlining, paraphrasing, note taking and writing paragraph headings" (Stosky 1983, cited in Craver 1989, 15). Reading strategies that have proved especially useful for student learning in information contexts are skimming (Kulleseid 1986) and note taking (Lavoie & Good 1988). Although no one strategy has been proven consistently superior for all students, Nagel (1972, cited in Craver 1989) found that "students showed greater comprehension when they summarized paragraphs in a single sentence" than when they "wrote nothing" (15).

Summarizing information is a difficult skill[2] for some students to learn, but it is also an information skill that can and should be taught in an "information curriculum."

According to Brown and Day (1983, cited in Baker & Brown 1984), useful strategies for instruction include teaching students how to delete information that is redundant or peripheral; how to create abstract or superordinate categories for objects, events, and activities; and how to look for topic sentences as clues to the main idea.

Although reading well is certainly an essential skill for information seeking, the ability to read critically is required if students are to make judgments about the relevance, point of view, authority, and bias of the sources they encounter. As Goodman (1976, cited in Baker & Brown 1984) notes, critical reading is often inadequately taught and seldom practiced, and the lack of this important skill poses "a barrier to [student] development of an adequate repertoire of study skills" (372). This lack of adequate instruction in reading critically perhaps explains why the first common belief listed in the *Standards for the 21st Century Learner* (AASL 2007) is "reading is a window to the world" (1):

> Reading is a foundational skill for learning, personal growth, and enjoyment. The degree to which students can read and understand text in all formats (e.g., picture, video, print) and all contexts is a key indicator of success in school and in life. As a lifelong learning skill, reading goes beyond decoding and comprehension to interpretation and development of new understandings. (1)

The emphasis placed by the profession's leadership and consequently by school librarians "in the trenches" on the skill of reading may perhaps help to bridge the critical reading gap that has long been the rule rather than the exception for students.

Strategies for Independent Information Seeking

If students are going to develop the skills in searching that will enable them to find the most pertinent information to meet their information needs in everyday life and in school-related tasks, they will have to develop more sophisticated techniques than serendipitous browsing. Bates, Ellis, and Foster have developed models and strategies based on their observations of real-world searching. Although most researchers encounter the works of these scholars in undergraduate or graduate school programs, there is no reason why they cannot be introduced to middle and high school students with good effect.

Searching Strategies: Bates's Idea Tactics

Contemporary LIS scholars and practitioners hold that information literacy is a complex cognitive process that must be taught if students are to develop this important life skill. Bates (1979b, 1989) has created a useful framework for information seeking by observing how successful searchers seek information. According to Bates (1989), in real-world settings, information searchers may begin broadly and then narrow the focus of their inquiries, or they may change their focus entirely as they encounter information or the lack of it along the way. Bates has described as "berry-picking" these sorts of searches, which seem to evolve over time in response to information as each additional piece is retrieved and reviewed. In fact, searchers who engage in this kind of process may not wish an overview of a research domain at all, nor desire a wide range of sources; instead, they employ a "serialist" (Pask 1972, cited in Eisenberg & Berkowitz 1990) approach, searching for "just enough" information to answer their specific information need or research question.

According to Bates (1979a), information providers can assist users in their searches by suggesting or teaching strategies to use when searchers get "stuck" or when their search strategies do not produce the desired results. Bates's "idea tactics" is a facilitation model comprised of "heuristics," or "rules of thumb," for searching. These tactics can help learners think more clearly (e.g., think, brainstorm, meditate, consult, rescue, and wander), alter the direction of the search (e.g., catch, break, breach, and/or reframe), or think more creatively (e.g., notice, jolt, change, focus, dilate, skip, and stop) (see Figure 8.1). The model is of use to school librarians in the wide range of specific suggestions it offers for both novice and expert searchers. "Thinking" refers to planning ahead in order to save time and energy later. "Brainstorming" helps students generate new ideas, new search terms, and new sources and types of sources; these can prove very useful in the presearch phases as well as later on, if the search stalls or if the beginning strategy is blocked.

"Meditating" may help students use both sides of their brains in adding imagination and hunches to logic in planning the search strategy. "Consulting" as a tactic accepts the validity and value of discussing the research task with others and is a forthright admission that no one person, neither student nor teacher, can know everything. In light of Solomon's (1994) finding that youngsters may not think to ask for help, reminding students that consulting presents a viable option seems wise. "Rescuing" is an effort to make sure that any early frustration or failure a student experiences initially does not result in the premature closure of an otherwise promising search.

"Wandering" recognizes that quite frequently ideas may be generated as one pursues various resources and materials if only the researcher is open to the possibilities. Allowing for this sort of flexibility may spark interesting ideas and directions. "Catching" oneself is the awareness that an approach is no longer yielding the desired results. "Breaking" suggests that when one line of approach is not working, it is time to risk going off in another direction or perhaps searching in a different way. "Breaching" requires the searcher to get out of one set of domain resources and into another, for example, to search a different website or a different database. "Reframing" asks a student to take another look at the question that is being posed and to ask it in a different way. "Noticing" indicates that students must appreciate what they learn about the topic or question as they move through the search and to make use of the new information to enrich the scope or the depth of their approach. By "jolting," students change their points of view, perhaps by considering how the question might be addressed by different groups, in different formats, or in other domain fields. "Changing" requires students to try new terms, new types of sources, and different disciplines when current ones fail to provide the needed information.

"Focusing" asks students to narrow the current search or the topic itself, perhaps by looking at or considering only one part of it. Limiting the scope of the topic by specific time, era, or epoch; by a specific group of people; or by a particular geographic location are all useful ways to reframe a topic in a more targeted way. "Dilating" calls on students to do the reverse: to expand the question or the search, perhaps by looking at the larger issues involved in the research question or by taking a more general approach to the topic. "Skipping" asks students to move around in a topic and to look at different aspects or subtropics involved in order to get a handle on the "big picture." "Stopping" acknowledges the fact that fatigue plays a role in any search situation and that in some instances stopping for now and coming back fresh on another day is the best strategy possible.

Figure 8.1
Searching Strategies Based on Bates's (1979a) Idea Tactics

Thinking	Thinking about the search will generate new ideas
Brainstorming	Getting ideas and considering alternative ideas can enrich understanding and approaches
Mediating	Thinking logically/rationally and creatively/intuitively activates both sides of the brain
Consulting	Talking ideas over with others provides valuable information and feedback for ideas
Rescuing	Persistence can prevent the premature abandonment of a useful approach
Wandering	Browsing in a variety of resources can help stir the imagination and ignite thinking
Catching	Realizing that the current approach isn't working or that a mistake has been made in a citation
Breaking	Doing something different perhaps searching in a different way
Breaching	Considering a different subject area or domain, database, or discipline when a given search strategy is exhausted
Reframing	Reexamining the question to get rid of distortions or erroneous assumptions
Noticing	Attending to what is being learned about the topic as information is encountered
Jolting	Changing the point of view by looking at the question as it has been addressed for different age groups or in different formats or in different disciplines
Changing	Breaking whatever patterns are in use in terms of the types of sources, the disciplines, and the terms being used in searching
Focusing	Narrowing the search or the concept or looking at only one part of it
Dilating	Expanding the search to widen the focus or considering larger issues
Skipping	Looking at another aspect of the same topic or considering subtopics as a way to view the whole
Stopping	Doing something else while your mind continues to work on the problem

Ellis's Research Strategies

Ellis (1989) has identified "starting," "chaining," "browsing," "differentiating," "monitoring," and "extracting" as useful search strategies to assist searchers in pre-search planning and in locating sources and finding information during the search process itself. "Starting" activities employed at the beginning of the search include identifying key articles and key authors in bibliographies, abstracts, indexes, and catalogs. "Chaining" refers to a strategy for using citations as clues to other information on the same topic. In "backward chaining," searchers follow up citations listed at the end of the documents they initially find; "forward chaining" involves the perusal of citation indexes to find articles or research based on the original study or publication. In these ways, relevant information on the same subject can be located in an efficient manner. "Browsing," within Ellis's meaning, is a sort of semidirected searching of resources and books in an area of potential interest. Using differences between sources as an indication of their nature and quality is a strategy that calls for searchers to "differentiate" among the alternatives to select those that are likely to be the most useful. Ellis suggests "monitoring," which requires that searchers check to see that the most recently published information in a field is not overlooked. Finally, "extracting" involves the systematic perusal of each source to locate information of interest. Any or all of these strategies can be of use to both novice and seasoned searchers and should become part of the instructional regimen of an information skills program.

An article by Meho and Tibbo (2003) describes a study following up on Ellis's (1989) pre-Web research on information behavior and suggests some additions to Ellis's model: "accessing, networking, verifying, and information managing" (583). "Accessing" acknowledges the many strategies that information seekers employ in obtaining relevant resources identified through starting, chaining, browsing, monitoring, and extracting activities as well as the problems searchers may encounter in acquiring relevant documents and sources. "Accessing" specifically addresses activities, issues, and problems inherently a part of information seeking outside major research libraries. "Networking" activities, once the terrain reserved for invisible colleges of scholars, are now possible through access to the Internet and Web 2.0 technologies, such as social networking sites. "Verifying" deals directly with problems related to the reliability, accuracy, and authenticity of information that seekers locate on the Internet. Finally, "information managing" involves the arrangement and storage of information located during a search. "Although," as the authors point out, information management "processes are the exact opposite of information searching or gathering activities, they are activities that have a significant role in enhancing information retrieval" (584).

The elements involved in information seeking first identified by Ellis (1989) and expanded by Meho and Tibbo (2003) are not sequential; for this reason, the latter have suggested a four-stage recursive model that groups the activities relative to various stages in the information-seeking process: searching, accessing, processing, and ending. "Searching" activities include starting, chaining, browsing, monitoring, differentiating, extracting, and networking. "Accessing" involves decision making with regard to direct and indirect resources. "Processing" activities might include chaining, extracting, differentiating, verifying, and information managing as well as analyzing and synthesizing information and initial writing activity. "Ending" involves the completion of search tasks and projects.

Foster's Model

Foster (2004) has created a model for information seeking that differs in dramatic ways from those considered in this text and familiar to most school librarians. Based on in-depth interviews of academic researchers involved in interdisciplinary information-seeking activities, the model takes into account the complexities of researching in online as well as print-based collections within a framework of personal abilities and preferences and situational constraints. As we have seen, Kuhlthau's (2004) process model includes cognitive, behavioral, and affective dimensions and in its basic form does not explicitly consider context. Bates's (1979a, 1979b) models offer powerful alternatives to employ while searching but ignore the situation that launched or indeed surrounds the search; they also make no allowances for the role that others may play in search activities. Ellis's (1989) model presents valuable techniques for search success but does not look at the process holistically. Foster's model addresses some of these limitations in potentially useful ways and also describes behaviors that, although characteristic of interdisciplinary research approaches, also have applications within the context of more mundane and everyday search activities that may or may not involve the creation of a research project or product. Given that contemporary teenagers rely so heavily on the Web in information seeking related to their own continuing interests, this model might well assist these opportunistic and serendipitous searchers. (See Figure 8.2.)

Within Foster's (2004) framework, information seeking is approached holistically, as nonlinear and nonsequential sets of activities. In diagramming his model, Foster presents a set of three nested squares to show that a person's thinking takes place within a context that has cognitive, internal, and external dimensions. Cognitive contexts relate to the searcher's personal learning styles and preferences, cognitive abilities, mental flexibility and openness to new ideas and resources, the ability to look at topics and problems from a variety of perspectives, and the ability to bring disparate ideas together to further understandings or identify new questions and directions. This model also aligns with the dispositions or "habits of mind" outlined in the new *Standards for the 21st Century Learning in Action* (AASL 2008, 40).

Internal context elements include the searcher's experience, prior knowledge of the topic or issue, understanding, feelings of uncertainty or confidence, self-perception, perception of the information need, and so on. Issues related to an "external" context include the amount of time that the person can spend on the search task, the nature and goals of the search, the organization of the information, the possibilities that exist for networking, and so on.

For Foster (2004), searching itself revolves around activities that he labels "orienting," "opening," and "consolidating." Orienting activities within Foster's framework involve the searcher in identifying key themes, determining the necessary steps to take in getting a search under way, choosing resources, choosing a focus, mapping out a course of action, recognizing what one knows and what gaps exist in necessary knowledge, and so on as preliminaries to beginning a search itself. Orienting activities do not end when openings begin but may be revisited any number of times over the course of an information-seeking episode.

For Foster (2004), openings do not mark the beginning moves in a search or exploration action. Rather, they are characterized by the choosing of key words, the selection of useful sources, and the undertaking of searching behaviors (e.g., networking, chaining, and so on), which might include simply browsing. Consolidation activities are strategies the searcher uses in deciding when enough information has been located and will often include sifting through the information for relevant items and then drawing some conclusions based the information. Thinking and writing are two options that can occur during consolidation.

Many school-age information seekers can be thought of as predisciplinary in that their inexperience in searching and their often superficial understandings of a

Figure 8.2
Foster's (2004) Framework for Information Seeking

- **Dimensions of the Information-Seeking Context:**
  - *Cognitive*: learning-style preference, mental ability and flexibility, and analytical and synthesis skills
  - *Internal*: prior experience, prior knowledge, self-awareness and self-confidence
  - *External*: time available, research goals, availability and organization of information, etc.
- **Information-Seeking Activities**:
  - *Orienting*: identifying themes, finding a focus, determining strategies, assessing personal knowledge state, etc.
  - *Opening:* preparing to search, choosing key words and resources, searching for information, etc.
  - *Consolidating*: deciding when enough information is "enough," reviewing and reading information found, selecting relevant portions, drawing conclusions, writing up search results, etc.

topic place them at a disadvantage when engaging in information projects that have the development of subject content learning as a goal. Orientation activities in Foster's (2004) model resemble the kinds of presearch activities that LIS researchers have found so helpful for novice researchers. Foster's construct of openings also creates a space within which novice searchers can enact orientation plans and maps and begin to move forward in their investigations Consolidation activities, which call on searchers to read, review, make sense of, and take stock of where they are in a search process, are also useful strategies to the novice student researcher.

Information-Handling Skills

Providing support to students in tasks involving information use is an important aspect of the school librarian's job. Some of the same strategies that assist learners in comprehending what they read are also useful in helping them become competent in handling the information they find. These include skimming, underlining, highlighting, paraphrasing, and note taking (Irving 1985). Although outlining has been found useful in focusing attention, Bretzing, Kulhavy, and Caterino (1987, cited in Thomas 1993) indicate that activities such as summarizing, "cognitive monitoring," and note taking are more often "associated with significant gains in achievement" (577).

Students frequently find narrowing a topic or finding a frame very difficult. In fact, Irving (1985) regards this step in the information-seeking process as "the most sophisticated skill" (41) and suggests that it is made even more problematic when one is compelled to do it in the absence of deep understanding of the topic or field. Irving suggests that breaking down the task and the topic is exceedingly important. "Unless we know clearly what we are looking for," she writes, "finding out" about a topic may be virtually "impossible" (42) even when students have an opportunity to choose their own topics.

Knowing what to do with the information is also a critical task (Wesley 1991). Until constructivist scholars called attention to the importance of information seeking as a process, a great deal of student time was devoted to the location and access of resources. With the shift in paradigm has come the acknowledgment that the use of the information gathered is the most critical aspect of information seeking (Haycock 1991). In a very real sense, it is through the arrangement, organization, and presentation of information (first as an outline, sketch, or diagram and then as a finished paper or project) that students create a synthesis and repackage the information in meaningful and "learningful" ways.

Irving (1985) has conceptualized steps in this important task as "presentation skills": organizing information, ordering and arranging it, outlining the project, writing it up, creating sentences, creating paragraphs and writing topic sentences, editing, and proofreading. Information handling also includes attention to the appropriate use of quotations and the proper form and use of citations and footnotes. In this way, students learn to give credit to their sources in an intellectually honest manner. All these are skills that school librarians are eminently qualified to help students acquire.

Information Overload: Pitfalls and Problems

Akin's (1998) research considers the issue of information overload as a problem for youngsters engaged in information-seeking activities. In this context, information overload may occur when too many topics are offered as research alternatives, too many resources are suggested as relevant, or too much information is retrieved as a result of information seeking. Akin's study sought to learn through survey data how fourth and eighth graders in two Texas public schools felt about information overload and what they did about it. It was Akin's view that "knowing how the child feels can help the librarian be more empathetic. But knowing what the child does allows the school media specialist to respond with instruction" (6). Particularly, Akin was looking for strategies that students used and the relationship of gender to the overload experience. Results indicated that 80 percent of students surveyed reported the experience of information overload, with girls and younger students "more likely than boys" and older students "to have felt overloaded" (4). Techniques reported by students in easing overload included selecting a few items from all those available, "filtering" and "chunking" the information, or linking "large amounts of information into some common shape" (e.g., "a teacher-supplied outline").

Feelings reported by fourth-grade students in Akin's (1998) study included confusion, frustration, depression, anger, and physical distress ("bulging," "bursting," " exploding," "headache," "fatigue"). As Akin notes, "These visceral responses speak to the degree of disillusionment or disappointment with the information at hand and the expectations of the child." Eighth graders experienced similar reactions to overload, although the expression of their reactions tended to the vulgar in boys and to reflect stress, tension, and panic in girls. "The eighth graders reported additional feelings of being stuffed and bored." Akin concluded that some kinds of inattention and acting out, swearing, or physical ailments necessitating trips to the school nurse might be the result of overload.

Although limited in terms of the number of students and the self-report method involved in survey research, Akin's (1998) study is interesting in that it indicates that overload does, indeed, affect children and that admitting and discussing the overload issue and possible strategies for coping with this syndrome are an important part of library and information skills sessions. Kuhlthau (1999) describes this feeling as "the dip" in confidence that searchers experience when encountering new and confusing information; "Advances in information systems that open access to a vast assortment of resources has ... in many cases ... intensified the sense of confusion and uncertainty." This is especially true when information retrieval systems overwhelm "the user with everything all at once, rather than an offering a few well-chosen introductory pieces for initial exploration."

Taking the availability of information into account in structuring lessons and information tasks also seems reasonable. According to Akin (1998), it may be useful to teach students to reduce the number of types of materials to be considered, change the topic, seek assistance, and take a break as ways to cope when the demands of the task overwhelm them. Brainstorming such coping techniques in advance would also assist learners "identify the overload reduction strategies on their own, learn more about manipulating information products, and adopt a proactive response to information overload." Gordon (2000) has identified an effective presearch strategy that helps children cope with overload: concept mapping. In fact, Gordon's informants indicated experiencing less overload when concept maps were used. Gordon indicated that this technique is one way to provide an overview of both general and specific terms that describe the topic.

Conclusion

As previously noted, Eadie (1990, quoted in Sauer 1995) has voiced his concern over the move by librarians to take on the responsibility for creating programs to teach information literacy skills in academic libraries. "I'm not sure," he has written, that "we should be 'educating' students but I am sure we should answer their questions. I think that we should dismantle barriers rather than train people to climb over them" (137–38). While few would argue with the goal of simplifying systems to enhance student abilities in using the library as independently as possible, most school librarians would assert that today's students encounter far more difficulties in searching for information than those posed exclusively by the idiosyncrasies of information systems and the ambiguities of the Web. In fact, research indicates that since students frequently lack an understanding of the research process (Kuhlthau 1993b; Pitts 1995) as a whole, they both need and would welcome assistance in understanding the processes required in seeing their projects through to completion. Moreover, Eadie's comments appear to reflect a view that considers information as an objective entity and research as fact-finding rather than the constructivist view of student investigation as a set of learning activities that require students to make sense of information as they seek evidence to support a personal perspective.

Mancall, Lodish, and Springer (1992) have asserted that "the task of the school is to be sure that students leave grade 12 ready for the information-rich environment in which they will live" (527). If we accept this statement as a goal as well as a challenge, then as educators we must take the responsibility for instructing students in information seeking, information handling, and information use. Eadie's (1990) angst serves a useful purpose in that it draws attention to the tension between service and instructional models of professional intervention that is created when we assume that the two reflect disparate and mutually exclusive views of the librarian's proper role. Some might argue that the "service-only model" is appropriate for "knowledge as fact," "while "knowledge as process" (Buckland 1983) requires more intensive levels of support and instruction. Certainly, where the "barriers" to system access have been removed, the student can concentrate on the attainment of content and process skills and, perhaps more importantly, learn to ask the right questions rather than to "find" the right answers (Keefer 1993, cited in Sauer 1995). However, constructivist approaches to education—particularly in terms of modeling and coaching, demonstrating, and scaffolding—represent the bridging or the blending of the service/instruction dichotomy, preserving the best intentions of both in ways that support the development of student competence, independence, and learning. When constructivist environments are well established, school libraries can develop into arenas for posing questions, discussing ideas, and pursuing understandings, thus becoming places (both physical and virtual) where students can come to solve the sorts of ill-defined problems (Carey 1998) that arise in the real world.

The realization that information skills are "survival skills" (Irving 1985, 115) and essential for the development of lifelong learners created a sense of urgency at the turn of the new century among many library professionals responsible for planning programs of instruction. Perhaps for this reason, LIS theorists sought to change the terms we use to describe the skills students need to develop. Breivik (1989), for example, insisted that using the terms "bibliographic instruction" and "library instruction" only perpetuated the notion that what goes on in the library is separate from what goes on in the classroom and indeed in life, effectively rendering contributions the library can make to student learning peripheral or superfluous. For this reason, the profession began using the term "information literacy skills" to describe more accurately what we actually want students to learn as a result of our intervention (Irving 1985). The concept of multiple literacies skills—"including digital, visual, textual, and technological" (AASL 2007, 2)—has since emerged to accompany information literacy skills in order to incorporate those abilities that are now necessary for learning in media-centered environments.

Carey (1998) claims that the differences inherent in the terms "library skills" and "information literacy" are philosophical and substantive, denoting two distinct wings of cognitive psychology: the objectivist wing and the constructivist wing. In Carey's view, the now defunct scope and sequence approach to instruction is objectivist, as is an approach that calls for the sorts of lesson planning frameworks that specify in advance the goals and outcomes of instruction, the skills required for the implementation of the activity, the ability levels and needs of student learners, and the tasks to be undertaken in implementing the lesson. On the contrary, constructivist approaches, including inquiry learning, focus on problem solving and call on the students to struggle through the complexities of the problem and themselves to come up with the "tactics and strategies" (7) they will need in resolving research questions for which no single answer exists.

As is evident, the instructional design involved in the case of constructivist lesson planning is entirely different from the sort of preplanning to which school librarians in the 20th century had become accustomed. Carey describes this planning in terms of "a learning environment" or "problem scenario" (8) for which the instructor furnishes the guidelines. Because there is value in both approaches to instruction, Carey articulates a middle ground that calls for the teaching and learning of a given model in constructing understandings from a variety of sources. "It appears that the approach to learning the problem-solving process is quite objectivist in its design, while the approach to learning from a variety of sources is quite constructivist" (8).

Finally, contemporary understandings of teaching and learning rely on theories that recognize "the inescapably social nature of cognitive development and of cognition itself" (Belmont 1989, 142). For this reason, school librarians in particular need to rethink what constitutes instruction and adopt roles that meet the exigencies of the task and the needs of specific groups of learners. Balancing the roles of instructor and coach, of expert and peer, and of partner and authority will be challenging and exciting. Knowing students and observing "their responses to instruction" (143) will be especially important in assessing learning and planning for further instructional interventions.

Notes

1. Delpit (1995) has taken exception to a blanket approach that values the use of process-oriented models over or at the expense of student-created products as evidence of learning. Arguing that diversity in the classroom demands diversity in instructional strategies, Delpit argues that "teachers do students no service to suggest, even implicitly, that 'product' is not important" (31). "There is little research data supporting the major tenets of process approaches over other forms of literacy instruction," Delpit writes, "and virtually no evidence that such approaches are more efficacious for children of color. . . . In this country, students will be judged on their products regardless of the process they utilized to achieve it. And that product, based as it is on the specific codes of a particular culture, is more readily produced when the directives of how to produce it are made explicit" (28). Although she is discussing the emphasis on process over product in contexts other than information seeking, Delpit's concerns have important implications for planning information literacy skills instruction in today's ethnically diverse schools.

2. According to Delpit (1995), some Native Americans may experience difficulties in summarizing tasks based on a community-based "prohibition against speaking for someone else" (170). It was apparently for this reason that college students in a study by Basham (cited in Delpit) offered their opinions of "various works rather than the summaries of the authors' words" (170) they were assigned to create.

In an updated edition of *Other People's Children* (Delpit & Kohl 2006), the authors argue that "giving voice to alternative worldviews is essential if the skill needs of minority children are to be met. These include knowledge of "discourse patterns, interactional styles, and spoken and written language codes that will allow them success in the larger society" (29). Delpit does not reject process skills, nor "advocate a simplistic 'basic skills' approach for children outside the culture of power. . . . Rather [she suggests] that schools must provide these children the context that other families from a different cultural orientation provide at home. This does not mean separating children according to family background, but instead ensuring that each classroom incorporate strategies appropriate for all children in its confines (3).

Given the continuous emphasis on process approaches in school library instruction, it is essential that school librarians honor diverse learning styles and skill needs in meaningful ways. This will require involving black teachers, administrators, librarians and parents in discussions involving the library curriculum objectives and instructional strategies. "Cross cultural communication is key, and the white educational establishment needs to take the initiative in opening up meaningful discussion" (Delpit & Kohl, 46).

9 Evaluating Library Services and Programs

It may be that by shifting the paradigm of education reform and teaching from one modeled after the clocklike character of the assembly line into one that is closer to the studio or innovative science laboratory might provide us with a vision that better suits the capacities and the futures of the students we teach.

—Elliot Eisner (2004)

National concerns for evaluating every aspect of the educational enterprise have increased pressures on public school librarians to demonstrate their contributions to the creation of information literate students and links between an "information age" literacy skills curriculum and student achievement. Thus, librarians who were in earlier times preoccupied with creating collections of a certain size and programming that reached a certain number of students are today focusing their attention on ensuring that outcomes are learned and competencies developed. Within such a context, assessment has become a priority. This chapter considers contemporary approaches to educational assessment, in particular as they relate to outcomes-based educational initiatives and authenticity. It also describes the evolution of school library evaluation, the roles for librarians in assessment, the continuing role of standards for library media programs in recent publications of the American Association of School Librarians (AASL), and the research findings related to library and information skills instruction. A concluding section summarizes Todd's views on the implications of school library research for instructional programming, student achievement, and lifelong learning.

Concern for Student Achievement

The claim that American public schools are no longer graduating students capable of competing in the global workplace has led to widespread demands for "school improvement" from worried parents, taxpayers, and politicians. Site-based management, charter schools, magnet schools, teacher accountability, and school choice are just a few contemporary approaches to restructuring public school systems; at the same time, educators have instituted instructional reforms related to basic skills, literature- or resource-based instruction, outcomes-based education, early childhood education, and national guidelines for curricular content and student achievement. Increasing teacher competence has also been a focus. Improving instructional expertise through the creation of certification benchmarks has been the goal of the National Board for Professional Teaching Standards, which rewards excellence for accomplished teachers and school librarians.

There is little consensus or research to support the educational efficacy of any of these remedies; indeed, many educators have criticized those who seek a single model for public education designed to cure the nation's disparate educational ills or create "quick-fix" solutions to the complex problems involved in educating 21st century children. Many educators believe that the nationalization of curriculum and curricular objectives is not the answer and claim that performance norms, as exemplified in standardized tests, used as a sort of "national yardstick" of achievement for decades, have in fact not served well the needs of educational systems trying to cope with student diversity, emerging technologies, and public ambivalence. Their views clash with certain federal programs, such as the 2010 Race to the Top initiative, which provides funding for school districts that present evidence of increased levels of student achievement in alignment with national standards. These initiatives fly in the face of views espoused by nationally known educators for decades. For example, in 1993, Stanford professor Elliot Eisner challenged educators to abandon the notion of national standards, which themselves imply a parity across school districts that does not exist, in order to "create schools that excite both teachers and students and provide the conditions that improve the quality of teaching" (23). And that same year, Harold Howe II (1993) opined that "tests have become the tail that wags the dog in the public discussion of educational change in the United States" (9).

Nonetheless, educators continue to invest time and effort in seeking national solutions for problems experienced at the local level. Of course, criticisms aimed at public education in the United States are hardly new; in fact, since the launching of *Sputnik* in 1957, every decade has witnessed similar demonstrations of what amounts to a sort of national educational angst (Madaus & Tan 1994). As Madaus and Tan have succinctly explained, the civil rights movement of the 1960s produced evidence of educational inequities; in the 1970s, national concern focused on an apparent decline in students' SAT scores; in the 1980s, they centered on concerns for quality in *A Nation at Risk*; while in the 1990s, educational pundits predicted the future failure of American students to compete in the global marketplace.

The emphasis on standardized testing peaked in the early years of the new millennium in the federal mandate for higher achievement and greater accountability embedded in the No Child Left Behind Act passed in 2001. In brief, this legislation called for states to create educational standards, implement annual progress testing (for students in grades 3 through 8), and impose penalties on schools whose students failed to meet required state minimums. The program emphasized literacy and reading, early childhood education, and staff development for K–3 teachers in reading instruction. The impact of the No Child Left Behind initiative's emphasis on standardized testing has led to changes in curriculum and instruction and has left library media specialists to find a niche in helping schools achieve goals outlined by the law.

What makes the most recent round of educational criticisms so compelling is that it comes at a time when the schools are struggling to deal effectively with increasingly diverse school populations amid concerns for educational equity in an economic climate that demands not only that schools educate students "better" but also that they do it for "less" (Craver 1995, 13). Given a situation that many consider a crisis of national confidence in public education, it is perhaps not surprising that the methods by which academic achievement and student progress are assessed have also come under scrutiny. In some places, new assessment methods have also been instituted as a way to push school reform agendas, with the idea that if assessment changes, so must instruction and ultimately school culture.

Educational Assessment: The Standardized Testing Imperative

For years, the public has relied on standardized achievement tests to take the educational pulse of virtually every school district in the country. The appeal of this type of testing, which has grown in popularity since its introduction in the early part of the 20th century, lies not only in its comparatively low cost and the administrative ease with which it can be accomplished but also in the apparent capacity of such tests to quantify educational achievement across a playing field that encompasses all students, all subject area content, all grade levels, and all school districts. Indeed, Madaus and Tan (1994) and Killaghan (1992, cited in Madaus & Tan 1994, 4) assert that bureaucratic rather than educational motives frequently drive interest in standardized test scores. So complete has public confidence risen in the results of standardized tests over time that most states have implemented testing programs (O'Neil 1992), and results that were once employed in creating programs of remediation are now being used in making a spate of crucial educational decisions, from the placement of individual students in alternative programs to the renewal of teacher's contracts and the allocation of resources among school districts (Madaus & Tan 1994).

Why have American educators and parents set such store by standardized test results? One answer surely lies in their apparent reliability—that is, the consistency of test results across situations, time, and context. The fact that standardized tests produce numbers, which at least on their face seem so objective, straightforward, and unambiguous, partially explains their appeal as well. However, critics of this type of testing have become increasingly vocal, calling into question the practice of using single-measure "IQ" tests as predictors of ability and challenging, convincingly, the fairness of test items on the grounds of gender, culture, and socioeconomic status. While in at least some cases test makers have made an effort to create instruments which are more culturally "fair," Neuman (1994) argues that such efforts do not ameliorate the deleterious effects of using assessment models that both encourage instructors to "teach to the test" (O'Neil 1992, 15) and skew instructional attention in the direction of basic skills rather than problem solving and critical thinking.

Importantly, Neuman (1994) goes on to assert that the short-answer format of most tests undermines instructional goals by reinforcing the notion that "knowledge consists simply of identifying the one and only correct answer to a question formulated by someone else" (68). In her view, defining learning in this way stands in direct opposition to constructivist theories, which hold that learning is a complex activity involving the creation of personal understandings. Herman (1992) agrees, suggesting further that the "narrowing" of the curriculum to basic skills, the recall of facts, and test preparation activities are particularly detrimental "in schools serving at-risk and disadvantaged students, where there is the most pressure to improve test scores" (74). For this reason, some critics believe that standardized testing may actually exacerbate inequities "for minorities and non-English speakers" (Madaus & Tan 1994, 5).

Outcomes-Based Education

A major initiative in schools across the country since the early 1990s has been the adoption of variations of a model for curricular reform based on the "outcomes" rather than "inputs" of instruction. According to Grover (1994), outcomes-based education focuses attention on the student as a learner and provides a "comprehensive approach to teaching and learning and to instructional management that has its origin in mastery learning and competency-based education" (Burns & Wood, 1990, quoted in Grover 1994, 174). Outcomes differ from behavioral objectives, which created a focus for instruction in the 1970s and 1980s, in their concern for ensuring that students actually acquire the skills that are the focus of instruction; in addition, the "skills" that students are to "master" relate less to *content* than they do to critical thinking and problem solving *processes*. Since outcomes-based educational strategies necessarily call for the assessment of "student progress toward the stated outcomes" (174), the evaluation techniques used to chart this project must be redesigned. In fact, a variety of new assessment models that build in opportunities for the remediation and enrichment deemed necessary for the achievement of skill mastery are clearly required. Grover also suggests "multi-dimensional" assessment strategies that "accommodate the various learning styles" (175) and multiple intelligences of students. Because outcomes-based education moves the emphasis from rote learning of traditional course content to critical thinking, it has proven to be very controversial in some school districts.

Alternative Models for Student Assessment

Attempts to answer the challenges posed by new instructional initiatives such as outcomes-based education have sparked a number of innovative "alternatives," which will undoubtedly continue to shape school efforts to assess student achievement for years to come. A major difference between "alternative assessment "measures and more "traditional" paper-and-pencil testing procedures is that the former allow students to show what they have learned in a variety of different ways. As noted above, these include portfolios of a student's written and graphic work; student projects of various kinds; student journals and "learning logs" that record their responses, thinking, and activities; and oral and dramatic presentations of their work. An important element in this form of assessment is the active involvement of students in planning and designing rubrics, as well as self-evaluation and peer evaluation as part of the learning process. As Maeroff (1991) suggests, with alternative assessment, "students, under the tutelage of their teachers, are trained to provide evidence of their own learning" (274).

Although the creation of alternate models for evaluating students are many and varied, all share an intent to substitute for the indirect means represented by the usual types of test questions some form of direct measurement of learning through the "performance" of what has been learned (Grover et al. 1996). One of the advantages of alternative assessment models that are increasingly finding support in school districts across the country (Maeroff 1991) and often cited in the literature is that such methods are not add-ons, "busy work," or "gotcha games" (274) that interrupt the flow of ongoing classroom instruction; instead, they are classroom activities that, because they are actually "embedded in instruction" (276), grow directly out of the curriculum rather than appearing as a single, stressful, end-of-unit or end-of-term event. For this reason, they can be used formatively to serve as a basis for improving instruction as the activities proceed.

Moreover, a number of assessment alternatives also propose to provide "in-progress" ongoing measures of student learning as it continues over time. In fact, these kinds of "test" activities themselves can have a positive impact on student performance (Chapman 1991; Quellmaltz & Burry, cited in Herman 1992) when conducted within the framework of ongoing classroom activity because they provide students an additional opportunity "to practice the knowledge and skills learned" (Grover et al. 1996, 2). When implemented properly, "the line between curriculum and assessment" (Krechevsky 1991, 45) practically disappears.

Alternative assessment techniques also provide an additional dimension to many traditional types of assessments in that they aim specifically to measure critical thinking and process skills as well as student acquisition of subject "content." According to Neuman (1994),

> [T]his focus on the student's direct and purposeful involvement is consistent with current cognitive theory, which holds that deep understanding occurs only when learners actively construct their own knowledge rather than passively absorbing facts and ideas presented by others. (Grady 1992; Wiggins 1989; Wolf et al. 1991). (69–70)

Grover et al. (1996) agree, asserting that the types of alternate assessment models that require the performance of the learning tasks are more likely than traditional kinds of testing methods to tap into critical thinking and the other complex processes that are inevitably involved in information seeking. Finally, Frazier and Paulson (1992) argue that the opportunities that assessment alternatives provide allow students to gain practice in self-evaluation and encourage "ownership, pride, and high self-esteem" (64), all of which are related to school success and achievement.

In addition to focusing attention on critical thinking and active participation on the part of the student learner, alternative assessment models return the professional responsibility for student learning to the educators in the classroom (Grady 1992; Perrone 1991; Wiggins 1989, cited in Neuman 1994) in ways that allow differentiated approaches to instruction. Many leaders in education have advocated the importance of this approach to instructional design. For instance, Eisner (1993) has argued that assessment must take into account "where [a] student started, the amount of practice and effort expended, the student's age and developmental level, and the extent to which his or her current work displays progress" (23).

Authentic Assessment

What is authentic assessment, and how does it differ from alternative and performance assessment strategies? The goals and strategies of alternative and authentic assessment are very similar in that they both aim to allow the presentation of "a reliable picture of a student's understandings" (Stripling 1994a, 79). That is, they measure how well instructional objectives have been mastered by allowing students to demonstrate what they know. The difference between the alternative and authentic forms of assessment is that in the latter, students are asked to enact the specific skills in question instead of answering questions related to that skill or performing specific behaviors in contrived contexts (Meyer 1994).

To a great extent, the success of authentic assessment lies with teachers who have the ability to make the connections between an academic subject and real-world applications at levels appropriate and consistent with a student's development and background knowledge. In addition, authentic assessments of student performance necessarily presuppose and demand an "authentic" curriculum and one that allows students access to the same sorts of information and resources that would be "available in real-life, problem-solving situations"(Stripling 1994a, 80). Other conditions that support authentic curriculum are frameworks for collaboration among students, teachers, and community members; student discretion in what work will be used in assessing learning; and flexibility in terms of time limits for completion of products and processes.

Authentic Assessment Models

Data collection for authentic assessment requires teachers to evaluate student learning on authentic tests, "questionnaires, interviews, ratings, observations, performance samples, and work products (Crittenden, 1991)" (Stripling 1994a, 79). Assessment models can include a variety of evaluative instruments and approaches, including one or a combination of locally produced and standardized tests, student-created portfolios, student performances and exhibitions, and personal contacts between the students and their instructors.

Authentic Tests

To be authentic, tests must provoke or stimulate problem solving, critical thinking, and writing. In addition, they must (1) allow students to demonstrate their strengths through the employment of multiple measures, including the student's self-assessment; (2) apply reasonable real-world standards in the assignation of grades; and (3) allow for different approaches to learning. According to Stripling (1994a), authentic tests should also be enjoyable activities in themselves. Reliability for "authentic tests" needs to be established through a pretesting of the test items and through the creation of scoring rubrics so that the outcomes of the testing can be used to inform future instruction.

Authentic Portfolios

Valencia (1991) notes that portfolios not only allow teachers to the track student cognitive, affective, social, and motivational progress but also make teachers more "sensitive to processes of learning" in ways that allow them to "select and create measures of students' talents and weaknesses so that appropriate instructional opportunities can be provided" (680). At the same time, authentic portfolios may actually increase the time students spend in reading and writing and provide the vehicles for monitoring more closely and accurately their progress in developing these literacy skills.

Two types of portfolios have been described in the literature. The first represents a compilation of student work carried out over time, with specific items selected by students to meet goals they themselves establish in collaboration with the teacher. Students are usually asked to write an introduction to the portfolio that reflects their own evaluation as well as evaluation by the instructor. A second portfolio model, suggested by Gardner (1991, cited in Stripling 1994b), documents the thinking and activity involved in the creation of major projects and may contain records of original brainstorming sessions, early and current drafts, written critiques by instructors and peers, "works by others that particularly inspired or influenced the project," and student self-assessments, instructor evaluation, and student thoughts on future projects (106). The arrangement of portfolio documents (e.g., finished pieces, drafts, revisions, and journals) is usually an individual matter chosen by the student, who may opt to present items by topic, by format, by achievement level, or chronologically (Stripling 1994a).

Authentic Performances

Authentic performances and exhibitions, defined as "prepared demonstration[s] of student learning" (Stripling 1994b, 106) as options to more traditional models of assessment, are suitable for activities and learning that do not easily lend themselves to paper-and-pencil assessments or to portfolios. These might include musical activities, speech and debate exercises, and physical expression in athletics, dance, or drama (especially the re-creation or reenactment of historical events).

Student Profiles

Project Spectrum, a joint educational initiative created by educators from Harvard University and Tufts University in 1984, uses the creation of student profiles to assess the strengths and weaknesses of student skills. Based on Gardner's (1983) multiple intelligences theory and the theory of development in nonuniversal domains of Feldman (1994), a program of activities is created for individual students that capitalizes on their strengths and develops areas where skills need to be improved (Krechevsky 1991). Student profiles log the linguistic and mathematical aspects of student progress as well as the "mechanical, spatial, bodily, musical, social and scientific abilities" (44) in "a short description of the child's participation in the project's activities" (46).

Personal Contacts

Personal contacts, observations, conferencing, and diagnostic interviews allow students and teachers to explore student achievement interactively and can provide an index of student strengths and weaknesses, an opportunity for support for student thinking, and a forum for the discussion of student ideas. Observation is a particularly valuable way of assessing interactions between and among individuals and between groups and to monitor the activity and operation of student participation in multistudent projects (Stripling 1994a). Interviews can be formal or informal and may involve students and teachers or peers.

Alternate/Authentic Assessment: Difficulties and Disadvantages

A number of difficulties often accompany efforts to implement alternative and authentic assessment models. Staff development and support are almost always necessary since new ways to measure achievement usually necessitate changes in instructional strategies and lesson plans (Herman 1992, 77). Maeroff (1991) has addressed these issues, identifying preparation and training time, expense, complexity, and imprecision as some of the costs of implementing alternative assessment formats. She also voices a concern that lies at the heart of many of the arguments against attempts to adopt alternative assessment models; because they lack a comparative aspect, they do not allow parents and teachers to chart a child's progress against the levels achieved by his or her peers. Indeed, "psychometricians have raised serious questions about establishing the validity, reliability, generalizability, and comparability of assessments conducted according to methods that are individualized and dependent upon human judgment (Koretz et al., 1992; Linn, Baker, & Dunbar, 1991; Moss 1992)" (Neuman 1994, 71).

In point of fact, alternative assessment strategies may not be suitable for all assessment needs, and critics have also noted that non–norm-referenced assessments are open to inequities and misrepresentations. In addition, while creative efforts at assessment abound, research on the resulting evaluation is minimal at the present time. For these reasons, Maeroff (1991) hopes "that alternative assessment is not rushed onto the battlefield of testing so hastily as to produce in its unperfected form friendly fire that harms the very children who are supposed to be the beneficiaries" (276).

The School Librarian and Alternative Assessment

Stripling (1994a, 1994b, 2006) clearly considers alternative assessment as *the* model for the future and sees a central role for school librarians in helping to anticipate the changes that the implementation of new assessment models will require. "If the primary goal of education is to cultivate thoughtfulness and understanding, and if the school library media center is at the core of that effort, then the school library media specialist must lead in changing assessment techniques" (Stripling 1994b, 106). In fact, Neuman (1994) suggests that school librarians have roles to play in the creation of an "assessment culture" (Wolfe et al., 1991, quoted in Neuman 1994, 73) that relies on "new understandings of learning and intelligence, new standards of evidence" and "sensitivity and rigor in the application of [assessment] alternatives" (73). And "since learning theory shows that students learn far more by 'doing' than by any other method," librarians can "provide the logical information laboratory for practice within an educational setting" (Markuson 1986, 39).

Stripling (1994b) posits a three-level taxonomy of involvement for library media specialists in the initiation and progress of authentic assessment (see Figure 9.1). At the Initial level, the school librarian does not play a role in instructional design of projects but can provide information on the use of assessment alternatives, perhaps developing a professional collection of materials and resources upon which school staff can draw. In addition, the media specialist can facilitate discussion on assessment alternatives and create collections that support students involved in the creation of "alternative" projects.

At the Moderate Level, school librarians collaborate in planning instruction and assessment and otherwise provide professional assistance by teaching production techniques (e.g., word processing; video production), and by monitoring student performance practices. At the highest, or In-depth, level, Striping (1994a) suggests that school librarians are intimately involved in designing "authentic assessment strategies" (92) with teachers, in helping students select their work for inclusion in their portfolios, in providing assistance with evaluating student

Figure 9.1
Stripling's (1994b) Taxonomy of Library Media Specialist (LMS) Assessment Involvement

Initial Level	LMS provides information on assessment alternatives
Moderate Level	LMS collaborates on instruction and assessment planning
In-depth Level	LMS designs assessment alternatives and strategies; conducts staff development

products, and in conducting in-service instruction to staff on alternate assessment techniques and strategies. In creating evaluative measures for alternative projects, Stripling suggests that rubrics be developed that allow comments on the overall framework of the project (clarity and achievement of goals and the organization of information), reflection (student assessments and depth of comments), content, style (originality, creativity, and personal connection or "voice"), and presentation (fluency and form).

Neuman (1994) notes the basic compatibility of the move to create alternatives to traditional methods of assessment with contemporary library information skills curricula in that "library media center programs are grounded in many of the same assumptions that undergird alternative assessment" (72). This affinity should not be surprising, as both initiatives draw on constructivism as a theory base and focus on the processes of learning. Nor has this new approach to information skills instruction, with its emphasis on collaboration and instructional intervention, gone unnoticed in the education community. Theodore Sizer (1990, quoted in Stripling 1994b), the creator of the Coalition of Essential Schools, has observed, "One good way to start designing an Essential School is to plan a library and let its shadow shape the rest"(105).

It is interesting to note that the techniques for data collection (e.g., observation, interviewing, and analyzing student projects) as suggested by Kuhlthau (1993b) and others are fundamentally the same as those used in alternative assessment approaches. Moreover, these techniques mirror approaches to "qualitative inquiry," which is achieving greater acceptance in the fields of education and school librarianship (Neuman 1994).

Evaluating the School Library

Three major approaches to library evaluation characterize the research literature in school librarianship: library standards, library use measures, and library skills achievement measures. As has typically been true with innovations in educational assessment, evaluation methods employed by researchers and librarians reflect passions and preoccupations in educational vogue at various times and over time. During the 1940s and 1950s, which in many respects constituted the formative years of school librarianship, the primary concerns lay in establishing a well-stocked central facility staffed by certified library personnel. For this reason, assessment attention turned to comparisons between individual schools or school districts and national or state library standards as measures of a quality library "presence" (Gallivan 1974). Once most schools had installed centralized facilities for school resources and libraries opened their doors to students and school staff, librarians tended to follow the public library model, often employing circulation and library visits as measures of a library's value. Since the 1960s, however, there have been a number of research efforts to show the impact of library programming on the acquisition of library skills, library use, and student attitudes. Assessments since the 1980s have focused on student learning as measured on the library skills portion of standardized tests. This shift in evaluation focus reflected *Information Power*'s (AASL 1988) emphasis on the teaching role of the school librarian.

Library Standards

As originally conceived, library standards for collection size, library staff, and library facilities were at one time thought to be the essentials of quality and value in public libraries (Joeckel 1943). Over time, a number of researchers have sought to relate library collection size to exemplary library programs (Greve 1974; Loertscher, Ho, & Bowie 1987) and the presence of certified staff to both programming excellence (Loertscher et al. 1987) and higher levels of service (Loertscher & Land 1975). Although useful, at least initially, in supporting budgetary requests, employing standards as evaluation measures has been problematic in that a causal linkage between such standards and the improvement of library services has never been definitely established (Baker & Lancaster 1991). For one thing, the findings of "standards" studies are often ambiguous, having meant different things to different people at different times. To some, evaluation standards represent the "ideal" in terms of collections and services; to others, they represent the "minimum" required to open a library's doors. Another problem is that standards tend to become obsolete quickly. This is particularly true in and across school settings, where communities change, enrollments fluctuate, curricula shift, and instructional approaches and innovations wax and wane. Furthermore, library standards represent types of "input" measures, which focus on materials but do not assess the value of these materials for student learning. In some cases, the invocation of standards has even created problems, especially in situations where a desire to maintain numerical minimums discourages librarians from discarding outdated or inappropriate resources and equipment.

Library Use: Circulation and Library Visits

From time to time, counting the circulation and library contacts in the aggregate and per student has been advanced as an appropriate assessment measure in some school libraries. Although such data are relatively easy to gather and document, they do not necessarily indicate use of information nor indicate why some resources are chosen over others. Indeed, they reveal next to nothing about the value of a collection for the curricular needs of a particular school nor the ability of the resources to match the developmental levels of particular students. In schools where library policies, library hours, or other situational factors constrain visits, library use as a measure is also problematic. Additionally, library contacts do not always reflect a positive attitude toward the library and library materials (or their utility for that matter), especially where children are compelled to come to the library as part of regularly scheduled "library skills" classes. Finally, when teachers require students to check out a prescribed book or a number of books for classroom or recreational use, circulation statistics can often be misleading or useless as measures of student performance.

The first edition of *Information Power* (AASL & AECT 1988) suggested that libraries attempt to document library use and utility in a different way through patterns of planning and teaching. Quantitative measures, such as the number of students and teachers served, the number and frequency of group activities in the library, the number of collaborative projects, the extent of collaborative planning, and student use of library resources to meet classroom objectives, were all advanced as alternatives to tracking the circulation of library materials. More recently, professionals and researchers have argued that these approaches are themselves too indirect to support persuasive arguments of program value. As Berkowitz (1994) has argued, such measures do not reveal anything about what students learn as a result of library "lessons" nor document the impact of that instruction on students' success as learners (36).

Standardized Tests

According to Jackson (1994), the content of standardized measures used to assess library skills is usually based on curricular guides and textbooks in general use across the United States, and a multiple-choice structure for test items is the form most often employed. The fact that "the cognitive skill most [easily and therefore] frequently" (25) tested through multiple-choice questions is recall has made problematic their use in assessing student thinking in terms of analysis, synthesis, and evaluation skills. In a review of the Iowa Test of Educational Development (1989), the Tests of Achievement and Proficiency (1990), and the Comprehensive Tests of Basic Skills, Fourth Edition (1989), Jackson found that, although test items aim to address process skills (e.g., identification of information problems, evaluation of sources, note taking, analysis of information, synthesis of ideas, and information use), the limited number of short-answer test items did not address the complexities of information seeking as it has been described in the work of Irving (1985), Kuhlthau (1993b), and other LIS theorists. In particular, Jackson noted the failure of these tests to assess information retrieval, search strategies, the "process of narrowing or broadening a topic" (30), selecting a research thesis, or creating researchable research questions.

Focusing on the Educational Value of School Library Programs

According to Berkowitz (1994), school librarians can establish the educational value of the library only if they undertake a more broad-based assessment plan that demonstrates how the use of "library resources help[s] to advance the district and school goals" and the "achievement, attitudes, and behaviors" of students (37). Indeed, in Berkowitz's view it is *only* outcomes in terms of student learning that will ensure that libraries continue to receive administrative support and adequate funding. In short, intuitive understandings that library programs and collections contribute to student learning are not enough. Ultimately, as Berkowitz points out, school librarians and researchers alike must find ways to make the effectiveness of information skills instruction both "describable and visible" (33).

Determining the Value of the School Library Program

Research in library and information skills instruction has generally shown that a positive relationship exists between library programming and student achievement; and, at least in a general way, the types of measures used can tell us which teaching strategies are or are not effective. Less frequently, however, do such measures offer insights into how learning can be enhanced or how programs might be improved. In addition, the types of skills often tested are not those that contemporary librarians regard as the most important. For example, despite the fact that for many years educators have known that "being able to locate information was of little intellectual benefit to students" (Henne 1966, cited in Jackson 1994, 26), assessment questions that ask students to identify specific reference sources or demonstrate the acquisition of location and access skills are still being used as measures of students' information competence. In addition, changes in the structure of library and information skills instruction, particularly the redefinition of literacy to include information-seeking and technology skills, a process approach to information skills instruction (Kuhlthau 1993b), and an inquiry-based (Kuhlthau, Maniotes, & Caspari 2007) "critical thinking curriculum" (Callison 1994, 43) argue for the development of new approaches to information skills assessment.

When applied within the context of the school library, Grover (1993, 1994) sees assessment as part of the overall program requiring school librarians to: diagnose the student's information needs in ways that help achieve curricular goals, design customized learning opportunities, and assess the outcomes of instructional interventions. "The library media specialist," according to Grover, "must be able to diagnose or analyze the information skills level of individuals or groups, prescribe or recommend appropriate learning activities, teach or assist with the implementation of work for teaching information skills . . . and [develop] a framework for assessing instruction" (187). Given the challenges of assessing a multidimensional program of instruction and an information skills curriculum focused on developing critical thinkers and problem solvers, librarians are faced with a question: What kinds of measures can be devised that will provide such information?

The truth is that the processes underlying contemporary models of information seeking and teaching a process approach to library skills instruction are difficult to measure using paper-and-pencil tests conducted at the local level. One solution to this assessment conundrum clearly lies with alternative testing initiatives that are now a part of contemporary educational reform efforts in many states (Grover 1994; Maeroff 1991). These include a multimodal menu of strategies for gathering data on student progress: observations, interviews, journals, projects, formal tests, self-evaluation and peer evaluation, and portfolios. Information obtained through these means can be used to plan "additional learning activities" (187), class groupings, and peer tutoring pairs.

As will be seen, a major strength of these assessment models, which assume the expertise of a master teacher, is the opportunity they provide for students to reflect on their own work, skills, or progress as well as on the work of their peers. Indeed, contemporary assessment models must be inclusive of the various talents that students may have. The valuing of alternative intellectual, artistic, and social "gifts" has been duly noted in *Empowering Learners: Guidelines for School Library Programs* (AASL 2009a), which suggests that "[w]hile school curricula often test analytical, mathematical, or linguistic skills, many learners excel in areas outside of these traditional fields. Instructional design must address a variety of learning styles, giving every student a chance to find his or her own strengths."

Measuring Student Achievement

Although research efforts in library and information science continue to grow in number and sophistication, studies designed to establish a relationship between information skills instruction and student learning are only just beginning to yield results to which librarians can point as justification for their programs (for an overview of early studies, see Didier 1985). One problem has been the fragmentary nature of the research (Aaron 1982; Eisenberg & Brown 1992; Kuhlthau 1987). With the exception of recent studies by Lance and his colleagues and research based on Kuhlthau's (1993a) information search process, few studies have been either theory-based or replicable, while the use of natural settings where variables are hard to control have yielded results that are not generalizable beyond a specific context. In the early 1990s, Haycock (1992) also complained that studies too often addressed issues of peripheral interest. And while scholars and practitioners concede that student achievement is the appropriate yardstick for assessing value, particularly as the teaching role has become the standard for school librarianship, until recently few studies were able to show that such links actually exist (Eisenberg & Brown; Vandergrift & Hannigan 1986).

Shifting the Evaluation Paradigm

Among the earliest of the research efforts "to evaluate the effectiveness of elementary school libraries" were studies by Mary Gaver (1963), who found a positive relationship between the presence of school libraries and student achievement. In her studies, Gaver attempted to determine the impact of centralized library facilities on student reading and library skills by surveying 271 schools in 13 states. Findings of the study revealed that students experienced "higher educational gain in schools with school libraries" (Gallivan 1974). In another study, Willson (1965) used survey instruments developed by Gaver to compare reading achievement and library skills proficiency of sixth graders in 12 schools to assess the impact of a library program administered by a professional librarian. Willson's study found that students with access to a central library and organized instruction achieved higher scores on skills and reading as measured on the Iowa Test of Basic Skills than those who lacked such programs.

Since these early studies, library practitioners and scholars have launched a spate of studies across many states. The first major study that sought to link the presence of an active library professional, the presence of library materials, and student learning was conducted by educators in Colorado schools in 1992. Results of this research verified "the importance of the library media specialist's instructional role" and the expenditure of funds to maintain school library collections and staff in "promoting academic achievement" (Lance, Welborn, & Hamilton-Pennell 1992). In a second Colorado study, Lance, Rodney, and Hamilton-Pennell

(2000a) sought to remedy the methodological shortcomings critics noted in the first study while replicating their research in Alaska (Lance et al. 2000), Pennsylvania (Lance, Rodney, & Hamilton-Pennell 2000b), New Mexico (Lance et al. 2003), Oregon (Lance et al. 2001), Texas (Smith 2001), and Iowa (Rodney, Lance, & Hamilton-Pennell 2002). These studies confirm that student competency test scores improve in schools where school library programs are clearly developed, where students have access to information technology, where libraries are run by qualified professionals, where librarians and teachers collaborate to integrate technology into the curriculum, where librarians provide in-service training in technology integration, and where independent use of the library is encouraged and supported.

A study of New York school librarians and library programs extended the Lance studies by exploring not only the impact of school libraries and librarians on student achievement but also "(1) the influence of the SLMS on technology use, (2) the relationship between principals and their SLMSs and (3) the level of service to students with disabilities" (Small, Shanahan, & Stasak 2010; Small and Snyder 2009; Small, Snyder, & Parker 2009). The primary research included more than 1,600 schools, while a qualitative component was conducted in 10 selected schools to gather information on motivation and learning. Findings indicate that

> (1) all groups perceive greater emphasis on skills for finding information than on skills for using or evaluating information; (2) elementary students perceive the SLMS as more autonomy supportive than middle or high school students; (3) students are largely unaware of librarian–teacher collaboration; (4) 69 percent of students visit their school library at least once a week, and most to do research; (5) students perceive "maintaining a neat and orderly collection" and "maintaining a quiet study environment" as the two most important services provided by the LMS; and (6) there is a lack of library services to students with disabilities. (Small & Snyder 2009, 1)

Additionally, the study supports the notion that school libraries and librarians positively influence students' motivation for research and inquiry, their reading development, and their development of reading interests (Small et al. 2010).

Another important study was undertaken in selected schools in Ohio during the 2002–2003 academic year (Kuhlthau & Todd 2005a, 2005b). Kuhlthau and Todd, two major researchers in the field of school librarianship, directed the research, which was funded through a grant from the Library Services and Technology Act/Institute of Museum and Library Services. In essence, the study aimed "to provide comprehensive and detailed empirical evidence of how libraries help students learn, and to provide recommendations for further research, educational policy development, and tools for the school librarian to chart how their school library impacts learning" (Todd 2002). Of particular interest as well was the study's effort to ascertain the value of libraries to student learning from the student point of view and as such is the "first comprehensive study based on students' evaluation of their media centers" (Whelan 2004). According to Todd (2002), *Student Learning through Ohio School Libraries* provided significant findings that demonstrate "the multidimensional relationship between an effective school library instructional program and student learning outcomes." For their part, students reported that the information skills instruction they received in the library "helped them with using and accessing information for their research assignments" (Todd, quoted in Whelan 2004) and helped them do better on class work and tests. African American youngsters in the study also reported getting help for their reading in the school library. Overall, students reported that access to and instruction in technology was especially valued (Todd & Kuhlthau 2003).

A study to link school library services to student achievement is reported in a dissertation by Achterman (2009), who looked at different levels of professional practice across public schools in California and noted that where staffing levels and library services were robust, students at all grade levels scored higher on "California criterion-referenced state-wide tests." Indeed, "the strength of the correlations between both certified and total staffing tend to increase with grade level; at the high school level, correlations were among the strongest reported in any statewide study to date." The key in this study, as with Lance's early work, is the presence of qualified library staff. "At every level," Achterman asserts, "certified and total staffing levels were associated with the strength of library program elements."

A similar theme can be found in Dow, Lakin, and Court's (2010) longitudinal study, which aimed to determine how Kansas school libraries contribute to student achievement. These researchers analyzed quantitative and qualitative data in an effort to examine linkages between an aligned state curriculum and established library media and technology standards. Recently reported findings established links between the presence of licensed school librarians and student gains in achievement across the curriculum.

Reading Achievement and School Libraries

The most powerful case currently being made in American public education is embedded in the work of Stephen Krashen, whose extensive research has provided evidence that school libraries promote reading behavior in students at all levels. Simply stated, Krashen believes that the availability of reading resources in the school library results in an increase in student reading. As evidence, Krashen (1993) reported the results of a meta-analysis of reading research in *The Power of Reading*, published in 1993. On the basis of his research, Krashen concluded that higher reading gains were made by children with access to high-quality collections of books in the school library. He also found the library superior to classroom collections because of children's comparative ease of access to these materials and their ability to "provide a comfortable and relaxing reading environment" and "qualified school librarians." Two other studies reported by Krashen also linked reading achievement and the presence of a certified school librarian in the library. In 1995, Krashen found a correlation between reading comprehension scores and high-quality collections, while an international study of more than 200,000 children in 32 countries in 1992 found that the size of school libraries had a positive impact on reading achievement scores (Elley 1992, cited in Krashen 1993). A later study using data obtained in the earlier research (Novlijan 1998, cited in Krashen 1993) found that students with access to a library professional within the school library scored higher on reading tests than did students those whose libraries were staffed by a teacher. This led Novlijan to conclude "that the presence of a professional school librarian in the school library was a positive factor in the development of reading literacy."

Although these studies do not address the teaching of library and information skills as having an impact on reading achievement, there is limited evidence for this connection in longitudinal studies in school libraries conducted by both Thorne (1967) and Yarling (1968). Thorne used a purposive sample of two schools, randomly selecting 640 students for a two-year study. Pretest and posttest reading comprehension instruments were used to determine the effects of augmented library services on reading comprehension. Thorne found that augmented services resulted in significant gains in reading comprehension and knowledge of library skills. Thorne also noted gender differences in terms of achievement. Girls improved their library skills to a greater degree than did boys, while the boys' reading comprehension scores advanced more than did those of the girls.

Yarling's (1968) study, on the other hand, compared groups of children within and between two elementary schools over three years. One school had a library, and one did not. As a result of exposure to a program that ostensibly provided practice in library location skills, index use, and a variety of study techniques, students in the school with a library performed significantly better on tests in library skills and language competence than groups in the same school tested previously and as compared with groups in the control school. During the same period, the control groups did not show a significant increase in their achievement on the same instruments.

Some studies have considered both reading achievement and study skills. For example, Didier (1982) looked at the relationship between students' reading achievement (measured by standardized test scores) and study skills and library skills instruction. The seventh graders in Didier's study demonstrated higher levels of achievement in reading and study skills and use of newspapers than did students in the control group, who had limited exposure to media centers or professional library staff. In a study two years later, Gifford and Gifford (1984) randomly selected and assigned 26 students in selected classes in one school to control and experimental groups. These researchers used a posttest design to determine the effect of a two-week program of bibliographical instruction on library use and ease of use by students. Dependent measures in this study were the use of specific library resources (e.g., card catalog, newspapers, magazines, vertical file, dictionaries, fiction, and nonfiction) and the number of times students requested assistance in the library. Findings revealed that the experimental group asked for less help and used some specific types of resources significantly more often than did students in the control group.

Gilliland's (1986) informal study of groups of California high school seniors found that test scores on the "study-locational portion of a state-wide mandated test rose appreciably after students had completed an exercise in which they reviewed basic library skills" (67). The exercise, the Senior Library Review, was a worksheet activity that "require[d] students to participate actively, to act and think independently," to use reading and writing skills, and "to use some higher order thinking skills such as analysis, and problem solving skills that would result in a product that they could use to write a paper or speech" (67).

Dewees (1987) employed an experimental research design to compare groups of randomly assigned students in fifth-grade classes in a single elementary school. The experimental group received six weeks of process-oriented instruction, which culminated in the production of a research paper. Student learning was assessed on a standardized achievement test. Results indicated that the experimental group scored significantly higher on the research skills portion of the test. Finally, Brodie (1988) also employed standardized test scores as measures in a study that compared student knowledge of library skills and the amount of library use by two groups of youngsters involved in special programs for gifted fourth- and fifth-grade students.

In this study, Brodie found that "students in the experimental group" increased their "use of the media center . . . and [the] use of six types of library materials: fiction, nonfiction, reference, encyclopedias, periodicals, and audiovisual materials" (Bracy 1990, 128).

Curriculum Integration

It is widely assumed that teaching information literacy skills within the context of ongoing classroom activities increases student learning. A number of researchers have investigated the relationship of instructional intervention, library use, and achievement. In a study in the late 1980s, Nolan (1989) looked at the effects of type of instructional design on patterns of student use of the media center. This researcher found that students for whom research skills instruction was delivered within the context of curricular tasks tended to use the library more, had better attitudes about the library, and had higher expectations as to its accessibility and utility than did students taught library skills in stand-alone lessons.

Todd, Lamb, and McNicholas (1993, cited in Todd 1995) reported research that concludes that an integrated information skills approach to teaching and learning can have a positive effect on a variety of learning outcomes, including improvement of student test scores, recall, concentration, focus on the task, and reflective thinking. In a second study, Todd (1995) compared the effectiveness of a "conventional approach" to information skills instruction and an "integrated approach" on student achievement, attitudes, and motivation. The study itself was undertaken in a culturally diverse girls' Catholic secondary school in Australia. Study participants were divided into treatment groups and control groups, with the former receiving instruction in a six-step process model for information seeking "explicitly aimed at the development of information skills as a basis for the meaningful learning of science" (134). The lessons were planned and taught collaboratively by the science teachers and the school librarian. Students in the control group learned the same science content but without an integrated program of library skills intervention. Science concepts were measured on annual science tests given at midyear and on end-of-year exams. Information literacy skills were assessed through the use of a problem-solving technique Todd devised to show student use of the information process model. Results of Todd's study indicate that students in the treatment group achieved significantly higher scores on both science content and information skills than those in the control groups. Thus, Todd concluded that, within this specific research context and for the specific students involved, integrated information skills instruction appeared to have a significant positive impact on students' mastery of prescribed science content and on their ability to use a range of information skills (37). While Todd calls for additional studies to test his conclusions, his study is particularly significant in that it ties information skills instruction and an integrated, process-oriented instructional program to student achievement within the context of the regular school curriculum. (See Table 9.1.)

New Emphasis on Evidence-Based Practice

School librarianship has not been immune from nor outside the scope of pressures to prove quality, as noted in recent writings by Todd (2008a), beginning with his *Evidence-Based Manifesto for School Librarians*, which reported on discussions at the School Library Leadership Summit held in Phoenix, Arizona, in 2007. Todd's recent

Table 9.1.
The Benefits of Library Instruction: Summary of Major Research Findings

- School libraries have a positive effect on student achievement (Gaver 1963; Greve 1974; Hall-Ellis & Berry 1995; Lance, Rodney, & Hamilton-Pennell 2000a, 2000b; Lance, Welborn, & Hamilton-Pennell 1992).

- Student achievement is higher in schools where library services and instruction are provided by school library professionals (Achterman 2009; Dow, Lakin, & Court 2010; Willson 1965).

- Library skills instruction has a positive effect on student achievement in reading comprehension (Didier 1982, 1985; Gaver 1963; Thorne 1967; Yarling 1968), language development (Didier 1982, 1985; Yarling 1968), and knowledge of library skills (Gaver 1963; Thorne 1967; Yarling 1968).

- Where school libraries are well funded and librarians participate in the instructional process, academic achievement is higher (Hall-Ellis & Berry 1995; Lance, Welborn, & Hamilton Pennell 1992; Smith 2001).

- Integration of library skills and classroom curriculum resulted in an increase in library use (Nolan 1989) and higher achievement in information-gathering skills and chart and graph readings (Becker 1970).

- Instruction in library resources resulted in more independence and increased use of specific types of library resources (Brodie 1988; Didier 1982; Gifford & Gifford 1984).

- Library skills instruction resulted in more positive attitudes about the library and its usefulness (Nolan 1989) and higher test scores on locational skills (Gilliland 1986), research skills (Dewees 1987), and study skills (Didier 1982);

- An integrated approach to library and information skills instruction has a positive effect on student learning related to test scores, recall, concentration, focus on the task, and reflective thinking (Todd, Lamb, & McNicholas 1993).

- Library skills instruction using a six-step process model can have a positive impact on student learning of science content (Todd 1995).

- School libraries and school librarians help students become better learners by providing resources in a variety of media to support curricular tasks and leisure reading and providing instruction in the search process, problem solving, and technology; by engaging students with information and assisting with research projects; by promoting reading; and by individualizing and personalizing instruction (Todd & Kuhlthau 2003).

focus on evidence-based practice within the context of school libraries calls attention to the many deficits in the school library literature that scholars have noted over time (Callison 2006). Callison in particular characterizes most research in school librarianship as falling well below the "gold standard" in terms of "rigorous evidence of randomly assigned students" (Todd 2009, 91), the use of control groups, and scientific and experimental methods. In the main, small samples, qualitative methods, uneven quality, focus on inputs rather than outcomes related to student learning, and failure to replicate studies certainly compromise the issuing of definitive statements about what works across student groups and schools. Whether a single, uniform, standardized model for library skills instruction is a desirable goal, to the contrary notwithstanding, Todd's message and model for evidence-based practice is a formidable challenge for school library scholars in addressing research deficits.

Of course, a number of barriers exist to the conduct of research that will yield generalizable findings. Many of the small-scale studies are the work of solitary researchers with limited funding. However, it is Todd's (2009) view that one remedy is the creation of a "sustained research culture" (92). Such a community would be able to take a more coordinated approach to the planning of research and provide for systematic data. In this way, research scholars would be in a position to demonstrate more definitely how instructional interventions increase students' knowledge and produce young learners with "competences and skills for thinking, living and working" (88). Such a community would necessarily involve individual schools and districts as well as professionals across regions, states, and the nation. Unfortunately, mechanisms for the collection of such rich data are not yet in place.

Todd's (2009) agenda is an ambitious one, and its success means rethinking how research in school librarianship is planned and funded and building the research capacity of school library professionals so that practitioners themselves can use the data they collect locally within the larger frameworks of nationwide studies. Todd also believes that the AASL's new *Standards for 21st Century Learners* will focus the attention of library professionals on student outcomes and "provide a framework for identifying evidence of the professional work of school librarians" (86).

Todd (2009) has created a three-phase model that categorizes research evidence as it relates to the basis, practice, and evaluation of instruction. Within this model, evidence for practice is comprised of theories and models that create frameworks for instruction. Evidence in practice is use of research findings in shaping the content and direction of instruction. Research data that mark learning and knowledge outcomes of instruction make up evidence of practice.

The importance that Todd places in the anchoring of school library practice in evidence provided by research probably cannot be overstated. As Todd (2008a) asserts,

> A profession without reflective practitioners who are willing to learn about relevant research is a blinkered profession—one that's disconnected from best practices and best thinking, and one which, by default, often resorts to advocacy rather than evidence to survive.

As noted, Todd is not alone in calling for added rigor in research and systematicity in data collection. As long ago as the mid-1990s Berkowitz urged librarians to find and use "measures of effectiveness" (Berkowitz 1994) such as those tested by Todd (1995), which can show that information skills instruction results in student achievement and an improvement in test results in content areas. Berkowitz also urges librarians to share the results with others in the school and the community.

Research in Practice

One assessment model currently being tested is the *Tool for Real-Time Assessment for Information Literacy Skills (TRAILS)*, developed by Schloman and Gedeon (2010), through a grant funded by the Institute for Library and Information Literacy Education, the Institute of Museum and Library Services, and the U.S. Department of Education. Their assessment tool, launched in 2004, ties specific library and information assessment questions to the Ohio state academic standards and also aligns with standards outlined in *Information Power* (1998) and *Standards for the 21st Century Learner* (AASL & AECT 2007).

Students in grades 6 and 9 may take an online assessment designed to provide teachers and school librarians with baseline data indicating areas of strengths and weaknesses. "TRAILS is designed as a classroom tool that enables a library media specialist easily to obtain a snapshot of skills levels in order to better tailor instructional efforts" (Schloman & Gedeon 2007, 45). A third-grade assessment is currently being developed. TRAILS is notable in that assessments were co-created with practitioners in the field within the context of state curricular standards. The assessment tool was created for students in Ohio public schools but has also been used nationwide to help school librarians determine how to proceed with integrated instruction. The program, which is made free to all educators (http://www.trails-9.org/), instantly provides individual, class, and school data. Project developers are working on a set of national benchmarks, allowing for comparison with schools throughout the United States.

The authors of TRAILS have examined data from 2006–2007 assessment results (32,000 students) and report the following:

- Seniors performed best in two areas: identifying potential sources and recognizing how to use information legally, responsibly, and ethically.

- It was more difficult for students to answer questions that asked them to develop, use, and revise search strategies.

- Students had the most trouble correctly identifying a topic and evaluating sources and information according to specific criterion (Schloman & Gedeon 2010).

Assessing the School Librarian

Within the realm of assessment, school librarians also need to be concerned about their own performances and ways they might ascertain whether or not they are providing expert services for their clientele. Inherent in this self-assessment are the uses of evidence-based practice, strategic planning, environmental scans, data analysis, and continuing evaluation (AASL 2009a). Evidence gathered from practice informs the development of a strategic plan. In order to develop and revisit the plan, however, school librarians must first perform an environmental scan by examining community analysis data that describe the school's surrounding community, stakeholders, and culture.

The next step is conducting a needs assessment, which takes into account budgeting, information access, staffing, collection, and instructional practices. "The [school library media specialist] analyzes data from the needs evaluation, identifies strengths and weaknesses of the program, and writes a plan of action that includes long-term goals and short-term (annual) objectives, and the monies needed to finance specific components of the program" (AASL 2009a, 31). In an effort to help school librarians include self-assessment within the context of overall program evaluation, the AASL (2010b), joining with Britannica, has created *A Planning Guide for Empowering Learners*, an interactive online tool to be used by the library professional to evaluate all aspects of an effective library program. Additionally, the AASL (2009b) has developed an Essential Links Wiki (http://aasl.ala.org/essentiallinks/index.php?title=Main_Page) to provide a toolbox of sorts as a resource for this purpose. Listed are links for school librarian evaluation tools provided by several school districts. It is important to note that school districts often have their own policy guidelines for evaluating teachers, including school librarians. However, *A Planning Guide for Empowering Learners* and the AASL Essential Links Wiki provide additional coverage of this topic for those programs that are being developed in some districts. Woolls (2008) explains that the most effective form of evaluation may be direct observation and also notes that it may cause discomfort both for the practitioner and for the evaluator while adding, "However, media professionals must be evaluated as they interact with students and teachers" (118).

Conclusion

Clearly, there is a need for more research not only in terms of the effectiveness of library skills instruction but also in terms of the impact that library programs can have on the contexts for learning. Information skills instruction based on a process approach to information seeking and inquiry learning certainly addresses the need for improving critical thinking and problem-solving skills that have purchase in real-world contexts. However, Herman (1992) notes that changes in assessment are only part of the answer to improved instruction and learning. Schools need support to implement new instructional strategies and to institute other changes to ensure that all students can achieve the complex skills that these new assessments strive to represent (77). Most particularly, school librarians and teachers must take into account the outcomes that the AASL set forth in 2007 as well as the guidelines provided in 2009 and together provide assignments and activities that demand critical thinking and problem-solving skills.

10 Attending to the Social and Emotional Needs of Today's Learners

[S]tudents value professional, respectful, and courteous interactions and appear to engage more readily with library services when their needs are met in a supportive, constructive, and pleasant manner.

—Todd and Kuhlthau (2003)

One sign, observed on the desk of a middle school librarian, sums up concerns that make manifest the social nature of library activities: "Our students," the sign reads, "may not remember whether or not you found the information they were seeking in the library, but they will never forget how you treated them." The simplicity of this idea and the commonsense aspect of such a message tend to obscure its importance, and perhaps it is for that reason that the relational aspects of library-student interactions have so seldom been addressed in the scholarly literature on school librarianship. Indeed, it is fair to say that most of the research interest in the area of school library instruction takes as a focus the cognitive aspects of information seeking and learning.

Acknowledging the Social Dimension of School Library Work

The contemporary emphases on the development of mental models and on information seeking as a cognitive task have proved extremely valuable in providing direction for school librarians in creating meaningful programs of instruction. It seems likely that the excitement generated by the advances in our understanding of the information search process and concomitant pressures related to information literacy issues have made inquiries into the relational nature of teaching and the service aspects of the school library programs appear peripheral, at best. However, Frohmann (1992) and others have cautioned against reducing to "a narrative of mental events" the "complexities of real practices, conduct, accomplishments and actions of information seeking, information use, and 'information processing' " (375).

For example, Crow (2009b) suggests that school librarians necessarily invoke an interactional model when using the relational aspects of play, humor, and group-related project assignments to foster intrinsic motivation for information seeking in the learning environment. Interest in the social and psychological aspects of library service has also surfaced in the work of Agosto and Hughes-Hassell (2006a, 2006b), whose study of information seeking in everyday life found that social, affective, and psychological needs form the focus of adolescent information seeking; to ignore these elements is to present a far too narrow view of information issues, particularly as they relate to children and youth.

It is true that over time a number of scholars have attempted to incorporate a concern for the affective experience of information users into their research and models. For example, Nahl-Jakobovits and Jakobovits (1993) noted the "serious affective information needs" that students have related to their own abilities in accessing library resources. Specifically, these researchers found that students "fear making mistakes," are often "intimidated by the complexity of search tools," and lack "confidence in their ability to find information" (83). Kuhlthau's (1993b, 2004) research also focused attention on the anxieties experienced by many students at the initial stages of the information search process and stresses the importance of providing support for students experiencing the dip in confidence during the initiation and exploration phases of the research activity. However, in other respects, Kuhlthau's emphasis is squarely on those uncertainties that are directly related to information and information tasks rather than those arising from or in librarian-student interactions or from aspects of the social context. Even those studies that have included "attitudes" toward the library as measures of its value (e.g., Todd 1995) have as their primary concern the relationship between student attitudes and the library's resources or a particular instructional approach; only secondarily is attention paid to the social experiences that may contribute to the creation of those attitudes.

In *Empowering Learners: Guidelines for School Library Programs* (American Association of School Librarians 2009a), there is certainly the suggestion that in their roles as leaders, school librarians need to be advocates for youth and embrace increased communication with students and all elements of the school community and in electronic as well as face-to-face interactions. However, the document seldom directly addresses the need for compassion and sensitivity in dealing day to day with the students who are not only the primary clientele of the school library but its raison d'être as well. In fact, enacting the librarian's role as information "intermediary" in assisting students with complex searches is appropriate and necessarily invokes a service orientation.

Chelton (1999) has noted that pressures to promote the independence of students as information seekers have sometimes led to a reluctance on the part of library professionals to provide the kinds of service support to students that are frequently available to adult users in public libraries (see Chapter 1 for a discussion of service models in academic and public libraries). In fact, Chelton asserts that the school librarian often "defines her role as helping people find information on their own." Yet given the increasing complexities of the information universe, one questions, with Liesener (1985), the efficacy of predicating all services related to information seeking in school libraries on a "selfsufficiency" (17) model. This is particularly the case where, as in Chelton's study, there is "little follow up by library staff to see if users" (283) actually find the information being sought.

Information Seeking as a Social Activity

As we have seen, contemporary trends in teaching emphasize inquiry and the "active" and "constructed" nature of learning as well as the importance of interaction among students and between students and teachers (Bruner 1975, 1977; Kuhlthau, Maniotes, & Caspari 2007; Vygotsky 1978). And there is an increasing awareness and valuing of group processes and social engagement as essential parts of the instructional context, thanks to input from many education researchers. This seems logical when one considers that the very act of teaching is itself inherently social and interactive. For example, the importance of "affective bonds" between adults and students has been recognized by Winograd and Gaskins (1992, 232), who assert that "the need for a supportive, trusting advocate is particularly important for students experiencing academic difficulties." Suggesting that schools need to become as concerned about being "high touch" as they are about being "hi-tech" (232), Mann (1986, cited in Winograd & Gaskins 1992) argues that reaching out to less successful students and providing personal contact constitute essential parts of all successful intervention programs. Delpit (1995) and others note that this may be especially true for some minority students. All too often, however, "even advocates of systemic change . . . often leave off of their agenda any recognition of the importance of having schools see students as people" (Howe 1993, 130). And unhappily, even in the few studies where the social aspects of library service and instruction are reflected in the data, as, for example, in Nahl-Jakobovits and Jakobovits's (1993) finding "that students fear talking to librarians," they are often ignored by practitioners and seldom pursued further by researchers.

Having said that, there are some exceptions. For example, the interactive nature of the school librarian's role has been marked in a study of achievement effects by Ryan (1991, cited in Bialo & Sivin-Kachala 1996), who identified social interaction among students and between students and teachers and/or librarians as one of the three characteristics essential for the creation and maintenance "of the most effective learning environments" (54). Kulleseid (1986) has also noted the contribution of the librarian's interpersonal skills to the successful modeling and facilitation of student-student and teacher-student interactions. Gehlken's (1994) examination of library programs in three exemplary schools in South Carolina called attention to the importance of "proactivity and commitment in meeting student needs." Indeed, Gehlken observed that "in every case, student samples overwhelmingly identified the single most important service provided by the library media program as help from the media specialist." Students surveyed by Todd and Kuhlthau (2003) felt the same way. "It wasn't really the library," reported one student, "it was the librarians that helped" (22). Finally, esteem needs appear to be implicated in Todd and Kuhlthau's conclusion that "students value professional, respectful, and courteous interactions and appear to engage more readily with library services when their needs are met in a supportive, constructive, and pleasant manner" (15).

Kuhlthau's (1996) intervention model, which describes tutoring and counseling activities for librarians in supporting students in seeking information, clearly assumes high-level communication and interactional skills. This model is based on Vygotsky's (1978) assertion that the most effective teaching activities are structuring interactions that enable students to function at a higher level than could be managed if they were left to struggle along on their own. Swain's (1996) extension of Kuhlthau's (1993a) research provides further insights into the role of social interaction in information seeking. In particular, Swain noted the importance of the social relationships that developed between students and library staff members who provided assistance in helping relieve the stresses and anxieties that the students experienced in selecting their topics, using library tools, and conducting their searching activities.

Social Identity Issues in the School Library

Issues of identity construction, which are usually considered of paramount interest and importance in other contexts, have seldom been the objects of interest in school library research. Recently, however, a number of scholars, including Radford (2006), Connaway et al. (2008), Radford and Connaway (2007), and Crow (2009b), have expressed a concern for this important aspect of librarianship, and their explorations of service interactions provide evidence that there is often more at stake in library encounters than simply the transfer of information. If, as Haycock (1992) suggests, interactional skills are essential elements in the librarian's professional tool kit and if librarians wish to implement programs that are truly learner centered, then the social experiences that students have in school libraries should be studied and the findings used, where necessary, to rethink and reshape professional attitudes and behavior. The rest of this chapter reviews some of the salient studies related to interactional aspects of the library experience in the hope that the insights they provide will raise sensitivity and spark discussion among both researchers and practitioners.

Interpersonal Interactions in the School Library Context

Writing in the *School Library Media Quarterly*, in 1982, Martin was one of the first to recognize the relational nature of teaching and learning in the library. Specifically, she considered the value of interpersonal relationships with students, school administrators, faculty, parents, and community members in creating trust, communicating clearly, building influence, and solving problems essential to the creation of exemplary library programs. According to Martin, self-acceptance, self-confidence, the ability to exhibit warmth, a sense of caring, and sensitivity to the feelings of others are all characteristics fundamental for establishing a context of support for information-seeking activities. In providing assistance, Martin admonished readers to attend "to the affective domain, valuing each person as unique, then showing individuals that you know their worth, and accepting them, recognizing their accomplishments, and helping them to develop self esteem" (54). Strategies that Martin suggested for librarians to use in making library visitors feel welcome included responding positively to their interests, respecting their rights and needs in terms of acceptance and valuing, and taking care to "avoid interrupting, shaming, name calling, commanding, moralizing, lecturing, arguing, or criticizing" (56).

Martin (1982) also called attention to the variety of paralinguistic (e.g., voice tone, rate of speech, and modulation) and nonverbal behaviors (e.g., gestures, expressions, posture, personal distance, style of dress, and so on) that have a bearing on the ways in which librarians relate to their users. In fact, she asserted that "nonverbal messages may be more powerful in communicating feelings than verbal ones" (54). But Nahl-Jakobovits and Jakobovits (1990) and Thomas (1996, 2002) have also urged librarians to attend to textual "messages" librarians direct at users in the form of signage, notes, list of rules, and directions. Stating "rules" or prohibitions in positive rather than negative ways, personalizing library messages, and minimizing the punitive aspects of library postings are suggested as techniques that contribute to the creation of welcoming and confirming library environments.

Library Encounters as Communicative Action

Research studies by Mokros, Mullins, and Saracevic (1995), Radford (1996, 1998, 1999, 2006), Radford and Connaway (2007), and Chelton (1997) address issues identified by Martin (1982) and others as barriers to "exemplary library program[s]" (56). These studies draw on communication theory as explained in the work of Goffman (1967) and Watzlawick, Beavin, and Jackson (1967) to investigate interactions in a variety of library contexts. Within this framework, an act of communication includes not only the expression of the report, or informational content, within a given utterance but also the "relational content," the feelings participants have about themselves, each other, and the interactive situation in which they find themselves. For this reason, the manner in which words are spoken (e.g., whether deferential and respectful or condescending and demeaning) are at least as powerful as the meanings of the words themselves. In addition, these researchers understand that language in use is, itself, value laden rather than merely representational, "even though such 'valuing' proceeds out of awareness and is seldom explored" (Thomas 2002, 80).

According to interactionists, *social identity*, the sense of who one is in relation to social others, arises in knowing how we regard ourselves and how we are ourselves regarded in social situations (Goffman 1967). There is a possibility in every social interaction that an individual will be accepted, respected, and honored or, conversely, rejected, shamed, or ignored and that there will be consequences in terms of personal identity formation depending on which treatment an individual perceives him- or herself to have received. For this reason, the "selves" of all interactants are potentially "at risk" in every social engagement. Mokros et al.'s (1995) and Radford's (1996, 1998, 2006) studies are significant for what each contributes to our understandings of the instructional context and to the relational aspects embedded within each informational encounter. As noted above, these scholars would argue that the "self" needs of library users are at least as important as their information needs (Thomas 2000b).

Acknowledging the role of communication in creating meaning, context, and the self, Mokros et al. (1995) studied interactions between librarians and students involved in an online searching activity in an academic library. In the view of these researchers, library activities that are undertaken with such frequency that they are enacted routinely and "unconsciously" are nonetheless charged with relational messages about who is in control and the nature of the relationship between the interactants (e.g., parity or asymmetry) within the context of the activity. Through an analysis of videotaped reference encounters, researchers concluded that the opening moments of service interactions are particularly significant in setting the stage for all the activities that follow. Their study revealed that in some cases the librarians' own self-identity and control needs took precedence, resulting in personally disaffirming experiences for the library users who had come to them for research assistance. Considered as personally affirming for both librarians and users in the study were those interactions that demonstrated, through words and gestures, a sense of parity in terms of status between the interactants and marked them as coparticipants in the shared research activity.

Approachability: A Key Aspect of Library Service

Radford (1998) explored the dimensions of approachability in a study among high school and college students, all of whom were engaged in a reference activity that required the use of library resources. Citing the uncertainty and anxiety that Kuhlthau (1993b) identified as common experiences for users in the initial and exploratory phases of a research task, and the important role that librarians can play in mediating these experiences for users as they contemplated the complexities of the contemporary library, Radford sought to determine what barriers might exist for users in seeking reference assistance. Her results indicated that the librarians in her study exhibited nonverbal "gestures," such as eye contact, manner, and deference, to which library users were extremely sensitive. In addition, the students Radford interviewed revealed that they used these nonverbal cues in assessing the "approachability" of the librarians and planned their information-seeking strategies accordingly. In short, they avoided some reference librarians and sought assistance from others on the basis of whether or not they thought a particular librarian seemed open and friendly. Significantly, the students in Radford's study considered that obtaining the desired information in a reference interaction, while important, was not as important as having their relational needs met. This led Radford (1996) to conclude that library users "may still leave the interaction with a negative impression of the librarian and of the library experience in general" (125) regardless of the informational outcome of a library visit.

Self-Esteem Needs of Library Users

The "negative attitudes" identified by Radford's (1996) informants included "(a) having no time, (b) unhelpful, (c) uncaring, (d) sour, (e) abrupt, and (f) impatient" (130). These kinds of behaviors seem to reflect those described in a study by Mellon (1990, cited in Chelton 1997) in which high school students reported that librarians tended to respond only to direct questions, made disparaging remarks about the kinds of questions that students posed, and made them feel stupid. Similarly, research conducted by the Pew Research Center (2001) indicated that the "bad attitude" of librarians led many students to abandon libraries altogether in favor of information seeking on the Internet.

Respecting Students in the School Library

In her dissertation research, Chelton (1997) confirmed the multidimensional nature of the school media specialist's job and the many kinds of interactions that take place in high school libraries. Drawing on the works of Kuhlthau (1993a), Radford (1996), and Mokros et al. (1995), Chelton used communication frameworks to explore these interactions, particularly as they involved issues of identity construction of the adolescents she observed. In her study, Chelton (1997, 1999) noted in particular many library interactions she observed in which the adults assumed "authority" positions in enforcing school and library rules. She then considered the ways in which these manifestations of authority might interfere with a librarian's ability to support information seeking predicated on a participatory, interactional model.

Chelton's (1997) adolescent informants expressed, sometimes poignantly, sometimes angrily, their sensitivity to deference issues and the disrespect many had themselves encountered in all kinds of service settings. The specific behaviors of which the youngsters complained included being ignored, being watched, and being stereotyped. These same students identified listening skills, courteous behavior, niceness, helpfulness, and promptness as important elements in positive service encounters.

It is especially important to note here that although the students themselves identified "respect" as their primary information need in library interactions, the adults Chelton (1997) interviewed failed to recognize this as an aspect of their encounters with students. Thus, while the adolescents appeared to want "an identity-confirming, emotional connection to adult service providers" (179) in the library as elsewhere, the librarians tended to view student needs as primarily informational in nature and isomorphic with the questions that the students asked! This is a significant disconnect and may well explain the differences in how library interactions are perceived by students and librarians.

Echoing Mokros et al. (1995), Chelton (1997) argued that the opening "moves" of a library interaction, when the participants greeted or failed to greet each other, established the nature of the relationship (e.g., who is in control of the interaction), signaled the deference with which students would be treated, and defined the "situation" or interactional context as potentially productive or adversarial. Chelton concluded that where expectations created in these interactional openings are negative, the chances for productivity later in the encounters are severely compromised.

An important aspect of Chelton's (1997) research is the concern it expresses with regard to the impact of "everyday" types of library interactions and routine activities on the selves of the youngsters involved. Thus, Chelton concludes,

> Helping an adolescent to use the photocopy machine, or checking out a book or asking to see a pass may seem mundane and tedious to someone who does it constantly. The young person receiving the service, however, is neither mundane nor tedious, but rather, another person who wants an emotional connection (Scheff 1990). Providing library service without it is otherwise a very empty and possibly meaningless activity. (208)

The Cultural Dimensions of Relational Work

The fact that in some cultures the relational "work" to establish a basis for further interaction must precede information tasks (Bialo & Sivin-Kachala 1996; Delpit 1996; Salvatore 2000) appears to suggest that the social aspects of service are especially important for school librarians serving multicultural/multiethnic school communities. In light of the research findings of Bialo and Sivin-Kachala and Salvatore, direct inquiries by the librarian, which constitute the warp and woof of the traditional reference interview and which frequently characterize the opening moves in other kinds of school library interactions, may be seen by some minority students as overly inquisitive, inappropriate, or rude. Using neutral questions as a reference technique in such instances, as explained in the work of Dervin and Dewdney (1986), might well be a useful way to interact with students for whom a more direct line of questions would be construed as disrespectful (for a discussion of Dervin and Dewdney's neutral questioning model, see Chapter 6).

Building Self-Esteem through Library Interactions

The psychological dimension of library-student interaction created a focus for the dissertation work of Diane McAfee Hopkins (1989). In particular, Hopkins's work considered the contributions that library programming and services could make to the development of feelings of self-worth in student users and the importance of establishing a positive atmosphere in the school library. Hopkins's research identified the provision of appropriate library materials, maintaining the accessibility to a variety of resources, and the creation of a welcoming physical setting as contributing to students' feelings of being valued in the library. In addition, Hopkins's research found that students also experienced a sense of affirmation and acceptance through participation in library activities that fostered cooperation and independence (McAfee, 1981, cited in Haycock 1992). Irving (1990) also noted the importance of this kind of library activity in her observation that learning to obtain "information personally" created a "tremendous sense of independence" (86) and was an important by-product of information skills instruction; while students in Nahl-Jakobovits and Jakobovits's (1990) study found "deeply rewarding" those "required course-integrated library research" tasks that led them to "an enlarged conception of their capacity to learn and succeed" (80).

Fourie and Kruger (1995) identified a number of psychosocial, cognitive, and affective needs behind the information-seeking behavior of secondary school students. They theorized that the fulfillment of these needs is the basis of teens' motivation to choose particular books and media. The more recent work of Agosto and Hughes-Hassell (2006a, 2006b) confirms insights from this earlier study.

Reference Interactions Online: Teenage Experiences and Preferences

Some of the most interesting and potentially disturbing research findings to date can be found in the work of Radford (2006) and Radford and Connaway (2007), who took as their research focus the experience of online information-seeking encounters between young adults and reference librarians. Citing Rushkoff (1996) for coining of the term "screenagers" to describe Millennial generation youngsters who thrive on social networking, cell phone conversations, instant messaging, and texting, Radford and Connaway's research centered on library users' experiences with chat reference. Data in these studies came from focus group interviews as well as from transcripts of chats recorded in virtual reference service settings in public libraries. Citing her own work as well as studies by Dewdney and Ross (1994), and Walter and Mediavilla (2005), Radford asserts that "interpersonal aspects have been shown to be critical to client's perceptions of success in both face-to-face reference interactions and virtual environments."

Unfortunately, comments by the informants in her study led Radford (2006) to conclude that in many cases Millennials not only make "limited use of libraries" but also tend to "view librarians in negative terms." Even where students reported preferring face-to-face interactions with school and public librarians as a general rule, they continued to be concerned for "face" (Goffman 1967) issues in interacting with library professionals. Fears of ridicule or humiliation at the hands of insensitive service providers made youngsters reluctant to ask for additional assistance even when they felt the need to do so. However, such feelings were lessened for students who had developed a relationship with specific reference librarians.

Millennials in Radford's study preferred the independence of online searching to asking for help from a librarian and were mixed in their perceptions of librarians' information-seeking expertise and knowledge; thus, while some appreciated the quality of the information that librarians could help them find, others preferred to trust information they found online on their own. Data from the recorded chat sessions also indicated problems between cyberlibrarians and Millennials. A number of negative interactions led Radford (2006) to conclude that when librarians reacted negatively and reproached youthful information seekers online for chat behaviors of which they disapproved, these reprimands actually exacerbated rude behavior.

The fact that many students in Radford's (2006) study reported a reluctance to engage via e-mail or other online chat strategy when adolescents today are often so comfortable in other kinds of online environments was surprising. Radford's informants tended to explain this behavior in terms of the more impersonal dimension of mediated communication with librarians and expressed concerns for privacy in dealing online with strangers.

The chat reference data collected by Radford and Connaway (2007) documented the interactions of students from primary school through college. Radford analyzed transcripts to identify what she called "relational facilitators" and "relational inhibitors" in interactive reference sessions online. Among those behaviors that fostered positive interactions were "greeting rituals" (e.g., hello, hi, and so on); "closing rituals" (e.g., good-bye, bye, thanks for the help, and so on); "deference demonstrations" (e.g., politeness); "rapport building" ("conversational give and take, self-disclosure-inclusive language" such as "we" and "us"); use of informal language and other strategies one commonly observes in face-to-face dialogic interactions, including the mutual use of nonverbal behaviors such as emoticons; and "phrase abbreviations" (e.g., LOL for "laugh out loud"). "Relational barriers" revealed in Radford's data included "failing to encourage give and take, establish mutual understanding, and engage in relationship development," "ending the chat interaction without a closing ritual or exchange of farewell or goodbye," and "negative closure" in terms of abrupt endings, such as the "disappearance of the information seeker." Where school librarians are in a position to provide virtual reference service for students, an awareness of the sometimes exquisite sensitivity of youth and knowledge of relational facilitators and inhibitors should greatly increase the chances for positive outcomes for both the information seeker and the information provider.

How We Describe Library Users Matters

Chelton (conversation with author, August 24, 1997) has argued that the ways in which adolescents are discussed in the media and popular culture create stereotypes and expectations, frequently negative, which are then reflected in treatment adolescents receive at the hands of service providers. This theme appears in an article by Marcus (2002). This author identifies titles such as *Unglued and Tattooed: How to Save Your Teen from Raves, Ritalin, Goth, Body Carving, GHB, Sex and 12 Other Emerging Threats, Parenting Your Out-of-Control Teenager, Yes, Your Teen Is Crazy,* and *Now I Know Why Tigers Eat Their Young: Surviving a New Generation of Teenagers* as not only pejorative, in the sense that they condition service providers to view all adolescents with suspicion, but also grossly insensitive to youngsters who are striving, often successfully, to navigate the often turbulent waters of adolescence.

The idea that the choice of words we use in describing library clients often has unintended consequences for library service delivery has been the subject of an

Table 10.1
Research Insights Related to Social Interaction in the Library Context

- Information seeking is affective and social as well as cognitive an informational.
- The relational aspects of a library encounter are at least as important as the information aspects.
- Students have self needs and want to feel respected in all kinds of service encounters.
- The opening moments of a library interaction establish the relational nature (adversarial, participatory; expert, novice; superior, inferior) of the encounter.
- Approachability and negativity are expressed in verbal and nonverbal actions and are "read" by students and considered when they plan their information-seeking strategies.
- The portrayal of library users in the research literature can promote asymmetry in librarian-user interactions.
- The pejorative characterizations of teenagers in and by media create narratives that, if unchallenged by library professionals, can condition attitudes that jeopardize service provision to teens in school libraries.
- Service providers need to be as sensitive to the deference needs of adolescents in online interactions as they are in face-to-face encounters.
- The use of relational facilitators online is an especially important aspect of mediated communication in libraries.
- Face-to-face interactions between librarians and youth within the framework of a physical library space remain a vital part of service in school libraries.

interesting study by Tuominen (1997). Drawing on communication theory, Tuominen applied a discourse-analytic lens to the vocabulary that Kuhlthau (1993b) and others have employed in studies related to information seeking in libraries. Discourse analysis acknowledges the constitutive and value-laden character of language and argues that the terms we employ in describing our experience actually create and constitute one version of reality: our own. Tuominen suggests that characterizing the library user as "uncertain," "anxious," "confused," and "unfocused," while at the same time identifying the librarian as an "expert," "rational," problem solver," and "teacher," creates a context for relational asymmetry that may actually stymie our ability to delivery effective library services. This asymmetry is especially problematic where successful service interventions are predicated on a model of shared responsibility and cooperation between users and librarians. Tuominen also argues that when anxiety is considered as a personal characteristic of the library user rather than as an outcome of the interaction between the library user and the more complex and arcane aspects of an information system or environment, librarians are released from the responsibility of examining the very practices that make libraries and information seeking intimidating for many people.

Conclusion

Table 10.1 summarizes the research findings related to social interaction in the library context. Taken together, this research underscores the importance of students' experiences in library settings. Considering the interactional issues related to instruction and service encounters serves to confirm not only the complexities of the librarians' tasks but also the significant roles that librarians can play in creating opportunities for positive encounters between their students and the school. Librarians devoted to helping students achieve educational and life goals must pay serious attention to this very important aspect of school librarianship. As Haycock (1991) reminds us, in the final analysis we are in the business of teaching kids, not content (15).

Epilogue

As school leaders, it is critical that we advocate articulately and passionately for our programs and, more importantly, for the youngsters we meet in the library on a daily basis. To do the job well demands that we set for ourselves both service and instructional goals as we strive to make our libraries supportive and caring places for all children.

—Thomas (2011)

Over time, many have commented on the lack of communication between research scholars and practicing school librarians. Durrance (1988), for example, asserts that "researchers most often write for other researchers and librarians for other librarians," resulting in "two sets of literatures, one based on practice the other on research" (161), resulting. Although it may be true that researchers and librarians sometimes seem to represent different constituencies, they are surely bound together in a shared concern for children and for improving the quality and effectiveness of information literacy instruction. To achieve this goal, scholars and professionals must rely on each other, for it is in practice that theories are verified, and it is theory that makes practice credible. To improve the quality of both, the exchange of ideas, insights, and information between researchers and practitioners is critically important.[1]

Todd (2008a, 2009) and others advocate grounding contemporary instructional approaches and the information literacy curriculum in research evidence. This has been discussed in some detail in the preceding chapters, and its importance cannot be overstated. As we enter the second decade of the 21st century, our commitment to research as the basis for reflective practice remains strong. Comer's (2001) challenge—to structure educational practice on understandings of how children grow and learn—continues to inspire us as we strive to put research insights to work within the context of contemporary school librarianship.

From its inception, *Information Skills and Information Literacy Instruction* has attempted to build a bridge between researchers in library and information studies and school library practitioners by making available basic theories and models to use in creating an effective information literacy curriculum and accessible research insights based on observations of students and practices over time. While there is an increasing emphasis on research and school librarianship, most scholars and practitioners agree that there is an enormous need for continuing our efforts. Longitudinal studies are particularly important if we are to prove that what we do makes a difference in preparing students for the business of living in an information-rich and technologically complex world. Further testing of process models and inquiry learning, as well as research related to information seeking among underserved and often overlooked user populations, will go a long way in helping school librarian achieve the spirit and the letter of the 21st century standards that the American Association of School Librarians has created for them.

A review of the research relating to instruction and learning in the modern media center reminds us that we are indeed accountable for empowering students through their acquisition of essential information and learning competencies. Helping students engage in skill building for a lifetime reminds us that we are in the business of educating youngster for the long haul. However, we must also be concerned about the short term, that is, helping students meet their immediate goals, only some of which will involve their school assignments. For these reasons, additional studies focused on motivation and on the independent information-seeking activities of students outside the confines of school-related information would be of special value.

As we have seen, an inquiry approach to teaching and learning relies on co-operation and collaboration of instructional teams and relationships, all of which require both initiative and investments of time and energy. Making changes that will result in higher levels of achievement for students often—and sometimes inevitably—demands that we take the lead in instructional team building. As librarians, we rely on teachers to provide the curricular context for the integration of information skills, while they can count on our technological expertise and knowledge of information-seeking processes and resources in helping to educate information-literate students. Thinking strategically, acting collaboratively, and communicating effectively will aid school librarians in this important endeavor. Assessing and capitalizing on our own strengths and developing new skill sets when necessary is a professional responsibility and one that will lead to increased levels if professional competence and self-confidence.

As school leaders, it is critical that we advocate articulately and passionately for our programs and, more importantly, for the youngsters we meet in the library on a daily basis. To do the job well demands that we set for ourselves both service and instructional goals as we strive to make our libraries supportive and caring places for all children. To ensure such outcomes, our library volunteers and aides must come to embrace our service models and ethics as enthusiastically as we do ourselves. It is our responsibility to see that this is so.

Because we have access to all the students in our schools, school librarians are in a position to make real differences in the lives of every one of these children every day. Vandergrift and Hannigan (1986) have acknowledged this aspect of school librarianship and the role librarians can take in helping students "develop the kind of educated imagination that empowers them to consider alternatives and to construct possible models of a better and more humane world" (171). The challenges of such an opportunity are striking and should surely shift our focus from the mundane aspects of "the job" to much loftier and more meaningful goals.

As a career path, school librarianship should not be undertaken casually: our commitments to children and their educational success must be total. Indeed, our tasks are complex—requiring wisdom as well as intelligence and empathy as well as patience in addition to advanced communication skills, creativity, stamina, humor, sensitivity, and a loving heart—and yet it is this very complexity that makes our professional lives both exciting and fulfilling.

On a final note, we offer one caveat: as important an activity as establishing unequivocally the educational value of school libraries is in ensuring support for the profession at large and as critical as it is to help prepare our students for the jobs of tomorrow, we should also take time to savor the joy of helping to educate children. We have much to learn from them, just as they have much to learn from us. Of the latter, one of the most important is introducing youngsters to literary works—works that inspire as well as instruct—as they embark on their personal intellectual journeys. It is in this way that we can advance the common good and secure for future generations the values that may well have drawn us into the field of school librarianship in the first place. Finally, we must not overlook or fail to appreciate fully the satisfactions inherent in positive interpersonal interactions with the children we meet in our libraries, for it is these that will enrich both their lives and our own.

Note

1. In 2010, school librarians and college and university librarians from Kansas and Missouri met in an effort to begin sharing information about what students know and what they need to know in terms of beginning and completing university-level reading and writing. The group plans to meet again for continuing discussion and collaboration and has created a wiki, available at http://collegehighschoollibrarians.pbworks.com/w/page/ 30847868/College-Readiness-Dialogue-Wiki.

References

Aaron, S. L. (1982). Review of Selected Doctoral Dissertations about School Library Media Programs and Resources January 1972–December 1980. *School Library Media Quarterly, 10*, 210–240.

Abram, S., & Luther, J. (2004). Born with the Chip. *Library Journal, 129*, no. 8, 34–37.

Achterman, D. L. (2009). *Haves, Halves, and Have-Nots: School Libraries and Student Achievement in California*. PhD diss., University of North Texas.

Agosto, D. E. (2001). Propelling Young Women in the Cyber Age: Gender Considerations in the Evaluation of Web-Based Information. *School Library Media Research, 4*. Available: http://www.ala.org/ala/mgrps/divs/aasl/aaslpubsandjournals/slmrb/slmrcontents/volume42001/agosto.cfm (accessed May 26, 2010).

Agosto, D. E. (2002). Bounded Rationality and Satisficing in Young People's Web-Based Decision Making. *Journal of the American Society for Information Science and Technology, 53*, no. 1, 16–27.

Agosto, D. E., & Hughes-Hassell, S. (2006a). Toward a Model of the Everyday Life Information Needs of Urban Teenagers, Part 1: Theoretical Model. *Journal of the American Society for Information Science and Technology, 57*, no. 10, 1394–1403.

Agosto, D. E., & Hughes-Hassell, S. (2006b). Toward a Model of the Everyday Life Information Needs of Urban Teenagers, Part 2: Empirical Model. *Journal of the American Society for Information Science and Technology, 57*, no. 11, 1418–1426.

Akin, L. (1998). Information Overload and Children: A Survey of Texas Elementary School Students. *School Library Media Quarterly, 1*. Available: http://www.ala.org/ala/mgrps/divs/aasl/aaslpubsandjournals/slmrb/slmrcontents/volume11998slmqo/akin.cfm (accessed May 26, 2010).

American Association of School Librarians. (1960). *Standards for School Library Media Programs*. Chicago: American Library Association.

American Association of School Librarians. (2007). *Standards for the 21st Century Learner*. Chicago: American Library Association.

American Association of School Librarians. (2009a). *Empowering Learners: Guidelines for School Library Media Programs*. Chicago: American Library Association.

American Association of School Librarians. (2009b). *Essential Links: Resources for School Library Media Program Development*. Available: http://aasl.ala.org/essentiallinks/index.php?title=Main_Page.

American Association of School Librarians. (2009c). *Standards for the 21st Century Learner in Action*. Chicago: American Library Association.

American Association of School Librarians. (2010a). *AASL Votes to Adopt the Professional Title School Librarian* [Press release, January 16]. Available: http://www.ala.org/ala/newspresscenter/news/pressreleases2010/january2010/adopt_aasl.cfm (accessed February 16, 2010).

American Association of School Librarians. (2010b). *A Planning Guide for Empowering Learners*. Available: http://www.info.eb.com/html/product_online_aasl.html.

American Association of School Librarians & Association for Education Communications and Technology. (1975). *Media Programs: District and School*. Chicago: American Library Association.

American Association of School Librarians & Association for Educational Communications and Technology. (1988). *Information Power: Guidelines for School Library Media Programs*. Chicago: American Library Association.

American Association of School Librarians & Association for Educational Communications and Technology. (1998). *Information Power: Building Partnerships for Learning*. Chicago: American Library Association.

American Library Association. (1945). *School Libraries for Today and Tomorrow: Functions and Standards*. Chicago: Author.

American Library Association. (1969). *Standards for School Library Media Programs*. Chicago: Author.

Anderson, J. A. (1988). Cognitive Styles and Multicultural Populations. *Journal of Teacher Education, 39*, no. 1, 2–9.

Anderson, L. W., & Krathwohl, D. R. (Eds.). (2001). *A Taxonomy for Learning, Teaching, and Assessing: A Revision of Bloom's Taxonomy of Educational Objectives*. Boston: Allyn & Bacon.

Armstrong, M., & Costa, B. (1983). Computer Cat at Mountain View Elementary School. *Library Hi Tech, 1*, no. 3, 47–52.

Arnone, M. P., & Reynolds, R. (2009). Empirical Support for the Integration of Dispositions in Action and Multiple Literacies into AASL's *Standards for the 21st Century Learner*. *School Library Media Research, 12*, 1–8. Available: http://www.aasl.org/ala/mgrps/divs/aasl/aaslpubsandjournals/slmrb/slmrcontents/volume12/arnone_reynolds.cfm (accessed March 31, 2010).

Arnone, M. P., Reynolds, R., & Marshall, T. (2009). The Effect of Early Adolescents' Psychological Needs Satisfaction upon Their Perceived Competence in Information Skills and Intrinsic Motivation for Research. *School Libraries Worldwide, 15*, no. 2, 115–134.

Asselin, M., & Doiron, R. (2008). Towards a Transformative Pedagogy for School Libraries 2.0. *School Libraries Worldwide, 14*, no. 2, 1–18.

Baker, L., & Brown, A. L. (1984). Metacognitive Skills and Reading. In P. D. Pearson (Ed.), *Handbook of Reading Research* (pp. 353–394), New York: Longman, 1984.

Baker, S. L., & Lancaster, F. W. (1991). *The Measurement and Evaluation of Library Services*. Arlington, VA: Information Resources Press.

Barron, D. D. (1994). School Library Media Specialists and The Internet: Road Kill or Road Warriors? *School Library Media Activities Monthly, 10*, no. 9, 48–50.

Bates, M. J. (1979a). Idea Tactics. *Journal of the American Society for Information Science, 30*, no. 5, 280–289.

Bates, M. J. (1979b). Information Search Tactics. *Journal of the American Society for Information Science, 30*, no. 4, 205–214.

Bates, M. J. (1989). Design of Browsing and Berrypicking: Techniques for the Online Search Interface. *Online Review, 13*, no. 4, 407–423.

Baumbach, D. T. (1986). Information Skills for the Information Age: The State of Our States. In S. L. Aaron & P. R. Scales (Eds.), *School Library Media Annual* (Vol. 4, pp. 278–285). Littleton, CO: Libraries Unlimited.

Becker, D. E. (1970). *Social Studies Achievement of Pupils in Schools with Libraries and Schools without Libraries.* PhD diss., University of Pennsylvania.

Belkin, N. J. (1980). Anomalous State of Knowledge for Information Retrieval. *Canadian Journal of Information Science, 5*, no. 13, 133–143.

Belkin, N. J., Oddy, R. N., & Brooks, H. M. (1982a). Ask for Information Retrieval: Part II. *Journal of Documentation, 38*, no. 3, 145–164.

Belkin, N. J., Oddy, R. N., & Brooks, H. M. (1982b). Information Retrieval: Part I. Background and Theory. *Journal of Documentation, 38*, no. 2, 61–71.

Belmont, J. M. (1989). Cognitive Strategies and Strategic Learning: The Socio-Instructional Approach. *American Psychologist, 44*, no. 2, 142–148.

Benton Foundation. (1996). *Buildings, Books, and Bites: Librarians and Communities in the Digital Age.* Available: http://benton.org/archive/publibrary/kellogg/buildings.html (accessed March 24, 2011).

Berkowitz, R. E. (1994). From Indicators of Quantity to Measures of Effectiveness: Ensuring Information Power's Mission. In C. C. Kuhlthau, M. E. Goodin, & M. J. McNally (Eds.), *Assessment in the School Library Media Center* (pp. 33–42). Englewood, CO: Libraries Unlimited.

Berkowitz, R. E., & Serim, F. (2002). *Moving Every Child Ahead: The Big6 Success Strategy.* Available: http://www.infotoday.com/MMSchools/may02/berkowitz.htm (accessed May, 26, 2010).

Berlyne, D. E. (1960). *Conflict, Arousal and Curiosity.* New York: McGraw-Hill.

Bernier, A. (2007). Introduction: "Not Broke by Someone Else's Schedule": On Joy and Young Adult Information Seeking. In M. K. Chelton and C. Cool (Eds.), *Youth Information-Seeking Behavior II: Context, Theories, Models, and Issues* (pp. xiii–xxviii). Lanham, MD: Scarecrow Press.

Bialo, E. R., & Sivin-Kachala, J. (1996). The Effectiveness of Technology in Schools: A Summary of Recent Research. *School Library Media Quarterly, 25*, no. 1, 51–57.

Biggers, D. (2001). The Argument against Accelerated Reader. *Journal of Adolescent & Adult Literacy, 45*, no. 1, 72–75.

Bilal, D. (1998). Children's Search Processes in Using World Wide Web Search Engines: An Exploratory Study. *Proceedings of the ASIS Annual Meeting* (Vol. 35, pp. 45–53). Medford, NJ: Information Today.

Bilal, D. (1999). Web Search Engines for Children: A Comparative Study and Performance Evaluation of Yahooligans!, Ask Jeeves for Kids™, and Super Snooper™. *Proceedings of ASIS Annual Meeting* (Vol. 36, pp. 70–83). Medford, NJ: Information Today.

Bilal, D. (2000). Children's Use of the Yahooligans! Web Search Engine: I. Cognitive, Physical and Affective Behaviors on Fact-Based Search Tasks. *Journal of the American Society for Information Science and Technology, 51*, no. 7, 646–665.

Bilal, D. (2001). Children's Use of the Yahooligans! Web Search Engine: II. Cognitive, and Physical Behaviors on Research Tasks. *Journal of the American Society for Information Science and Technology, 52*, no. 2, 118–136.

Bilal, D. (2002a). Children's Use of the Yahooligans! Web Search Engine: 1. Cognitive, and Physical Behaviors on Fully Self-Generated Search Tasks. *Journal of the American Society for Information Science and Technology, 53*, no. 13, 1170–1183.

Bilal, D. (2002b). Perspectives on Children's Navigation of the World Wide Web: Does the Type of Search Task Make a Difference? *Online Information Review, 26,* no. 2, 108–117.

Bilal, D. (2005). Children's Information Seeking and the Design of Digital Interfaces in the Affective Paradigm. *Library Trends, 54,* no. 2, 197–208.

Bilal, D., & Watson, J. S. (1998). Children's Paperless Projects: Inspiring Research via the Web. In *Proceedings of the 64th IFLA General Conference, August 16–21, 1998, Amsterdam, The Netherlands* (101–107, Booklet 3). Amsterdam: Xerox. Available: – http://archive.ifla.org/IV/ifla64/009–131e.htm (accessed November 10, 2010).

Bishop, K. (2001). *Inquiry-Based Learning: Lessons from Library Power.* Worthington, OH: Linworth.

Bishop, W. W. (1986). Training in the Use of Books. In L. L. Hardesty, J. P. Schmitt, & J. M. Tucker (Eds.), *User Instruction in Academic Libraries: A Century of Selected Readings* (pp. 69–85). Metuchen, NJ: Scarecrow Press.

Bloom, B. (1956). *Taxonomy of Educational Objectives.* New York: David McKay.

Bobotis, N. C., (1978). *Relationship of Modes of Instruction and Bilingualism to Achievement in Library Skills.* PhD diss., University of New Mexico.

Bodi, S. (1992). Collaborating with Faculty in Teaching Critical Thinking: The Role of Librarians. *Research Strategies, 10,* no. 2, 69–76.

Bogen, J. E. (1969). Some Educational Aspects of Hemispheric Specialization. *UCLA Educator, 17,* 24–32.

Boggiano, A. K., Flink, C., Shields, A., Seelbach, A., & Barrett, M. (1993). Use of Techniques Promoting Students' Self-Determination: Effects on Students' Analytic Problem-Solving Skills. *Motivation and Emotion, 17,* no. 4, 319–336.

Bondy, E. (1984). Thinking about Thinking: Encouraging Children's Use of Metacognitive Processes. *Childhood Education, 60,* no. 4, 234–238.

Borgman, C. L., Hirsh, S. G., Walter, V. A., & Gallagher, A. L. (1995). Children's Searching Behavior on Browsing and Keyword Online Catalogs: The Science Library Catalog Project. *Journal of the American Society for Information Science, 46,* no. 9, 663–684.

Bowie, M. M. (Comp.). (1986). *Historic Documents of School Libraries.* Fayetteville, AR: Hi Willow Research Publishing.

Bracy, P. (1990). Completed Research Pertinent to School Library Media Programs. In J. B. Smith (Ed.), *School Library Media Annual* (Vol. 8, pp. 126–134). Littleton, CO: Libraries Unlimited.

Branch, J. L. (2003). Instructional Intervention Is Key: Supporting Adolescent Information Seeking. *School Libraries Worldwide, 9,* no. 2, 47–61.

Breivik, P. S. (1989). Politics for Bridging the Gap. *Reference Librarian, 10,* no. 24, 5–16.

Breivik, P. S. (1991). Literacy in an Information. *Society. Community, Technical, and Junior College Journal, 61,* no. 6, 28–29, 32–35.

Brien, D. P. (1995). *The Teaching and Learning Processes Involved in Primary School Children's Research Projects.* EdD diss., University of New South Wales.

Broch, E. (2000). Children's Search Engines from an Information Search Process Perspective. *School Library Media Research.* Available: http://www.ala.org/ala/mgrps/divs/aasl/aaslpubsandjournals/slmrb/slmrcontents/volume32000/childrens.cfm (accessed May 26, 2010).

Brodie, C. S. (1988). *Library Programs for the Gifted and Talented: Differentiated versus Traditional.* PhD diss., Texas Women's University.

Brown, J. S., Collins, A., & Duguid, P. (1989). Situated Cognition and the Culture of Learning. *Educational Researcher, 18,* no. 1, 32–42.

Bruce, H. (1994). Media Center Automation: A Watershed for the School Library Media Specials. *School Library Media Quarterly, 22*, no. 4, 206–212.

Bruffee, K. A. (1984). Collaborative Learning and the "Conversation of Mankind." *College English, 46*, no. 7, 635–652.

Bruner, J. (1975). *Toward a Theory of Instruction.* Cambridge, MA: Harvard University Press.

Bruner, J. (1977). *The Process of Education.* Cambridge, MA: Harvard University Press.

Bruner, J. (1980). *Beyond the Information Given.* New York: Norton.

Bruner, J. (1986). *Actual Minds, Possible Worlds.* Cambridge, MA: Harvard University Press.

Buckland, M. K. (1983). *Library Services in Theory and Context.* New York: Pergamon Press.

Burdick, T. A. (1996). Success and Diversity in Information Seeking: Gender and the Information Search Styles Model. *School Library Media Quarterly, 25*, no. 1, 19–26.

Burdick, T. A. (1997). Snakes and Snails and Puppy Dog Tails: Girl and Boys Expressing Voice in Information Research Projects. *Journal of Youth Services in Libraries, 11*, no. 1, 28–36.

Butler, P. (1933). *An Introduction to Library Science.* Chicago: University of Chicago Press.

Buzan, T. (1991). *Use Both Sides of Your Brain.* New York: Dutton.

Callison, D. (1986). School Library Media Programs and Free Inquiry Learning. *School Library Media Quarterly, 15*, no. 6, 20–24.

Callison, D. (1990). A Review of the Research Related to School Library Media Collections: Part I. *School Library Media Quarterly, 19*, no. 1, 57–62.

Callison, D. (1994). Expanding the Evaluation Role in the Critical-Thinking Curriculum. In C. C. Kuhlthau, M. E. Goodin, & M. J. McNally (Eds.), *Assessment in the School Library Media Center* (pp. 43–57). Englewood, CO: Libraries Unlimited.

Callison, D. (1995). Expanding the Evaluation Role in the Critical-Thinking Curriculum. In Fifteenth Anniversary Task Force, Library Instruction Round Table, American Library Association (Comp.), *Information for a New Age: Redefining the Librarian* (pp. 153–169). Englewood, CO: Libraries Unlimited.

Callison, D. (1999). Key Instructional Term: Motivation. *School Library Media Activities Monthly, 16*, no. 1, 37–39.

Callison, D. (2006). Editor's Choice: Enough Already? Blazing New Trails for School Library Research: An Interview with Keith Curry Lance, Director, Library Research Service, Colorado State Library & University of Denver. *School Library Media Research, 1–12.* Available: http://www.ala.org/ala/mgrps/divs/aasl/aaslpubsandjournals/slmrb/editorschoiceb/lance/interviewlance.cfm (accessed January 23, 2010).

Carey, J. O. (1997, April). *From Library Skills to Information Literacy: Implications for Teaching and Learning.* Presentation at Treasure Mountain Research Retreat. Portland, OR.

Carey, J. O. (1998). Library Skills, Information Skills, and Information Literacy: Implications for Teaching and Learning. *SLMQ Online.* Available: http://www.ala.org/ala/mgrps/divs/aasl/aaslpubsandjournals/slmrb/slmrcontents/volume11998slmqo/slmqvolume1.cfm (accessed May 26, 2010).

Carroll, F. L. (1981). *Recent Advances in School Librarianship.* Oxford: Pergamon Press.

Carson, C. H., & Curtis, R. V. (1991). Applying Instructional Design Theory to Bibliographic Instruction: Microtheory. *Research Strategies, 9*, no. 2, 20–76.

Carvin, A. (2000a). *Beyond Access: Understanding the Digital Divide.* Keynote Address, New York University Third Act Conference, May 19, 2000.

Carvin, A. (2000b). *Mending the Breach: Overcoming the Digital Divide.* Available: http://www.edutopia.org/mending-breach-overcoming-digital-divide (accessed May 26, 2010)

Cecil, H. L., & Heaps, W. A. (1940). School Library Service in the United States: An Interpretive Survey. In M. M. Bowie (Comp.), *Historic Documents of School Libraries.* Fayetteville, AR: Hi Willow, 1986.

Chelton, M. K. (1997). *Adult-Adolescent Service Encounters. The Library Context.* PhD diss., Rutgers University.

Chelton, M. K. (1999). Structural and Theoretical Constraints on Reference Service in a High School Library Media Center. *Reference & User Services Quarterly, 38,* no. 3, 275–287.

Chelton, M. K., & Thomas, N. P. (1999). Introduction: Why a Special Issue on Youth Services? In M. K. Chelton & N. P. Thomas (Eds.), Special Issue: Youth Issues in Information Science. *Journal of the American Society for Information Science, 50,* no. 1, 7–9.

Chen, S.-H. (1993). A Study of High School Students' Online Catalog Searching Behavior. *School Library Media Quarterly, 22,* no. 1, 33–40.

Clark, L. A., & Halford, G. S. (1983). Does Cognitive Style Account for Cultural Differences in Scholastic Achievement? *Journal of Cross-Cultural Psychology, 14,* no. 3, 279–296.

Clarke, J., Martell, K., & Willey, C. (1994). Sequencing Graphic Organizers to Guide Historical Research. *The Social Studies, 85,* no. 5, 70–78.

Claxton, C. S. (1990). Learning Styles, Minority Students, and Effective Education. *Journal of Developmental Education, 14,* no. 1, 6–8, 35.

Clements, D. H., & Nastasi, B. K. (1988). Social and Cognitive Interaction in Educational Computer Environments. *American Educational Research Journal, 25,* no. 1, 87–106.

Coleman, J. G. (1989). Library Media Personnel: The Essential Ingredient. In J. B. Smith (Ed.), *School Library Media Annual* (Vol. 7, pp. 46–56). Englewood, CO: Libraries Unlimited.

Collins, A., Brown, J. S., & Newman, S. E. (1989). Cognitive Apprenticeship: Teaching the Crafts of Reading, Writing, and Mathematics. In L. B. Resnick (Ed.), *Knowing, Learning, and Instruction: Essays in Honor of Robert Glaser* (pp. 453–494). Hillsdale, NJ: Lawrence Erlbaum Associates.

Comer, J. P. (2001). Schools That Develop Children. *The American Prospect Online, 12,* no. 7 (April 22). Available: http://www.prospect.org/cs/articles?article=schools_that _develop_children (accessed May, 26, 2010).

Connaway, L. S., Radford, M. L., Dickey, T. J., Williams, J. D., & Confer, P. C. (2008). Sense-Making and Synchronicity: Information-Seeking Behaviors of Millennials and Baby Boomers. *Libri, 58,* 123–135.

Cookson, P. (2009). What Would Socrates Say? *Educational Leadership, 56,* no. 2, 8–19.

Cooper, L. Z. (2002). A Case Study of Information-Seeking Behavior in 7-Year-Old Children in a Semi-Structured Situation. *Journal of the American Society for Information Science and Technology, 53,* no. 11, 904–922.

Cottrell, J. R., & Eisenberg, M. B. (2001). Applying an Information Problem-Solving Model to Academic Reference Work: Findings and Implications. *College & Research Libraries, 62,* no. 4, 334–347.

Craver, K. W. (1989). Critical Thinking: Implications from Research. *School Library Media Quarterly, 18,* no. 1, 13–18.

Craver, K. W. (1995). Shaping our Future: The Role of School Library Media Centers. *School Library Media Quarterly, 24,* no. 1, 13–18.

Creanor, L., Durndell, H., Henderson, F. P., Primrose, C., Brown, M. I., Draper, S. W., & McAteer, E. (1995). *A Hypertext Approach to Information Skills: Development and Evaluation.* Glasgow: University of Glasgow Series, TLT Publications.

Creative Commons. (2010). *About*. Available: http://creativecommons.org/about (accessed November 10, 2010).

Crow, S. R. (2004). The Colorado Children's Book Award Program: Why All the Shouting? *Colorado Libraries*, Spring, 17–20.

Crow, S. R. (2009a). *Exploring the Experiences of Upper Elementary School Children Who Are Intrinsically Motivated to Seek Information*. Presentation at the American Association of School Librarians (AASL) National Conference. November 5–9, Charlotte, NC.

Crow, S. R. (2009b). Relationships That Foster Intrinsic Motivation for Information Seeking. *School Libraries Worldwide*, *15*, no. 2, 91–112.

Crow, S. R. (2010). Children's Choice Book Award Programs: Effective Weapons in the Battle to Get and Keep Kids Reading. *School Library Monthly*, *26*, no. 9, 12–13.

Csikszentmihalyi, M. (1975). *Beyond Boredom and Anxiety*. San Francisco: Jossey-Bass, 1975.

Csikszentmihalyi, M. (1990). *Flow: The Psychology of Optimal Experience*. New York: Harper & Row.

Csikszentmihalyi, M., & Hermanson, K. (1999). Intrinsic Motivation in Museums: Why Does One Want to Learn? In E. Hooper-Greenhill (Ed.), *The Educational Role of the Museum* (2nd ed., pp. 147–160). New York: Routledge.

Davies, R. A. (1974). Educating Library Users in the Senior High School. In J. Lubans (Ed.), *Educating the Library User* (pp. 39–52). New York: Bowker.

Davies, R. A. (1979). *The School Library Media Program: Instructional Force for Excellence* (3rd ed.). New York: Bowker.

Deci, E. L. (1975). *Intrinsic Motivation*. New York: Plenum Press.

Deci, E. L., Nezlek, J., & Scheinman, L. (1981). Characteristics of the Rewarder and Intrinsic Motivation of the Rewardee. *Journal of Personality and Social Psychology*, *40*, 1–10.

Deci, E. L., & Ryan, R. M. (1985). *Intrinsic Motivation and Self-Determination in Human Behavior*. New York: Plenum Press.

Deci, E. L., Schwartz, A. J., Sheinman, L., & Ryan, R. M. (1981). An Instrument to Assess Adults' Orientations toward Control versus Autonomy with Children: Reflections on Intrinsic Motivation and Perceived Competence. *Journal of Educational Psychology*, *73*, 642–650.

Delpit, L. D. (1995). *Other People's Children: Cultural Conflict in the Classroom*. New York: New Press.

Delpit, L. D., & Kohl, H. (2006). *Other People's Children: Cultural Conflict in the Classroom, Updated Edition*. New York: The New Press.

Denning, R., Shuttleworth, M., & Smith, P. (1998). Interface Design Concepts in the Development of a Web-Based Information Retrieval System. *Bulletin of the American Society for Information Science*, *24*, no. 4, 17–20. Available: http://www.asis.org/Bulletin/Apr-98/design.html (accessed May 26, 2010).

Dervin, B. (1983). *An Overview of Sense-Making Research: Concepts, Methods, and Results to Date*. Seattle: School of Communication, University of Washington.

Dervin, B. (1989). Users as Research Inventions: How Research Categories Perpetuate Inequities. *Journal of Communication*, *39*, no. 3, 216–232.

Dervin, B. (1999). The Implications of Connecting Metatheory to Method. *Information Processing & Management*, *35*, no. 6, 727–750.

Dervin, B., & Dewdney, P. (1986). Neutral Questioning: A New Approach to the Reference Interview. *Research Quarterly*, *35*, no. 4, 506–513.

Dervin, B., & Nilan, M. (1986). Information Needs and Uses. In M. E. Williams (Ed.), *Annual Review of Information Science and Technology (ARIST)* (Vol. 21, pp. 3–33). White Plains, NY: Knowledge Industry Publications.

Dewees, K. B. (1987). *The Effect of Teaching Library Skills Using "The Pooh Step-by-Step Guide for Writing the Research Paper" at Lieder Elementary School in the Cypress Fairbanks Independent School District. A Research Report.* Houston: Prairie View A & M University. (ERIC ED 284 577)

Dewey, J. (1915). *The School and Society.* Chicago: University of Chicago Press.

Dewey, J. (1916). *Democracy and Education: An Introduction to the Philosophy of Education.* New York: Macmillan.

Dewey, J. (1933). *How We Think.* Lexington, MA: Heath.

Dickinson, D. W. (1981). Library Literacy: Who? When? Where? *Library Journal, 106,* no. 8, 853–855.

Didier, E. K. (1982). *Relationships between Student Achievement in Reading and Library Media Programs and Personnel.* PhD diss., University of Michigan.

Didier, E. K. (1985). An Overview of Research on the Impact of School Library Media Programs on Student Achievement. *School Library Media Quarterly, 14,* no. 1, 33–36.

Dike, V. W. (1993). School Libraries/Media Centers. In *World Encyclopedia of Library and Information Science* (3rd ed., pp. 743–753). Chicago: American Library Association.

Donham, J., Bishop, K., Kuhlthau, C. C., & Oberg, D. (2001). *Inquiry-Based Learning: Lessons from Library Power.* Worthington, OH: Linworth.

Dow, M. J. (2008). Teaching Ethical Behavior in the Global World of Information and the New AASL Standards. *School Library Media Activities Monthly, 25,* no. 4, 49–52.

Dow, M. J. I., Lakin, J. M., & Court, S. (2010). *Kansas School Library Media Statewide Study.* Presentation at KSDE Annual Conference, October 26–27, Wichita, KS.

Doyle, C. S. (1994). Information-Literate Use of Telecommunications. *CMLEA Journal, 17,* no. 2, 17–20.

Driver, R., Asoko, H., Leach, J., Mortimer, E., & Scott, P. (1994). Constructing Scientific Knowledge in the Classroom. *Educational Researcher, 23,* no. 1, 8–14.

Dunn, R., Beasley, M., & Buchanan, K. (1994). What Do You Believe about How Culturally Diverse Students Learn? *Emergency Librarian, 22,* no. 1, 8–14.

Dunn, R., & Smith, J. B. (1990). Learning Styles and Library Media Programs. In J. B. Smith (Ed.), *School Library Media Annual* (Vol. 8, pp. 32–49). Englewood, CO: Libraries Unlimited.

Durrance, J. C. (1988). Information Needs: Old Song, New Tune. In *Rethinking the Library in the Information Age: Issues in Library Research. Proposals for the 1990s* (pp. 159–177). Washington, DC: Government Printing Office.

Dutilloy, J. (2003). Implementing a Plagiarism Policy at the United Nations International School. *Knowledge Quest, 31,* no. 4, 44–45.

Dwyer, D. (1994). Apple Classroom of Tomorrow: What We've Learned. *Educational Leadership, 51,* no. 7, 4–10.

Eadie, T. (1990). Immodest Proposals: User Instruction for Students Does Not Work. *Library Journal, 115,* no. 17, 42–45.

Edmonds, L., Moore, P., & Balcom, K. M. (1990). The Effectiveness of an Online Catalog. *School Library Journal, 36,* no. 10, 28–32.

Eisenberg, M. B., & Berkowitz, R. B. (1990). *Information Problem-Solving: The Big Six Skills Approach to Library and Information Skills Instruction.* Norwood, NJ: Ablex.

Eisenberg, M. B., & Berkowitz, R. B. (1996). *Helping with Homework: A Parent's Guide to Information Problem-Solving.* Syracuse, NY: ERIC Clearinghouse in Information and Technology.

Eisenberg, M. B., & Brown, M. K. (1992). Current Themes Regarding Library and Information Skills Instruction: Research Supporting and Research Lacking. *School Library Media Quarterly, 20,* no. 2, 103–109.

Eisenberg, M. B., Johnson, D., & Berkowitz, R. (2010). Information, Communications, and Technology (ICT) Skills Curriculum Based on the Big6Skills Approach to Information Problem-Solving.*Library Media Connection.* Available: http://www.big6 .com/.../2010/.../LMC_Big6–ICT_Curriculum_LMC_MayJune2010.pdf (accessed June 2, 2010).

Eisenberg, M. B., & Spitzer, K. L. (1991). Information Technology and Service in Schools. In M. E. Williams (Ed.), *Annual Review of Information Science and Technology (ARIST)* (Vol. 26, pp. 243–285). Medford, NJ: Learned Education.

Eisner, E. W. (1993). Why Standards May Not Improve Schools. *Educational Leadership, 50,* no. 5, 22–23.

Eisner, E. W. (2004). "Artistry in Teaching," *Cultural Commons.* In M. K. Smith, Elliot W. Eisner, Connoisseurship, criticism and the art of education, the encyclopedia of informal education, www.infed.org/thinkers/Eisner/htm.

Ellis, D. (1989). A Behavioural Approach to Information Retrieval Systems Design. *Journal of Documentation, 45,* no. 3, 171–212.

Ely, D. P. (1992). Response 1 to Ann Irving. In J. B. Smith (Ed.), *School Library Media Annual* (Vol. 10, pp. 46–47). Englewood, CO: Libraries Unlimited.

Engledinger, E. A. (1988). Bibliographic Instruction and Critical Thinking: The Contribution of the Annotated Bibliography. *Research Quarterly, 28,* no. 2, 195–202.

Engledinger, E. A., & Stevens, B. R. (1984). Library Instruction within the Curriculum. *College & Research Libraries, 45,* no. 11, 593–598.

Entwhistle, N. (1981). *Styles of Learning and Teaching: An Integrative Outline of Educational Psychology.* Chichester: Wiley.

Eriksen, E. H. (1968). *Identity, Youth, and Crisis.* New York: Norton.

Everhart, N. (2003). Students and Plagiarism. *Knowledge Quest, 31,* no. 4, 43–44.

Everhart, N. (2005). A Cross-Cultural Inquiry into the Levels of Implementation of Accelerated Reader and Its Effect on Motivation and Extent of Reading: Perspectives from Scotland and England. *School Library Media Research, 8,* 1–15. Available: http://www.ala .org/ala/aasl/aaslpubsandjournals/slmrb/slmrcontents/volume82005/reader.htm (accessed September 10, 2010).

Farber, E. I. (1995). Bibliographic Instruction, Briefly. In Fifteen Fifteenth Anniversary Task Force, Library Instruction Round Table, American Library Association (Comp.), *Information for a New Age: Redefining the Librarian* (pp. 153–169). Englewood, CO: Libraries Unlimited.

Feldman, D. H. (Ed.). (1994). *Beyond Universals in Cognitive Development* (2nd ed.). Westport, CT: Ablex.

Fidel, R., Davies, R. K., Douglass, M. H., Holder, J. K., Hopkins, C. J., Kushner, E. J., Miyagishima, B. K., & Toney, C. D. (1999). A Visit to the Information Mall: Web Searching Behavior of High School Students. *Journal of the American Society for Information Science, 50,* no. 1, 24–37.

Fisher, K. E., Marcoux, E., Meyers, E., & Landry, C. F. (2006). Tweens and Everyday Life Information Behavior: Preliminary Findings from Seattle. In M. K. Chelton & C. Cool (Eds.), *Youth Information Seeking Behaviors: Contexts, Theories, Models and Issues* (Vol. 2, pp. 1–26). Lanham, MD: Scarecrow Press.

Fitzgerald, M. A. (1999). Evaluating Information: an Information Literacy Challenge. *School Library Media Research*, 2. Available: http://www.ala.org/ala/mgrps/divs/aasl/aaslpubsandjournals/slmrb/slmrcontents/volume21999/ALA_print_layout_1_202785_202785.cfm (accessed May 26, 2010).

Flink, C., Boggiano, A. K., & Barrett, M. (1990). Controlling Teaching Strategies: Undermining Children's Self-Determination and Performance. *Journal of Personality and Social Psychology, 59*, 916–924.

Ford, D. Y. (1996). *Reversing Underachievement among Gifted Black Students*. New York: Teachers College Press.

Forehand, G. A., Regosta, M., & Rock, D. A. (1976). *Conditions and Processes of Effective School Desegregation: Final Report*. Princeton, NJ: Educational Testing Service.

Foster, A. (2004). A Nonlinear Model of Information-Seeking Behavior. *Journal of the American Society for Information Science and Technology, 55*, no. 3, 228–237.

Fourie, J. A., & Kruger, J. A. (1995). Basic and Developmental Information Needs of Secondary School Pupils. *Mousaion, 13*, nos. 1/2, 225–249.

Frazier, D. U., & Paulson, F. L. (1992). How Portfolios Motivate Reluctant Writers. *Educational Leadership, 49*, no. 8, 62–65.

Freedman, K., & Liu, M. (1996). The Importance of Computer Experience, Learning Processes, and Communication Patterns in Multicultural Networking. *ETR & D, 44*, no. 1, 43–59.

Freud, S. (1925). Instincts and Their Vicissitudes. In *Collected Papers* (Vol. 4). London: Hogarth.

Freud, S. (1957). On Narcissism. In *The Standard Edition of the Complete Works of Sigmund Freud* (Vol. 14). London: Hogarth Press.

Frohmann, B. (1992). The Power of Image: A Discourse Analysis of the Cognitive Viewpoint. *Journal of Documentation, 48*, no. 4, 365–386.

Gallivan, M. F. (1974). Research on Children's Services in Libraries: An Annotated Bibliography. *Top of the News, 30*, no. 3, 275–293.

Gardner, H. (1983). *Frames of Mind: The Theory of Multiple Intelligences*. New York: Basic Books.

Gardner, H. (1996), Probing More Deeply into the Theory of Multiple Intelligences. *NASSP Bulletin, 80*, no. 583, 1–7.

Gardner, H. (1999). *Intelligence Reframed: Multiple Intelligences for the 21st Century*. New York: Basic Books.

Gardner, H. (2003, April 21). *Multiple Intelligences after Twenty Years*. Paper presented at the annual meeting of the American Educational Research Association, Chicago, IL. Available: http://www.pz.harvard.edu/PIs/HG_MI_after_20_years.pdf (accessed November 8, 2010).

Garland, K. (1995). The Information Search Process: A Study of Elements Associated with Meaningful Research Tasks. In B. J. Morris, J. L. McQuiston, & C. L. Saretsky (Eds.), *School Library Media Annual* (Vol. 13, pp. 171–183). Englewood, CO: Libraries Unlimited.

Gaver, M. V. (1963). *Effectiveness of Centralized Library Service in Elementary Schools*. New Brunswick, NJ: Rutgers University Press.

Gedeon, R. (2000). Accessing the Right Brain with Bibliographic Instruction. *Research Strategies, 16*, no. 4, 259–269.

Gehlken, V. S. (1994). *The Role of the High School Library Media Program in Three Nationally Recognized South Carolina Blue Ribbon Secondary Schools*. PhD diss., University of South Carolina.

Ghikas, M. W. (1989). Collection Management for the 21st Century. In P. Woodrom (Ed.), *Managing Public Libraries in the 21st Century* (pp. 119–135). New York: Haworth Press.

Giese, R. N., Cothron, J. H., & Rezha, R. J. (1992). Take the Search Out of Research: A Guide to "Checking Out" the Library. *The Science Teacher, 59*, no. 1, 32–37.

Gifford, V., & Gifford, J. (1984). *Effects of Teaching a Library Usage Unit to Seventh Graders.* Paper presented at the annual conference of the Mid-South Educational Research Association, New Orleans, LA. (ERIC ED 254 230)

Gillespie, J. T., & Spirt, D. L. (1973). *Creating a School Media Program.* New York: Bowker.

Gilligan, C. (1982*). In a Different Voice.* Cambridge, MA: Harvard University Press.

Gilliland, M. J. (1986). Can Libraries Make a Difference? Test Cores Say "Yes"! *School Library Media Quarterly, 15*, no. 2, 67–70.

Goffman, E. (1967). *Interaction Ritual: Essays in Face-to-Face Behavior.* New York: Pantheon.

Goodin, M. E. (1987). *The Transferability of Library Skills from High School to College.* PhD diss., Rutgers University.

Goodin, M. E. (1991). The Transferability of Library Research Skills from High School to College. *School Library Media Quarterly, 20*, no. 1, 33–41.

Gordon, C. (1999). Students as Authentic Researchers: A New Perspective for the High School Research Assignment. *School Library Media Research, 2*. Available: http://www.ala.org/ala/mgrps/divs/aasl/aaslpubsandjournals/slmrb/slmrcontents/volume21999/vol2gordon.cfm (accessed March 31, 2010).

Gordon, C. (2000). *The Effects of Concept Mapping on the Searching Behavior of Tenth-Grade Students. School Library media Research.* Available: http://www.ala.org/ala/mgrps/divs/aasl/aaslpubsandjournals/slmrb/slmrcontents/volume32000/mapping.cfm (accessed November 7, 2010).

Gordon, C., & Lu, Y. (2008). "I Hate to Read—or Do I?": Low Achievers and Their Reading. *School Library Media Research, 11*, 1–13. Available: http://www.aasl.org/ala/mgrps/divs/aasl/aaslpubsandjournals/slmrb/slmrcontents/volume11/gordon_lu.cfm (accessed March 31, 2010).

Gordon, H. (1996). Hemisphericity. In J. G. Beaumont, P. M., Kenealy, & M. K. Rogers (Eds.), *The Blackwell Dictionary of Neuropsychology* (pp. 388–395). Cambridge, MA: Blackwell.

Greer, R. C., Grover, R. J., & Fowler, S. G. (2007). *Introduction to the Library and Information Professions.* Westport, CT: Libraries Unlimited.

Greve, C. L. (1974). *The Relationship of the Availability of Libraries to the Academic Achievement of Iowa High School Seniors.* PhD diss., University of Denver.

Gross, M. (1995). The Imposed Query. *Research Quarterly, 35*, no. 2, 236–243.

Gross, M. (1997). Pilot Study on the Prevalence of Imposed Queries in a School Library Media Center. *School Library Media Quarterly, 25*, no. 3, 157–166.

Gross, M. (1999). Imposed Queries in the School Library Media Center: A Descriptive Study. *Library and Information Science Research, 21*, no. 4, 501–521.

Grover, R. (1993). A Proposed Model for Diagnosing Information Needs. *School Library Media Quarterly, 21*, no. 2, 95–100.

Grover, R. (1994). Assessing Information Skills Instruction. *The Reference Librarian, 20*, no. 44, 173–189.

Grover, R., Blume, S., Dickerson, J., Lakin, J., & Schumacher, M. (1996). *An Interdisciplinary Model for Assessing Learning.* Paper presented at the Library Research Seminar I. Tallahassee, FL.

Hagiopian, G., Iandoli, A., Wellins, C. L., & Williams, H. B. (1996). *Four Phase Study: Impact of Learning Styles on Teaching and Learning in an Urban District.* Paper presented at the National Development Council Annual Conference, Vancouver, British Columbia, December.

Hale-Benson, J. E. (1982). *Black Children: Their Roots, Culture, and Learning Styles.* Provo, UT: Brigham Young University Press.

Hanchett, T. W. (1988). The Rosenwald Schools and Black Education in North Carolina. *North Carolina Historical Review, 64,* 4.

Harada, V. H. (2002). Personalizing the Information Search Process: A Case Study of Journal Writing with Elementary-Age Students. *School Library Media Research, 5.* Available: http://www.ala.org/ala/mgrps/divs/aasl/aaslpubsandjournals/slmrb/slmrcontents/volume52002/harada.cfm (accessed November 7, 2010).

Hardesty, L. L., Schmitt, J. P., & Tucker, J. M. (Comps.). (1986). *User Instruction in Academic Libraries: A Century of Selected Readings.* Metuchen, NJ: Scarecrow Press.

Harmon, C. T., & Bradburn, F. B. (1988). Realizing the Reading and Information Needs of Youth. *Library Trends, 37,* no. 1, 19–27.

Harter, S. (1980). *A Scale of Intrinsic versus Extrinsic Orientation in the Classroom* (Available from Susan Harter, Department of Psychology, University of Denver, Denver, CO 80208).

Harter, S. (1981). A New Self-Report Scale of Intrinsic versus Extrinsic Orientation in the Classroom: Motivational and Informational Components. *Developmental Psychology, 17* (3), 300–312.

Hartzell, G. N. (1994). *Building Influence for the School Librarian.* Worthington, OH: Linworth Publishing.

Havighurst, R. I. (1953). *Human Development and Education.* New York: McKay

Haycock, C. A. (1991). Resource-Based Learning: A Shift in the Roles of Teacher, Learner. *NASSP Bulletin, 75,* no. 535, 15–22.

Haycock, K. (1992). *What Works: Research about Teaching and Learning through the School's Library Resource Center.* Vancouver: Rockland Press.

Heeks, P. (1997). School Libraries. In J. Feather & P. Sturges (Eds.), *International Encyclopedia of Information and Library Science* (pp. 410–412). London: Routledge.

Heinström, J. (2006a). Fast Surfing for Availability or Deep Diving into Quality: Motivation and Information Seeking among Middle and High School Students. *Information Research, 11,* no. 4, 1–12. Available: http://information.net/ir//11-4/paper265.htm (accessed April 1, 2011).

Heinström, J. (2006b). Broad Exploration of Precise Specifity: Two Basic Information Seeking Patterns among Students. *Journal of the American Society for Information Science and Technology, 57,* no. 11, 1440–1450.

Hensley, R. (1991). Learning Style Theory and Learning Transfer Principles during Reference Interview Instruction. *Library Trends, 39,* no. 3, 203–209.

Herman, J. L. (1992). What Research Tells Us about Good Assessment. *Educational Leadership, 48,* no. 5, 74–78.

Hidi, S., & Baird, W. (1986). Interestingness—A Neglected Variable in Discourse Processing. *Cognitive Science, 10,* no. 2, 179–194.

Hirsh, S. G. (1997). How Do Children Find Information in Different Tasks? Children's Use of the Science Catalog. *Library Trends, 45,* no. 4, 725–745.

Hirsh, S. G. (1998). Relevance Determinations in Children's Use of Electronic Resources: A Case Study. *Proceedings of the ASIS Annual Meeting* (Vol. 35, pp. 63–72). Medford, NJ: Learned Information.

Hirsh, S. G. (1999). Children's Relevance Criteria and Information Seeking on Electronic Resources. *Journal of the American Society for Information Science, 50*, no. 14, 1265–1283.

Hoerr, T. R. (1996). Introducing the Theory of Multiple Intelligences. *NASSP Bulletin, 80*, no. 583, 8–9.

Holliday, W., & Li, Q. (2004). Understanding the Millennials: Updating Our Knowledge about Students. *Reference Services Review, 32*, no. 4, 356–366.

Honebein, P. (1996). Seven Goals for the Design of Constructivist Learning Environments. In B. G. Wilson (Ed.), *Constructivist Learning Environments: Case Studies in Instructional Design* (pp. 11–24). Englewood Cliffs, NJ: Educational Technology Publications.

Hooten, P. A. (1989). Online Catalogs: Will They Improve Children's Access? *Journal of Youth Services in Libraries, 2*, no. 3, 267–272.

Hopkins, D. M. (1989). Elementary School Library Media Programs and the Promotion of Positive Self-Concept: A Report of an Exploratory Study. *Library Quarterly, 59*, no. 2, 131–147.

Howe, H. II. (1993). *Thinking about Our Kids*. New York: Free Press.

Hull, C. L. (1943). *Principles of Behavior: An Introduction to Behavior Theory*. New York: Appleton-Century-Crofts.

Huston, M. M. (1989). Search Theory and Instruction of End Users of Online Bibliographic Information Retrieval Systems: A Literature Review. *Research Strategies, 7*, no. 1, 14–32.

Huston, M. M., & Oberman, C. (1989). Search Theory and Instruction for End Users of Online Bibliographic Information Retrieval Systems: A Literature Review. *Research Strategies, 7*, no. 1, 14–32.

Hyland, A. H. (1978). Recent Directions in Educating the Library Use: Elementary Schools. In J. Lubans Jr. (Ed.), *Progress in Educating the Library User* (pp. 29–44). New York: Bowker.

Hyldegärd, J. (2009). Beyond the Search Process: Exploring Group Members' Behavior in Context. *Information Processing & Management: An International Journal, 45*, no. 1, 142–158.

Inhelder, B., & Piaget, J. (1958). *The Growth of Logical Thinking: From Childhood to Adolescence*. New York: Basic Books.

Irvine, J. J., & Irvine, R. W. (1995). Black Youth in School: Individual Achievement and Instructional/Cultural Perspectives. In R. L. Taylor (Ed.), *African-American Youth: Their Social and Economic Status in the United States* (pp. 129–142). Westport, CT: Praeger.

Irving, A. (1983). Educating Information Users in Schools. In *British Library Research Reviews* (Vol. 4). London: British Library.

Irving, A. (1985). *Study and Information Skills Across the Curriculum*. London: Heinemann.

Irving, A. (1990). *Wider Horizons: Online Information Services in Schools. Library and Information Research Report 80*. London: British Library.

Irving, A. (1991). The Educational Value and Use of Online Information Services in Schools. *Computers and Education, 17*, no. 3, 213–225.

Jackson, M. M. (1994). Library Information Skills and Standardized Achievement Tests. In C. C. Kuhlthau, M. E. Goodin, & M. J. McNally (Eds.), *Assessment in the School Library Media Center* (pp. 25–32). Englewood, CO: Libraries Unlimited.

Jacobson, F. F. (1997). Introduction. *Library Trends, 45*, no. 4, 575–581.

Jacobson, F. F., & Ignacio, E. N. (1997). Teaching Reflection: Information Seeking and Evaluation in a Digital Library Environment. *Library Trends, 45*, no. 4, 771–802.

Jacobson, F. F., & Jacobson, M. J. (1993). Representative Cognitive Learning Theories and BI: A Case Study of End User Searching. *Research Strategies, 11*, no. 3, 124–137.

Jacobson, T. E., & Mark, B. L. (1995). Teaching in the Information Age: Active Learning Techniques to Empower Students. *The Reference Librarian*, no. 51–52, 105–120.

Jakobovits, L. A., & Nahl-Jakobovits, D. (1990). Measuring Information Searching Competence. *Research Libraries, 51*, no. 5, 448–462.

Jay, M. E. (1986). The Elementary School Library Media Teacher's Role in Educating Students to Think. *School Library Media Quarterly, 15*, no. 1, 28–32.

Joeckel, C. B. (1943). *Post-War Standards for Public Libraries*. Chicago: American Library Association.

Johnson, L. (1986). Stephens College Library Experiment. In L. L. Hardesty, J. P. Schmitt, & J. M. Tucker (Comps.), *User Instruction in Academic Libraries: A Century of Selected Readings* (pp. 110–120). Metuchen, NJ: Scarecrow Press.

Jonassen, D. H., Myers, J. M., & McKillop, A. M. (1996). From Constructivism to Constructionism: Learning with Hypermedia/Multimedia Rather Than from It. In B. Wilson (Ed.), *Constructivist Learning Environments: Case Studies in Instructional Design* (pp. 93–106). Englewood Cliffs, NJ: Educational Technology Publications.

Joyce, M. Z., & Tallman, J. I. (1997). *Making the Writing and Research Connection with The I-Search Process*. New York: Neal-Schuman.

Julien, H. E. (1999). Barriers to Adolescents' Information Seeking for Career Decision-Making. *Journal of the American Society for Information Science, 50*, no. 1, 38–48.

Jung, C. G. (1923). *Psychological Types*. New York: Harcourt & Brace.

Kafai, Y., & Bates, M. J. (1997). Internet Web-Searching Instruction in the Elementary Classroom: Building a Foundation for Information Literacy. *School Library Media Quarterly, 25*, no. 2, 103–111.

Kaiser Family Foundation. (2002). *See No Evil: How Internet Filters Affect the Search for Online Health Information: A Kaiser Family Foundation Study*. Available: http://www.kff.org/entmedia/upload/See-No-Evil-How-Internet-Filters-Affect-the-Search-for-Online-Health-Information-Executive-Summary.pdf (accessed May 26, 2010).

Kansas Association of School Librarians Research Committee (2001). *The Handy 5: Planning and Assessing Integrated Information Skills Instruction* (R. Grover, C. Fox, & J. M. Lakin, Eds.). Lanham, MD: Scarecrow Press.

Kapitzke, C. (2009). Rethinking Copyrights for the Library through Creative Commons Licensing. *Library Trends, 58*, no. 1, 95–108.

Keil, F. C. (1979). *Semantic and Conceptual Development: An Ontological Perspective*. Cambridge, MA: Harvard University Press.

Keller, J. M. (1987). The Systematic Process of Motivational Design. *Performance and Instruction, 26*, no. 8, 1–8.

Kelly, G. A. (1963). *A Theory of Personality: The Psychology of Personal Constructs*. New York: Norton.

Kennedy, J. R., Jr. (1986). Integrated Library Instruction. In L. L. Hardesty, J. P. Schmitt, & J. M. Tucker (Comps.), *User Instruction in Academic Libraries: A Century of Selected Readings* (pp. 231–242). Metuchen, NJ: Scarecrow Press.

Kester, D. D. (1994). Secondary School Library and Information Skills: Are They Transferred from High School to College? *The Reference Librarian*, no. 44, 9–17.

Kleifgen, J. A. (1989). *Computers and Opportunities for Literacy Development*. ERIC/CUE Digest, no. 54. New York: ERIC Clearinghouse on Urban Education

Knapp, P. B. (1966). *The Monteith College Library Experiment*. New York: Scarecrow Press.

Knapp, P. B. (1986). A Suggested Program of College Instruction in the Use of the Library. In L. L. Hardesty, J. P. Schmitt, & J. M. Tucker (Comps.), *User Instruction in Academic Libraries: A Century of Selected Readings* (pp. 151–166). Metuchen, NJ: Scarecrow Press.

Koch, S. (1956). Behavior as "Intrinsically" Regulated: Work Notes toward a Pre-Theory of Phenomena Called "Motivational." In M. R. Jones (Ed.), *Nebraska Symposium on Motivation* (Vol. 4). Lincoln: University of Nebraska Press.

Koch, S. (1961). Psychological Science vs. The Science-Humanism Antinomy: Intimations of a Significant Science of Man. *American Psychologist, 16,* 629–639.

Koestner, R., Ryan, R. M., Bernieri, F., & Holt, K. (1984). Setting Limits on Children's Behavior: The Differential Effects of Controlling versus Informational Styles on Intrinsic Motivation and Creativity. *Journal of Personality, 52,* no. 3, 233–248.

Kohlberg, L. (1969). *Development of Moral Thought and Action.* New York: Holt, Rinehart & Winston.

Kolb, D. A. (1983). *Experiential Learning.* Englewood Cliffs, NJ: Prentice Hall.

Kolb, D. A., & Fry, R. E. (1975*). Toward an Applied Theory of Experiential Learning.* In C. Cooper (Ed.), *Theories of Group Process* (pp. 33–57). London: Wiley.

Kozol, J. (1994). *Savage Inequities: Children in America's Schools.* New York: Harper.

Kozol, J. (1996). *Amazing Grace: The Lives of Children and the Conscience of the Nation.* New York: Harper

Kozol, J. (2000). An Unequal Education. *School Library Journal.* Available: http://www.schoollibraryjournal.com/article/CA153042.html (accessed May 27, 2010).

Kozol, J. (2006). *The Shame of the Nation: The Restoration of Apartheid in America.* New York: Three Rivers Press.

Krapp, A., & Fink, B. (1992). The Development and Function of Interests during the Critical Transition from Home to Preschool. In K. A. Renninger, S. Hidi, & A. Krapp (Eds.), *The Role of Interest in Learning and Development* (pp. 397–429). Hillsdale, NY: Lawrence Erlbaum Associates.

Krashen, S. (1993). *The Power of Reading: Insights From Research.* Littleton, CO: Libraries Unlimited.

Krashen, S. (2003). The (Lack of) Experimental Evidence Supporting the Use of Accelerated Reader. *Journal of Children's Literature, 29,* no. 2, 9–30.

Krechevsky, M. (1991). Project Spectrum: An Innovative Assessment Alternative. *Educational Leadership, 48,* no. 5, 43–48.

Kuhlthau, C. C. (1985). *Teaching the Library Research Process: A Step-by-Step Program for Secondary School Students.* West Nyack, NY: Center for Applied Research in Education.

Kuhlthau, C. C. (1987). An Emerging Theory of Library Instruction. *School Library Media Quarterly, 16,* no. 1, 23–27.

Kuhlthau, C. C. (1988a). Longitudinal Case Studies of the Information Search Process of Users in Libraries. *Library and Information Science Research, 10,* no. 3, 257–304.

Kuhlthau, C. C. (1988b). Perceptions of the Information Search Process in Libraries: A Study in Changes from High School through College. *Information Processing & Management, 24,* no. 4, 419–427.

Kuhlthau, C. C. (1991). Inside the Search Process: Information Seeking from the User's Perspective. *Journal of the American Society for Information Science, 42,* no. 5, 361–371.

Kuhlthau, C. C. (1993a). Implementing a Process Approach to Information Skills: A Study Identifying Indicators of Success in Library Media Programs. *School Library Media Quarterly, 22,* no. 1, 11–18.

Kuhlthau, C. C. (1993b). *Seeking Meaning.* Norwood, NJ: Ablex.

Kuhlthau, C. C. (1994). Assessing the Library Research Process. In C. C. Kuhlthau, M. E. Goodin, & M. J. McNally (Eds.), *Assessment and the School Library Media Center* (pp. 59–65). Englewood, CO: Libraries Unlimited.

Kuhlthau, C. C. (1995). The Process of Learning from Information. *School Libraries World Wide, 1,* no. 1, 1–13.

Kuhlthau, C. C. (1996). The Concept of a Zone of Intervention for Identifying the Role of Intermediaries in the Information Search Process. *Proceedings of the ASIS Annual Meeting.* Available: http://www.asis.org/annual-96/ElectronicProceedings/kuhlthau.html (accessed May 27, 2010).

Kuhlthau, C. C. (1997). Learning in Digital Libraries: An Information Search Process Approach. *Library Trends, 45,* no. 4, 708–724.

Kuhlthau, C. C. (1999). Accommodating the User's Information Search Process: Challenges for Information Retrieval Systems Designers. *Bulletin of the American Society for Information Science, 25,* no. 3. Available: http://www.asis.org/Bulletin/Feb-99/kuhlthau.html (accessed May 27, 2010).

Kuhlthau, C. C. (2001). *Rethinking Libraries for the Information Age School: Vital Roles in Inquiry Learning.* Keynote Address, International Association of School Librarians: Conference and International Research Forum on Research in School Librarianship, Auckland, New Zealand, July 9. Available: http://www.iasl-online.org/events/conf/keynote-kuhlthau2001.html (accessed May 27, 2010).

Kuhlthau, C. C. (2004). *Seeking Meaning: A Process Approach to Library and Information Services* (2nd ed). Westport, CT: Libraries Unlimited.

Kuhlthau, C. C. (2005). Information Search Process. In K. E. Fisher, S. Erdelez, & L. McKechnie (Eds.). *Theories of Human Information Behavior.* Medford, NJ: Information Today.

Kuhlthau, C. C., Goodin, M. E., & McNally, M. J. (Eds.). (1996). *Assessment and the School Library Media Center.* Englewood, CO: Libraries Unlimited.

Kuhlthau, C. C., Heinström, J., & Todd, R. (2008). The "Information Search Process Revisited": Is the Model Still Useful? *Information Research, 13,* no. 4. Available: http://informationr.net/ir/13–4/paper355.html (accessed June 2, 2010).

Kuhlthau, C. C., Maniotes, L. K., & Caspari, A. K. (2007). *Guided Inquiry: Learning in the 21st Century.* Westport, CT: Libraries Unlimited.

Kuhlthau, C. C., & Todd, R. J. (2005a). Student Learning through Ohio School Libraries. Part 1: How Effective School Libraries Help Students. *School Libraries Worldwide, 11,* no. 1, 63–68.

Kuhlthau, C. C., & Todd, R. J. (2005b). Student Learning through Ohio School Libraries. Part 2: Faculty Perceptions of Effective School Libraries. *School Libraries Worldwide, 11,* no. 1, 89–110.

Kulleseid, E. R. (1986). Extending the Research Base: Schema Theory, Cognitive Styles, and Types of Intelligence. *School Library Media Quarterly, 15,* no. 1, 41–48.

Kuykendall, C. (2001). *Improving Black Student Achievement by Enhancing Student's Self Image.* Available: http://www.maec.org/achieve/achieve.html (accessed May 27, 2010).

Lance, K. C. (2002). What Research Tells Us about the Importance of School Libraries. In *Proceedings, The White House Conference on School Libraries, June 4, 2002* (pp. 17–22). Washington, DC: Institute of Museum and Library Services.

Lance, K. C., Hamilton-Pennell, C., Rodney, M. J., Peterson, L., & Sitter, C. (2000). *Information Empowered: The School Librarian as an Agent of Academic Achievement in Alaska Schools.* Available: http://www.library.state.ak.us/dev/infoemp.html (accessed May 27, 2010).

Lance, K. C., Rodney, M. J., & Hamilton-Pennell, C. (2000a). *How School Libraries Help Kids Achieve Standards. The Second Colorado Study.* Denver: Colorado Department of Education. Available: http://www.lrs.org/documents/lmcstudies/CO/execsumm.pdf (accessed May 27, 2010).

Lance, K. C., Rodney, M. J., & Hamilton-Pennell, C. (2000b). *Measuring Up to Standards: The Impact of School Library Programs and Information Literacy in Pennsylvania Schools.* Pennsylvania Department of Educations Office of Commonwealth Libraries. Gainsburg, PA: Pennsylvania Citizens for Better Libraries. Available: http://www.lrs.org/impact.php (accessed May 27, 2010).

Lance, K. C., Rodney, M. J., & Hamilton-Pennell, C. (2001). *Good Schools Have School Librarians: Oregon School Libraries Collaborate to Improve Academic Achievement.* Salem: Oregon Educational Media Association. Available: http://www.lrs.org/impact.php (accessed May 27, 2010).

Lance, K. C., Rodney, M. J., & Hamilton-Pennell, C. (2003). *How School Librarians Improve Outcomes for Children: The New Mexico Study.* Santa Fe: New Mexico State Library.

Lance, K. C., Welborn, L., & Hamilton-Pennell, C. (1992). *The Impact of School Library Media Centers on Academic Achievement.* Denver: State Library and Adult Education Office, Colorado Department of Education.

Large, A. (2002). Gender Differences in Collaborative Web Searching Behavior: An Elementary School Study. *Information Processing & Management, 38*, no. 3, 427–443.

Large, A., & Beheshti, J. (2000). The Web as a Classroom Resource: Reactions from the Users. *Journal of the American Society for Information Science, 51*, no. 12, 1069–1080.

Large, A., Beheshti, J., & Breuleux, A. (1998). Information Seeking in a Multimedia Environment by Primary School Students. *Library and Information Science Research, 20*, no. 343–376.

Large, A., Beheshti, J., & Rahman, T. (2002). Design Criteria for Children's Web Portals: The Users Speak Out. *Journal of the American Society for Information Science and Technology, 53*, no. 2, 79–94.

Latham, D., & Gross, M. (2008). Broken Links: Undergraduates Look Back on Their Experiences with Information Literacy in K–12 Education. *School Library Media Research, 11.* Available: http://www.ala.org/ala/mgrps/divs/aasl/aaslpubsandjournals/slmrb/slmrcontents/volume11/lathamgross.cfm (accessed June 2, 2010).

Latrobe, K., & Havener, W. M. (1997). The Information-Seeking Behavior of High School Honors Students: An Exploratory Study. *Youth Services in Libraries, 10*, no. 2, 188–200.

Lavoie, D. R., & Good, R. (1988). The Nature and Use of Prediction Skills in a Biological Computer Simulation. *Journal of Research in Science Teaching, 25*, no. 5, 335–360.

Lazarus, W., & Mora, F. (2000). *Online Content for Low-Income and Underserved Americans: The Digital Divide's New Frontier.* Available: http://www.childrenspartnership.org (accessed May 27, 2010).

Lazear, D. (1991). *Seven Ways of Knowing: Teaching for Multiple Intelligences.* Palatine, IL: Skylight Publishing.

Lazear, D. (1999). *Multiple Intelligence Approaches to Assessment: Solving the Assessment Conundrum.* Chicago: Zephyr Press.

Lepper, M. R., Corpus, J. H., & Lyengar, S. S. (2005). Intrinsic and Extrinsic Motivational Orientations in the Classroom: Age Differences and Academic Correlates. *Journal of Educational Psychology, 97*, no. 2, 184–196.

Lieberman, M. (1989). *Reports on the Fairfax County Area III 4MAT Geometry and Algebra Projects, 1988 and 1989.* Available from the Excel Office, 200 W. Station St., Barrington, IL 60010.

Liebscher, P., & Marchionini, G. (1988). Browse and Analytical Search Strategies in a Full-Text CD-ROM Encyclopedia. *School Library Media Quarterly*, *16*, no. 4, 223–233.

Liesener, J. W. (1985). Learning at Risk: School Library Media Programs in an Information World. *School Library Media Quarterly*, *14*, no. 1, 11–20.

Limberg, L. (1999). Model School Libraries: Tools or Threats? Reflections on a Development Project in Sweden. *School Libraries Worldwide*, *5*, no. 1, 49–65.

Lin, P. (1994). Library Instruction for Culturally Diverse Populations: A Comparative Approach. *Research Strategies*, *12*, no. 3, 168–173.

Lindlof, T. R. (1995). *Qualitative Communication Research Models*. Thousand Oaks, CA: Sage.

Loerke, K. (1994). Teaching the Library Research Process in Junior High. *School Libraries in Canada*, *14*, no. 2, 23–26.

Loertscher, D. V. (1985). Collection Mapping: An Evaluation Strategy for Collection Development. *Drexel Library Quarterly*, *21*, no. 2, 9–21.

Loertscher, D. V. (1996). A Farewell Challenge. *School Library Media Quarterly*, *24*, no. 4, 192, 194.

Loertscher, D. V., Ho, M. L., & Bowie, M. M. (1987). "Exemplary Elementary Schools" and Their Library Media Center: A Research Report. *School Library Media Quarterly*, *16*, no. 3, 147–153.

Loertscher, D. V., & Land, P. (1975). An Empirical Study of Media Services in Indiana Elementary Schools. *School Library Media Quarterly*, *4*, no. 1, 8–18.

Logan, D. K. (2010). A Measure of Success. *Library Media Connection*, *28* (5), 7.

Lohr, U. G. (2006). *Media Multitasking among American Youth: Prevalence, Predictors and Pairings*. Kaiser Family Foundation. Available: www.kff.org/entmedia/upload/7592.pd (accessed May 13, 2010).

Loranger, A. L. (1994). The Study Strategies of Successful and Unsuccessful High School Students. *Journal of Reading Behavior*, *26*, no. 2, 347–360.

Lu, Y-L., & Gordon, C. (2007). Reading Takes You Places: A Study of a Web-Based Summer Reading Program. *School Library Media Research*, *10*, 1–14. Available: http://www.aasl.org/ala/mgrps/divs/aasl/aaslpubsandjournals/slmrb/slmrcontents/volume10/lu_reading.cfm.

Lubans, J. (Ed.). (1974). *Educating the Library User*. New York: Bowker.

Madaus, G. F., & Tan, A. G. A. (1994). The Growth of Assessment. In C. C. Kuhlthau, M. E. Goodin, & M. J. McNally, (Eds.), *Assessment in the School Library Media Center* (pp. 1–24). Englewood, CO: Libraries Unlimited.

Maeroff, G. I. (1991). Assessing Alternative Assessment. *Phi Delta Kappan*, *73*, no. 4, 273–281.

Mallette, M., Henk, W., & Melnick, S. (2004). The Influence of Accelerated Reader on the Affective Literacy Orientations of Intermediate Grade Students. *Journal of Literacy Research*, *36*, no. 1, 73–84.

Mancall, J. C., Aaron, S. L., & Walker, S. A. (1986). Educating Students to Think: The Role of the School Library Media Program. *School Library Media Quarterly*, *15*, no. 1, 18–27.

Mancall, J. C., Lodish, E. K., & Springer, J. (1992). Searching across the Curriculum. *Phi Delta Kappan*, *73*, no. 7, 526–528.

Maniotes, L. (2005). *The Transformative Power of Literary Third Space*. PhD diss., University of Colorado.

Marchionini, G. (1987). An Invitation to Browse: Digital Text Systems for Novice Users. *Canadian Journal of Information Science*, *12*, nos. 3–4, 69–79.

Marchionini, G. (1989). Information-Seeking Strategies of Novices Using a Full-Text Electronic Encyclopedia. *Journal of the American Society for Information Science, 40,* no. 1, 54–66.

Marchinoni, G., & Teague, J. (1987). Elementary Students' Use of Electronic Information Service: An Exploratory Study. *Journal of Research in Computing in Education, 20,* no. 2, 139–155.

Marcus, D. L. (2002). Her Parents Look at Her as a Problem. *Knowledge Quest, 30,* no. 5, 19–21.

Mark, B. L., & Jacobson, T. E. (1995). Teaching Anxious Students Skills for the Electronic Library. *College Teaching, 42,* no. 1, 28–31.

Markless, S., & Streatfield, D. R. (2007). Three Decades of Information Literacy: Redefining the Parameters. In S. Andretta (Ed.), *Change and Challenge: Information Literacy for the 21st Century* (pp. 15–36). Adelaide. Auslib Press. Available: http://www.informat .org/pdfs/streatfield-markless.pdf (accessed June 2, 2010).

Markuson, C. (1986). Making It Happen: Taking Charge of the Information Curriculum. *School Library Media Quarterly, 15,* no. 1, 37–40.

Martin, B. (1982). Interpersonal Relations and the School Library Media Specialist. *School Library Media Quarterly, 11,* no. 1, 43–44, 53–57.

Martin, L. A. (1984). *The Organizational Structure of Libraries.* Metuchen, NJ: Scarecrow Press.

Martinez, M. E. (1994). Access to Information Technologies Among School-Age Children: Implications for a Democratic Society. *Journal of the Association for Information Science, 45,* no. 6, 393–400.

Marzano, R. J. (1992). *A Different Kind of Classroom: Teaching with Dimensions of Learning.* Alexandria, VA: Association for Supervision and Curriculum Development.

Marzano, R. J. (2000). *Designing a New Taxonomy of Educational Objectives.* Thousand Oaks, CA: Corwin Press.

Maslow, A. H. (1970). *Motivation and Personality.* New York: Harper and Row.

McCarthy, B. (1987). *The 4MAT System: Teaching Learning Styles with Right/Left Mode Techniques.* Barrington, IL: Excel, Inc.

McCarthy, B. (1990). Using the 4MAT System to Bring Learning Styles to Schools. *Educational Leadership, 48,* no. 2, 31–37.

McCarthy, B. (1996). *About Learning.* Barrington, IL: Excel, Inc.

McCarthy, B. (2000). *About Teaching: 4MAT in the Classroom.* Wauconda, IL: About Learning, Inc.

McDonald, F. B. (1988). Information Access for Youth: Issues and Concerns. *Library Trends, 37,* no. 1, 28–42.

McGill-Frantzen, A., Allington, R., Yokoi, L., & Brooks, G. (1999). Putting Books in the Classroom Seems Necessary but Not Sufficient. *Journal of Educational Research, 93,* no. 2, 67–74.

McGregor, J. H. (1994a). Cognitive Processes and the Use of Information: A Qualitative Study of Higher Order Thinking Skills Used in the Research Process by Students in a Gifted Program. *School Library Media Annual, 12,* pp. 124–133.

McGregor, J. H. (1994b). Information Seeking and Use: Students' Thinking and Their Mental Models. *Youth Services in Libraries, 8,* no. 1, 69–76.

McKenzie, J. (1999). The Research Cycle. *From Now On: The Educational Technology Journal, 9,* no. 4. Available: http://questioning.org/rcycle.html (accessed May 28, 2010).

McKenzie, J. (2000). *Beyond Technology: Questioning, Research and the information Literate School.* Bellingham, WA: FNO Press.

McNally, M. J. (2004). *Analysis of Students' Mental Models: Using the Internet in an Authentic Learning Situation*. PhD diss., Rutgers University.

McNally, M. J., & Kuhlthau, C. C. (1994). Information Search Process in Science Education. *The Reference Librarian, 20*, no. 44, 53–60.

Means, B., & Olson, K. (1994). The Link between Technology and Authentic Learning. *Educational Leadership, 51*, no. 7, 15–18.

Meho, L. I., & Tibbo, H. R, (2003). Modeling the Information Seeking Behavior of Scientists: Ellis' Study Revisited. *Journal of the American Society for Information Science and Technology, 54*, no. 6, 570–587.

Mendrinos, R. (1994). *Building Information Literacy Using High Technology: A Guide for Schools and Libraries*. Englewood, CO: Libraries Unlimited.

Meyer, C. A. (1994). What's the Difference between "Authentic" and "Performance" Assessment. In C. C. Kuhlthau, M. E. Goodin, & M. J. McNally (Eds.), *Assessment in the School Library Media Center* (pp. 99–101). Englewood, CO: Libraries Unlimited.

Mokros, H. B., Mullins, L. S., & Saracevic, T. (1995). Practice and Personhood in Professional Interaction: Exploring Social Identities in the Addressing of Information Needs. *LISR, 17*, no. 3, 237–257.

Montgomery, P. (1997). Use of Information: The Information Literacy Phenomenon. In A. E Tepe & J. Calarco (Eds.), *A Handbook for Pathways to Knowledge* (pp. 8–10). McHenry, IL: Follett Software.

Moore P. (1993). Information Problem Solving: A Wider View of Library Skills. *Contemporary Educational Psychology, 20*, no. 1, 1–31.

Moore, P. A., & St. George, A. (1991). Children as Information Seekers: The Cognitive Demands of Books and Library Systems. *School Library Media Quarterly, 19*, no. 3, 161–168.

Moran, M. (2010). *Young Learners Need Librarians, Not Just Google*. Available: http://forbes.com/2010/03/22/moran-librarian-skills-intelligent-investing-google.html (accessed June 2, 2010).

Morton, C. (1996). The Modern Land of Laputa: Where Computers Are Used in Education. *Phi Delta Kappan, 77*, no. 6, 416–419.

Nahl, D., & Harada, V. H. (1996). Composing Boolean Search Statements: Self Confidence, Concept Analysis, Search Logic, and Errors. *School Library Media Quarterly, 24*, no. 4, 199–207.

Nahl-Jakobovits, D., & Jakobovits, L. A. (1990). Learning Principles and the Library Environment. *Research Strategies, 8*, no. 2, 74–81.

Nahl-Jakobovits, D., & Jakobovits, L. A. (1993). Bibliographic Instructional Design for Information Literacy: Integrating Affective and Cognitive Objectives. *Research Strategies, 11*, no. 2, 73–88.

Nastasi, B K., Battista, M. T., & Clements, D. H. (1990). Social-Cognitive Interactions, Motivation and Cognitive Growth in Logo Programming and CAI Problem-Solving Environments. *Journal of Educational Psychology, 82*, no. 21, 150–158.

National Education Association and North Central Association of Colleges and Secondary Schools. (1920). *Standard Library Organization and Equipment for Secondary Schools of Different Sizes*. (C. C. Certain, Chair) Chicago: American Library Association.

Neuman, D. (1994). Alternative Assessment, Promises and Pitfalls. In C. C. Kuhlthau, M. E. Goodin, & M. J. McNally, *Assessment in the School Library Media Center* (pp. 67–75). Englewood, CO: Libraries Unlimited.

Neuman, D. (1995a, October). *High School Students' Use of Databases: Competing Conceptual Structures*. Paper presented at the annual meeting of the American Society for Information Science, Chicago, IL.

Neuman, D. (1995b). High School Students' Use of Databases: Results of a National Delphi Study. *Journal of the American Society for Information Science, 46*, no. 4, 284–298.

Neuman, D. (1997). Learning and the Digital Library. *Library Trends, 45*, no. 4, 687–707.

Neuman, S. B., & Celano, D. (2001). Access to Print in Low-Income and Middle-Income Communities: An Ecological Study of Four Neighborhoods. *Reading Research Quarterly, 36*, no. 1, 8–26.

Newell, T. S. (2010). Examining Information Problem-Solving Instruction: Dynamic Relationship Patterns Mediated by Distinct Instructional Methodologies. *School Libraries Worldwide, 15*, no. 2, 49–76.

Nolan, J. P. (1989). *A Comparison of Two Methods of Instruction in Library Research Skills for Elementary School Students*. PhD diss., Temple University.

Norris, S. P. (1985). Synthesis of Research on Critical Thinking. *Educational Leadership, 2*, no. 8, 40–45.

Nowicki, S. (2003). Student vs. Search Engine: Undergraduates Rank Results for Relevance. *Libraries and the Academy, 3*, no. 3, 503–515.

Oberman, C. (1995). Avoiding the Cereal Syndrome; Or, Critical Thinking in the Electronic Environment. In Fifteenth Anniversary Task Force, Library Instruction Round Table, American Library Association (Comp.), *Information for a New Age: Redefining the Librarian* (pp. 107–119). Englewood, CO: Libraries Unlimited.

Oliver, R., & Oliver, H. (1997). Using Context to Promote Learning from Information-Seeking Tasks. *Journal of the American Society for Information Science, 48*, no. 6, 519–526.

O'Neil, J. (1992). Putting Performance Assessment to the Test. *Educational Leadership, 49*, no. 8, 14–19.

Pack, S. (2000). Public Library Use, School Performance, and the Parental X-Factor: A Bio-Documentary Approach to Children's Snapshots. *Reading Improvement, 37*, no. 4, 161–171.

Pane, D. M. (2009). Third Space: Blended Teaching and Learning. *Journal for the Research Center for Educational Technology, 5*, no. 1, 64–92.

Pappas, M. (1997). *Introduction to Pathways to Knowledge: Follett's Information Skills Model*. McHenry, IL: Follett Software.

Pappas, M. L., & Tepe, A. E. (1997). *Pathways to Knowledge: Follett's Information Skills Model* (3rd ed.). McHenry, IL: Follett Software.

Pappas, M. L., & Tepe, A. E. (2002). *Pathways to Knowledge® and Inquiry Learning*. Englewood, CO: Libraries Unlimited.

Pask, G. (1972). A Fresh Look at Cognition and the Individual. *International Journal of Man-Machine Studies, 4*, 211–216.

Pask, G. (1975). *Conversations, Cognition, and Learning*. Amsterdam: Elsevier.

Pask, G., & Scott, B. C. E. (1972). Learning Strategies and Individual Competence. *International Journal of Mathematics and Mathematical Sciences, 4*, 217–253.

Patrick, B. C., Skinner, E. A., & Connell, J. P. (1993). What Motivates Children's Behavior and Emotion? Joint Effects of Perceived Control and Autonomy in the Academic Domain. *Journal of Personality and Social Psychology, 65*, no. 4, 781–791.

Peck, K. L., & Dorricott, D. (1994). Why Use Technology? *Educational Leadership, 51*, no. 7, 11–14.

Peter D. Hart Research Associates & Public Opinion Strategies (2005). *Rising to the Challenge: Are High School Graduates Prepared for College and Work? A Study of Recent High School Graduates, College Instructors, and Employers*. Available: http://www.achieve.org/node/548 (accessed June 2, 2010).

Pew Research Center. (2001). *The Internet and Education: Findings of the Pew Internet & American Life Project*. Available: http://www.pewinternet.org/Reports/2001/ The-Internet-and-Education.aspx (accessed May 28, 2010).

Pfau, D. W. (1967). Effects of Planned Recreational Reading Programs. *The Reading Teacher, 21*, no. 1, 34–39.

Pipher, M. (1994). *Reviving Ophelia: Saving the Selves of Adolescent Girls*. New York: Putnam.

Pitts, J. M. (1995). Mental Models of Information: The 1993–94 AASL/Highsmith Research Award Study. *School Library Media Quarterly, 23*, no. 3, 177–184. Available: http://www.ala.org/ala/mgrps/divs/aasl/aaslpubsandjournals/slmrb/editorschoiceb/ infopower/selctpittsshtml.cfm (accessed November 16, 2010).

Radford, M. L. (1996). Communication Theory Applied to the Reference Encounter: An Analysis of Critical Incidents. *Library Quarterly, 66*, no. 2, 123–137.

Radford, M. L. (1998). Approach or Avoidance? The Role of Nonverbal Communication in the Academic Library User's Decision to Initiate a Reference Encounter. *Library-Trends, 46* no. 4, 699–717.

Radford, M. L. (1999). *The Reference Encounter: Interpersonal Communication in the Academic Library*. Publications in Librarianship, no. 52. Chicago: American Library Association and Association of College and Research Libraries.

Radford, M. L. (2006). Encountering Virtual Users: A Qualitative Investigation of Inter-personal Communication in Chat Reference. *Journal of the American Society for Information Science and Technology, 57*, no. 8, 1046–1059.

Radford, M. L., & Connaway, L. S. (2007). "Screenagers" and Live Chat Reference: Living Up to the Promise. *Scan, 26*, no. 1, 31–39.

Ranganathan, S. R. (1957). *The Five Laws of Library Science*. Madras: Madras Library Association.

Ray, J. T. (1994). Resource-Based Teaching: Media Specialists and Teachers as Partners in Curriculum Development and the Teaching of Library and Information Skills. *The Reference Librarian, 44*, 19–27.

Renninger, K. A., Hidi, S., & Krapp, A. (Eds.). (1992). *The Role of Interest in Learning and Development*. Hillsdale, NY: Lawrence Erlbaum Associates.

Robbins, E., & Thompson, L. (1991). *A Study of the Indianapolis-Marion County Public Library's Summer Reading Program for Children*. East Lansing, MI: National Center for Research on Teacher Learning. (ERIC Document Reproduction Service No. ED355647)

Rodney, M. J., Lance, K. C., & Hamilton-Pennell, C. (2002). *Make the Connection: Quality School Library Programs Impact Academic Achievement in Iowa*. A Research Project by Iowa Area Education Agencies. Bettendorf, IA: Mississippi Bend Area Education Agency.

Rothstein, S. (1955). *The Development of Reference Services through Academic Traditions, Public Library Practice, and Special Librarianship*. Chicago: Association of College and Research Libraries.

Rothstein, S. (1994). Reference Services. In W. A. Wiegand & D. G. Davis Jr. (Eds.), *Ency-clopedia of Library History* (pp. 541–546). New York: Garland.

Ryan, R. M., & Deci, E. L. (2000). Self-Determination Theory and the Facilitation of Intrinsic Motivation, Social Development, and Well-Being. *American Psychologist, 55*, no. 1, 68–78.

Salmon, L. M. (1986). Instruction in the Use of a College Library. In L. L. Hardesty, J. P. Schmitt, & J. M. Tucker (Comps.), *User Instruction in Academic Libraries: A Century of Selected Readings* (pp. 86–101). Metuchen, NJ: Scarecrow Press.

Salvatore, C. L. (2000). *Community, Institutions, and Identity in the Chamorro Speech Community: An Ethnographic Study of How They Shape information-Seeking Discourses in the Library.* PhD diss., University of Texas.

Saracevic, T., Mokros, H. B., & Su, L. (1990). Nature of Interaction between Users and Intermediaries in Online Searching: A Qualitative Analysis. *Proceedings of the American Society for Information Science, 27,* 47–54.

Sauer, J. A. (1995). Conversation 101: Process, Development, and Collaboration. In Fifteenth Anniversary Task Force, Library Instruction Round Table, American Library Association (Comp.), *Information for a New Age: Redefining the Librarian* (pp. 135–151). Englewood, CO: Libraries Unlimited.

Savolainen, R. (2003). Book Review: Looking for Information: A Survey of Research in Information Seeking, Deeds, and Behavior. By D. O. Case. *Journal of the American Society for Information Science and Technology, 54,* no. 7, 695–697.

Schack, G. D. (1993). Involving Students in Authentic Research. *Educational Research, 50,* no. 7, 29–31.

Schacter, J., Chung, K. W. K., & Dorr, A. (1998). Children's Internet Searching on Complex Problems: Performance and Process Analyses. *Journal of the American Society for Information Science, 44,* no. 9, 840–849.

Schiefele, U., & Csikszentmihalyi, M. (1995). Motivation and Ability as Factors in Mathematics Experience and Achievement. *Journal of Research in Mathematics Education, 26,* no. 2, 163–181.

Schiller, A. (1986). Reference Service: Instruction or Information. In L. L. Hardesty, J. P. Schmitt, & J. M. Tucker (Comps.), *User Instruction in Academic Libraries: A Century of Selected Readings* (pp. 189–203). Metuchen, NJ: Scarecrow Press.

Schloman, B. F., & Gedeon, J. A. (2007). Creating TRAILS: Tool for Real-Time Assessment of Information Literacy Skills. *Knowledge Quest, 35,* no. 5, pp. 44–47.

Schloman, B. F., & Gedeon, J. A. (2010). *TRAILS—Tool for Real-Time Assessment of Information Literacy Skills.* Available: http://www.trails-9.org (accessed June 10, 2010).

Schmidt, R. (2008). Really Reading: What Does Accelerated Reader Teach Adults and Children? *Language Arts, 85,* no. 3, 202–211.

Schön, D. A. (1983). *The Reflective Practitioner: How Professionals Think in Action.* New York: Basic Books.

Scott, M., & VanNoord, G. (1996). Conducting Original Research at the High School Level—The Student's Perspective. *The American Biology Teacher, 58,* no. 4, 217–219.

Sein, M. K., & Bostrom, R. P. (1989). Individual Differences and Conceptual Models in Training Novice Users. *Human-Computer Interaction, 4,* no. 3, 197–229.

Shaw, C. B. (1986). Bibliographic Instruction for Students. In L. L. Hardesty, J. P., Schmitt, & J. M. Tucker (Comps.), *User Instruction in Academic Libraries: A Century of Selected Readings* (pp. 107–109). Metuchen, NJ: Scarecrow Press.

Sheingold, K. (1986). Keeping Children's Knowledge Alive through Inquiry. *School Library Media Quarterly, 15,* no. 1, 80–85.

Shenton, A. K., & Dixon, P. (2003). A Comparison of Youngster's Use of CD-ROM and the Internet as Information Resources. *Journal of the American Society for Information Science and Technology, 54,* no. 11, 1029–1049.

Shores, L. (1986). The Liberal Arts College: A Possibility in 1954? In L. L. Hardesty, J. P., Schmitt, & J. M. Tucker (Comps.), *User Instruction in Academic Libraries: A Century of Selected Readings* (pp. 121–129). Metuchen, NJ: Scarecrow Press.

Sillars, M. O. (1991). *Messages, Meanings, and Culture: Approaches to Communication Criticism.* New York: HarperCollins.

Silverstein, J. (2005). Just Curious: Children's Use of Digital Reference for Unimposed Queries and Its Importance in Informal Education. *Library Trends, 54,* no. 2, 228–244.

Slavin, R. V. (1990). *Cooperative Learning: Theory, Research, and Practice.* Needham, MA: Allyn & Bacon.

Small, R. V. (1998). Designing Motivation into Library and Information Skills Instruction. *School Library Media Quarterly.* Available: http://www.ala.org/ala/mgrps/divs/aasl/ aaslpubsandjournals/slmrb/slmrcontents/volume11998slmqo/small.cfm (accessed May 28, 2010).

Small, R. V. (1999). An Exploration of Motivational Strategies Used by Library Media Specialists during Library and Information Skills Instruction. *School Library Media Research, 2,* 1–23. Available: http://www.ala.org/ala/aasl/aaslpubsandjournals/slmrb/ slmrcontents/volume21999/vol2small.htm (accessed June 2, 2010).

Small, R. V., Shanahan, K. A., & Stasak, M. (2010). The Impact of New York's School Libraries on Student Achievement and Motivation: Phase III. School Library Media Research, 13, 1–27. Available: http://www.ala.org/ala/mgrps/divs/aasl/ aaslpubsandjournals/slmrb/slmrcontents/volume13/small_phase3.cfm (accessed September 11, 2010).

Small, R. V., & Snyder, J. (2009). The Impact of New York's School Libraries on Student Achievement and Motivation: Phase II—In-Depth Study. *School Library Media Research, 12,* 1–17. Available: http://www.nyla.org/content/user_4/Impact%20Phase%202.pdf (accessed June 2, 2010).

Small, R. V., Snyder, J., & Parker, K. (2009). *The Impact of New York's School Libraries: Phase I.* Available: http://www.aasl.org/ala/mgrps/divs/aasl/aaslpubsandjournals/slmrb/ slmrcontents/volume12/small.cfm (accessed June 2, 2010).

Smith, E. G. (2001). *Texas School Libraries: Standards, Resources, and Students' Performance.* Austin: Texas State Library and Archives Commission. Available: http:// www.tsl.state.tx.us/ld/pubs/schlibsurvey/survey.pdf (accessed May 28, 2010).

Smith, J. B. (1987). Higher Order Thinking Skills and Nonprint Media. *School Library Media Quarterly, 16,* no. 1, 38–42.

Solomon, P. (1992). On the Dynamics of Information System Use: From Novice to? In D. Shaw (Ed.), *Proceedings of the ASIS Annual Meeting* (Vol. 29, pp. 162–170). Medford, NJ: Learned Information.

Solomon, P. (1993). Children's Information Retrieval Behavior: A Case Analysis of an OPAC. *Journal of the American Society for Information Science, 44,* no. 5, 245–264.

Solomon, P. (1994). Children, Technology, and Instruction: A Case Study of Elementary School Children Using an Online Public Access Catalog (OPAC). *School Library Media Quarterly, 23,* no. 1, 43–51.

Springer, S. P., & Deutsch, G. (1993). *Left Brain, Right Brain.* New York: Freeman.

Staino, R. (2010, January 21). *AASL Adopts "School Librarian" as Official Term for the Profession.* Available: http://www.schoollibraryjournal.com/article/CA6715763.html (accessed November 4, 2010).

Stead, T. (2005). *Reality Checks: Teaching Reading Comprehension with Nonfiction K–5.* Portland, ME: Stenhouse Publishers.

Stoan, S. K. (1984). Research and Library Skills: An Analysis and Interpretation. *College and Research Libraries, 45,* no. 2, 99–108.

Stripling, B. K. (1994a). Assessment of Student Performance: The Fourth Step in the Instructional Design Process. In C. C. Kuhlthau, M. E. Goodin, & M. J. McNally (Eds.), *Assessment in the School Library Media Center* (pp. 77–97). Englewood, CO: Libraries Unlimited.

Stripling, B. K. (1994b). Practicing Authentic Assessment in the School Library. In C. C. Kuhlthau, M. E. Goodin, & M. J. McNally (Eds.), *Assessment in the School Library Media Center* (pp. 103–118). Englewood, CO: Libraries Unlimited.

Stripling, B. K. (1995). Learning-Centered Libraries: Implications from Research. *School Library Media Quarterly, 23*, no. 3, 163–170.

Stripling, B. K. (2006). Formative Assessment for Learning. AASL Fall Forum, Warwick, RI: October 13–15.

Stripling, B. K., & Pitts, J. M. (1988). *Brainstorms and Blueprints: Teaching Library Research as a Thinking Process*. Englewood, CO: Libraries Unlimited.

Swain, D. E. (1996). Information Search Process Model: How Freshmen Begin Research. In *Proceedings of the ASIS Annual Meeting*. Available: http://www.asis.org/annual-96/ElectronicProceedings/swain.html (accessed May 28, 2010).

Tallman, J., & Henderson, L. (1999). *Constructing Mental Model Paradigms for Teaching Electronic Resources*. Chicago: American Association of School Librarians. Available: http://www.ala.org/ala/mgrps/divs/aasl/aaslpubsandjournals/slmrb/slmrcontents/volume21999/vol2tallman.cfm (accessed May 28, 2010).

Tapscott, D. (1998). *Growing Up Digital: The Rise of the Net Generation*. New York: McGraw-Hill.

Tapscott, D. (2009). *Growing Up Digital: How the Net Generation Is Changing Your World*. New York: McGraw Hill.

Taylor, R. S. (1968). Question-Negotiation and Information Seeking in Libraries. *College and Research Libraries, 29*, no. 3, 178–194.

Teele, S. (1996). Redesigning the Educational System to Enable All Students to succeed. *NASSP Bulletin, 80*, no. 583, 65–75.

Thomas, J. W. (1993). Promoting Independent Learning in the Middle Grades: The Role of Instructional Support Practices. *The Elementary School Journal, 93*, no. 5, 575–591.

Thomas, N. P. (1996). *Reading Libraries: An Interpretive Study of Discursive Practices in Library Architecture and the Interactional Construction of Personal Identity*. PhD diss., Rutgers, the State University of New Jersey.

Thomas, N. P. (2000a). A Multiplicity of (Research) Models: Alternative Strategies for Diverse Learners. *School Library Media Activities Monthly, 17*, no. 1, 25.

Thomas, N. P. (2000b). Teaching "Kids" Not Content: Recreating the School Library Media Center as a Caring Context for Student Learning. *School Library Media Activities Monthly, 1*, no. 2, 23.

Thomas, N. P. (2001). Learning Styles and the Big6: Combining the 4MAT Approach and the Big6Skills to Plan Projects for Diverse Learners. *The Big6© Newsletter*, E-2, no. 2.

Thomas, N. P. (2002). Design Matters: Relational Projections in Library Environments. In H. B. Mokros (Ed.), *Identity Matters: Communication-Based Explorations and Explanations* (pp. 77–108). Creskill, NJ: Hampton Press.

Thomas, N. P., Vroegindewey, D., & Wellins, C. (1997, April 4). *4MATing the Big Six©: Tailoring Research Assignments to Student Learning Styles*. Paper presented at the annual conference of the American Association of School Librarians, Portland, OR.

Thorne, L. M. (1967). *The Influence of the Knapp School Libraries Project on the Reading Comprehension and the Knowledge of Library Skills of the Pupils at the Farrar Junior High School, Provo, Utah*. PhD diss., Brigham Young University.

Tierney, R. J., & Cunningham, J. W. (1984). Research in Teaching Reading Comprehension. In P. D. Pearson (Ed.), *Handbook of Reading Research* (Vol. 1, pp. 609–655). New York: Longman.

Todd, R. J. (1995). Integrated Information Skills Instruction: Does It Make a Difference? *School Library Media Quarterly, 23,* no. 2, 133–139.

Todd, R. J. (1998). WWW, Critical Literacies and Learning Outcomes. *Teacher Librarian, 26,* no. 2, 16–21.

Todd, R. J. (2002). Press release. Available: http://www.oelma.org/OhioResearchStudy .htm (accessed May 29, 2010).

Todd, R. J. (2003). *Student Learning through Ohio School Libraries.* Summary of the Ohio Research Study presented to the Ohio Educational Library MediaAssociation. Available: http://www.oelma.org/studentlearning.htm (accessed November 16, 2010).

Todd, R. J. (2008a). The Evidence-Based Manifesto for School Librarians. *School Library Journal, 4* (1). Available: http://www.schoollibraryjournal.com/article/CA6545434 .html (accessed November 3, 2010).

Todd, R. J. (2008b). Youth and Their Virtual Networked Worlds: Research Findings and Implications for School Libraries. *School Libraries Worldwide, 14,* no. 2, 19–34.

Todd, R. J. (2009). School Librarianship and Evidence Based Practice: Progress, Perspectives, and Challenges. *Evidence Based Library and Information Practice, 4,* no. 2, 78–96.

Todd, R. J., & Kuhlthau, C. C. (2003). *Student Learning through Ohio School Libraries: Background, Methodology, and Report of Findings.* Columbus: Ohio Educational Library Media Association.

Todd, R. J., Lamb, E., & McNicholas, C. (1993). Information Skills and Learning: Some Research Findings. *Access, 7,* no. 1, 14–16.

Tucker, J. M. (1994). Library Instruction. In W. A. Wiegand & D. G. Davis Jr. (Eds.), *Encyclopedia of Library History* (pp. 364–366). New York: Garland.

Tuckett, H. W., & Stoffle, C. J. (1984). Learning Theory and the Self-Reliant Library User. *RQ, 24,* no. 1, 58–66.

Tuominen, K. (1997). User-Centered Discourse: An Analysis of the Subject Positions of the User and the Librarian. *Library Quarterly, 67,* no. 4, 352–371.

Turkle, S. (1984). *The Second Self.* New York: Simon and Schuster.

Turner, P. M. (1990). Research Reviews from the Treasure Mountain Research Retreat. In J. B. Smith (Ed.), *School Library Media Annual* (Vol. 8, pp. 139–153). Englewood, CO: Libraries Unlimited.

Twist, K. L. (2004). *Disparities along the Information Age Career Path.* Digital Divide Network.

Valencia, S. W. (1991). Portfolio Assessment for Young Readers. *The Reading Teacher, 44,* no. 9, 680–682.

Vandergrift, K. E., & Hannigan, J. A. (1986). Elementary School Library Media Centers as Essential Components in the Schooling Process. *School Library Media Quarterly, 14,* no. 2, 171–173.

Von Glasersfeld, E. (1995). *Radical Constructivism: A Way of Knowing and Learning.* London: Falmer.

Vroom, V. H. (1964). *Work and Motivation.* New York: Wiley.

Vygotsky, L. (1978). *Mind in Society: The Development of Higher Psychological Processes.* Cambridge, MA: Harvard University Press.

Walter, V. A, (1994). The Information Needs of Children. In I. P. Godden (Ed.), *Advances in Librarianship* (pp. 111–129). San Diego, CA: Academic Press.

Walter, V. A., Borgman, C. L., & Hirsh, S. G. (1996), The Science Library Catalog: A Springboard for Information Literacy. *School Library Media Quarterly, 24,* no. 2, 105–110.

Watson, J. S. (1998). "If You Don't Have It, You Can't Find It": A Close Look at Students' Perceptions of Using Technology. *Journal of the American Society for Information Science, 49*, no. 11, 1024–1036.

Watson, J. S. (2003). Examining Perceptions of the Science Fair Project: Content or Process? *School Library Media Research*, 6. Available: http://www.ala.org/ala/mgrps/divs/aasl/aaslpubsandjournals/slmrb/slmrcontents/volume62003/sciencefair.cfm (accessed September 11, 2010).

Watzlawick, P., Beavin, J. H., & Jackson, D. D. (1967). *Pragmatics of Human Communication: A Study of Patterns, Pathologies, and Paradoxes.* New York: Norton.

Weiner, B. (1992). *Human Motivation: Metaphors, Theories, and Research.* Newbury Park, CA: Sage.

Wells, J., & Lewis, L. (2006). *Internet Access in U.S. Public Schools and Classroomss: 1994–2005* (NCES 2007-020). U.S. Department of Education. Washington, D.C.: National Center for Educational Statistics.

Wesley, T. (1991). Teaching Library Research: Are We Preparing Students for Effective Information Use? *Emergency Librarian, 18*, no. 3, 23–30.

Wesson, C. L., & Keefe, M. J. (1995). *Serving Special Needs Students in the School Library Media Center.* Westport, CT: Greenwood Press.

Whelan, D. L. (2004). 130,000 Kids Can't Be Wrong: A New Ohio Study Shows How School Librarians Help Students Learn. *School Library Journal, 50*, no. 2. Available: http://www.schoollibraryjournal.com/article/CA377858.html (accessed November 4, 2010).

White, R. W. (1959). Motivation Reconsidered: The Concept of Competence. *Psychological Review, 6*, no. 5, 297–323.

Wigfield, A., & Asher, S. R. (1984). Social and Motivational Influences on Reading. In P. D, Pearson, (Ed.), *Handbook of Reading Research* (Vol. 1, pp., 423–452). New York: Longman.

Wiggins, G., & McTighe, J. (1998) *Understanding by Design.* Arlington, VA: Association for Supervision and Curriculum Development.

Wilhelm, T., Carmen, D., & Reynolds, M. (2002). *Annie E. Casey Foundation and Benton Foundation Connecting Kids and Technology: Challenges and Opportunities. Kids Count Snapshot.* Available: http://www.eric.ed.gov/ERICDocs/data/ericdocs2sql/content_storage_01/0000019b/80/1a/42/a5.pdf (accessed May 30, 2010).

Wilkerson, R., & White, K. (1988). Effects of the 4MAT System of Instruction on Students' Achievement, Retention, and Attitudes. *Elementary School Journal, 88*, 257–368.

Willson, E. J. (1965). *Evaluating Urban Centralized Elementary School Libraries.* PhD diss., Wayne State University.

Wilson, L. R. (1933). The Development of Research in Relation to Library Schools. *Library Journal, 58*, no. 22, 817–821.

Winograd, P., & Gaskins, R. W. (1992). Metacognition: Matters of the Mind, Matters of the Heart. In A. L. Costa, J. A., Bellanca, & R. Fogarty (Eds.), *If Minds Matter: A Foreword to the Future* (Vol. 1, pp. 225–238). Palatine, IL: IRI/Skylight Publishing.

Winsor, J. (1986). The College Library. In L. L. Hardesty, J. P. Schmitt, & J. M. Tucker (Comps.), *User Instruction in Academic Libraries: A Century of Selected Readings* (pp. 5–16). Metuchen, NJ: Scarecrow Press.

Woolls, B. (2008). *The School Library Media Manager* (4th ed.). Westport, CT: Libraries Unlimited.

Woronov, T. (1994). Machine Dreams: Six Myths (and Five Promising Truths) about the Uses of Educational Technology. *Harvard Education Letter, 10*, no. 5, 1–3.

Wyer, J. (1930). *Reference Work: A Textbook for Students of Library Work and Libraries.* Chicago: American Library Association.

Yarling, J. R. (1968). *Children's Understandings and Use of Selected Library-Related Skills in Two Elementary Schools, One with and One without a Centralized Library.* PhD diss., Ball State University.

Yucht, A. H. (1997). *FLIP IT! An Information Skills Strategy for Student Researchers.* Worthington, OH: Linworth.

Yucht, A. H. (2002). *Flip It!™ for Information Skills Strategies.* Available: http://www.aliceinfo.org/flipit (accessed November 4, 2010).

Author Index

Subject Index

About the Authors

NANCY PICKERING THOMAS is Professor Emeritus in the School of Library and Information Management, Emporia State University. She received her PhD in communication, information and library studies from Rutgers, The State University of New Jersey, and has taught graduate courses in theoretical foundations of service, children's literature and programming, managing the school library, and services for special populations. Her articles have appeared in *Advances in Library Administration and Organization*, *Journal of Education for Library and Information Science*, *School Library Media Activities Monthly*, and the *Big6Newsletter* in addition to a special issue on youth for the *Journal of the American Society for Information Science and Technology*, which she coedited with Dr. Mary Kay Chelton. She has chaired dissertations related to issues in school libraries, including student motivation and organizational culture.

SHERRY R. CROW received her PhD in library and information management from Emporia State University and is currently assistant professor of school library science and coordinator of the school librarian endorsement program at the University of Nebraska at Kearney (UNK). Author of *Information Literacy: A Guide for the Library Media Specialist* (2005), she was named Colorado Librarian of the Year in 2004 and has presented her research at national and international conferences. Her articles have been published in *School Library Media Research*, *School Libraries Worldwide* and *School Library Monthly*. She was named UNK's Outstanding Scholar of the College of Education in 2010.

LORI L. FRANKLIN is a working school librarian at Olathe East High School, a large, suburban high school in the Kansas City metro area that was recently chosen by the International Center for Leadership in Education as one of "20 Model High Schools" in the nation. A national board-certified teacher with more than 15 years of experience in school libraries at all levels, she was a district finalist for master teacher of the year in 2006 and received an Educator to Excellence Award for the 2006–2007 academic year. In addition, she is a PhD student at the School of Library and Information Management at Emporia State University, where her research focus centers on the everyday life information seeking practices of 21st century learners.